☆ ☆ ☆

Beyond
Confederation

☆ ☆ ☆ ☆

Beyond Confederation
Origins of the Constitution and American National Identity

EDITED BY

RICHARD BEEMAN,

STEPHEN BOTEIN, AND

EDWARD C. CARTER II

Published for the Omohundro
Institute of Early American
History and Culture,
Williamsburg, Virginia,
by the University of
North Carolina Press,
Chapel Hill & London

*The Omohundro Institute of Early
American History and Culture is sponsored
jointly by The College of William and Mary
and the Colonial Williamsburg Foundation.*

02 01 00 99 98   8 7 6 5 4

Library of Congress Cataloging-in-Publication Data
Beyond confederation
   "Published for the Institute of Early American
History and Culture, Williamsburg, Virginia."
   Includes index.
   1. United States—Politics and government—1783–
1789. 2. United States. Constitution. 3. United
States—Constitutional history. I. Beeman, Richard R.
II. Botein, Stephen. III. Carter, Edward Carlos, II
1928–   . IV. Institute of Early American History
and Culture (Williamsburg, Va.)
E303.P85   1987   973.3'18   86-16150
ISBN 0-8078-1719-8
ISBN 0-8078-4172-2 (pbk.)

*Publication of this book was assisted by
a grant from the William Nelson Cromwell Foundation.*

To the memory of Stephen Botein

☆ ☆ ☆
Acknowledgments

All but two of the essays in this volume were initially presented at a conference in Philadelphia in October 1984, "The Creation of the American Constitution." That conference was jointly sponsored by the American Philosophical Society, the Philadelphia Center for Early American Studies, and the Institute of Early American History and Culture and was partially funded by the National Endowment for the Humanities and the Andrew W. Mellon Foundation. The John Ben Snow Foundation provided additional support to underwrite publication of these essays. We thank all of those institutions for their generous support.

We would also like to acknowledge the invaluable help of Sharon Holt and Alan Karras of the University of Pennsylvania, who contributed mightily of their labors during the conference, and of Hobart Cawood, Superintendent of the Independence National Historical Park, who generously opened his domain to the conferees. Finally, we would like to thank the members of the staff at the Institute of Early American History and Culture—Gil Kelly, Martha King, Philip D. Morgan, Wendy Sacket, and Thad W. Tate—for their substantial editorial contributions to the volume.

Most of us who contributed to this volume possessed a high regard for the scholarly abilities of Stephen Botein well before work on this collection of essays commenced. Over the course of the year and a half in which the volume had been going through the editorial process we came to appreciate not only his considerable intellect and his incisive but nevertheless gentle manner as a critic, but also, and most important, his warmth, good humor, and decency as a human being. We were shocked and saddened to learn of his death, which occurred only a few days after the major part of the editorial work was completed and the manuscript sent to the printer. We will miss Steve terribly, but at the same time we hope this book will stand as partial monument to his accomplishments as teacher, scholar, and friend.

☆ ☆ ☆

Contents

☆ ☆ ☆

Beyond
Confederation

☆ ☆ ☆

Introduction

RICHARD BEEMAN

The bicentennial of the United States Constitution is upon us, and we are, as a consequence, already hearing a good many pieties about the "living Constitution" and the "legacy" laid down for us by the framers of that document. It may be, though, as we approach the end of the twentieth century, that the founding fathers appear *more removed* from the lives of most Americans than ever before. Their motives, always a source of controversy among scholars, seem no clearer to us; and their essential concerns—with the balancing and limiting of political power, with the "filtration of talent," and with the maintenance of that old-fashioned notion of "virtue"—seem somehow distant from our own preoccupations.

One important cause of our estrangement from this important moment in our past is the extraordinary transformation that has occurred—and occurred only recently—in our conception of "federalism." As Lance Banning reminds us in his fine essay, "The Practicable Sphere of a Republic," even James Madison, one of the most aggressive proponents of a radically strengthened central government, possessed by virtually any standard conceivable in our twentieth-century world an extraordinarily *limited* view of the sphere of action of that government. Although it is plain that the accumulation of power in the hands of the federal government—often but not always at the *expense* of state governmental power—has been a consistent process from 1789 to the present, it seems nevertheless that a *qualitative* change in our conception of federal-state relations has taken place only within the past few decades.

To be sure, there have been other significant milestones in the history of federalism. The Civil War would, for practical if not for rhetorical purposes, end discussion about where ultimate sovereignty rested. But the northern-imposed consensus respecting ultimate sovereignty notwithstanding, virtually all Americans of the post–Civil War era continued to pay homage to the notion, articulated most forcefully and explicitly in *The Federalist Papers*, that their government was "part-national" and "part-federal." Most Americans, north and south, Republican and Democrat, would have assented to the proposition of John Dickinson in the Philadelphia Convention, that the federal system could be likened "to the Solar System, in which the States were the planets, and ought to be left to move freely in their proper orbits."[1]

Just as the explicit language of the Constitution in prescribing where the orbits of state governmental authority should be drawn remained directly pertinent to matters of public policy, so too were the founders' own views on that subject of more than mere rhetorical or academic interest. In the half-century following the Civil War, the United States Supreme Court would take a number of curious twists and turns in its interpretations of the boundaries separating federal and state jurisdictions—the most notable, controversial, and curious of these being in its judgments on the application of the Fourteenth Amendment to state government attempts at economic regulation. But whether one favored doctrines of "declarative" or "sociological" jurisprudence, one could hardly ignore issues of the "intent" of the framers of either the original Constitution or the subsequent amendments to it.[2]

When Charles Beard began work on *An Economic Interpretation of the Constitution of the United States*, he was hardly unaware of or unconcerned with the Supreme Court's recent visions of the intent of the framers. When he referred to the Constitution as "an economic document for economic ends," issues of federal-state power and, in his view, of the inability of the federal government to assume an activist role in restraining the abuses of

1. James Madison, *Federalist* No. 39, in Jacob E. Cooke, ed., *The Federalist Papers* (Middletown, Conn., 1961); Dickinson's analogy was made in a speech to the convention on June 7, 1787, and reported in James Madison, *Notes of Debates in the Federal Convention of 1787*, ed. by Adrienne Koch, rev. ed. (Athens, Ohio, 1984), 84. The subsequent scholarly commentary on the deliberations in the convention that led to the "part-national, part-federal" equation is voluminous. For a sampling of that commentary, see Harry N. Scheiber, "Federalism and the Constitution: The Original Understanding," in Lawrence M. Friedman and Harry N. Scheiber, eds., *American Law and the Constitutional Order: Historical Perspectives* (Cambridge, Mass., 1978), 85–98; Martin Diamond, "What the Framers Meant by Federalism," in Robert A. Goldwin, ed., *A Nation of States: Essays on the American Federal System* (Chicago, 1963), 24–41; Alpheus Thomas Mason, "The Federalist— A Split Personality," *American Historical Review*, LVII (1951–1952), 625–643.

2. The best textbook surveys of the changes occurring in American constitutional law respecting issues of economic regulation are Alfred H. Kelly *et al.*, *The American Constitution: Its Origins and Development*, 6th ed. (New York, 1983), esp. 397–418, 465–475; and Paul Brest and Sanford Levinson, *Processes of Constitutional Decision-making: Cases and Other Problems*, 5th ed. (Boston, 1984), esp. 195–265. See also Edward S. Corwin, "The Supreme Court and the Fourteenth Amendment," *Michigan Law Review*, VII (1909), 643–672; Keith Jurow, "Untimely Thoughts: A Reconsideration of the Origins of Due Process of Law," *American Journal of Legal History*, XIX (1975), 265–279.

capitalism were hardly of mere academic interest. As Max Lerner noted long ago:

> If it was true that even the founding fathers were human beings governed by their sense of economic interest, it was a fortiori even truer of the Supreme Court justices who passed on the validity of federal and state legislation that sought to control Big Property. Thus, it [*An Economic Interpretation*] dealt a blow to the strongest panoply in which property in Beard's day clothed itself—the inviolate panoply of Constitutional "due process of law."[3]

Although Beard and other Progressive politicians no doubt hoped that the United States Supreme Court would take a more sympathetic view toward federal government regulation of the capitalist economy, they nevertheless continued to look primarily to the *state governments* for those reforms; they did so, not because state governments were necessarily friendlier to reform, but, rather, because those governments represented the orthodox constitutional path to economic regulation.

In fact, the publication of *An Economic Interpretation* coincided with the beginnings of a significantly expanded federal role both in economic regulation and in the protection of individual civil liberties. In a series of decisions in the first two decades of the twentieth century the Supreme Court began to interpret Congress's regulatory powers under the commerce clause in a more expansive fashion; and, in the majority opinion in *Gitlow* v. *New York* (1925), the Court began a long (and relatively slow) process by which the First Amendment was incorporated into the due process clause of the Fourteenth Amendment, thus protecting those First Amendment rights from impairment by laws emanating from the state legislatures.[4]

Those trends, of course, received their greatest propulsion during the New Deal and were further consolidated in the Truman-Eisenhower years.

3. Charles A. Beard, *An Economic Interpretation of the Constitution of the United States* (New York, 1913); Max Lerner, "Charles Beard's Political Theory," in Howard K. Beale, ed., *Charles A. Beard: An Appraisal* (Lexington, Ky., 1954), 35. Also directly pertinent to this issue is Beard, *The Supreme Court and the Constitution* (New York, 1912).

4. Kelly *et al.*, *The American Constitution*, 419–444, 468–475, 527–534; John E. Semonche, *Charting the Future: The Supreme Court Responds to a Changing Society, 1890–1920* (Westport, Conn., 1978); for the incorporation of the Bill of Rights into the Fourteenth Amendment, see Richard C. Cortner, *The Supreme Court and the Second Bill of Rights: The Fourteenth Amendment and the Nationalization of Civil Liberties* (Madison, Wis., 1981); and, for a highly critical view of those same developments, Charles Fairman and Stanley Morrison, *The Fourteenth Amendment and the Bill of Rights: The Incorporation Theory* (Stanford, Calif., 1949).

Yet, viewed from the perspective of 1986, even these dramatic increases in the sphere of activity of the central government amount to no more than alterations in degree and not alterations in the essential character of the federal-state equation. When William W. Crosskey published the first two volumes of his extraordinary work, *Politics and the Constitution in the History of the United States*, in 1953, he plainly did not feel that the issue of federal versus state governmental power was anywhere close to being resolved. Plainly too, though many scholars and public policy-makers may have disagreed with the interpretation laid down in his work, his method of proof— the marshaling of historical evidence to reveal the original intent of the framers—was accepted by both strict constructionists and broad constructionists as the most appropriate, indeed, as the *only* appropriate, avenue of inquiry.[5]

Crosskey was neither a crank nor a fool, yet the zealousness with which he pursued his thesis—that Madison and the other principal architects of the Constitution steadfastly and purposely sought to create a government with a broad grant of power under the commerce clause—strikes most readers today as more than a little curious. It is not so much that Crosskey was *wrong* about Madison's intent, though most scholars today would probably conclude that he *was* wrong, but, rather, that such an extraordinarily long and labored exegesis on Madison's intentions on these matters seems so much beside the point.

Clearly, it mattered to Crosskey and to a good many broad constructionist liberals of his generation, just as it continued to matter to American politicians up through at least the mid-1960s. When the Civil Rights Act of 1964 was being debated in the United States Congress, a good many congressmen (most, but not all, from the South) vehemently opposed it because they saw in it a fundamental threat to the system of segregation that had for them come to stand for much of what they valued in their way of life. When they invoked a strict constructionist view of the commerce clause and of the equal protection clause of the Fourteenth Amendment, they may have been guided by some considerations—racism, misguided paternalism, self-interest—that had little to do with pure constitutional abstractions. Yet the doctrine of strict constructionism as a principle with a history and rationale of its own continued to have a vitality, a substantive meaning, to many Americans in 1964 that it altogether lacks in 1986.

One is likely, of course, to find in any past era a wide range of both respectable and sordid self-interests lurking behind lofty constitutional pronouncements defining the boundaries of federalism, but what is striking

5. William Winslow Crosskey, *Politics and the Constitution in the History of the United States*, 3 vols. (Chicago, 1953–1980). Vol. III was published posthumously, with William Jeffrey, Jr., as coauthor.

about our present constitutional situation is how unlikely it is that arguments turning on notions of the proper spheres of federalism are even to be invoked on any issue before the public. Even in the case of public education, the one area in which both the funding and the control over policy decisions has tended to remain with state and local governments, there appear to be few constitutional barriers to a larger federal role should the government decide to exert its power in that area. It is notable, for example, that the bulk of the opposition to Secretary of Education William Bennett's proposal for a voucher system—a plan which would dramatically transform both public and private education through the means of the federal government's power over the purse—comes not from those concerned about defending traditional notions of federalism, but, rather, from those who either dislike the substance of the policy or who see in it a potential breach of First Amendment guarantees of separation of church and state.

And it is there, with the First Amendment, that we discover the most fundamental difference between our present constitutional circumstance and that of any generation that has preceded it. From 1787 until the mid-1960s, questions of the proper definition of *federalism* constituted much of the sum and substance of the constitutional discourse; from the mid-1960s to the present, the principal constitutional problems occupying the public mind have been outgrowths of an expansive view of the Bill of Rights, of the First, Fourth, Fifth, and Sixth Amendments in particular.

Though the views of the founding fathers on questions of federal-state power may have been rendered increasingly problematic by trends toward nationalization in our economy and politics, the basic character of the debate over federalism from 1787 until the mid-twentieth century remained the same, and few would have conceived the framers' views to be irrelevant to those decisions. Can we say the same, though, about the currently relevant constitutional issues involving church-state relations, free speech, or criminal rights? Though Edwin Meese might derive some rhetorical satisfaction from his calls for a return to the "original intent of the framers" on these issues, that notion may be a chimera in the current constitutional context. One of the most striking impressions that one gains from reading Stephen Botein's essay in this volume on separation of church and state is just how radically different the framers' notions of a Christian republic were from our present conception of the church-state relationship. And, if in that area we at least have the pronouncements of a Jefferson or a Madison to remind us of the spirit of the founders, we lack even that ephemeral concept as a guide when we confront pornography issues or current debates on what constitutes probable cause and proper protection against self-incrimination.[6]

---

6. There are, it should be noted, some legal historians who continue to hold to the centrality of notions of original intent in constitutional decision-making. The

One of the consequences of this shift in constitutional direction has been a rather pronounced change in patterns of historical writing on the Constitution. Our own increasing sense of distance from the problems and perspectives of the founding fathers, while causing much of the recent scholarship on the subject of the making of the Constitution to appear less immediately relevant to current problems, has at the same time allowed historians, perhaps for the first time, to evaluate the eighteenth-century *context* of American constitutional thought in a manner remarkably free from the encumbrances of the nineteenth- and twentieth-century *consequences* of that thought.

The rediscovery of the meaning and vitality of "republican" ideas for the American Revolutionary generation, a rediscovery which began with the work of scholars such as Caroline Robbins and J. G. A. Pocock on seventeenth- and early eighteenth-century England and Bernard Bailyn and Pauline Maier on America during the Revolution, has now pushed forward to comprehend American behavior during the early stages of nation-building. Historians such as Gordon Wood, Lance Banning, and Drew McCoy have brought about a remarkable revision of the way in which we conceive of the world in which the founding fathers operated.[7] It was a world in which neither Whig nor Progressive categories of analysis, with

---

most vehement of these is perhaps Raoul Berger, who in *Government by Judiciary: The Transformation of the Fourteenth Amendment* (Cambridge, Mass., 1977) mounts a vigorous attack on judicial activism and calls for a return to a closer adherence to original intent. See also Henry P. Monaghan, "Our Perfect Constitution," *New York University Law Review*, LVI (1981), 353–396.

7. That body of scholarship constituting what has been called "the republican synthesis" has been admirably surveyed by Robert Shalhope in two articles, "Toward a Republican Synthesis: The Emergence of an Understanding of Republicanism in Early American Historiography," *William and Mary Quarterly*, 3d Ser., XXIX (1972), 49–80; and "Republicanism and Early American Historiography," *WMQ*, 3d Ser., XXXIX (1982), 334–356. But see, particularly, J.G.A. Pocock, *The Machiavellian Moment: Florentine Political Thought and the Atlantic Republican Tradition* (Princeton, N.J., 1975); Caroline Robbins, *The Eighteenth-Century Commonwealthman: Studies in the Transmission, Development, and Circumstance of English Liberal Thought from the Restoration of Charles II until the War with the Thirteen Colonies* (Cambridge, Mass., 1959); Bernard Bailyn, *The Ideological Origins of the American Revolution* (Cambridge, Mass., 1967); Pauline Maier, *From Resistance to Revolution: Colonial Radicals and the Development of American Opposition to Great Britain, 1765–1776* (New York, 1972); Gordon S. Wood, *The Creation of the American Republic, 1776–1787* (Chapel Hill, N.C., 1969); Lance Banning, *The Jeffersonian Persuasion: Evolution of a Party Ideology* (Ithaca, N.Y., 1978); and Drew R. McCoy, *The Elusive Republic: Political Economy in Jeffersonian America* (Chapel Hill, N.C., 1980).

their preoccupations with modern notions of democracy, nationalism, and pluralism, were very useful as a conceptual frame. In some senses the central concerns of the eighteenth-century republican world—the restraint of the ceaselessly aggressive tendencies of power, the maintenance of the public virtue, and the filtration of talent—were timeless in their application to the problems of governance at any point in human history. But those concerns were, in the way in which they were formulated by Americans of the Revolutionary era and in the logic they imposed on those who assumed the reins of government after the Revolution, nevertheless peculiar to a world that is now very distant from our own.

The most powerful single statement of the content and dynamic of republican ideology during the Revolutionary era remains Bernard Bailyn's *Ideological Origins of the American Revolution*, but Bailyn's original formulation had only a limited applicability to the problems associated with the framing and ratification of the Constitution. Indeed, his only mention of the Constitution was confined to a passing aside that American preoccupations with divided sovereignty "would continue the effort to make federalism a logical as well as a practical system of government."[8] Moreover, by depicting republicanism as an ideological world view shared in all of its particulars by all Americans, Bailyn provided his readers with scant basis for assessing the differing perspectives of Federalists and Antifederalists during the debates of 1787–1788.

It was Gordon Wood, in *The Creation of the American Republic, 1776–1787*, who began the task of tracing the evolution of republican ideas in the post-Revolutionary period. Although Wood shared with Bailyn the conviction that Americans shared a common republican ideological tradition, he recognized, in a way not acknowledged by Bailyn, that that tradition itself was sufficiently varied—both in England and, even more pointedly, in a rapidly changing American society—to allow for some dramatically differing political prescriptions for the young nation.

The Federalists, increasingly obsessed with the need to stem disorder in America and continuing to cling to a notion of political representation that depended heavily on deference, were most obviously working within a traditional and elitist conception of republicanism. Their traditionalism was, however, offset in important ways by their more cosmopolitan view of America's economic and political destiny and, ultimately, by James Madison's dramatic articulation of the advantages of an extended republic. Such a republic, with its ability to give "such an extent to its sphere, that no one common interest or passion will be likely to unite a majority of the whole number in an unjust pursuit," was, according to Wood, altogether novel.

---

8. Bailyn, *Ideological Origins*, 228.

"The stability of government no longer relied, as it had for centuries, upon its embodiment of the basic social forces of the state. Indeed, it now depended upon the prevention of the various social interests from incorporating themselves too firmly in the government." The result, in Wood's view, was the creation of a governmental system with a "more modern and more realistic sense of political behavior in the society itself," a system which marked the end "of the classical conception of politics."[9]

The Antifederalists, distrustful of the machinations of an aristocratical element within America and increasingly willing to resort to aggressive, popular styles of electoral conduct in order to defeat the forces of aristocracy, were, in Wood's view, moving toward a definition of republicanism that was more explicitly connected with America's democratic future. At the same time, however, their essential parochialism—their attachment to state and local, rather than continental interests—left them at a substantial practical disadvantage in communicating their vision of the Republic to their fellow citizens. They were, according to Wood, "politicians without influence and connections, and ultimately politicians without social and intellectual confidence." There may have been, imbedded within their railings against the aristocratic leanings of their opponents, a positive democratic faith, but their platform in the struggle over ratification was nevertheless a singularly negative one.[10]

Wood's book was successful, in ways far more striking than the writings of Charles Beard and his adherents, in causing us to appreciate the Antifederalist contribution to American political thought. While we can, after reading his book, admire the ways in which Federalists like James Madison modernized traditional conceptions of both governmental structure and function, we are also reminded that Madison, like most of his Federalist colleagues, continued to be preoccupied with elitist notions of virtue and the filtration of talent. Conversely, though earlier commentators such as Cecelia Kenyon may have been partially accurate in labeling the Antifederalists as "Men of Little Faith" in democracy, Wood has made a convincing case for the proposition that, while few individuals in republican America were unabashed advocates of pure democracy, it was on the Antifederalist side that one encountered a definition of republicanism that granted to ordinary citizens a large measure of direct political power.[11]

9. Wood, *Creation of the American Republic*, esp. 471–564, 606 (quotations on 504, 606).

10. *Ibid.*, 483–492.

11. The most influential argument stressing the weakness of the Antifederalists' faith in democracy is Cecelia M. Kenyon, "Men of Little Faith: The Antifederalists on the Nature of Representative Government," *WMQ*, 3d Ser., XII (1955), 3–43. More recently, James H. Hutson, in "Country, Court, and Constitution: Antifeder-

The Creation of the American Republic, by the strength of its erudition and the vigor of its argument, has succeeded in substantial measure in turning the traditional formulation of the ideological division between Federalists and Antifederalists on its head. Most scholars today, in looking for the historical roots of America's transition from an elitist to a democratic republic, would probably turn to the writings of the Antifederalists and not the Federalists. While acknowledging the genius of a Madison or a Hamilton in constructing a republican government capable of operating in vigorous fashion over an extended territory, they would turn to Samuel Bryan's *Centinel* or to the arguments of Abraham and Robert Yates against ratification of the Constitution in New York for statements about the role of democracy in both legitimating and limiting national governmental power.[12]

In the years since the publication of *The Creation of the American Republic* a number of historians have sought to expand and to refine Wood's views on the evolution of American ideology during the early national period. Scholars such as Lance Banning and Drew McCoy, following closely Bailyn's and Wood's notions of republicanism, have illuminated the continuing vitality of those ideas during the early years of the operation of the new national Republic. And, more recently, Joyce Appleby, Isaac Kramnick, and, from rather different perspectives, Forrest McDonald and Garry Wills have sought to provide us with a broader and more varied conception of the sources of the Americans' ideological tradition at the time of the making of the Constitution. While acknowledging the importance of classical republican ideas in shaping American thought, they have traced other important lines of influence—classical liberalism, Scottish common sense philosophy, English common law, a myriad of theories in the newly emerging intellectual battleground of political economy—on American Revolutionary and constitutional thinking.[13]

---

alism and the Historians," *WMQ*, 3d Ser., XXXVIII (1981), 337–368, has questioned the Antifederalists' commitment to democracy.

12. The pieces by Bryan and the Yateses can be found in Herbert J. Storing, ed., *The Complete Anti-Federalist* (Chicago, 1981), II, 136–213, VI, 37–41, 89–121. Storing's introduction to those volumes has been published separately as *What the Anti-Federalists Were For* (Chicago, 1981).

13. Banning, *The Jeffersonian Persuasion*; "Republican Ideology and the Triumph of the Constitution, 1789 to 1793," *WMQ*, 3d Ser., XXXI (1974), 167–188; "Jeffersonian Ideology Revisited: Liberal and Classical Ideas in the New American Republic," *WMQ*, 3d Ser., XLIII (1986), 3–19; McCoy, *Elusive Republic*; Joyce Appleby, *Capitalism and a New Social Order: The Republican Vision of the 1790s* (New York, 1984); and "What Is Still American in the Political Philosophy of Thomas Jefferson?" *WMQ*, 3d Ser., XXXIX (1982), 287–309; Isaac Kramnick, "Republican Revisionism Revisited," *AHR*, LXXXVII (1982), 629–664; Forrest McDonald, *Novus*

Several of the essays in this volume, though drawing some of their inspiration from Bailyn's and Wood's earlier work, nevertheless demonstrate an inclination to move beyond the insights yielded by the "republican synthesis." Drew McCoy and Jack Rakove, each the author of a book drawing heavily on the storehouse of republican ideas, suggest in their essays in this volume the need for a closer look at the relationship between ideology and interests. McCoy's essay, "James Madison and Visions of American Nationality in the Confederation Period," looks at a familiar issue in American political history—regional and sectional division—and illuminates some of the optimistic assumptions that informed many southerners, and James Madison in particular, as they calculated their region's role in the new Republic. Similarly, Jack Rakove, in "The Structure of Politics at the Accession of George Washington," highlights the wide gulf that separated the founding fathers' belief in classical republican notions of disinterested public service and in the filtration of talent from the actual patterns of service in the national Congress following ratification of the Constitution.

Stanley Katz, writing from the perspective of American legal history, reminds us that there were also traditions of American legal thought—many of them distinct from though not contrary to republican ideas—which served as an important foundation for American constitutional thought. While obviously appreciative of the work of Bernard Bailyn, he suggests nevertheless that Bailyn's cavalier dismissal of the constitutional logic of the colonists as "abstruse" has caused us to ignore a significant, *real* cause of the Revolution and an important substantive basis for the subsequent constitutional system that emerged in the new Republic. And finally, in an essay likely to provoke wide discussion if not uniform assent, Ralph Lerner mounts a vigorous and broad-gauged attack on nearly the whole of the "ideological school," claiming that Bailyn, Wood, and others have mistakenly depicted the founding fathers as "prisoners" of ideology, a depiction which has unnecessarily debased "the significance of thought and thoughtfulness in political discourse and action."

Most recent studies of the ideological origins of Federalist and Antifederalist thought, though insightful in their analyses of the transmission of *ideas*, have not brought us much closer to agreement on the *social* underpinnings of those two divergent ideologies. Gordon Wood, though he speaks of the Federalists as representing a "preponderance of wealth and respectability," has not himself assayed a systematic analysis of the social composition of the two groups.[14] Similarly, Lance Banning, whose study *The Jeffersonian Persuasion* traces the evolution of republican ideology in the 1790s, has been relatively unconcerned with questions relating to the social context of that ideology. And Joyce Appleby, though she has performed a notable service by steering us away from too extensive a reliance on traditional notions of classical republicanism, revealing for us the optimistic sense in which the founding fathers confronted the promise of liberal capitalism, has nevertheless been more intent on tracing the evolution of *ideas* than on identifying Federalist and Republican *interests*.

Janet Riesman's contribution to this volume, "Money, Credit, and Federalist Political Economy," though written primarily from the perspective of intellectual history, does begin to move us somewhat closer to a junction between political rhetoric and economic reality. Arguing that Americans in the 1780s were every bit as much concerned with prosperity as they were with virtue, Riesman traces the important changes in the way in which Americans—and Antifederalists in particular—came to regard the benefits and the perils of credit, indebtedness, and wealth itself during the early national period.

Riesman's analysis of the Federalists' and Antifederalists' grapplings with political economy is perhaps the most sophisticated that we have to date, yet it is nevertheless hard to avoid the conclusion that the intellectual history of the Constitutional period—which has undergone an extraordinarily active and creative recrudescence during the past twenty years—still remains largely disconnected from that body of Progressive historical scholarship inspired by Charles Beard three-quarters of a century ago.[15] After two or three generations of debate over both the specifics and the implications of Beard's initial assessment of the social and economic underpinnings of the Constitution—a span of time which has witnessed the publication of scores of books and articles purporting to test his thesis about economic interests and the Constitution—there seems to be a scholarly consensus on two points:

1. That Beard's description of the *precise* configuration of economic interests both at the Philadelphia Convention and in the ratification process—a

---

14. Wood, *Creation of the American Republic*, 498.

15. The most compelling call for a synthesis of Progressive and idealist approaches to the Revolutionary and constitutional periods remains Gordon Wood's "Rhetoric and Reality in the American Revolution," *WMQ*, 3d Ser., XXIII (1966), 3–32; and while Wood, in his recent work (including, most particularly, his essay in this volume), has himself moved a bit closer to that synthesis, it does nevertheless seem that the two traditions have been continuing to move along separate tracks.

configuration revolving around the categories of "personalty" and
"realty"—was badly flawed.

2. That Beard's more general contention—that there was *some* sort of
relationship between an individual's socioeconomic position and political
behavior on the matter of the Constitution—has some merit.

One might, however, add a third area of consensus, namely, that most
historians find the debate over economic interests and the Constitution, at
least in its current form, increasingly uninteresting and unhelpful. In the
1950s, when Robert E. Brown and Forrest McDonald launched their massive assaults on the empirical basis of Beard's contentions, there may have
been some (such as Brown himself) who believed that the act of rescuing
the founding fathers from charges of self-interest was of immediate, practical importance; but as time has passed, those historiographical debates have
seemed important to ever-decreasing numbers.[16] Those who have rallied to
Beard's defense, trying to salvage at least a few of his insights from amidst
the litter of his specific errors of fact and overstatement of opinion, have
been only partially successful in doing so. Some, like Jackson Turner Main,
have stuck with the basics of Beard's economic interpretation but have
sought to broaden his categories, substituting "commercial and cosmopolitan" interests for "personalty," and "agrarian and provincial" interests for
"realty."[17] Most historians would probably agree that these newly refined

16. The scholarly literature provoked by Beard's book is, of course, immense.
Perhaps the three most influential of the assessments of that book are Robert E.
Brown, *Charles Beard and the Constitution: A Critical Analysis of "An Economic Interpretation of the Constitution"* (Princeton, N.J., 1956); Forrest McDonald, *We the
People: The Economic Origins of the Constitution* (Chicago, 1958); and Lee Benson,
Turner and Beard: American Historical Writing Reconsidered (Glencoe, Ill., 1960). In
fact, each of the three, though critical of Beard's findings, is based on rather different
assumptions. Brown's was unabashedly hostile to every aspect—ideological, methodological, and empirical—of *An Economic Interpretation*. McDonald, though he
emphatically rejected Beard's empirical findings, nevertheless conducted his analysis
wholly within Beard's assumptions about the relationship between economic interests and political behavior. Benson, though he rejected Beard's methodology as
too simplistic, was nevertheless as committed as Beard to developing a theory of
political behavior which incorporated "interest."

17. Jackson Turner Main, *The Antifederalists: Critics of the Constitution, 1781-1788*
(Chapel Hill, N.C., 1961); and *Political Parties before the Constitution* (Chapel Hill,
N.C., 1973). For other examinations of political division in the 1780s in which
interests assume paramount importance, see H. James Henderson, *Party Politics in
the Continental Congress* (New York, 1974); Joseph L. Davis, *Sectionalism in American
Politics, 1774-1787* (Madison, Wis., 1977); and Stephen R. Boyd, *The Politics of*

categories are improvements over the originals, yet they too remain open to exceptions at every turn. While most would perhaps agree that Alexander Hamilton, and in a slightly different way, James Madison, were "cosmopolitans," and that Patrick Henry and George Clinton were "provincials," what is one to do with a Federalist such as John Adams, whose classical republican principles impelled him toward behavior—whether at the Court of St. James's or at the seat of government in Philadelphia—that made him seem anything but a cosmopolite? Conversely, what is one to do with an Antifederalist like William Findley of Pennsylvania who, as Gordon Wood demonstrates in his essay "Interests and Disinterestedness in the Making of the Constitution," was as aggressively entrepreneurial and fearlessly future-oriented as anyone in America? Indeed, Wood's essay in this volume challenges the traditional formulation of "cosmopolitan" Federalists and "provincial" Antifederalists directly, arguing that it was the Antifederalists who broke most decisively with traditional patterns of thought in the areas of *both* politics and the economy.

The most recent effort at providing a synthesis of the ideological and social bases of Federalist and Antifederalist thought has been inspired in part by comparable work on the social and ideological bases of political division in eighteenth-century England. John Murrin, in a widely cited and elaborately titled essay, "The Great Inversion, or Court versus Country: A Comparison of the Revolution Settlements in England (1688–1721) and America (1776–1816)," suggests that the Federalist-Antifederalist divisions have their analogue in the eighteenth-century English divisions between the court and country parties in Parliament.[18] Following up on Murrin's suggestion, James Hutson has sought to use the court-country dichotomy to explain both the social and ideological bases of Federalist and Antifederalist thought and thus, in his claim, to reconcile "the conflicting contributions of the Progressive and consensus historians." According to Hutson, the court Whigs of England, "patrons not only of commerce but of strong government," shared with the Federalists a determination "to endow the government with the resources and vigor necessary to command great respect abroad and maintain order at home." Even more pointedly, the country party, whose *interests and ideology* were rooted in agriculture and the owner-

---

Opposition: Antifederalists and the Acceptance of the Constitution (Millwood, N.Y., 1979).

18. John M. Murrin, "The Great Inversion, or Court versus Country: A Comparison of the Revolution Settlements in England (1688–1721) and America (1776–1816)," in J.G.A. Pocock, ed., *Three British Revolutions: 1641, 1688, 1776* (Princeton, N.J., 1980), 368–453.

ship of real property, provided the model for the Antifederalists' views on central government. The Antifederalists' distrust of commerce, their fears of influence and corruption, and their fear of governmental power all had their analogues in country ideology.[19]

Like the earlier distinctions between "cosmopolitan" and "localist" political leaders, the terms "court" and "country" do have the virtue of blending (though perhaps *blurring*) the behavioral and ideological characteristics of Federalist and Antifederalist thought. More important, they remind us of the strong influence that eighteenth-century English political thought and political conflict had on American Revolutionary and constitutional thought. However, like notions of classical republicanism, or even of Lockean liberalism, the court-country categories of analysis do carry with them a number of the liabilities that come with any imported ideology. Although an understanding of the rhetoric of court and country is helpful in reminding us that Federalist fears of disorder or Antifederalist anxieties about the corrupting influences of commerce were not produced in a cultural vacuum, those perspectives do very little to help us understand some of the distinctively *American* sources of political division during the early national period.

The bitter debates between advocates of a broad and of a strict construction of the Constitution—debates that would divide both Federalists and Republicans and later Democrats and Whigs—simply cannot be comprehended through the lenses of English politics. Similarly, the increasingly clear divisions between North and South over issues relating both to economic development and political control of the new nation were obviously outgrowths of conditions peculiar to the spacious American Republic; and the rhetorical stances of defenders of the northern or southern position, while they might occasionally evoke those of partisans of the court or the country interest, certainly cannot be explained adequately by those categories. Indeed, in reading Paul Finkelman's detailed analysis in "Slavery and the Constitutional Convention," it is difficult to escape the conclusion that at least some aspects of our original constitutional system were shaped by ideologies and interests—racism and a slave-based agricultural system— that were nearly wholly outside the experience of court *and* country politicians alike.

Hutson also argues, in sharp contrast to Wood, Herbert Storing, and most other recent analysts of the Federalist-Antifederalist division, that there was little connection between either of the two camps and the acceptance of a democratic ethic in American politics.[20] It is certainly true that "democ-

19. Hutson, "Country, Court, and Constitution," *WMQ*, 3d Ser., XXXIX (1982), 337–368.
20. *Ibid.*, 350–356.

racy" had little place in the rhetorical arsenals of either the court or country factions in England, for the members of those factions were still working within an avowedly elitist political system, but it seems clear that the political context in which Federalists and Antifederalists operated, while by no means unreservedly egalitarian, was nevertheless far more open to popular influences than in England.

Ultimately, the court-country categories run afoul of the same difficulties as any of the dichotomous categories yet formulated to explain ideological or social division in America during the Revolutionary and constitutional period. Though Americans were, for a fleeting moment, forced by the yes-or-no nature of the decision on the Constitution to identify themselves as Federalists or Antifederalists, the array of crosscutting interests and ideological and cultural perspectives represented within those two camps was so diverse as to defy simple categorization. And thus, tempting as it may be to come up with matching sets of dichotomous interests and ideologies for each of the two sides, we are likely to do so only at the risk of obscuring much of the diversity that coexisted within those two camps.

The essays that this volume comprises reflect, we think, both the vigor of recent work on the ideology of the Revolutionary and constitutional periods and much of the current dissatisfaction with existing behavioral categories of analysis of those periods. And, while nearly all of the essays try in one way or another to ground their discussion of American ideology in the more earthly contexts of experience, they are, uniformly, unwilling to adopt Progressive categories as a means to that end. Though the range of subject matter and interpretation of the twelve essays defies easy categorization, there is, finally, one other theme—perhaps self-evident to historians of eighteenth-century America but assuredly not so to most Americans of the late twentieth century—that runs through many of the essays. The new part-national, part-federal government created in Philadelphia in 1787 was one of extraordinarily limited powers. It had to be so, since ancient fears of distant, uncontrollable tyranny remained intense among the common people of America, such as the inland farmers whom Richard D. Brown describes in his contribution to this volume, "Shays's Rebellion and the Ratification of the Federal Constitution in Massachusetts." The warnings of Antifederalists such as Patrick Henry that the new Constitution would bring about the "consolidation" of the states into a single, overpowering national government, though gaining some plausibility in the late twentieth century, were in fact greatly exaggerated in the contexts of the late eighteenth and early nineteenth centuries.[21] As John Murrin notes in his Epilogue to the volume,

21. See, for example, Henry's speech in the Virginia ratifying convention in

the Constitution itself would, soon after its drafting and ratification, become an important symbol of national unity, but the American nation, qua nation, was a roof without walls, a remarkably heterogeneous collection of generally sovereign and independent-minded states.

To be sure, Alexander Hamilton's financial programs seemed to some to threaten that sovereignty and independence, but viewed from the perspective of 1820 or even 1840, Hamilton's programs in fact altered the balance of power between the state and national governments only slightly. As Richard Ellis's essay "The Persistence of Antifederalism after 1789" indicates, the concerns expressed by the Antifederalists in 1787–1788 remained very much alive during the first half of the nineteenth century; but far from representing a backward-looking, rearguard action against an inevitable centralization of power, Antifederalist ideas persisted precisely because the locally oriented principles upon which they were based remained alive and well in the early Republic.

Historians of the American constitutional system can profit, I think, from a sharper recognition of the limits of early federal power. By far the greatest portion of the *existing* body of American constitutional scholarship has focused on the federal judiciary, and on Supreme Court interpretations of the U.S. Constitution in particular. The reasons for this emphasis are fairly obvious. Within the historical community in general there has been an understandable inclination to go where the action is, and the steady growth of federal power has quite naturally led historians to conclude that most of the action has been occurring within the various branches of the federal government. Moreover, within the legal profession itself, constitutional studies have been heavily tilted toward Supreme Court history, a mode of history which itself has been part of the tendency of American law schools to exalt the notion of an objectified body of law and of a nonpartisan judiciary charged with interpreting that law.

It seems possible, however, that all this may be about to change. While constitutional histories focusing on the evolution of federal power will always be essential to an understanding of how we arrived at our present constitutional destination, it is now becoming apparent that it may only be through studies of legal and constitutional development in the individual *states* that we will be able to discover where we have been. Stephen Botein's essay on early understandings of the relationship between church and state gives us one indication of the necessity of going this route; but even so recent, and controversial, a topic as the current Supreme Court stands on

---

Jonathan Elliot, ed., *The Debates in the Several State Conventions on the Adoption of the Federal Constitution* . . . , 2d ed. (Philadelphia, 1876–1881), II, 21–23.

the introduction of illegally seized evidence in criminal prosecutions is better comprehended against the background of earlier developments in state courts. As John P. Frank has noted in a contribution to a symposium on the emergence of state constitutional law, "When the United States Supreme Court finally 'created' an exclusionary rule for illegally seized evidence in state prosecutions, it followed a result that twenty-two states already had reached" in previous judicial and legislative acts at the state level. Similarly, though it may please some current critics of the Supreme Court to suppose that the ban on Bible reading in the public schools was an invention of that Court, it must be remembered that no fewer than seven state courts had issued such bans before the Supreme Court passed judgment on the issue.[22]

It is, I suspect, not surprising that the essays in this volume—most of which were written by historians whose previous work has focused on early America—should emphasize the distinctively *eighteenth-century* character of the Americans' understanding of their new federal union. Nor should it be much of a surprise to discover that a significant component of that eighteenth-century character was related to concerns about *limiting* governmental power. Manifestly, that "original understanding" is not in itself sufficient as a guide to the dilemmas that confront a complex society in the late twentieth century, but our clearer comprehension of the component parts of that understanding—a comprehension that must include *both* sides of the federal-state equation—may nevertheless provide us with a logical starting point.

22. The proceedings of the symposium "The Emergence of State Constitutional Law" are printed in *Texas Law Review*, LXIII, Nos. 6, 7 (1985). See, in particular, Stanley Mosk, "State Constitutionalism: Both Liberal and Conservative," 1081–1093; Robert F. Williams, "Equality Guarantees in State Constitutional Law," 1195–1224; and John P. Frank, review, 1339–1346. For additional indications of the revival of interest in state constitutional law, see Robert C. Palmer, "Liberties as Constitutional Provisions, 1776–1791," *Monographs of the Institute of Bill of Rights Law*, II (forthcoming); and Donald Lutz, *Popular Consent and Popular Control: Whig Political Theory in the Early State Constitutions* (Baton Rouge, La., 1980).

☆ ☆ ☆

PART I

Ideologies

☆ ☆ ☆ ☆ ☆

The American Constitution

A Revolutionary Interpretation

STANLEY N. KATZ

The year 1987 promises to be easier for Americans than 1976. The Constitutional Bicentennial should be more persuasive than the Revolutionary commemoration more than a decade ago. Is that because the first revolutionary new nation is not eager to think of itself as revolutionary? The Constitution, on the other hand, symbolizes stability and continuity, more comfortable values these days, values carrying less explicit ideological baggage. Although we will not reenact battles fought against the redcoats over the next several years, we also will not have to repress the fact that many of the most important Revolutionary battles were fought among Americans.

Indeed, the instinct to downplay the revolutionary character of the 1770s long ago suggested historical emphasis upon late eighteenth-century constitutionalism. In the late nineteenth century, a naive romantic nationalism disguised historians' ambivalence about revolution. But during the destabilized early years of the twentieth century, Progressive historians and political scientists sought to articulate more plausible links between a revolutionary past and a restabilizing present. The spiritual godfather of this academic trend was doubtless Woodrow Wilson of Princeton, with his admiration of Edmund Burke and Walter Bagehot, and his disdain for revolutionary philosophy. Perhaps younger scholars noted Wilson's prescription for the introduction of democracy into the Philippines: "They can have liberty no cheaper than we got it. They must first take the discipline of law, must first

This essay is based upon a lecture delivered as the first Charles and Jessica Swift Lecture in Constitutional Law at Middlebury College on May 7, 1985. I wish to express gratitude to Middlebury College and especially to Murray Dry for the invitation to deliver the lecture, and for permission to publish this expanded and revised version.

love order and instinctively yield to it. . . . We are old in this learning and must be their tutors."[1]

In any case, the scholarly instinct to explore the constitutional aspects of the Revolutionary era did not really mature until the decade between World War I and the early years of the New Deal. Then, when political scientists were undertaking the serious study of constitutional law for the first time, a liberal-legalist ethos dominated. It must have seemed natural for scholars of public law, searching for the origins of the 1787 system, to reach back to the apparently liberal principles of the Revolution, rooted in traditional English constitutionalism.

During this heyday of interest in revolutionary constitutional theory, debate was waged among such prominent scholars as Charles G. Haines, Andrew C. McLaughlin, Randolph G. Adams, Robert Livingston Schuyler, Charles F. Mullett, and Benjamin F. Wright.[2] For the purposes of this essay, however, I will focus upon the work of Charles H. McIlwain and *The American Revolution: A Constitutional Interpretation*, which won the Pulitzer Prize for History for him in 1923.

The most brilliant of the constitutionalists, McIlwain was educated as an undergraduate at Princeton (A.B., 1894) and did his graduate work at Harvard (Ph.D., 1911). Briefly in practice (like Wilson) as a lawyer, he taught history at Miami of Ohio (1903–1905), Princeton (where he was one of Wilson's preceptors, 1905–1910), Bowdoin (1910–1911), and thereafter at Harvard (in history and government) until 1946. McIlwain's deepest interest was in medieval and early modern English legal-political theory, but

1. As quoted by Arthur S. Link, in *Wilson: The Road to the White House* (Princeton, N.J., 1947), 28, from Wilson, "The Ideals of America," *Atlantic Monthly*, XC (1902), 730.

2. Charles Grove Haines, *The Revival of Natural Law Concepts . . .* , Harvard Studies in Jurisprudence, IV (Cambridge, Mass., 1930); Andrew Cunningham McLaughlin, *The Confederation and Constitution, 1783–1789* (New York, 1905), Vol. X of Albert Bushnell Hart, ed., *The American Nation: A History*; McLaughlin, *The Foundations of American Constitutionalism* (New York, 1932); Randolph Greenfield Adams, *Political Ideas of the American Revolution: Britannic-American Contributions to the Problem of Imperial Organization, 1765 to 1775* (Durham, N.C., 1922); Robert Livingston Schuyler, *Parliament and the British Empire: Some Constitutional Controversies concerning Imperial Legislative Jurisdiction* (New York, 1929); Charles F. Mullett, *Fundamental Law and the American Revolution, 1770–1776* (New York, 1933); Benjamin Fletcher Wright, Jr., *American Interpretations of Natural Law: A Study in the History of Political Thought* (Cambridge, Mass., 1931); Wright, *The Growth of American Constitutional Law* (New York, 1942). There were, of course, a great many other historians writing in the constitutional vein, and I do not intend to suggest that they formed a closely knit school.

throughout his career he insisted upon the historian's responsibility to relate his professional work to current political imperatives. Most notable, from this point of view, were articles written for *Foreign Affairs* during the 1930s, invoking the importance of Anglo-American constitutional values as a bulwark against the tyranny of fascism: "In this world struggle between arbitrary will and settled law, it is true that liberalism and democracy are deeply involved. The triumph of will over law must mean the end of both. But our present crisis is not merely the crisis of liberalism or of democracy; it is a struggle for every human right against despotism."[3]

As early as 1923, McIlwain had approached the problem of the American Revolution from the perspective of contemporary constitutionalism. McIlwain's summary analysis of the problem typifies the approach:

> The Americans denied the authority under English constitutional law of the Parliament at Westminster to bind Englishmen beyond the realm. They also asserted that parts of that law were wholly beyond Parliament's reach, were "fundamental," and that any act of Parliament in contravention of these parts was void. English statesmen asserted in reply that there was nothing beyond the power of the English Parliament, whether in the Realm or "in the Dominions thereunto belonging."[4]

McIlwain discerned three stages of development in the colonists' constitutional theory. First, and for most of the eighteenth century prior to 1765, they relied upon their charter rights; next, they turned to "the general Whig argument that the English constitution, founded on natural law, was a free constitution, guaranteeing to all its subjects wherever they might be the fundamental rights incident to free government"; finally, by 1774 they developed the notion that, although Parliament had no legal authority to legislate for colonies outside the realm, an exception could be made for the regulation of imperial trade ("one expressly declared to be not of right but only by way of voluntary concession") by colonial consent ("except in matters of 'internal polity'"). The final appeal to natural rights McIlwain considered altogether political and nonconstitutional, "no longer as a part of the British constitution, but as the rights of man in general."[5]

---

3. C. H. McIlwain, "Government by Law," *Foreign Affairs*, XIV (1935–1936), 186. See also "The Reconstruction of Liberalism," *ibid.*, XVI (1937–1938), 167–175.

4. McIlwain, *The American Revolution: A Constitutional Interpretation* (1923; paper rpt., Ithaca, N.Y., 1958), 16.

5. *Ibid.*, 152, 116–117. The 1774 document is the Oct. 1 Declaration of Colonial Rights and Grievances, article 4, reprinted in Merrill Jensen, ed., *American Colonial Documents to 1776* (London, 1965), Vol. IX of David C. Douglas, ed., *English Historical Documents* (Oxford, 1953–), 806–807.

This hurried survey does justice neither to McIlwain nor to his contemporaries, but it does suggest four characteristics that they shared. The first was an insistence upon the fundamental law function of the Constitution as a limitation on the power of the sovereign over individuals. The second was a belief that the ultimate constitutional problem of the Revolution was the imperial question: how could the colonists exercise all the rights of Englishmen as though they lived within the realm? Put another way, how could Americans avoid the constitutional disaster of Ireland? Third, there was a tendency to constitutional formalism. McIlwain listed as "constitutional non-essentials" the economic, social, and political causes of the Revolution.[6] The final and probably most basic characteristic of the constitutionalist position was that it derived from analogy between the American colonies in the mid-eighteenth century and England in the middle third of the seventeenth century, between the American Revolution and the era of the English Civil War–Glorious Revolution. The unspoken question put to the American Revolution was why it was not amenable to constitutional resolution as the internal English conflict ultimately had been.

Perhaps McIlwain and his contemporaries had gone as far as it was then possible for constitutional historians to go. Their predilection for interpreting the Revolutionary struggle as a succession of legal precedents has, however, alienated (or bored) more modern historians—even those who were and are not committed to the notion that Revolutionary rhetoric is best discounted as propaganda. In a 1972 essay, Bernard Bailyn twice in three pages stigmatized certain Revolutionary constitutional ideas as "abstruse."[7] Perhaps more important, the constitutionalists' preoccupation with the imperial problem has made it seem as if constitutional history had little to contribute to the study of the domestic side of the Revolution, and their stress on precedent has made them appear biased toward a conservative interpretation of the Revolution, viewing the conflict as a "movement wrought by practitioners of the common law and devoted to preserving it, and the ancient liberties embedded in it, intact."[8]

In truth, the intellectual history of the Revolution was almost totally ignored in the 1940s and 1950s. For most historians of my own generation, it consisted in the classroom assignment of the few Revolutionary pamphlets reprinted in Samuel Eliot Morison's ubiquitous little book of sources and an offhand reference or two to Randolph G. Adams and Moses Coit Tyler.

6. McIlwain, *American Revolution*, v, 5.

7. Bernard Bailyn, "The Central Themes of the American Revolution: An Interpretation," in Stephen G. Kurtz and James H. Hutson, eds., *Essays on the American Revolution* (Chapel Hill, N.C., 1973), 5–7.

8. Bernard Bailyn, *The Ideological Origins of the American Revolution* (Cambridge, Mass., 1967), vii.

We memorized the strategic ploys of Revolutionary "propagandists" and argued over whether the colonists had distinguished between the competence of Parliament to regulate internal and its competence to regulate imperial trade.[9]

With the publication of Caroline Robbins's *Eighteenth-Century Commonwealthman* in 1959, however, interest in political theory was renewed, and intellectual interpretations of the American Revolution were dramatically revised.[10] Although a great many scholars have taken part in the reinterpretation, it is most widely associated with Professor Bailyn (*The Ideological Origins of the American Revolution*) and Gordon S. Wood (*The Creation of the American Republic*),[11] and its characteristic feature is the identification of early eighteenth-century English political radicalism (right *and* left opposition to Robert Walpole) as the critical determinant of American political thought. In a summary of his view, Bailyn contended:

Almost—but not quite—all of the ideas and beliefs that shaped the American Revolutionary mind can be found in the voluminous writ-

9. S. E. Morison, ed., *Sources and Documents Illustrating the American Revolution, 1764-1788, and the Formation of the Federal Constitution* (Oxford, 1923); Adams, *Political Ideas*; Moses Coit Tyler, *The Literary History of the American Revolution, 1763-1783*, 2 vols. (New York, 1897); Edmund S. Morgan and Helen M. Morgan, *The Stamp Act Crisis: Prologue to Revolution* (Chapel Hill, N.C., 1953).

10. Caroline Robbins, *The Eighteenth-Century Commonwealthman: Studies in the Transmission, Development, and Circumstance of English Liberal Thought from the Restoration of Charles II until the War with the Thirteen Colonies* (Cambridge, Mass., 1961). See also Corinne C. Weston, *English Constitutional Theory and the House of Lords, 1556-1832* (London, 1965); Betty Kemp, *King and Commons, 1660-1832* (London, 1957); J. W. Gough, *Fundamental Law in English Constitutional History* (Oxford, 1955); J.G.A. Pocock, *The Ancient Constitution and the Feudal Law: A Study of English Historical Thought in the Seventeenth Century* (1957; paper rpt., New York, 1967); Jack P. Greene, introduction to Greene, ed., *The Nature of Colony Constitutions* (Columbia, S.C., 1970), 1-55. I should note here that R. R. Palmer, *The Age of the Democratic Revolution: A Political History of Europe and America, 1760-1780*, 2 vols. (Princeton, N.J., 1959-1964), in revivifying interest in American constitutional history has probably been underestimated.

11. Gordon S. Wood, *The Creation of the American Republic, 1776-1787* (Chapel Hill, N.C., 1969). See also H. Trevor Colbourn, *The Lamp of Experience: Whig History and the Intellectual Origins of the American Revolution* (Chapel Hill, N.C., 1965); Richard Buel, Jr., "Democracy and the American Revolution: A Frame of Reference," *William and Mary Quarterly*, 3d Ser., XXI (1964), 165-190; Elisha P. Douglass, *Rebels and Democrats: The Struggle for Equal Political Rights and Majority Rule during the American Revolution* (Chapel Hill, N.C., 1955); Pauline Maier, *From Resistance to Revolution: Colonial Radicals and the Development of American Opposition to Britain, 1765-1776* (New York, 1972).

ings of the Exclusion Crisis and in the literature of the Glorious Revolution. . . . [But] there remains still another decisive moment. . . . in the
writings of the [Walpole opposition, which constituted a] populist cry
against what appeared to be a swelling financial-governmental complex
fat with corruption, complaisant and power-engrossing.

From their reading of the anti-Walpole pamphleteers the colonists discerned
the two complaints that seemed best to describe their own situation in the
emerging imperial crisis: that "all power . . . was evil . . . in the threat it would
always pose to the progress of liberty" and that corruption "threatened to
destroy the free British constitution."[12]

Bailyn's hypothesis directly impinges upon the relationship of constitutionalism and the Revolution. He acknowledges the relevance of late
seventeenth-century English political thought and certainly recognizes the
commitment of Revolutionaries to the ideal of the British constitution. As
Gordon Wood has pointed out, the Revolutionary generation "sincerely
believed they were not creating new rights or new principles prescribed only
by what ought to be, but saw themselves claiming 'only to keep their old
privileges,' the traditional rights and principles of all Englishmen, sanc-
tioned by what they thought had always been." Wood goes on to argue,
however, that "this continual talk of desiring nothing new and wishing only
to return to the old system and the essentials of the English constitution was
only a superficial gloss," belied by the "powerful revolutionary ideology"
which they had absorbed from the English opposition theorists.[13] Both Bailyn and Wood view the constitutional tradition as subordinate to Revolutionary political ideology and as having little explanatory value for understanding the actual progress of revolution.

It may be useful to point out some of the implications for constitutional
history that arise from the revisionism of the 1960s. The most significant
new contribution is the clarification of the successive English constitutional
theories from the late Middle Ages to the time of the American Revolution:
mixed government, separation of powers, the balanced constitution. This
analysis has quickly become accepted by American historians for its utility
in explaining early American governmental institutions, and it has been
immensely helpful in understanding the relevance of Montesquieu, Blackstone, and Burke to American intellectual development. Perhaps even more
important, it has shed an entirely new light on the meaning of separation of
power and the checks and balances in the American constitutional scheme.[14]

12. Bailyn, "Central Themes," in Kurtz and Hutson, eds., *Essays*, 8–9.
13. Wood, *Creation of the American Republic*, 13.
14. See Weston, *Constitutional Theory*; M.J.C. Vile, *Constitutionalism and the Sepa-*
ration of Powers (Oxford, 1967); W. B. Gwyn, *The Meaning of the Separation of Powers:*
An Analysis of the Doctrine from Its Origin to the Adoption of the United States Constitu-

More crucial for constitutional history, Bailyn contends that true constitutionalism (species *americanus*) was a result rather than a cause of Revolutionary ideology:

> Like their contemporaries in England and like their predecessors for centuries before, the colonists at the beginning of the Revolutionary controversy understood by the word "constitution" not, as we would have it, a written document or even an unwritten but deliberately contrived design of government and a specification of rights beyond the power of ordinary legislation to alter; they thought of it, rather, as the constituted—that is, existing—arrangement of governmental institutions, laws, and customs together with the principles and goals that animated them.[15]

This was James Otis's view of the constitution as expounded in the mid-1760s, but Bailyn argues that it was founded on already anachronistic notions of the judicial functions of Parliament and, in particular, of the subordination of Parliament to the constitution.[16] Other Americans perceived more clearly the political and constitutional implications of the mid-eighteenth-century sovereignty of Parliament and revised their constitutional attitudes accordingly:

> In 1770 the constitution was said to be "a line which marks out the enclosure"; in 1773 it was "the standing measure of the proceedings of government" of which rulers are "by no means to attempt an alteration ... without public consent"; in 1774 it was a "model of government"; in 1775 it was "certain great first principles" on whose "certainty and permanency ... the rights of both the ruler and the subjects depend; nor may they be altered or changed by ruler or people, but [only] by the whole collective body ... nor may they be touched by the legislator."[17]

The final step came in 1776, when Americans concluded that such novel limitations on government must be created by "an act of *all*" (by specially selected popular conventions, approved by popular referendum) and must be embodied in written documents.[18] For Bailyn and Wood, one of the

---

tion (New Orleans, La., 1965). See also Bailyn, *Ideological Origins*; and Wood, *Creation of the American Republic*. For a survey of the literature, see Stanley N. Katz, "The Origins of American Constitutional Thought," *Perspectives in American History*, III (1969), 474–490.

15. Bailyn, *Ideological Origins*, 67–68.

16. *Ibid.*, 176–180.

17. *Ibid.*, 182.

18. *Ibid.*, 182–184. On the importance of conventions and popular assent to constitutions, see especially Wood, *Creation of the American Republic*, 306–343.

transcendent achievements of the American Revolution was the creation of the modern conception of the constitution as something antecedent to government and drawing its authority immediately from the will of the people, against which no law or governmental action can prevail. The idea had been previously proclaimed, of course, and its elements are mostly present in McLaughlin's *Foundations of American Constitutionalism*, but never before had it been stated so elegantly, nor had its implications been so thoroughly explored.[19]

Despite the attractiveness and obvious utility of the revisionist theory of Revolutionary political thought, we would do well to avoid throwing the baby out with the bath water. What Bailyn and Wood are describing is not "constitutionalism" tout simple, but, rather, modern or democratic constitutionalism—perhaps, more narrowly, the constitutionalism of new nations. What necessitated the resort to the convention-written, document-ratification model of constitutionalism was the fact that the imperial crisis of 1775-1776 and the decision for Independence required popular agreement upon and identification of the fundamental law (as well as the creation of a mechanism for enforcing that law against the government). The "ancient constitution" and the common law would not do as the bulwarks against ministerial despotism, in part simply because they were English. From this point of view Revolutionary (at least, early Revolutionary) protestations of commitment to the divine British constitution were anything but "a superficial gloss."

As Professor Bailyn has repeatedly stressed in defense of his position, the importance of the Revolutionary ideology is that it was the triggering mechanism of the movement for Independence:

> American resistance in the 1760s and 1770s was a response to acts of power deemed arbitrary, degrading, and uncontrollable—a response, in itself objectively reasonable, that was inflamed to the point of explosion by ideological currents generating fears everywhere in America that irresponsible and self-seeking adventurers . . . had gained the power of the English government and were turning first, for reasons that were variously explained, to that Rhineland of their aggressions, the colonies.[20]

But we must not forget that McIlwain himself denied that the English constitutional tradition had been a cause of the rebellion. "So far then," he

19. McLaughlin, *Foundations*, chap. 4; Wood, *Creation of the American Republic*, 600-602.

20. Bailyn, "Central Themes," in Kurtz and Hutson, eds., *Essays*, 12. See also "A Comment," *American Historical Review*, LXXV (1969-1970), 361-363.

admitted "as America's final and fundamental constitutional demands as a part of the British Empire are concerned, our debt to England is slight, and rather to the Radicals than to the Whigs." Our debt to the Whig tradition, he concluded, lies "in those positive institutions of government whose foundations were laid long before the Revolutionary struggle." "These principles are still embodied in our present constitutional system."[21] English constitutionalism contributed significantly to both the libertarian-fundamental law tradition omnipresent in the colonies and to the American constitutional tradition that succeeded it. The constitutional tradition will surely not do as an explanation of the coming of the Revolution, but without it we can hardly begin to understand the basic theme in the development of American political institutions over the past two hundred years.

In his *Constitutionalism: Ancient and Modern*, McIlwain has given us a convenient (if oversimplified) account of the English constitutional heritage. It is based on the proposition that English constitutionalism can best be understood in terms of Henry de Bracton's distinction between *jurisdictio* and *gubernaculum*—between fundamental law and the power to govern. "Jurisdiction" is the proposition that "the king is under the law and yet under no man, that private right is determinable and enforceable by law, and is under the control of courts and parliaments." "Government" is the proposition that the management of public affairs is exclusively within the competence of the king.[22] So long as king, lords, and commons remained an organic whole, the theory (admittedly European rather than English) provided for the protection of private right within a monarchical structure. In England, jurisdiction was practically synonymous with the common law, whose authority derived from time immemorial.

By the mid-seventeenth century the traditional constitutional theory was violently revealed to have a fatal flaw—"the lack of sanction for the protection of the sphere of law from invasion by the power of government."[23] Jurisdiction was more or less sufficient to protect private property, but it was becoming increasingly clear that it could not protect individual freedom from the ravages of autocratic government. As a contemporary put it, "I shall have an estate of inheritance for life, or for years in my land, or propriety in my goods, and I shall be a tenant at will for my liberty; I shall have propriety in my house, and not liberty in my person."[24] In the end, of course, the only sanction to enforce jurisdiction against government was revolu-

---

21. McIlwain, *American Revolution*, 159.

22. McIlwain, *Constitutionalism: Ancient and Modern*, rev. ed. (1947; paper rpt., Ithaca, N.Y., 1961), 111.

23. *Ibid.*, 117.

24. *Ibid.*, 127 (quoting William Hakewill).

tion, and this was the accomplishment of the Civil War and, finally, of the Glorious Revolution. Thus, by the early eighteenth century the constitutional tradition had been (partially) modernized, for the king had been made "responsible in government as well as in jurisdiction, and responsible not merely to God, as had been held before, but to the law and to the people."[25]

McIlwain's paradigm (stretched to an extent that Bracton could never have imagined) can be usefully applied to the American situation—so long as one does not suppose that it was consciously employed by the colonists themselves. I believe that the jurisdiction-government dichotomy helps to explain why the 1689 solution to England's constitutional crisis was bound to be unsatisfactory on this side of the Atlantic. After all, it was by the transfer of much of the scope of government to Parliament and the courts that the crown was finally and effectively limited.

J. G. A. Pocock has explained to us how the English common law tradition of the early seventeenth century was expanded (one might almost say obfuscated) into an overarching protector of individual rights:

The search for precedents resulted in the building-up of a body of alleged rights and privileges that were supposed to be immemorial, and this, coupled with the general and vigorous belief that England was ruled by law and that this law was itself immemorial, resulted in turn in that most important and elusive of seventeenth-century concepts, the fundamental law.

The concept of fundamental law itself was then transformed with the Glorious Revolution, and soon "assertions that the law was immemorial tended to be replaced by assertions that parliament, and especially a house of commons representing the property-owners, was immemorial," with the result that "the concept of fundamental law therefore did much both to cloak and to delay the transition to a full assertion of parliamentary sovereignty."[26]

The Glorious Revolution doubtless marks a curious, almost invisible, turning point in American constitutional development. For most of the colonists, England's bloodless conflict meant nothing more than a change of distant rulers, and there was surely next to no colonial apprehension of the actual progress toward legislative sovereignty in the mother country. Yet, superficially, the inhabitants of Massachusetts, New York, and Maryland (at least) behaved as though they were zealous to overthrow the Catholic-Jacobite conspiracy against the rights of Englishmen. For Massachusetts, in particular, the parallel must have seemed compelling, since the Dominion of New England at which they hurled themselves had actually destroyed

25. *Ibid.*, 131.
26. Pocock, *Ancient Constitution*, 48, 49, 50.

the very basis of consensual, limited government as they had known it since 1630.

Everywhere, there was talk of the right of property and the rights of individuals, of the jurisdiction of courts and the protection of trial by jury, of the need for representation at least in matters of taxation, of the necessity of local legislatures. The colonial rhetoric of the seventeenth-century revolutionary era was derivative, and it surely seems unlikely that the social and political unrest of the period 1675–1692 was caused by these constitutional dissatisfactions. Furthermore, as David Lovejoy has eloquently pointed out, the Glorious Revolution was a theoretical failure in America:

> From a conception of empire based on an equality of Englishmen in dominions and realm, colonists sought a colonial policy which would honor Englishmen's rights in America. In these rights, they believed, besides protection *from* arbitrary power and troublesome "mutacons," lay sanction *for* government by law, equitable justice, economic opportunity, and the rights of property—a combination of political principle and material advantage. Prevented from realizing these guarantees before 1689, they championed the Glorious Revolution as a means to that end. In this, too, they were disappointed. Despite significant changes won by Englishmen in England, the lesson the Revolution taught the colonies was that they were dominions of the Crown to be dealt with as the King wished, with no assurance of Englishmen's rights on permanent bases.[27]

Ironically, the Glorious Revolution left the Americans trapped between a stone and a soft place. They had achieved only marginal constitutional gains (the demise of the Dominion, the establishment of an assembly in New York) and had been forced to abide by the traditional conception that the colonial dominions were directly under the prerogative of the crown. It was this latter fact, more than anything else, that accounts for the long-delayed American awareness of the parliamentary victory in England in 1689, since with the exception of a continuing series of toothless mercantile acts it was prerogative rather than legislative power that symbolized English authority to the colonists.

Imperial intervention was thus minimal at the very time that colonial political institutions entered the final phase of their development. The opening decades of the eighteenth century witnessed a general acceptance of the substantive common law and English procedural forms, the more formal

27. David S. Lovejoy, *The Glorious Revolution in America* (New York, 1972), 377–378. See especially the discussion of the draft Virginia charter of 1675, pp. 38–39, and the chapters on New York and Massachusetts, 235–270.

structuring of town and county governments, the establishment of news-papers, and the general improvement of communications—and the self-aggrandizement of the lower houses of legislatures, the much-discussed "rise of the assembly."[28]

Jack P. Greene finds in the development of the assemblies a conscious con-tinuation of the seventeenth-century parliamentary struggle for supremacy over the crown. He argues that the later Stuart opposition literature and par-liamentary commentaries "prescribed explicitly and in detail a whole set of generalized and specific institutional imperatives for representative bodies, a particular pattern of behavior for their members, and a concrete program of political action":

> The central assumptions behind this prescription were, first, that there was a natural antagonism between the "King's Prerogative" and the "Rights, Liberties and Properties of the People," and, second, that the primary function of the House of Commons, as Henry Care declared, was "to preserve inviolable our Liberty and Property, according to the known Laws of the Land, without any giving way unto or Introduction of that absolute and arbitrary Rule practised in Foreign Countries."[29]

It was therefore natural that the colonists (and particularly colonial legis-lators) should view their governors as surrogates of an almost uncontrollable prerogative descending directly from the Stuart tyrants, and their assemblies as "the main barrier of all those rights and privileges which British subjects enjoy."[30]

There is certainly no doubt that the colonists strove to increase the power and institutional sophistication of their legislatures, and it is clear that they were strongly influenced to do so by the example of Parliament in the Stuart era. It seems to me less obvious that they were "haunted" by "the specter of unlimited prerogative" or that their reliance was so exclusively upon legisla-tive defense of their liberties.[31] The passing of the Stuarts had, after all, been well remarked in America, and we are all aware of the relative powerlessness

28. Charles Worthen Spencer, "The Rise of the Assembly, 1691–1760," in A. C. Flick, ed., *History of the State of New York* (New York, 1933–1937), II, 153–199; Mary Patterson Clarke, *Parliamentary Privilege in the American Colonies* (New Haven, Conn., 1943); Jack P. Greene, *The Quest for Power: The Lower Houses of Assembly in the Southern Royal Colonies, 1689–1776* (Chapel Hill, N.C., 1963); Michael Kam-men, *Deputyes and Libertyes: The Origins of Representative Government in Colonial America* (New York, 1969).

29. Jack P. Greene, "Political Mimesis: A Consideration of the Historical and Cultural Roots of Legislative Behavior in the British Colonies in the Eighteenth Century," *AHR*, LXXV (1969–1970), 347.

30. *Ibid.*, 349 (quoting an address of the Pennsylvania assembly, 1728).

31. *Ibid.*, 351.

of colonial governors as compared even to the Hanoverian monarchs. Furthermore, the relatively limited segment of colonial society which controlled the assemblies (and used them for very restricted purposes) was infrequently capable of generating that feeling of identification with the entire nation that was surely the touchstone of success for the English parliamentary movement.

And, to return to our discussion of America and the Glorious Revolution, the "rise" of the assembly was limited by the colonial perception of the role of Parliament. As M. J. C. Vile has noted, one of the results of "the battle between King and Parliament" was that "the King, although he still had powerful and important prerogatives, must acknowledge the supremacy of the law, and, therefore, of the legislature."[32] But if one thinks the matter through, the assembly could never aspire to "supremacy" within the context of the British constitution. It was not only that political thinkers of the early eighteenth century could not conceive of divisible sovereignty, but, more important, that the colonists had never fully assimilated the implications of parliamentary victory—and when Blackstone pointed them out, they found them intolerable.

Parliament had moved steadily to the modern command notion of legislation, to the point at which the lord chancellor could oppose the repeal of the Stamp Act on Austinian grounds: "Every government can arbitrarily inpose laws on all its subjects; there must be a supreme dominion in every state; whether monarchical, aristocratical, democratical, or mixed. And all the subjects of each state are bound by the laws made by government."[33] The colonists, manifestly still under the sway of *gubernaculum*, retained a pre-Revolutionary commitment to *jurisdictio*. Their eighteenth-century romance with the common law, which is everywhere evident in colonial political controversies, deceived them into a Cokeian reliance upon tradition and law as a limitation on governmental excess—although, of course, they also sought to bolster themselves by legislative action. So little did they exaggerate the competence of their assemblies, however, that they doubted their competence to alter the common law. They held, as Gordon Wood has pointed out in discussing the views of James Otis, that law was not "the enacted will of the legislature but more in the nature of a judgment declaratory of the moral principles of the law by the high court of Parliament . . . that must be inherently just and equitable."[34] In America, the cloak of fundamental law

---

32. Vile, *Constitutionalism*, 53.

33. First earl of Northington, as quoted in *The Parliamentary History of England*, XVI (London, 1815), 170, and in McIlwain, *Constitutionalism*, 5.

34. Wood, *Creation of the American Republic*, 263; see also 262–267; William E. Nelson, *Americanization of the Common Law: The Impact of Legal Change on Massachusetts Society, 1760–1830* (Cambridge, Mass., 1975), chap. 2.

over parliamentary sovereignty was all but complete, and from the 1690s to the 1760s the colonists tended to base their most important claims to private right on the old common law tradition. Anyone who has read the newspapers, pamphlets, and assembly debates of the period will recognize the tedious parade of precedents drawn from Coke and his brethren. To this point the English constitutional tradition, partially perceived, had carried the Americans. But, of course, neither the lack of sanction against parliamentary power nor the necessity for such sanction was foreseen much before 1765. To resolve the contradiction between liberty and government the colonists would be forced to seek elsewhere.

It was when, following the Seven Years' War, Parliament began freely to exercise its power of government over the colonies that the Americans began thinking and acting their way toward revolution. As if they had been transported back to the seventeenth century, they came to acknowledge that, short of rebellion, they had no way of enforcing the fundamental law against a tyrannical government that treated their property as ruthlessly as their personal liberty. *Jurisdictio* was once again at war with *gubernaculum*, and the American solution to the problem was to devise a radically new mode of public law for keeping government under control and for linking fundamental law to popular consent. In doing so they explicitly rejected the Hanoverian solution and distinguished sharply between constitutional law and legislation.

There remains much in the traditional constitutional interpretation that rings true. One continues to be struck by the extent to which the colonists hewed so closely to Cokeian parliamentarianism that they failed to recognize its transformation to Whig parliamentarianism, and by their pre-1775 struggle to achieve constitutional "reformation by conservation."[35] We can still appreciate the importance of the royal charters (and even gubernatorial commissions and instructions) in the formation of the American notion of the written constitution. And, of course, the characteristic concern of the English tradition for fundamental law protection (and procedural legal guarantees) of the individual against the power of the state is self-evident in the colonial scene. By 1775 the Americans were out of constitutional synchronization with Great Britain, but they had good historical reason to believe that the liberties which they strove to defend against British corruption and power were the same as Pym and Sydney had striven for.

The values of the "ancient constitution" were properly a colonial birthright, and they were intensified by both their validity in the brief American

35. William Huse Dunham, Jr., "A Transatlantic View of the British Constitution, 1760–76," in Dafydd Jenkins, ed., *Legal History Studies, 1972: Papers Presented to the Legal History Conference, Aberystwyth, 18–21 July 1972* (Cardiff, 1975), 52.

experience and their mimicry during the pervasive Anglicization of early eighteenth-century America.[36] Colonial commitment to English constitutionalism made the apparent unconstitutionality of the ministerial program of the years following the Seven Years' War all the more poignant, as the Americans realized that they would have to forge the means to enforce the fundamental law against the governmental excesses of the new sovereign— Parliament.

At the end the colonists were confronted with a choice between an Irish submission to external authority, the reform of Parliament, and the assertion of American sovereignty. Their unhesitating acceptance of the English libertarian heritage rendered the first alternative impossible, just as the pace of English political and constitutional development made the second too difficult for accomplishment in the eighteenth century. Having discovered that their English contemporaries had wrenched law loose from its moral footings, the Americans came to the conclusion that there could be no guarantee of individual liberty in imperial Britain. They had to summon up a new conception of the relation between fundamental law and governmental power, but in doing so they were by no means without historic resources. Despite its well-recognized innovations and instrumentalism, in its origins the modern American constitutional tradition sought to achieve the traditional ideals that Englishmen had churlishly abandoned.

The constitutionalists of McIlwain's generation responded to the threat of revolution from the right; our own generation has been more concerned to erect barriers against the left. Ironically, then, the revolutionary origins of American constitutionalism now look like a fundamentalist, antirevolutionary tradition, the bold assertions of the Declaration of Independence to the contrary. The Constitution stands as a bulwark against revolution on the one hand and legislative sovereignty on the other. None of this was, however, historically inevitable, and the task of the historian is to see that the record is as clear as he can make it.[37] As McIlwain said in his 1937 presidential address to the American Historical Association: "Some 'lessons of history' we know will always be drawn, some 'lessons of history' will always be acted on. Our part is to see that these really are the lessons *of history*."[38]

36. See John M. Murrin, "Anglicizing an American Colony: The Transformation of Provincial Massachusetts" (Ph.D. diss., Yale University, 1966).

37. Forrest McDonald's brilliant approach to this problem appeared too late to be incorporated into this essay: *Novus Ordo Seclorum: The Intellectual Origins of the Constitution* (Lawrence, Kans., 1985).

38. C. H. McIlwain, "The Historian's Part in a Changing World," *AHR*, XLII (1936–1937), 208.

☆ ☆ ☆ ☆ ☆
The Constitution
of the Thinking
Revolutionary

RALPH LERNER

I

The quickened interest among students of American history in the political
writings of the Revolutionary and early national periods may fairly be traced
to the influential work of Bernard Bailyn and Gordon S. Wood. Reinforced
by the historical and methodological researches of J. G. A. Pocock and
Quentin Skinner, a regiment of scholars has for the past quarter-century
traversed the historical landscape to ferret out and account for the concerns
of that generation of Americans. Although these historians are a diverse lot,
marching indeed to different drummers, they share some beliefs—sharply
at odds with earlier modes—that make it useful to treat them *as* a group. In
marshaling them here under one banner I mean neither to trick them out in
one uniform nor to enlist them under false colors. Nor does this general
review imply that a closer inspection of such knowledgeable and sharp-
sighted scholars would be without value or interest. But such is not the
order of the day. My immediate concern is what I take to be the stance
adopted by these historians when they come to assess the significance of
thought and thoughtfulness in political discourse and action. Just as a common staging area testifies to a unity behind diverse forces going their several
ways, so too do these shared assumptions bespeak a deeper level of agreement. It is that often tacit agreement which serves as the point of departure
for this inquiry.

The new historians begin with a doubt. Can any generation be mindful
of its assumptions or premises? Can we as individuals find a platform at
some remove from our daily preoccupations, a platform from which we may

The author wishes to thank Marvin Meyers and Thomas S. Schrock for their
criticism and suggestions.

coolly observe our acts, our words, our fears and hopes? If not, it may be because we are enmeshed in a net of meanings, intentions, and significations largely not of our making and largely beyond our control. That very tool by which we mean to effect our will—language—may equally influence and limit how we think and what we think and hence even what we can imagine willing.

These observations or misgivings—and I present them here in a very simple, bare-bones fashion—raise large problems for the study of the past, and especially for the study of the American Revolutionary founders. The most prominent and vocal of those men and women acted as though they believed they knew what they were about, as though their own reasoned analyses might make a difference in the course of human affairs. On the whole, they were impressed more by their opportunities than by their entrapment. But this will not do for today's historians. Emboldened by the insights of late twentieth-century psychology, sociology, philosophy, and so forth, they claim to see through and beyond the delimiting mold of eighteenth-century thinking. They understand what those Revolutionary founders could never have grasped: that when those figures mounted their elaborate arguments—buttressed with classical references, historical examples, and citations from approved religious, political, and philosophical authorities—they were doing more than stating in enlightened fashion the common sense of the age. Unbeknownst to themselves, they were clarifying, while symbolizing, the inchoate feelings, urges, anxieties, and stresses of a world in flux. What they took to be high principle, even self-evident truth, was in fact ideology, a dramatic way of making sense of a world somehow gone awry. Useful research needs to begin with that insight.

Accordingly, the vast outpouring of argument that attended the struggle over Independence and the formation of a national government has been reviewed and scrutinized with the new eyes and in accord with the new purposes of our new historians. To be sure, this labor has not always been easy to sustain. It is hard to keep one's mind on, let alone take seriously, language and argument that seem so overwrought, fantastical, and "extravagant." Just as the eighteenth-century British country writers exhibited "obsessive concern" in harping upon their favorite theme of corruption in government, so too did the American colonists dwell "endlessly, almost compulsively" on the theme of containing power, fascinated perhaps by "its 'sado-masochistic flavor'" (Bailyn).[1] Our natural impulse is to want to look no further into a literature said to be rife with "irrational and hysterical

---

1. Bernard Bailyn, *The Origins of American Politics* (New York, 1968), 10–11; *The Ideological Origins of the American Revolution* (Cambridge, Mass., 1967), 48, 56 (see also 62 n. 7).

beliefs," "patent absurdity and implausibility," "exaggerated and fanatical rhetoric," "hysterical and emotional ideas," "violent seemingly absurd distortions and falsifications of what we now believe to be true," and "frenzied rhetoric." Nor are our spirits lifted to hear that "there is simply too much fanatical and millennial thinking even by the best minds"; that even John Adams and Thomas Jefferson were victims of "the enthusiastic extravagance —the paranoiac obsession," the "grandiose and feverish language" of their age (Wood).[2] We are more likely to pity Jefferson than to be fascinated by him on learning that his view of Saxon England, expressed in a pamphlet meant to propel people toward revolution and independence, "was a romantic diversion rather than a meaningful historical appeal" and, in any event, "too obscure to have ideological power" (Henderson). That pity may turn to contempt on learning how, in the last decade of his life, Jefferson's use of language provides "a classic example of symbolic action," growing ever more extreme, rigid, and inflexible (Shalhope).[3] The corpus of early American political writings begins to take on the character of a psychopathologist's cabinet of curiosa.

Yet it would, of course, be wrong to jump to conclude thus about Jefferson and, accordingly, about the new historians; for as these very historians would be the first to assert, our distaste or dismay or disbelief in the face of such language needs to be overcome. We must "listen with care" precisely because that language reflects how the world seemed to those eighteenth-century folk; they sincerely believed and acted on that appearance (Bailyn).[4] Thus "any idea or symbol . . . however irrational or silly" (Wood), however "archaic" or "anachronistic"—even, or especially, if it prevented contemporaries from reaching a realistic understanding of their situation (Berthoff) —holds special significance for the historian. Make-believe is as much part of the real world as tubs and taxes. In analyzing these peculiar notions, the historian makes the incredible intelligible and helps us to see "the inescapable limits circumscribing [a man's] ability to think and to act" (Shalhope).[5]

2. Gordon S. Wood, "Rhetoric and Reality in the American Revolution," *William and Mary Quarterly*, 3d Ser., XXIII (1966), 20-21, 25-27.

3. H. James Henderson, *Party Politics in the Continental Congress* (New York, 1974), 89; Robert E. Shalhope, "Thomas Jefferson's Republicanism and Antebellum Southern Thought," *Journal of Southern History*, XLII (1976), 538-539.

4. Bailyn, *Origins of American Politics*, 10-11, 148, 159-160; and *Ideological Origins*, 94-95; Lance Banning, "Republican Ideology and the Triumph of the Constitution, 1789 to 1793," *WMQ*, 3d Ser., XXXI (1974), 184; Gordon S. Wood, "Conspiracy and the Paranoid Style: Causality and Deceit in the Eighteenth Century," *WMQ*, 3d Ser., XXXIX (1982), 420-429; but see Wood, "Intellectual History and the Social Sciences," in John Higham and Paul K. Conkin, eds., *New Directions in American Intellectual History* (Baltimore, 1979), 33.

5. Wood, "Intellectual History," in Higham and Conkin, eds., *New Directions*,

Nor should one misunderstand the new historians' disinclination to ask—and answer—the question, Was there anything to those fears? Were they solely or principally matters of subjective perception? No one maintains they were merely neurotic fantasies. The solidity and appositeness of this anxious analysis were vindicated for eighteenth-century folk in a number of ways: by newspaper dispatches, by recent history, by the accounts of ancient historians—and also, let it be said, "by the testimony of direct experience." Here in 1768 was "in bold, stark actuality a standing army" (Bailyn). Here in 1791 was a permanently funded debt with its corrupt and corruptible swarm of Treasury dependents (Banning).[6]

Yet these particulars are not the most significant facts. Or, rather, their significance—for contemporaries then and for historians now—rests on the added credibility they gave to already cherished beliefs and on the heightened effect those beliefs accorded the events of the day. Beneath the legalistic polemics and the news dispatches, beneath the extreme intellectualism of the age, lay deep social strains aching for expression and relief. From this perspective, the things debated and bruited about—however much or little they were factually true—were at least "always psychologically true." Caught up by social and economic changes they understood little and could control less, the Americans like others before and since them fell into "a revolutionary syndrome." Indeed, it may be enough for us to know that people in the eighteenth century were especially distressed by the "discrepancy between the professed motives of an actor and the contrary effects of his actions," a distress intensified by their lack of "our modern repertory of explanations" (Wood).[7] Thus, if Richard Henry Lee seems to have been "mesmerized" by the notion that Grenville's ministry was trying to reduce the American colonists to slavery, that is to be understood as "an example of the alienation and distrust of established political institutions associated with ideological commitment." And if John Adams appears "excessive" in his "puritanical compulsions," that might better be seen as the expression of a desire "typical of the radical psychology" (Henderson). Once one recognizes the hyperbole of the founding generation as part of an effort by individuals or groups "to escape strain," the importance of ideology as a key to understanding becomes evident. Words and arguments and reasons can then

---

34; Rowland Berthoff, "Independence and Attachment, Virtue and Interest: From Republican Citizen to Free Enterpriser, 1787–1837," in Richard L. Bushman *et al.*, eds., *Uprooted Americans: Essays to Honor Oscar Handlin* (Boston, 1979), 101–105; Shalhope, "Jefferson's Republicanism," *Jour. So. Hist.*, XLII (1976), 556.

6. Bailyn, *Ideological Origins*, 87, 113; Banning, "Republican Ideology," *WMQ*, 3d Ser., XXXI (1974), 182–183.

7. Wood, "Rhetoric and Reality," *WMQ*, 3d Ser., XXIII (1966), 25–27, 31; "Conspiracy and the Paranoid Style," *WMQ*, 3d Ser., XXXIX (1982), 411, 425.

best be seen as parts of "highly selective, oversimplified, symbol systems which function primarily to integrate social systems," "to alleviate the strains engendered by ... social and economic changes" (Shalhope).[8]

Propelled by an aversion to earlier historians' preoccupation with elitist discourse and drawn by a hope of enlarging historical understanding, scholars of the ideological school have pushed away from eighteenth-century writing desks and gone outdoors. In that bright light, they promise to show us sights and truths undreamt of. At last we can see "how facile and how unreal were our predecessors' unexamined assumptions" about the relation of formal discourse to political life (Bailyn). We can then, with clear understanding and an even clearer conscience, descend from "the high-blown philosophy of life embodied in what are commonly called Natural Rights ideas" to the concerns of actual men and women in the real world. Indeed, why stop with the "elaborate, highly-abstracted, intellectualized" Commonwealth ideology? "Were there no 'mentalities' ... that achieved their expression on a level of historical abstraction?" (Ernst). Why stop even there? Progressively, we can detect the fulminations of distressed planters, merchants, and artisans, and finally even "the mob's effigy" (Wood) as a continuing social process of relieving strain and reconstituting social behavior. Similarly, we may come to see gesture, dress, play, and civic ritual as parts of a panorama wherein all segments of society act out their hopes and fears. We will then perhaps have come a long way from "the folly of projecting ideas in the heads of crowds from ideas in the heads of elites" (Lemisch).[9]

Of course, one might wonder at a certain asymmetry in the historians' treatment of those thoughts, ideas, symbols, and expressions after reducing them all to forms of public rhetoric (Wood). It might seem at times that the discount rate applied to the language of learned pamphlets could at least as properly be applied to the symbol making of a crowd burning down a royal official's house. "Looking at broken windowpanes is hanging a lot on a little" (Lemisch).[10] Why should extravagance in the inarticulate masses be

8. Henderson, *Party Politics*, 80, 82; Shalhope, "Jefferson's Republicanism," *Jour. So. Hist.*, XLII (1976), 533–535, 556.

9. Bernard Bailyn, "The Central Themes of the American Revolution: An Interpretation," in Stephen G. Kurtz and James H. Hutson, eds., *Essays on the American Revolution* (Chapel Hill, N.C., 1973), 10–11; Joseph Ernst, "Ideology and the Political Economy of Revolution," *Canadian Review of American Studies*, IV (1973), 143; Wood, "Intellectual History," in Higham and Conkin, eds., *New Directions*, 34; Jesse Lemisch, "Bailyn Besieged in His Bunker," *Radical History Review*, III (1976), 74.

10. Wood, "Intellectual History," in Higham and Conkin, eds., *New Directions*, 35; Lemisch, "Bailyn Besieged," *Radical History Review*, III (1976), 75.

treated as a reflection of their true beliefs (about a moral economy, for example), when the same presumption is denied to the productions of the better educated or more literate? Why indeed?

The new historians' reasons have to be divined from their premises. Any historical account that does not mislead must give the real concerns, the real activities, of the age their deserved weight and emphasis. Although those who fancy that "the history of an idea or event can ever be adequately written in terms of its leading actors" may gratify themselves with that conceit, they in fact mistake the actual historical situation. For those very "qualities of intelligence and presentation" that make a John Locke (or an Alexander Hamilton) so arresting and fascinating to a scholar are precisely the features that disqualify such characters from figuring large in the world of "real entities and activities" (Skinner). To assess properly the role of political thinking in political life *as lived*, one must circumvent the canon of great names and great works lest one fall victim to their "distorting perspective." Only by locating those men, writings, ideas, arguments, and activities within the broader social, economic, and linguistic context, only by reconceiving the past as "the history of ideologies" can we hope to reach some approximation of that past (Skinner).[11] In this sense the nuanced sophistications of the few stand in greater need of deflation than the jeers and cries of the many.

Those atypical great works and great men are cast aside, or transcended, in favor of the study of emerging symbolization. Not the ideas, but their formation or emergence is what matters. As turmoil in social life becomes more evident to people living in a revolutionary age, as words fail, individuals struggle to voice "an idea, which in turn must symbolize or grasp a complex of ineffable feelings" (Shalhope). A revolutionary struggle should perhaps be seen as a linguistic or "mental revolution," the revolutionary moment to be marked at the point when a people "suddenly blinked" and saw their familiar world in a new perspective (Wood).[12]

It is in this context of seeking what really matters that thought and the thinking human being are relegated to their newly assigned place. For if "human thought is necessarily rhetorical" and public, " 'and not, or at least not fundamentally, a private activity,' " we may properly subsume all that under the heading of communication. And if we are concerned to identify

---

11. Quentin Skinner, "The Limits of Historical Explanations," *Philosophy*, XLI (1966), 212–213, 215; and "Some Problems in the Analysis of Political Thought and Action," *Political Theory*, II (1974), 280. See also Joyce Appleby, "Republicanism in Old and New Contexts," *WMQ*, 3d Ser., XLIII (1986), 28.

12. Shalhope, "Jefferson's Republicanism," *Jour. So. Hist.*, XLII (1976), 538; Wood, "Rhetoric and Reality," *WMQ*, 3d Ser., XXIII (1966), 13.

the communications that really stirred men to action, we would do well to cast our eyes and nets beyond "just the literary terms expressed by a few supposedly representative thinkers." If we do, "mental worlds" beyond our imagining await our discovery. The full range of "symbolic actions" or "meanings," from a wink to an effigy, are thus fodder for our historians. Advisedly so, for in "this postpsychological age" no one with the dimmest awareness of "how people really behave" could accept the notion that "individuals acted as they did because they believed, 'sincerely' believed, in the ideas or principles they expressed" (Wood).[13] Least of all if those beliefs are expressed in stately Augustan prose.

Yet the very acceptance of "ideology" as the key term carries with it a train of assumptions and implications that effectively bar our ever recognizing the power of thought and of thoughtfulness. However one understands the term—whether as the pleasant-sounding nonsense with which devious folk deck out their darker purposes, or as the unintended energizing and symbolization of the hopes and anxieties of a faceless age—at bottom lies a common understanding, so common that it no longer needs express assertion: ideas may be important at a given moment or place, but they are not and can never be the central reality or the independent variable. An underlying reality—strain, anxiety, interest, whatever—*uses* thought and shapes *it* to its ends. Ideas, then, in the modern researcher's eyes, become "important for what they do rather than for what they are." Accordingly, the resort to explanation "in terms of the intentions and designs of particular individuals" becomes only a recurrence to the crude modes of eighteenth-century men obsessed with motives (Wood).[14]

The relative insignificance of individual thought and individual actors is amply illustrated by the work of the new historians. Thus, for example, when they turn to inspect the use eighteenth-century authors made of others' thoughts and writings, they are quick to dip beneath the surface appearance of things. They are not inclined to be overwhelmed by the show of learning—classical, secular, legal, or religious—with which those eighteenth-century controversialists adorned their speeches, letters, and pamphlets. They focus instead on what they take to be those authors' superficiality or tendentious selectivity. In fact, what appears, "at first glance, a massive, seemingly random eclecticism" turns out to be just about that: "clusters of ideas" marked by "striking incongruities and contradictions."

13. Wood, "Intellectual History," in Higham and Conkin, eds., *New Directions*, 29–30, 32–35.

14. *Ibid.*, 34; and "Rhetoric and Reality," *WMQ*, 3d Ser., XXIII (1966), 16–17. Contrast the noncrude examples in Bailyn, *Ideological Origins*, 150; and in Wood, "Conspiracy and the Paranoid Style," *WMQ*, 3d Ser., XXXIX (1982), 421.

We do not see men and women thinking hard about things they have heard or read, but citing what they have found useful for "illustrative, not determinative," purposes. Thus although Bailyn grants that not all learning was "superficial," that not all recurrence to learned citations was "offhand" or in order "to score points" against an adversary, he shows no instance in which a powerful searching mind engages with another such mind. Notwithstanding that he judges some earlier authors to have "contributed substantially" or to have been "in certain ways powerfully influential" or even (in the exceptional case of Locke) "authoritative" in some respect, those authors and their distinctive ideas remain strangely evanescent in his account (Bailyn).[15]

Even when an element of "the Revolutionary ideology" is described in some detail, its possible bearing on people's actions appears as both obscure and negligible. Our confidence that the men of '76 made good use of the "Puritan value system" gains little from the assurance that Sukarno manipulated "ancient Indic tradition to frame the 'sacred' ideological base for a newly independent" Indonesia. At issue is not whether the incorporation of "Puritan values" would fit in with "this nationalist revolutionary paradigm." Rather, the question is whether the changes effected by American independence and the establishment of the new state and federal governments were in fact "greatly facilitated by endowing the new form with cultural attributes of older institutions." Clearly, one cannot leave it at the observation that, "being many things to many men, . . . [the "Puritan value system"] was a superb instrument of Revolutionary ideology." For whatever made that old New England tradition "many things to many men" also made it unequally assimilable by all and unequally welcome to all (Henderson).[16]

The gist of the ideological interpretation is, of course, not that classical or Enlightenment or legal or religious sources mattered little, but that the "Country" or "classical republican" or English "Opposition" writers mattered more. This group was "unique in its determinative power"; its writings were "central to American political expression" (Bailyn). In its "complete and consistent Americanization," this "structured universe of classical thought continued to serve as the intellectual medium through which Americans perceived the political world." The political language the Americans inherited shaped their hopes, discontents, and the way they saw the world. As in the case of any intellectual universe, men find "some ideas are native and others are difficult to conceive." Paradoxically, but perhaps not surprisingly, the truth that would liberate individuals' bodies and minds from arbitrary and overbearing authority rendered people incapable of thinking differently. "The heritage of classical republicanism and English

15. Bailyn, *Ideological Origins*, 23–34, 36.
16. Henderson, *Party Politics*, 84–85.

opposition thought, shaped and hardened in the furnace of a great Revolution, left few men free" (Banning).[17]

Not all historians have been happy with this characterization, but their reservations have more to do with the monolithic quality ascribed to opposition ideology than to the adequacy of the concept of ideology as an explanatory device. Thus Joyce Appleby argues that there were "competing ideologies," that of an opposition at once reactionary and legalistic and that of a secular liberalism advocating a natural order of undifferentiated competitors. Another reading finds two country parties and two court parties at work in eighteenth-century Britain and thus a still more complex tradition to which Americans could refer. Another finds the options in Jeffersonian America ranging from "Burkeanism and the court party on the right through the country party and Smithian liberalism to Christian and secular radicalisms on the left," all drawing on the heady brew of "Scottish ideas" (Howe). At this stage of the inquiry the only consensus among these historians is that ideology is a prime explanation; there is none about which ideology was decisive (Shalhope).[18]

Fundamental to the concept of ideology is the premise that, however things happen and change, those outcomes are not properly attributable to deliberating individuals. This is not the same as asserting that "formal discourse and articulated belief" are merely weapons in a battle to manipulate men's minds, but then neither is it to assert that formal discourse "in some simple sense . . . constitutes motives" (Bailyn).[19] Rather, all that talk and writing should be viewed within the broader context of a "political culture" (or a "popular culture," depending on the historian's political leanings). Within that broader culture, and as shaped by it, transformations take place "indeliberately, half-knowingly," the workings of "in effect an intellectual switchboard" wired by no one in particular and to all appearances fully automatic. Changes in feeling, belief, and attitude occur somehow, but as far as we are told not as a result of anyone's deliberate intention (Bailyn).[20] It

17. Bailyn, *Ideological Origins*, 34, 43; Banning, "Republican Ideology," *WMQ*, 3d Ser., XXXI (1974), 172–173, 178–179.

18. Joyce Appleby, "The Social Origins of American Revolutionary Ideology," *Journal of American History*, LXIV (1977–1978), 937, 953–954; Daniel Walker Howe, "European Sources of Political Ideas in Jeffersonian America," *Reviews in American History*, X, No. 4 (December 1982), 34, 40–41; Robert E. Shalhope, "Republicanism and Early American Historiography," *WMQ*, 3d Ser., XXXIX (1982), 334–356.

19. Bailyn, "Central Themes," in Kurtz and Hutson, eds., *Essays on the American Revolution*, 10–11.

20. Bailyn, *Ideological Origins*, ix, 22, 160, 190, 302; and "Political Experience and Enlightenment Ideas in Eighteenth-Century America," *American Historical Review*, LXVII (1961–1962), 349.

may even turn out to be the case that the actors are "the languages rather than (or on an equal footing with) the human individuals who have used them" (Pocock). Nor, finally, do we need to distinguish between those expressing a "visceral reaction" and those acting in response to considered convictions. At the energizing level of ideology it does not matter whether some "*feel* Country ideology," thereby "giving voice to socio-economic grudges," while others syllogize their way to similar conclusions (Hutson).[21]

Such differences do not matter all that much for the same reason that ideas count in only limited ways. When historians realize that thinkers and actors are mistaken to believe they have direct access to ideas unmediated by ideology, when historians explode the illusion of autonomous thought conversing with autonomous ideas, when they realize that all mental activity and mental objects take place in or are given by ideology, they are thereby freed from the blinders of the past. Neither the eighteenth-century "obsession with motives," nor the "simple nineteenth-century intellectualist assumption," nor a "stifling judicial-like preoccupation with motivation and responsibility" need any longer impede the modern student from perceiving the more fundamental sociological, psychological, or economic determinants (Wood).[22] If some historical behavior perversely argues that deliberating individuals matter, if a Jefferson continues "to rely extensively on private correspondence for the dissemination of his views," and a Madison continues "to write learned pieces . . . for a restricted audience of educated gentlemen" (Wood),[23] that behavior is best understood as the fixed habits of old fogies, the intellectual equivalent of persisting in wearing breeches and wigs long gone out of fashion. Whether the botanizing founders of the Republican societies and the moving spirits behind Philip Freneau's *National Gazette* and the Virginia and Kentucky resolutions were oblivious of the democratization of mind in the early national period is not at issue. What is at issue is the historians' persistence in looking for ideology, a preoccupation that literally obscures the significance of those moments when "the best minds" are "compelled to ask . . . serious questions" (Wood).[24]

Such moments are neither reducible to, nor explicable in terms of, some

21. J.G.A. Pocock, "*The Machiavellian Moment* Revisited: A Study in History and Ideology," *Journal of Modern History*, LIII (1981), 52; James H. Hutson, "Country, Court, and Constitution: Antifederalism and the Historians," *WMQ*, 3d Ser., XXXVIII (1981), 366-367.

22. Wood, "Rhetoric and Reality," *WMQ*, 3d Ser., XXIII (1966), 16-17, 19-20, 22-23.

23. Gordon S. Wood, "The Democratization of Mind in the American Revolution," in Robert H. Horwitz, ed., *The Moral Foundations of the American Republic* (Charlottesville, Va., 1977), 122.

24. Wood, "Rhetoric and Reality," *WMQ*, 3d Ser., XXIII (1966), 24, 25.

"elaborate pattern of middle-level beliefs and ideas." Nor can one leave it at an ideology that reshapes and promotes "moods, attitudes, ideas, and aspirations that in some form, however crude or incomplete, already exist." For that only pushes the search for causes back in time, not out of mind. Do those moods and ideas have ideological origins as well? Did "the complex and integrated set of values, beliefs, attitudes, and responses that had evolved through a century and a half of Anglo-American history" (Bailyn) owe anything, at any point, to the abstractions and formal arguments of thoughtful, even purposefully thoughtful, individuals? Not, it would seem, if there is no such thing as thought trying to achieve knowledge, if we have only opinion growing out of an age's "conspiratorial fears and imagined intrigues" (Wood).[25] If that is the case, then what purports to be thought is in fact fundamentally derivative, little better than a patchwork of miscellaneous remnants, like the stuff quilts and dreams are made of.

In that event the subject of an intellectual historian's study ought to be the *invokers* of ideas, not some presumed great theoretical originators. Those invokers might differ little from casual marketers, people afflicted with the myopia of short-range concerns. Of course, one might still wonder where those middlemen get their stock in trade or, for that matter, whether they are after all and in every case mindless factors of other people's goods. Although it is worth examining how the historical accretion and evolution of a people's values, beliefs, attitudes, and responses may shape that people's view of themselves and of the world, that inquiry need not preclude the possibly significant part played by some purposive and maybe magisterial thinker in the history of those values, beliefs, and attitudes. Unless, of course, we know that such singular figures *can* not matter decisively (Wood).[26] But if we doubt that certainty or if we eschew that convenience,[27] then we are left with the need to come to terms with a first-class (or even second-class) mind in the act of thinking clearly, forcefully, and deliberately.

II

That coming to terms will not and cannot take place as long as we look and act on the premise of the new historians. Given that point of departure, it is

25. Bailyn, "Central Themes," in Kurtz and Hutson, eds., *Essays on the American Revolution*, 10–11; Wood, "Conspiracy and the Paranoid Style," *WMQ*, 3d Ser., XXXIX (1982), 407.

26. Wood, "Conspiracy and the Paranoid Style," *WMQ*, 3d Ser., XXXIX (1982), 408–409.

27. Alexis de Tocqueville, *Democracy in America*, trans. George Lawrence (New York, 1966), 463 (II, Pt. i, chap. 20).

no surprise, however striking, that these historians largely ignore, when they are not misconstruing, how their historical subjects viewed their principles and acts. The very gravity, even high-mindedness, with which the generations of '76 and '87 (and beyond) debated alternative principles and policies remains fundamentally alien to practitioners of the ideological approach. To be intelligible within the terms of that analysis, political thought and speech must be transmuted into something else.

Thus, for example, the debate over ratification of the Constitution turns out to be a court-country dispute that gave vent to "the social resentment and antagonism of the agrarian interests that were preponderant in the Country, in both England and America" (Hutson). Or it is at bottom a social conflict between those who would preserve a community of equals and those who would reinstitute hierarchical distinctions: in short, a debate on "an essential point of political sociology" (Wood).[28] Even the conversion of Anti-Federalists into strict constructionists is reduced to a "reflexive literalism," an instinctive inclination "that seems inevitable," given the Americans' upbringing on "a diet of opposition writings." Indeed, that heritage "left few men free" to think otherwise. But where that ideology required an "ancient constitution" as a bench mark by which to gauge political corruption and constitutional decay, those Americans, having only the newly minted Constitution to fall back on, "instinctively settled for the next best thing. Symbolically speaking, they made the Constitution old" (Banning).[29] By this account a sharp division over the character of the Union and the requirements of free government is transformed into an ideologically prescribed obsession with corruption. Of course, it was common doctrine that, over time, good constitutions would become worse and bad ones insufferable. But those former Anti-Federalists most apt to cry alarm at deviations from the constitutional text did not need classical republicanism or country ideology to prompt them. The most thoughtful and the most radical of the opponents of the Constitution could hardly have taken the amendments of 1789–1791 as meeting their major objections of 1787–1788. If they sought to hold the Constitution to its word, it was not out of some instinctive or reflexive impulse. Rather, they tried with great deliberateness to pre-

28. Hutson, "Country, Court, and Constitution," *WMQ*, 3d Ser., XXXVIII (1981), 368; Gordon S. Wood, *The Creation of the American Republic, 1776–1787* (Chapel Hill, N.C., 1969), 484–485; see Gary J. Schmitt and Robert H. Webking, "Revolutionaries, Antifederalists, and Federalists: Comments on Gordon Wood's Understanding of the American Founding," *Political Science Reviewer*, IX (1979), 215–229; and Herbert J. Storing, "What the Anti-Federalists Were *For*," in *The Complete Anti-Federalist* (Chicago, 1981), I, 4.

29. Banning, "Republican Ideology," *WMQ*, 3d Ser., XXXI (1974), 178–179, 182, 187.

vent what they believed the Constitution invited. This was Anti-Federalism in its postratification garb. Strict construction could not alone remedy what they had found most objectionable in the Constitution as proposed, but it was the best they had—short of resistance grounded on the right of self-preservation.

With such a stance toward authors and arguments, texts and thinking, it is altogether understandable that the necessary discriminations should often be gross or even lacking. By subsuming a broad range of intelligence under the heading of ideology, the ideological interpretation in effect disarms us for the task at hand. In order to discriminate those who merely absorbed what was useful, with little regard for coherence and consistency, from those who sought to trace the premises of their preferences and the consequences of their principles, a historian today must first recover the possibility of rank order among thinkers, and then listen carefully for intimations of rank. Especially and above all must he learn to attend to those historical actors who seem most to have considered what they were about and who, far from being the unconscious puppets of the presuppositions of their age, were most intent on reshaping those presuppositions—on replacing old intellectual precepts and societal purposes with new precepts and purposes of *their* design. Then, and only then, will the constitution of the thinking revolutionary finally hover into sight.

A closer look at an ideological interpretation of a major American thinker affords a singular opportunity to weigh alternative approaches. By abstracting from details in order to sketch the main features of the ideological mode of interpretation, I have, of course, hardly established the adequacy or shortcomings of that mode. Ultimately, any interpretation must be judged by its ability to illumine or account for things said and done, or for things left unsaid and undone. Specific cases are thus indispensable for testing plausibility and estimating relative superiority. But at the same time, such particular instances can be only illustrative, not conclusive; the choice of test cases is always open to cavil. Yet, in Gordon Wood's impressive analysis of the republicanism of John Adams we have a coherent, extended reading of America's "political scientist par excellence" (Wood), a reading that invites scrutiny and comparison. Eschewing for once the "encyclopedic historical method" by which big fish and small fry are netted into one swirling school (Schmitt and Webking),[30] Wood turns his attentive eye and ear to a political actor who knows his own mind and addresses ours. It is an instructive encounter.

30. Wood, *Creation of the American Republic*, 568; Schmitt and Webking, "Revolutionaries, Antifederalists, and Federalists," *Political Science Reviewer*, IX (1979), 224 n. 53.

The John Adams that emerges from Wood's nuanced presentation exudes complication and contradiction, invites pity and admiration, and altogether leaves us almost as bewildered as he himself is alleged to have been. True to the premises of the ideological school, Wood early on in *The Creation of the American Republic* insists on the need to look beyond "the nicely reasoned constitutional arguments" of an Adams or a Jefferson lest we miss "the enthusiastic and visionary extravagance" in those men's thinking (Wood).[31] Adams is presented as one who moved from hopeful enthusiasm to a redoubled anxiety and loss of republican faith (571, 575). But since neither Adams nor Wood's Adams was a simple fellow, those contrasting moods and casts of mind are themselves fairly complex. The title of Wood's thematic treatment puts the ambiguity plainly enough. "The Relevance and Irrelevance of John Adams" depicts the "bewilderment of a man whom ideas had passed by," one whose "unfortunate fate" it was "to have missed the intellectual significance of the most important event since the Revolution" (48, 567). Further discussion shows Adams's plight to have been less a matter of bad luck than of poor thinking. "Adams never really comprehended what was happening to the fundamentals of political thought in the years after 1776"; "he remained unaware" of its originality (568, 580). His "inability to understand" left him outside the mainstream, ensconced with his "superannuated idea" of mixed government, "thinking in old-fashioned terms," and rendered "seemingly immune" to new thought while "carrying on in a timeworn manner" (581, 583, 586, 587, 591). Far from being contemptuous of so perversely obsolete a thinker, Wood can barely conceal his admiration. He praises Adams for his clarity and insight, for his honest and correct social analysis, for his unflinching readiness "to tell his fellow Americans some truths about themselves that American values and American ideology would not admit" (568, 569, 592). The "obsolescence of Adams's political theory" in no way diminishes for Wood the truth of his observations (587). If he was irrelevant in the America of 1787 and after, it was for all the wrong reasons.

It would be a grave injustice—to Adams and to Wood's complex account —to conclude that Adams suffered the common plight of those who do not change with the times. In fact, the linchpin of Wood's analysis is the belief that Adams did indeed change. Depicting the character of that change compels Wood to bring to bear upon his vast knowledge of primary sources the analytical skills of a parser of texts. For the moment Wood is concerned less with detecting how Adams's beliefs may have reflected the contending passions of "his own tormented soul" (577, also 571) than with establishing

---

31. Wood, *Creation of the American Republic*, 121. All further parenthetical references in this section are to this work.

the depth and quality of that change. On the one hand, we have the sketch of a young Adams, fired with Revolutionary enthusiasm, convinced of the redemptive and regenerative powers of republican institutions and republican education, and ready to see in aristocracy a useful ally of the people in their struggle against executive aggrandizement (570, 579). On the other hand, there is a detailed portrait of an older Adams, one who had outgrown his illusions and somewhat naive enthusiasms. Though Wood deals at length with the changed Adams—the Adams that became irrelevant—the force of his analysis depends on the adequacy of his account of the Revolutionary Adams. Without the contrast, both "the relevance and irrelevance of John Adams" would have to be reconsidered.[32]

The bulk of what we learn in this chapter about the early views of Adams comes less from a direct examination of early writings (569–571, 579) than from an implied contrast with later writings. Hence the reader who wants to know *whether* Adams changed his political thinking is hard put to discover Wood's grounds for asserting it. A sentence such as this—"Within a few years after Independence, . . . whatever optimism Adams had had for the refinement of the American character was gone"—tells us both that the Adams of 1787 was no optimist *and* that he might have been taken for one in 1776. To be told that he "now saw" the futility of relying simply on popular virtue to sustain popular government implies that he once thought otherwise. Asserting that it was "now clear that there was 'no special providence for Americans, and their nature is the same with that of others'" is tantamount to saying that the earlier Adams had held Americans as a breed apart (571). By repeated recourse to this mode—what Alexander Hamilton in *Federalist* No. 32 called a "negative pregnant"—Wood leaves us with a John Adams who once had "faith in the inspirational and ameliorating qualities of republicanism" (575), who once thought education capable of "compelling the people to submerge their individual desires into a love for the

32. In focusing on Wood's broad theme of the Revolutionary Adams's dramatic reversal, I run the risk of appearing to ignore the other ways in which Adams figures in this work. Wood portrays as well a more equivocal Adams, one who persistently combined high hopes with deep doubts (121, 569–570). Indeed, Wood's last word on Adams—quoting his lament that he had lived in enemy country for fifty years (592)—at the very least leaves the thesis of a changing Adams up in the air. It also raises the possibility that Wood's larger purpose may lie in a different direction: showing the character of Adams's blind (if half-truthful) resistance to the compelling (if largely deceptive) message of the new, post-Revolutionary politics, both Federalist and Republican. Yet I am reluctant to dismiss as insubstantial or inconsequential the dozen closely worked pages that Wood devotes to detailing this purported change. Not one of the 300 other political figures mentioned in this book is held by Wood to so steady and prolonged a scrutiny; that judgment deserves consideration.

whole" (575), and who once thought of an aristocracy as "different from the people but by no means opposed to the people's welfare" (579).

Almost every one of these assertions can be seconded by citations to chapter and verse in Adams's writings, and yet, strange to say, this account of the earlier Adams is fundamentally awry. It can be shown to be so, not "in order to prove the moderation of the Revolution" (121), but in order to show the thoughtfulness of the revolutionary—as a young lawyer no less than as a mature diplomat or a retired president. It can be seen to be so by recurring to the young Adams's own coherent accounts of his political views.

In one of his earliest published newspaper essays, Adams reflected on the ingredients of public discourse. He held self-deceit, "the spurious offspring of *self-love*," to be the root cause of the ease and glee with which men impugn one another, all the while mistaking the impulses of their own "swarms of passions" for the dictates of conscience. Given this fundamental fact of human nature, it is futile to expect that even the purest or most needful reform will ever pass current in the world without being waylaid by opposition and slander. From this Adams drew a republican moral. Alluding to the antimonarchical parable of Jotham ben Jerubbaal (Judges 9:7–21), he concluded that "we can never be secure in a resignation of our understandings, or in confiding *enormous power*, either to the *Bramble* or the *Cedar*; no, nor to *any mortal*, however great or good." By the same token, predetermined hostility and discredit are equally unjust and unwise. "Let us not be bubbled then out of our reverence and obedience to Government, on one hand; nor out of our right to think and act *for ourselves*, in our own departments, on the other." It was a foregone conclusion for Adams that "ignorance, vanity, excessive *ambition* and venality, will in spight of all human precautions creep into government." This calls not for a politics of righteousness and indignation, but for a politics of attentive thoughtfulness. Like Hamilton in *Federalist* No. 1, Adams was here loath to cast political antagonists as the children of light against the children of darkness. Hence he was as wary of quick judgments as he was of indifference. Considering that "every step in the public administration of government, concerns us *nearly*," it behooves all to inspect all rulers strictly and, if need be, to oppose them soberly. "It becomes necessary to every subject then, to be in some degree a *statesman*: and to examine and judge for *himself* of the tendency of political *principles* and *measures*." [33]

This essay's sequel (for some reason unpublished) bears special relevance for any consideration of "the changing political thought of John Adams." Taking as his text, "All Men would be Tyrants if they could," Adams in-

33. John Adams, "U" to the *Boston Gazette*, Aug. 29, 1763, in Robert J. Taylor *et al.*, eds., *Papers of John Adams* (Cambridge, Mass., 1977–), I, 78–81.

quired into that old maxim's meaning and implications. The notion is not that "all the sons of Adam, are so many abandond Knaves regardless of all Morality and Right," but simply that man cannot be "left to the natural Emotions of his own Mind, unrestrained and uncheckd by other Power extrinsic to himself." Far from being a new discovery, this has been the view of "thinking Men" for many millennia. Heedful of the danger posed by power unchecked, "our Constitution" has wisely provided against all such, whether military, "casuistical," or civil. Its wisdom, Adams concluded, clearly lies in its recognition that "no simple Form of Government, can possibly secure Men against the Violences of Power." Some forty-four years later, the old republican warrior rummaging among his papers saw fit to append: "This last Paragraph has been the Creed of my whole Life and is now March 27 1807 as much approved as it was when it was written by John Adams."[34] What others might take to be obstinacy, Adams thought consistency.

This adherence to considered views is especially evident in the "Dissertation on the Canon and the Feudal Law." Written and published serially over a period of several months in 1765, it affords a close look at Adams's thoughts about knowledge and power, education and liberty. Its somber tone, heightened in all likelihood by news of the recently passed Stamp Act, smacks little of the enthusiastic extravagance we have been led to expect in the young Adams. And yet, it is for all that a pronouncedly revolutionary statement.

One of the most striking features of the "Dissertation" is its quiet assumption that the love of power, the spirit of liberty, and even knowledge itself are neutral forces capable of great good or great evil. "The desire of dominion," that very principle which "has always prompted the princes and nobles of the earth, by every species of fraud and violence, to shake off, all the *limitations* of their power," has also impelled the common people to try to confine them. As the people become "more *intelligent* in general," as they find ways of overcoming their ignorance and isolation, their own love of power may make it more difficult for "the great" to lord it over those whom they contemptuously call "the populace."[35] The spirit of liberty may be no less ambiguous. The "Dissertation" is, among other things, a paean to that spirit, seeking to rouse Americans out of their "habits of reserve, and a cautious diffidence of asserting their opinions publickly." But in urging "a manly assertion" of American rights, Adams was far from proclaiming the spirit of liberty an unqualified good. "This spirit . . . without knowledge,

34. Adams, "An Essay on Man's Lust for Power . . . ," post Aug. 29, 1763, *ibid.*, 81–83.

35. Adams, "A Dissertation on the Canon and the Feudal Law," No. 1, Aug. 12, 1765, *ibid.*, 111–112.

would be little better than a brutal rage." Brutish activity is not preferable to brutish indolence.[36]

Though knowledge may be indispensable for self-governance, it too was no simple good in the eyes of John Adams. An ignorant people is a vulnerable people, one easily seduced into projects leading to ruin or oppression. Yet the knowledge that would make them free is the other side of the science that holds them in thrall. Of all the "systems of iniquity" devised for tyrannizing the people, none had been more "successful," "sublime," "astonishing," and "calamitous to human liberty" than the union of those two vast products of human art and intelligence, the canon and the feudal law. Here was the amplest proof that the intellectual and moral virtues were quite distinct. The young lawyer of 1765 knew full well how knowledge—and the monopolization of knowledge—might be used by self-serving men to further their purposes.[37] It was no new disenchanting revelation that led a wary vice-president of 1789 to confess his misgivings about the regenerative "Influence of general Science." For where the political system itself was flawed (because "unballanced"), the heightened ability of partisans promised exacerbation rather than relief. Greater knowledge, an improved science, "would only increase and inflame" the defects of the political system by adding to the number of "able and ambitious Men, who would only understand the better, how to worry one another with greater Art and dexterity."[38]

With these important reservations in mind, one may then consider John Adams's early thoughts on education and republicanism. There is no denying that he held the struggle for liberty to be inseparable from the struggle against ignorance. The "wicked confederacy" that saw temporal and spiritual "grandees" reinforcing each other's dominion also left them vulnerable to the liberating forces unleashed by the Reformation. Whatever events made the people "more and more sensible of the wrong that was done them, by these systems," to that extent contributed to the cause of liberty. The Puritans' prominent part in that struggle was emphatically connected by Adams to that "sensible" people's intelligence, learning, knowledge, and dedication to inquiry and examination.[39] He made light of the charge that the Puritans were guilty of enthusiasm, but not by denying it. Most of Christendom, he asserted, had that trait in those earlier days; and, besides, "no great enterprize, for the honour or happiness of mankind, was ever achieved, without a

36. Adams, "Dissertation," No. 4, Oct. 21, 1765, *ibid.*, 123, 125–126.

37. Adams, "Dissertation," No. 1, *ibid.*, 111–113.

38. Adams to Benjamin Rush, June 19, 1789, in Alexander Biddle, ed., *Old Family Letters: Copied from the Originals . . .* , Ser. A (Philadelphia, 1892), 39.

39. Adams, "Dissertation," No. 1, in Taylor *et al.*, eds., *Papers of John Adams*, I, 113–114.

large mixture of that noble infirmity." It was, then, no canting zealot out of a Ben Jonson comedy that Adams held up as a model. Rather, it was a people praiseworthy for knowing "that government was a plain, simple, intelligible thing founded in nature and reason and quite comprehensible by common sense."[40]

To promote and secure that truth, and thereby "preserve their posterity from the encroachments of the two systems of tyranny," the Puritans had doubled their efforts on behalf of popular education. It is hard to resist the conclusion that Adams regarded this dedication as his ancestors' finest legacy. The Puritans made "knowledge diffused generally thro' the whole body of the people" into a commitment not only cherished by public opinion but supported by legislative enactment and public funds. In reducing principles to practice, they showed their republican descendants the road to follow.[41]

In what are Adams's people to be educated? If "every order and degree among the people" are to be roused to study and inquiry, it is clearly so that they might absorb "the ideas of right and the sensations of freedom." Some few, the "learned men," would come to concentrate their thoughts on "matters of power and of right." The many, instructed by the men of learning, would come in turn to see "they have a right, an indisputable, unalienable, indefeasible divine right to that most dreaded, and envied kind of knowledge, I mean of the characters and conduct of their rulers."[42] The result would be a citizenry: alert, assertive, and mindful of its honor, interest, and happiness. Only with such a people could be sustained those mixed forms of government so needful for preserving liberty. King, lords, commons, and people—none could be dispensed with; each had its contribution to make to prevent government from degenerating into an absolute monarchy, or an oligarchy or aristocracy, or a mixture of monarchy and aristocracy.[43]

Very much depended on "the temper and character of the people." No small part of the case for an independent judiciary, for example, turned on its role in molding "the morals of the people." Similarly, sumptuary legislation and laws providing public support for "the liberal education of youth, especially of the lower class of people," were alike viewed by Adams as means of forming a certain kind of citizenry. But overarching these as a shaping and educative force was the constitution itself. If founded on the right prin-

40. Adams, "Dissertation," No. 2, Aug. 19, 1765, *ibid.*, 115–117.

41. Adams, "Dissertation," No. 3, Sept. 30, 1765, *ibid.*, 118, 120.

42. Adams, "Dissertation," No. 4, *ibid.*, 126–127; "Dissertation," No. 3, *ibid.*, 121.

43. Adams, "The Earl of Clarendon to William Pym," No. 3, Jan. 27, 1766, *ibid.*, 167–169.

ciples, it would as a matter of course work toward making the people more knowing and more conscious of their worth as "Freemen." The prospect Adams held forth evokes positive feelings but promises no miraculous transfiguration. "A general emulation takes place, which causes good humour, sociability, good manners, and good morals to be general. That elevation of sentiment, inspired by such a government, makes the common people brave and enterprizing. That ambition which is inspired by it makes them sober, industrious and frugal. You will find among them some elegance, perhaps, but more solidity; a little pleasure, but a great deal of business — some politeness, but more civility." That would be a happy, a very happy outcome, but it is no Eden under a new dispensation of grace. Only in comparison with "the regions of domination, whether Monarchial or Aristocratical," would one fancy it an "Arcadia or Elisium."[44]

Adams has here depicted a people with the usual passions — but in a setting that tames or channels those passions in socially useful ways. This echoes the system of James Harrington, much admired by Adams, which sought to secure "the Liberty, Virtue, and Interest of the Multitude in all Acts of Government" by balancing the ownership of land and thereby balancing power in a society. If the hope and cautious expectation are that all will be happier as a result, it is not because people in the real world will have forgotten their self-interested projects or have become heedless of the arbitrariness and inequities of the general rules embodied in law. "So fruitfull a Source of Controversy and Altercation" remains just that as long as human nature retains its general character.[45]

None of this is to forget that John Adams was the author of the famous provision of the Massachusetts Constitution of 1780 proclaiming it "the duty of legislators and magistrates, in all future periods of this commonwealth, to cherish the interests of literature and the sciences, and all seminaries of them."[46] Nor is it to discount his expectation that the state constitution's arrangements and commitments might help make the body of the people more humane and sociable, even more generous, than they otherwise would be. John Adams surely had expectations, even revolutionary expectations, but they were grounded in a sober analysis of human character. Precisely because he did not give his fancies free rein, Adams's hopes and disappointments in these matters are to be distinguished sharply from those of a Mercy or James Warren.

His ardor for the Revolutionary cause typically expressed itself in a discus-

44. *Ibid.*, 165; "Thoughts on Government," Apr. 1776, *ibid.*, IV, 91-92.
45. Adams to James Sullivan, May 26, 1776, *ibid.*, IV, 210-212.
46. Charles Francis Adams, ed., *The Works of John Adams* (Philadelphia, 1874-1877), IV, 259.

sion of particulars, concrete proposals and policies, not as a general effusion of sentiment. Thus, he could assure Richard Henry Lee that in their adopting a plan of government along the lines Adams was proposing, "human Nature would appear in its proper Glory asserting its own real Dignity." Similarly, a hurried account of prospective European financing and of the present availability of gunpowder led Adams to conclude that "Patience and Perseverance, will carry Us through this mighty Enterprize—an Enterprize that is and will be an Astonishment to vulgar Minds all over the World, in this and in future Generations." Whatever this is, it is not a case, as Wood asserts, of "enthusiastic and visionary extravagance" brought on by Adams's "extraordinary reliance . . . on the eventual ameliorating influence of republican laws and government on men's behavior" (121). For the dignity that the people might ultimately come to display—to the astonishment of vulgar minds—would be of a whole people having learned "to reverence themselves." The people needed to be taught to admire, not heroes, but the nation that produces heroes. Yet the people could raise their estimation of themselves only if they had just cause for thinking better of themselves. Imagine a whole people taking "upon themselves the education of the whole people"—and being willing to bear the expenses of it. Imagine a people with "too high a sense of their own dignity ever to suffer any man to serve them for nothing."[47] It is on their *willingness* to think better of themselves and to act on it that Adams placed his hopes.

From this perspective, the story of the twists and turns of a man who insists on perfection and yet despairs of it comes closer to being an account of a Javanese puppet show than of the historical John Adams. No less than Mercy Warren, he believed that "a well regulated Commonwealth" promoted virtue even as it required it. But unlike Mrs. Warren, the young Adams knew that such perfection was neither to be expected nor mourned after. One might wish to counteract certain vices, most especially "Servility and Flattery," but the means for totally remaking the character of the people were simply not at hand.[48] Thus, too, Adams could admire along with Mrs. Warren the virtuous republic, where "a possitive Passion for the public

47. Adams to Richard Henry Lee, Nov. 15, 1775, in Taylor *et al.*, eds., *Papers of John Adams*, III, 308; Adams to James Warren, Mar. 31, 1777, in Worthington Chauncey Ford, ed., *Warren-Adams Letters: Being Chiefly a Correspondence among John Adams, Samuel Adams, and James Warren* (Massachusetts Historical Society, *Collections*, LXXII–LXXIII [Boston, 1917–1925]), I, 308 (hereafter cited as *Warren-Adams Letters*); Adams to John Jebb, Sept. 10, 1785, in C. F. Adams, ed., *Works of John Adams*, IX, 538–542.

48. Adams to Mercy Warren, Jan. 8, 1776, in Taylor *et al.*, eds., *Papers of John Adams*, III, 398.

good, the public Interest, Honour, Power, and Glory" overrode all "private Pleasures, Passions, and Interests." But speaking as plainly as a gentleman disagreeing with a lady could, the young Adams asked, "Is there in the World a Nation, which deserves this Character[?]" Mrs. Warren's cause could not be faulted in principle, but then again, neither could it be reduced to practice. Young Adams's litany of inconvenient facts drives that point home: "I have seen all along my Life, Such Selfishness, and Littleness even in New England"; the corrupting "Spirit of Commerce is as rampant in New England as in any Part of the World," even to the point that "Property is generally the standard of Respect there as much as any where."[49]

This clearly was a people who could stand some improvement. There is no reason to discount Adams's concern expressed to his reverend cousin that, if virtue could not "be inspired into our People, in a greater Measure, than they have it now, They may change their Rulers, and the forms of Government, but they will not obtain a lasting Liberty.—They will only exchange Tyrants and Tyrannies." Adams reiterated this apprehension in a letter written to Abigail on the very eve of Congress's declaration of independence. The new status of the American governments—and the consequent "unbounded Power" now to be vested in the people—required a "Purification from our Vices, and an Augmentation of our Virtues or they will be no Blessings." Yet given the extreme addiction of the people "as well as the Great" to corruption and venality, Adams could not and did not anticipate wholesale conversions.[50] In this respect Massachusetts or America was no exception. Early and late, John Adams understood that self-governance needed as good a people as one could muster and as many public-spirited individuals as one could press into the public's service. But to insist on that desideratum as an everyday requirement would guarantee, not the rule of the disinterested and the saintly, but the enthronement of hypocrites and knaves. Adams's steadily unsentimental view of things did not lead him to deny that there are disinterested men, but only to insist that "they are not enough in any age or any country to fill all the necessary offices." Only levelheadedness could keep the counsel of perfection in political life from turning into the triumph of madness and despotism.[51] Thanks too to this sobriety, the mature Adams was spared the kind of dark despair shown by James Warren at the time of Shays's Rebellion. "When We find

49. Adams to Mercy Warren, Apr. 16, 1776, *ibid.*, IV, 123–125.

50. Adams to Zabdiel Adams, June 21, 1776, in L. H. Butterfield *et al.*, eds., *Adams Family Correspondence* (Cambridge, Mass., 1963–), II, 21; Adams to Abigail Adams, July 3, 1776, *ibid.*, 27–28.

51. Adams to John Jebb, Aug. 21, 1785, in C. F. Adams, ed., *Works of John Adams*, IX, 535; Adams to Jebb, Sept. 10, 1785, *ibid.*, 539.

ourselves disposed to think there is a total Change of manners and Principles," Adams gently demurred, "We should recollect, what the manners and Principles were before the War." There had been no golden age in Massachusetts. Looking back unsentimentally to 1760 or 1755 or even back to 1745, "You will be very sensible that our Countrymen have never merited the Character of very exalted Virtue." If Adams had hardly expected them to have grown much better, neither was he inclined to believe they had grown much worse.[52]

Whatever shifts in nuance and emphasis we may detect in Adams's political thought, they remain as footnotes to his black-letter text. Contrary to the impression fostered by Wood's account, John Adams's writings display remarkable coherence and balance in analyzing and judging political behavior. This is no small achievement, considering the great uncertainties and frustrations that attended the American Revolutionary cause as a whole and Adams's undertakings in particular. He perceived clearly and welcomed the new decree "that a more equal Liberty, than has prevail'd in other Parts of the Earth, must be established in America. That Exuberance of Pride, which has produced an insolent Domination, in a few, a very few opulent, monopolizing Families, will be brought down nearer to the Confines of Reason and Moderation, than they have been used." That decree was irrevocable, however much the grandees and nabobs of this world might fret and foam.[53] The young revolutionary, being no mere ideologue, did not permit his pleasure at that prospect to blind him to more somber vistas. Adams already knew and was increasingly troubled by the skill and ease with which the rich and unscrupulous might turn democratic sentiments, credulity, and gratitude to their own corrupt purposes. From that standpoint, a constitutional provision such as Pennsylvania's condemnation of "offices of profit" was but a land mine planted by unthinking enthusiasts. "Hang well and pay well,. conveys to my understanding infinitely more sense and more virtue than this whole article of the Pennsylvania Constitution." Far from letting his unquestionable enthusiasm for the republican cause unbalance his judgment, John Adams thought from first to last that the cause demanded that "government must become something more intelligible, rational, and steady." And as though to mark that fact down to the very end, he responded to an invitation to celebrate the fiftieth anniversary of the Declaration of Independence with this fitting last reflection: "A memorable epoch in the annals of the human race; destined in future history to form the brightest or the blackest

52. Adams to James Warren, Jan. 9, 1787, in Ford, ed., *Warren-Adams Letters*, II, 280.

53. Adams to Patrick Henry, June 3, 1776, in Taylor *et al.*, eds., *Papers of John Adams*, IV, 235.

page, according to the use or the abuse of those political institutions by which they shall in time to come be shaped by the *human mind*."[54] Despite the old man's shaky syntax, Adams showed by his emphasis that he was still the very model of a thinking revolutionary.

III

The example of John Adams, rare individual though he was, suggests the difficulties attending the modern researcher's efforts to reconstruct earlier thought. At every turn we either must discriminate or risk losing sight of our object. If, then, we are to understand the past, we must first listen with care to its distant murmurings. On this, all seem to agree. But listening from afar, like viewing from afar, requires more than specialized apparatus. Without criteria of significance we condemn ourselves to being overwhelmed by a clutter of noise, static, and random lights that effectively conceals the thing being sought. In this respect the historian's problem resembles the astronomer's.

The shortcomings of the modes prevailing today among historians of thought may be traced in large measure to this, their studied reluctance to discriminate. The criticisms developed in the preceding pages suggest a more rewarding approach to the past. It is necessary, first, to separate out the rare and thoughtful from the ordinary and banal lest the former simply be subsumed under the latter. It is necessary, further, to distinguish the several ends and purposes being sought by those voicing common grievances lest a richly revealing variety be reduced to a monotone. Polemics and polemicists, too, call for discrimination lest all political rhetoric be indistinguishable from incantation. Finally, we modern researchers need to separate ourselves from our commonplaces lest the truisms and shortcomings of our age keep us from taking in the perspective of another.

The first act of discrimination, then, is urged upon the student of past thought when he confronts those thousands of whose doings and speeches some record remains. He might begin by noting which of those historical actors were held in special regard or notoriety by contemporaries. Taking note of his own judgment and applying criteria not very different from those he uses in his own life, he might further distinguish those who shape thought from those who merely market it. As suggested before, this disjunction is by no means complete. Some profound thinkers have not held

54. Adams to John Jebb, Aug. 21, 1785, in C. F. Adams, ed., *Works of John Adams*, IX, 532–536; Adams to Jebb, Sept. 10, 1785, *ibid.*, 542–543; Adams to John Whitney, June 7, 1826, *ibid.*, X, 417.

themselves above the task of popularizing or even proselytizing for their conclusions. Nor ought one to underestimate the ability of an intellectual middleman to reshape the thought of a greater or more original mind even while, so to speak, transmitting it. Earlier ages may have had their own John Lennons. But these indisputable complications do not themselves render suspect or invalid the basic distinction between those who are mindful of larger issues and longer-range consequences and those who are not.

The case for paying greater heed to the former than to the latter rests, not on elitist snobbery or on fallacious intellectualism, but on very down-to-earth considerations. Ultimately it is only clear and coherent thought that can be understood; the rest must to a greater or lesser extent remain obscure.[55] Further, insofar as private thought matters, insofar as it may and sometimes does alter how a larger public believes and thinks and acts, one ought to prefer the clearer and more considered expression of that thought. The distant observer needs all the help he can get in orienting himself in unfamiliar terrain—and by and large it *is* unfamiliar terrain. Or to put it more cautiously, it is a safer presumption to treat the past, including our national past, as different or as possibly even strange. In doing so we reduce the likelihood of our unwittingly smoothing away or overlooking whatever might be distinctive in that earlier period. By preserving some sense of possible alienness, we leave ourselves open to being surprised and even to learning something. Then, should we indeed find ourselves in alien territory, all the more certainly will we stand in need of any available farsighted guide.

None of this presumes anything about *who* such a guide might be or about where such an individual should be sought. It would be a very foolish student who confined his search to eighteenth-century graduates of Harvard or William and Mary, or even to good spellers. But it would not be foolish to place greater emphasis upon things said and written than upon deeds performed. For although words may be spoken with forked tongue, acts are often even more ambiguous. Again, this is not to deny that a civic ritual, as analyzed by a knowing and sensitive observer, may yield a wealth of insight. But the depth of analysis displayed in the opening chapters of *The Scarlet Letter* is hardly to be expected from scholars who probably know less of their subject than did Hawthorne and who operate under a more restricted license.

It is not, however, sufficient to identify the principal and most vocal participants in a controversy. A second act of discrimination is needed, for ends, too, have to be distinguished. The fact that diverse individuals or groups concur in a political proposal or even a program is no sure testimony

---

55. Nathan Tarcov, "Quentin Skinner's Method and Machiavelli's *Prince*," *Ethics*, XCII (1982), 693.

to the identity of their objectives. Without some effort at distinguishing agreement on principles from agreement on particular political arrangements, one runs the risk of assimilating and blurring much that might be revealing. Eighteenth-century Americans seem to have perceived this fact of political life most clearly. It was not enough for them to learn that a tax had been laid or lifted. What, they insisted on knowing, was the intention behind the bare act? That would make all the difference. Thus their preoccupation with motivations, far from being a simplistic obsession, can be seen, rather, as an effort on their part to discriminate among principles in the absence of clear and explicit statements.[56]

The different grievances of that generation (for example, those of Virginia revolutionaries or New York Anti-Federalists), ought likewise to be distinguished. One suspects that those people knew at least as well as modern scholars that they were not about to be reduced to the level of that distant brutalized people of whom they had so often heard—the Turks—or of that oppressed folk whom they so often saw at their very hearths. Yet they persisted in speaking of their own potential enslavement. That decision on their part to discriminate between the burden actually borne and "the general course and tendency of things" is now commonly dismissed as an expression of eighteenth-century paranoia, frenzy, or some other form of psychosocial disorder. In this, historians err. For the standard by which a grievance is identified and measured is not the burden itself, but the interpretation one puts on what was tolerable about one's previous condition. If Jefferson and others were correct in seeing the colonists in British America as having enjoyed virtual self-government, with very limited concessions to the imperial structure, then *that* condition becomes the measure of one's discontent. The test of reasonableness asks not whether a tax of so many pence upon paper, tea, or glass will bring this proud people to its knees. It asks, instead, Are the characterization of the past arrangements and the identification of what was most to be cherished in those arrangements correct? If so, it is no sign of madness to feel pain at every instance in that "long train of Abuses, Prevarications, and Artifices." Then may one rightly ask, "Are the People to be blamed, if they have the sence of rational Creatures, and can think of things no otherwise than as they find and feel them?"[57]

---

56. Appleby, "Republicanism," *WMQ*, 3d Ser., XLIII (1986), 29.

57. John Locke, *Two Treatises of Government*, II, secs. 225, 230. On this, thinking revolutionaries were insistent: "How ridiculous then is it to affirm, that we are quarrelling for the trifling sum of three pence a pound on tea; when it is evidently the principle against which we contend." Alexander Hamilton, "A Full Vindication of the Measures of the Congress . . . ," Dec. 15, 1774, in Harold C. Syrett *et al.*, eds., *The Papers of Alexander Hamilton* (New York, 1961–1979), I, 46, 48 (quote). Simi-

It is refreshing and chastening to turn from the new historians' account of these witless prisoners of a paranoiac age to Edmund Burke's portrait of a mercurial people's "fierce spirit of liberty." Like these historians, although for very different reasons, Burke chose not to discuss the abstract doctrine of liberty. Instead, he devoted a half-dozen pages in his speech on concilia-tion with the colonies to convey a sense and understanding of the temper and character of American resistance. The people there depicted, "snuff-[ing] the approach of tyranny in every tainted breeze," leap to life from those dazzling pages.[58] The contrast with the productions of our postpsy-chological age ought to be humbling.

Even in those instances where men great and small indulge in polemical speech, the need for discernment and distinction continues. There is a dif-ference between those who shouted the slogans and voiced the truisms of the age and those who knew that merely following "cultural imperatives" was the road to ruination. That difference is easy to overlook when con-fronted, for example, by John Adams's great catalogs of authorities, ancient and modern, in support of his "revolution-principles." Yet it is a serious misreading that would conflate a young lawyer's forensic overkill with an unquestioning acceptance of conventional maxims and truths. It was one thing to seek support from whatever quarter, catching up all who might to some extent share a common spirit, even while imposing one's own under-standing upon those authoritative names. But it was yet another thing to do so with an awareness of the limits and risks entailed. The best among the Revolutionary founders understood what the hacks and third-rate people never grasped: that there is no substitute for a clear, calm understanding of one's situation.

Far, then, from being mere reflections of their "political culture," the best took special pains to distance themselves from much of what everyone else opined. A James Madison would interrupt his polemics to remind overcon-fident friends and foes of the proposed Constitution of the limits of intellect and language in politics. He did this, not with a view to deconstructing rational discourse, but for the antiquated purpose of finding the measure of clarity and precision that the complex subject and the imperfect mind and

---

larly, James Madison: "The people of the U. S. owe their Independence and their liberty, to the wisdom of descrying in the minute tax of 3 pence on tea, the magni-tude of the evil comprized in the precedent." Elizabeth Fleet, ed., "Madison's 'De-tached Memoranda,'" *WMQ*, 3d Ser., III (1946), 557.

58. Edmund Burke, "Speech on Moving His Resolutions for Conciliation with the Colonies," Mar. 22, 1775, in *The Works of the Right Honourable Edmund Burke* (London, 1854–1856), I, 464–469.

medium would admit.[59] A John Adams would distinguish the respectable and necessary uses of rhetoric from nonsensical prating and manipulative chicanery. His penetrating analysis of ideology—named as such—remains a testimony to the power of good sense to form an independent judgment.[60] It was precisely in their conscious, deliberate effort not to be mere mouthers of givens that the men separated themselves from the boys.

How ironical and baffling it is that, in the cause of sophisticated rhetorical analysis as the key to meaning, the new historians should treat eighteenth-century masters of rhetoric as slaves to commonplaces. In their avidity to discover unintended meanings in the texts (and even scraps) that have come down to us, too many of these historians miss the rich subtleties to be detected in the founders' studied use of language to both persuade and teach. When a cultivated art is mistaken for children's finger painting, the consequences are predictable.

These were no garden-variety eighteenth-century ideologues flattering themselves they had an option to create a utopia. Knowing that they could neither stop history nor command it, these founders turned their thoughts to identifying sources of danger without fancying that they might overcome those dangers once and for all. Accordingly, they took thinking clearly to be their paramount duty. It was not enough to know a truth, such as that all political authority derives from the people, or an invaluable precept, such as that the branches of government ought to be separate and distinct. Nor would it do to guide one's policies by some simplistic definitions of regimes. Unless one thought through, with care and deliberation, how those truths and precepts would work in an actual world, one stood a good chance of ending up victim of one's own principles.

These thinking revolutionaries saw their task and opportunity in fashioning a new beginning, but without presuming a magical transmutation of the species. If they were impressed that their generation had the greatest opportunity since the First Pair, they also could never ask too often, What is the genius of this people for whom and to whom we mean to propose a constitution and government? What would this all too human people accept—and follow? In displaying this awareness of boundaries and limits, the thinking

59. James Madison, *Federalist* No. 37, in Jacob E. Cooke, ed., *The Federalist* (Middletown, Conn., 1961), 233–237.

60. John Adams to Benjamin Rush, June 22, Sept. 19, Nov. 11, 1806, in Biddle, ed., *Old Family Letters*, Ser. A, 99–100, 109–113, 114–117. Adams to Thomas Jefferson, July 13, 1813, in C. F. Adams, ed., *Works of John Adams*, X, 52–54; Adams to Jefferson, Mar. 2, 1816, *ibid.*, 211–212; Adams to James Madison, Apr. 22, 1817, *ibid.*, 256–257.

revolutionary was by no means simply parroting the conventions of the age, for within those broad limits lay a variety of paths and a variety of outcomes. It was precisely this awareness that accounts for the sense of heavy responsibility that so marks the founders' thinking and writing. They feared for the fragility of their political handiwork, not because they were caught in the grip of a paranoiac, conspiratorial age, but because their daring project was and always would be in jeopardy.

The goal, after all, was not to attain some minimal standard of cooperation and preservation. A den of wary thieves, properly organized, might manage as much for themselves. Because these thinking revolutionaries wanted so much more than that, it was all the more important that they start right, choose right, and with greatest deliberation forfend or minimize whatever might threaten or damage their new order. This meant, among other things, that the simple truths of the age—the ideologues' daily bread—had somehow or other to be qualified, even deviated from, if the cause of a self-governing people were to be preserved. The shouter of slogans, the mouther of maxims, may have believed sincerely, may have had a real grievance, but his thoughts were simple and his vision limited. He is in no way to be confused with our thinking revolutionaries, intent on complicating, refining, and elaborating those simple truths the better to make them true in practice. For this great task no useful device would be spurned. In the case of the separation of powers, for example, they relied not only on the slogan itself (proclaimed in half a dozen state constitutions) but on its embodiment in institutions and, not least, on the good use of power by other, later, thoughtful men. Here was a way by which this extraordinary experiment might correct itself and survive.

If we are, then, finally, to recover the constitution of the thinking revolutionary, we must indeed look and listen with care. Doing so may demand nothing less than shaking free of our familiar intellectual tackle, the fourth and most trying of these requisite acts of separation and discernment. We might begin by reconsidering the new historians' claim to be the first to understand the murky automatic writing of the past—and this, on the basis of a new revelation coming from (of all places) the abstract theoretical works of academic social science.[61] Following the lead of those thoughtful founders who attacked ideologues for not rising above the assumptions of their age, we present-day students might make a special effort to rise above our age's maxims and think anew. Following the lead of those thoughtful founders who insisted on the difference between levels of political discourse, we might discriminate between those who dealt only in ideals and those

61. John Patrick Diggins, *The Lost Soul of American Politics: Virtue, Self-Interest, and the Foundations of Liberalism* (New York, 1984), 364.

who, without abandoning ideals, considered a world peopled with real men and women. Those thoughtful founders were not above creating a political culture, but they were intent on its being a better one. If those men of the Enlightenment, declining to rely solely on the persuasiveness of reason, chose as well to form a political culture that would instill reverence for the laws, it was out of their recognition that the citizenry were mere mortals. But since these were to be self-governing mortals, they dared not wish for a nation of automatic believers. Far from it.

Those founders believed and acted on the premise that the highest activity of the thinking revolutionary is constitution making and constitution preserving. Neither was possible where mindlessness reigned. Without thinkers, and a population receptive to thoughtful argument, the brave experiment was doomed. Hence they taught through precept and example that a people might distinguish better from worse reasons and choose the better out of its understanding. They acted as though dedicated intelligence might make a difference. Those precepts and assumptions may well be controverted. But the thinking revolutionary would probably say their denial or denigration carries its own lesson to the broader public.[62]

It takes an act of considerable will and historical imagination for a historian to shake loose of prevailing intellectual modes. Looking beyond mere numbers, we can see that ours is no great age of founding and constitution making. It is almost natural that people today should take principles for granted and find it hard to envision an earlier world when many minds were filled with a sense of fundamentals contending as real alternatives and inviting reasoned choice. And as though this were not enough of a barrier to historical understanding and reconstruction, there is the further artificial difference between our age and that of the founders. Theirs was a period when thought was believed (rightly or wrongly) to be enlightenment; ours, when thought is believed (rightly or wrongly) to be ideology. Yet even if we are persuaded that we are correct, we are not free as students of another period and another way of thinking to ignore the consequences of that difference in belief. We are compelled as students of that other period to try to imagine what differences that difference in belief makes in how thought is conducted, transmitted, and applied.

Someone might wonder, finally, whether all this talk of ideology and ideas, reasons and thoughtfulness, is not itself an exaggeration. Did all that theorizing really matter beyond the handful who delighted in such things? Such misgivings are not the monopoly of sophisticated historians, for some founders confronted those very doubts at the time. To the charge that he

---

62. Tocqueville, *Democracy in America*, trans. Lawrence, 464–465 (II, Pt. i, chap. 20); see also Diggins, *Lost Soul*, 357.

and his like were "disaffected" incendiaries, young John Adams chose only to deny the implied passivity of the people. His premise was that "the people are capable of understanding, seeing and feeling the difference between true and false, right and wrong, virtue and vice"; it was to "the sense of this difference" that he and those like him had recurred. It was a mistake to view the people as so much flammable matter ready at any moment to be touched off and exploded. "I appeal to all experience, and to universal history, if it has ever been in the power of popular leaders, uninvested with other authority than what is conferred by the popular suffrage, to persuade a large people, for any length of time together, to think themselves wronged, injured, and oppressed, unless they really were, and saw and felt it to be so."[63]

For John Adams, reflection and the exchange of reasons were central to the age of founding and constitution making. Far from being an irrelevance, the capacity for thoughtful response was taken to be broadly distributed in society, albeit in different degrees and kinds. The counterpart of the thinking revolutionary in America was not some sodden peasantry. But by the same token, neither was that population a vast, continuous seminar in political theory. Newspapers were scarce, and books no less so; "Every class of men cannot be supposed to have been aided by extensive literary views." And yet a variety of social and political arrangements made it possible for Virginians, for example, "to catch the full spirit of the theories which at the fountainhead were known only to men of studious retirement."[64] In leaving their retirement and speaking as they did, the thinking revolutionaries sought to honor themselves and their public. On this basis rested their confident invitation to all—contemporaries and successors alike—to examine their principles and acts. That invitation still stands.

63. John Adams, "Novanglus," No. 1, Jan. 23, 1775, in Taylor *et al.*, eds., *Papers of John Adams*, II, 229. What began as an "apprehension," would then "arouse the attention, not only of the inquiring mind, but of the common people, and urge them to close thinking on the constitutional authority of parliament over the colonies." Adams to Jedidiah Morse, Dec. 2, 1815, in C. F. Adams, ed., *Works of John Adams*, X, 185.

64. Edmund Randolph, *History of Virginia*, ed. Arthur H. Shaffer (Charlottesville, Va., 1970), 193–194.

☆ ☆ ☆ ☆ ☆

Interests and Disinterestedness in the Making of the Constitution

GORDON S. WOOD

I

During our bicentennial celebrations of the Constitution we will gather many times to honor the makers of that Constitution, the Federalists of 1787-1788. We have certainly done so many times in the past. We have repeatedly pictured the founders, as we call them, as men of vision—bold, original, open-minded, enlightened men who deliberately created what William Gladstone once called "the most wonderful work ever struck off at a given time by the hand and purpose of man."[1] We have described them as men who knew where the future lay and went for it. Even those like Charles Beard who have denigrated their motives have seen the founders as masters of events, realistic pragmatists who knew human nature when they saw it, farsighted, economically advanced, modern men in step with the movement of history.

In contrast, we have usually viewed the opponents of the Constitution, the Antifederalists, as very tame and timid, narrow-minded and parochial men of no imagination and little faith, caught up in the ideological rigidities of the past—inflexible, suspicious men unable to look ahead and see where the United States was going. The Antifederalists seem forever doomed to be losers, bypassed by history and eternally disgraced by their opposition to the greatest constitutional achievement in our nation's history.

But maybe we have got it all wrong. Maybe the Federalists were not men of the future after all. Maybe it was the Antifederalists who really saw best

---

1. Gladstone, quoted in Douglass Adair, "The Tenth Federalist Revisited," in Trevor Colbourn, ed., *Fame and the Founding Fathers* (New York, 1974), 81.

and farthest. Is it possible that all those original, bold, and farsighted Federalists had their eyes not on what was coming, but on what was passing? Perhaps the roles of the participants in the contest over the Constitution in 1787-1788 ought to be reversed. If either side in the conflict over the Constitution stood for modernity, perhaps it was the Antifederalists. They, and not the Federalists, may have been the real harbingers of the moral and political world we know—the liberal, democratic, commercially advanced world of individual pursuits of happiness.

If this is true—if indeed the founders did not stand for modernity—then it should not be surprising that they are now so lost to us, that they should have become, as we continually lament, "a galaxy of public leaders we have never been able remotely to duplicate since."[2] Instead of being the masters, were they really the victims of events? Is it possible that their Constitution failed, and failed miserably, in what they wanted it to do?

Naturally, we are reluctant to admit that the Constitution may have failed in what it set out to do, and consequently we have difficulty in fully understanding its origins. To be sure, we readily accept the necessity for a new central government in 1787. Unable to imagine the United States as ever existing without a strong national government, we regard the creation of the new structure in 1787 as inevitable. (For us it is the Articles of Confederation that cannot be taken seriously.) But the new central government seems inevitable to us only for reasons that fit our modern preconceptions. As long as people in the 1780s explain the movement for the Constitution in terms of the weaknesses of the Confederation, we can easily understand and accept their explanations. But when people in the 1780s explain the movement for the Constitution in terms other than the palpable weaknesses of the central government—in terms of a crisis in the society—we become puzzled and skeptical. A real crisis? It hardly seems believable. The 1780s were, after all, a time of great release and expansion: the population grew as never before, or since, and more Americans than ever before were off in pursuit of prosperity and happiness. "There is not upon the face of the earth a body of people more happy or rising into consequence with more rapid stride, than the Inhabitants of the United States of America," Charles Thomson told Jefferson in 1786. "Population is increasing, new houses building, new lands clearing, new settlements forming, and new manufactures establishing with a rapidity beyond conception."[3] The general mood

2. Henry Steele Commager, *Jefferson, Nationalism, and the Enlightenment* (New York, 1975), xix.

3. Thomson to Jefferson, Apr. 6, 1786, in Julian P. Boyd *et al.*, eds., *The Papers of Thomas Jefferson* (Princeton, N.J., 1950-), IX, 380. On the demographic explosion of the 1780s, see J. Potter, "The Growth of Population in America, 1700-1860,"

was high, expectant, and far from bleak. No wonder then that historians of very different persuasions have doubted that there was anything really critical happening in the society.[4]

Yet, of course, we have all those statements by people in the 1780s warning that "our situation is critical and dangerous" and that "our vices" were plunging us into "national ruin." Benjamin Rush even thought that the American people were on the verge of "degenerating into savages or devouring each other like beasts of prey." But if we think that Rush is someone with a hyperactive imagination, here is the 1786 voice of the much more sober and restrained George Washington: "What astonishing changes a few years are capable of producing. . . . From the high ground we stood upon, from the plain path which invited our footsteps, to be so fallen! so lost! it is really mortifying."[5]

What are we to make of such despairing and excited statements—statements that can be multiplied over and over and that were often made not in the frenzy of public debate, but in the privacy of letters to friends? Many of those historians who, like Charles Beard, believe that such statements are a gross exaggeration can conclude only that the sense of crisis was "conjured up" by the Federalists, since "actually the country faced no such emergency." But such a conspiratorial interpretation of the Constitution is hardly satisfying and tells us nothing of what such statements of alarm and foreboding meant. Why did some men, members of the elite—those who saved their letters for us to read—think America was in a crisis?[6]

---

in D. V. Glass and D.E.C. Eversley, eds., *Population in History: Essays in Historical Demography* (Chicago, 1965), 640.

4. For examples of the various historians who have minimized the criticalness of the 1780s, see Charles A. Beard, *An Economic Interpretation of the Constitution of the United States* (New York, 1913), 48; E. James Ferguson, *The Power of the Purse: A History of American Public Finance, 1776–1790* (Chapel Hill, N.C., 1961), 337; Merrill Jensen, *The New Nation: A History of the United States during the Confederation, 1781–1789* (New York, 1950), 348–349; Bernard Bailyn, "The Central Themes of the American Revolution: An Interpretation," in Stephen G. Kurtz and James H. Hutson, eds., *Essays on the American Revolution* (Chapel Hill, N.C., 1973), 21.

5. "Amicus Republicae," *Address to the Public* . . . (Exeter, N.H., 1786), in Charles S. Hyneman and Donald S. Lutz, eds., *American Political Writing during the Founding Era, 1760–1805* (Indianapolis, Ind., 1983), I, 644; Rush to David Ramsay, [Mar. or Apr. 1788], in L. H. Butterfield, ed., *Letters of Benjamin Rush* (Princeton, N.J., 1951), I, 454; Washington to John Jay, Aug. 1, 1786, May 18, 1786, in John C. Fitzpatrick, ed., *The Writings of George Washington* . . . (Washington, D.C., 1931–1944), XXVIII, 503, 431–432.

6. Jackson Turner Main, *The Antifederalists: Critics of the Constitution, 1781–1788* (Chapel Hill, N.C., 1961), 177–178.

Certainly it was not the defects of the Articles of Confederation that were causing this sense of crisis. These defects of the Confederation were remediable and were scarcely capable of eliciting horror and despair. To be sure, these defects did make possible the calling of the Philadelphia Convention to amend the Articles. By 1787 almost every political leader in the country, including most of the later Antifederalists, wanted something done to strengthen the Articles of Confederation. The Confederation had no power to pay its debts, no power to tax, and no power to regulate commerce, and it was daily being humiliated in its international relationships. Reform of the Articles in some way or other—particularly by granting the Congress a limited authority to tax and the power to regulate commerce—was in the air. This desire to do something about the central government was the Federalists' opportunity: it explains the willingness of people to accede to the meeting at Annapolis and the subsequent convening of delegates at Philadelphia. In fact, so acceptable and necessary seemed some sort of change in the Confederation that later Antifederalists were remarkably casual about the meeting at Philadelphia. William Findley of western Pennsylvania, for example, later claimed he was selected to go to the convention but declined when he learned that "the delegates would have no wages." Thus the seven delegates Pennsylvania sent to the convention were all residents of the city of Philadelphia (including even one, Gouverneur Morris, who was really a New Yorker), and no one at the time complained.[7]

Thus the defects of the Confederation were widely acknowledged, and many looked to the Philadelphia Convention for a remedy. But these defects do not account for the elite's expression of crisis, nor do they explain the ambitious nature of the nationalists' Virginia Plan that formed the working model for the convention's deliberations. The nationalists' aims and the Virginia Plan went way beyond what the weaknesses of the Articles demanded. Granting Congress the authority to raise revenue, to regulate trade, to pay off its debts, and to deal effectively in international affairs did not require the total scrapping of the Articles and the creation of an extraordinarily powerful and distant national government, the like of which was virtually inconceivable to Americans a decade earlier. The Virginia Plan was the remedy for more than the obvious impotence of the Confederation; it was a remedy—and an aristocratic remedy—for what were often referred to as the excesses of American democracy. It was these excesses of democracy that lay behind the elite's sense of crisis.

7. Findley to Gov. William Plumer of New Hampshire, "William Findley of Westmoreland, Pa.," *Pennsylvania Magazine of History and Biography*, V (1881), 444; Jerry Grundfest, *George Clymer: Philadelphia Revolutionary, 1739–1813* (New York, 1982), 293–294; John Bach McMaster and Frederick D. Stone, eds., *Pennsylvania and the Federal Constitution, 1787–1788* (Philadelphia, 1888), 115.

What excesses of democracy? What on earth could have been happening to provoke fear and horror? Not Shays's Rebellion that broke out in the winter of 1786-1787. That was an alarming clincher for many Federalists, especially in Massachusetts, but it was scarcely the cause of the Federalists' pervasive sense of crisis, which existed well before they learned of Shays's Rebellion.[8] No, it was not mobs and overt disorder that really frightened the founders. They knew about popular rioting, and had taken such occurrences more or less in stride for years. What bothered them, what they meant by the excesses of democracy, was something more insidious than mobs. It was something that we today accept as familiar, ordinary, and innocuous, but the founders did not—good old American popular politics. It was popular politics, especially as practiced in the state legislatures, that lay behind the founders' sense of crisis. The legislatures were unwilling to do "justice," and this, said Washington, is "the origin of the evils we now feel." The abuses of the state legislatures, said Madison, were "so frequent and so flagrant as to alarm the most stedfast friends of Republicanism," and these abuses, he told Jefferson in the fall of 1787, "contributed more to that uneasiness which produced the Convention, and prepared the public mind for a general reform, than those which accrued to our national character and interest from the inadequacy of the Confederation to its immediate objects."[9] Hard as it may be for us today to accept, the weaknesses of the Articles of Confederation were not the most important reasons for the making of the Constitution.

Throughout the whole period of crisis, Madison, the father of the Constitution if there ever was one, never had any doubt where the main source of the troubles lay. In his working paper drafted in the late winter of 1787 entitled "Vices of the Political System of the United States," Madison spent very little time on the impotence of the Confederation. What was really on his mind was the deficiencies of the state governments: he devoted more than half his paper to the "multiplicity," "mutability," and "injustice" of the laws passed by the states.[10] Particularly alarming and unjust in his eyes were the paper money acts, stay laws, and other forms of debtor-relief legislation that hurt creditors and violated individual property rights. And he knew personally what he was talking about. Although we usually think of Madison

8. On this point, see Robert A. Feer, "Shays's Rebellion and the Constitution: A Study in Causation," *New England Quarterly*, XLII (1969), 388-410.

9. Washington to Jay, May 18, 1786, in Fitzpatrick, ed., *Writings of Washington*, XVIII, 432; Madison to Jefferson, Oct. 24, 1787, in Boyd *et al.*, eds., *Papers of Jefferson*, XII, 276.

10. Robert A. Rutland, editorial note to "Vices of the Political System of the United States," in William T. Hutchinson *et al.*, eds., *The Papers of James Madison* (Chicago, Charlottesville, 1962-), IX, 346.

as a bookish scholar who got all his thoughts from his wide reading, he did not develop his ideas about the democratic excesses of the state governments by poring through the bundles of books that Jefferson was sending him from Europe. He learned about popular politics and legislative abuses firsthand—by being a member of the Virginia Assembly.

During the years 1784 through 1787 Madison attended four sessions of the Virginia legislature. They were perhaps the most frustrating and disillusioning years of his life, but also the most important years of his life, for his experience as a Virginia legislator in the 1780s was fundamental in shaping his thinking as a constitutional reformer.

Although Madison in these years had some notable legislative achievements, particularly with his shepherding into enactment Jefferson's famous bill for religious freedom, he was continually exasperated by what Jefferson years later (no doubt following Madison's own account) referred to as "the endless quibbles, chicaneries, perversions, vexations, and delays of lawyers and demi-lawyers" in the assembly. Really for the first time, Madison found out what democracy in America might mean. Not all the legislators were going to be like him or Jefferson; many of them did not even appear to be gentlemen. The Virginia legislators seemed so parochial, so illiberal, so small-minded, and most of them seemed to have only "a particular interest to serve." They had no regard for public honor or honesty. They too often made a travesty of the legislative process and were reluctant to do anything that might appear unpopular. They postponed taxes, subverted debts owed to the subjects of Great Britain, and passed, defeated, and repassed bills in the most haphazard ways. Madison had enlightened expectations for Virginia's port bill in 1784, but the other legislators got their self-serving hands on it and perverted it. It was the same with nearly all the legislative proposals he sought to introduce, especially those involving reform of the legal code and court system. "Important bills prepared at leisure by skilful hands," he complained, were vitiated by "crudeness and tedious discussion." What could he do with such clods? "It will little elevate your idea of our Senate," he wrote in weary disgust to Washington in 1786, to learn that the senators actually defeated a bill defining the privileges of foreign ambassadors in Virginia "on the principle . . . that an Alien ought not to be put on better ground than a Citizen."[11] This was carrying localism to absurdity.

It was not what republican lawmaking was supposed to be. Madison con-

11. Jefferson quoted in Ralph Ketcham, *James Madison: A Biography* (New York, 1971), 162; Drew R. McCoy, "The Virginia Port Bill of 1784," *Virginia Magazine of History and Biography*, LXXXIII (1975), 294; Madison to Edmund Pendleton, Jan. 9, 1787, to Washington, Dec. 24, 1786, in Hutchinson *et al.*, eds., *Papers of Madison*, IX, 244, 225; A. G. Roeber, *Faithful Magistrates and Republican Lawyers: Creators of Virginia Legal Culture, 1680–1810* (Chapel Hill, N.C., 1981), 192–202.

tinually had to make concessions to the "prevailing sentiments," whether or not such sentiments promoted the good of the state or nation. He had to agree to bad laws for fear of getting worse ones, or give up good bills "rather than pay such a price" as opponents wanted. Today legislators are used to this sort of political horse-trading. But Madison simply was not yet ready for the logrolling and the pork-barreling that would eventually become the staples of American legislative politics. By 1786 he had "strong apprehensions" that his and Jefferson's hope for reforming the legal code "may never be systematically perfected." The legislature was simply too popular, and appealing to the people had none of the beneficial effects good republicans had expected. A bill having to do with court reform was, for example, "to be printed for consideration of the public"; but "instead of calling forth the sanction of the wise and virtuous," this action, Madison, feared, would only "be a signal to interested men to redouble their efforts to get into the Legislature." Democracy was no solution to the problem; democracy was the problem. Madison repeatedly found himself having to beat back the "itch for paper money" and other measures "of a popular cast." Too often Madison had to admit that the only hope he had was "of moderating the fury," not defeating it.[12]

Madison, like other enthusiastic Revolutionary idealists, emerged from his experience with democratic politics in the mid–1780s a very chastened republican. It was bad enough, he wrote in his "Vices of the Political System of the United States," that legislators were often interested men or dupes of the sophistry of "a favorite leader" (like Patrick Henry). Even more alarming for the fate of republican government, however, was the fact that such legislators were only reflecting the partial interests and parochial outlooks of their constituents. Too many of the American people could not see beyond their own pocketbooks or their own neighborhoods. "Individuals of extended views, and of national pride," said Madison (and he knew whom he meant), might be able to bring public proceedings to an enlightened cosmopolitan standard, but their example could never be followed by "the multitude." "Is it to be imagined that an ordinary citizen or even an assemblyman of R. Island in estimating the policy of paper money, ever considered or cared in what light the measure would be viewed in France or Holland; or even in Massts or Connect.? It was a sufficient temptation to both that it was for their interest."[13]

Madison's experience with the populist politics of the state legislatures

12. McCoy, "Virginia Port Bill" *VMHB*, LXXXIII (1975) 292; Madison to Washington, Dec. 7, 1786, to Pendleton, Jan. 9, 1787, to Washington, Dec. 24, 1786, to Jefferson, Dec. 4, 1786, in Hutchinson *et al.*, eds., *Papers of Madison*, IX, 200, 244, 225, 191; Ketcham, *Madison*, 172.

13. "Vices," in Hutchinson *et al.*, eds., *Papers of Madison*, IX, 354, 355–356.

was especially important because of his extraordinary influence in the writing of the Federal Constitution. But his experience was not unusual; indeed, the Federalists could never have done what they did if Madison's experience was not widely shared. By the mid-1780s gentlemen up and down the continent were shaking their heads in disbelief and anger at the "private views and selfish principles" of the men they saw in the state assemblies, "men of narrow souls and no natural interest in the society." Selfish, ignorant, illiberal state legislators—"Characters too full of Local attachments and Views to permit sufficient attention to the general interest"—were bringing discredit upon popular government. They were promoting their own or their locality's particular interest, pandering "to the vulgar and sordid notions of the populace," and acting as judges in their own causes. "Private convenience, paper money, and ex post facto laws" were the "main springs" of these state lawmakers. Many of the delegates to the Philadelphia Convention were so ready to accept Madison's radical Virginia Plan and its proposed national authority to veto all state laws precisely because they shared his deep disgust with the localist and interest-ridden politics of the state legislatures. "The vile State governments are sources of pollution which will contaminate the American name for ages. . . . Smite them," Henry Knox urged Rufus King sitting in the Philadelphia Convention, "smite them, in the name of God and the people."[14]

We today can easily appreciate the concerns of the founders with the weaknesses of the Confederation government: these seem real and tangible to us, especially in light of what we know our national government has become. But we have more difficulty in appreciating the fears the founders expressed over the democratic politics of the state legislatures—the scrambling of different interest groups, the narrow self-promoting nature of much of the lawmaking, the incessant catering to popular demands. Surely, this behavior cannot be accurately described as the "wilderness of anarchy and vice." This "excess of democracy" is, after all, what popular politics is about, and it is not different from what Americans in time came to be very used to.[15]

14. Washington to Henry Lee, Apr. 5, 1786, in Fitzpatrick, ed., *Writings of Washington*, XXVIII, 402; Grundfest, *Clymer*, 165, 164; E. Wayne Carp, *To Starve the Army at Pleasure: Continental Army Administration and American Political Culture, 1775-1783* (Chapel Hill, N.C., 1984), 209; Knox quoted in William Winslow Crosskey and William Jeffrey, Jr., *Politics and the Constitution in the History of the United States* (Chicago, 1980), III, 420, 421.

15. Rush to Jeremy Belknap, May 6, 1788, in Butterfield, ed., *Letters of Rush*, I, 461; Elbridge Gerry in Max Farrand, ed., *The Records of the Federal Convention of 1787* (New Haven, Conn., 1911, rev. ed., 1937), I, 48.

It may not have been different from what Americans came to be used to, and it may not even have been different from what some of the Revolutionary leaders had occasionally experienced in their colonial assemblies. But for most of the founding fathers, popular political behavior in the states during the 1780s was very different from what they expected from their republican Revolution, and for them that difference was what made the 1780s a genuine critical period.

II

Republicanism was not supposed to stimulate selfishness and private interests, but was to divert and control them. But in states up and down the continent various narrow factional interests, especially economic, were flourishing as never before, and, more alarming still, were demanding and getting protection and satisfaction from the democratically elected state legislatures. Although interest groups and factionalism had been common in the colonial legislatures, the interests and factions of post-Revolutionary politics were different: more numerous, less personal and family-oriented, and more democratically expressive of new, widespread economic elements in the society. The Revolution, it appeared, had unleashed acquisitive and commercial forces that no one had quite realized existed.

We are only beginning to appreciate the immense consequences that the Revolution and, especially, wartime mobilization had on American society. When all the articles and monographs are in, however, I think that we will find that the Revolutionary war, like the Civil War and the two world wars, radically transformed America's society and economy. The war effort was enormous. The war went on for eight years (the longest in American history until that of Vietnam); it eventually saw one hundred thousand or more men under arms, and it touched the whole of American society to a degree that no previous event ever had. The inexhaustible needs of the army—for everything from blankets and wagons to meat and rum—brought into being a host of new manufacturing and entrepreneurial interests and made market farmers out of husbandmen who before had scarcely ever traded out of their neighborhoods. To pay for all these new war goods the Revolutionary governments issued huge sums—four hundred million to five hundred million dollars—of paper money that made its way into the hands of many people who had hitherto dealt only in a personal and bookkeeping barter economy.[16] Under the stimulus of this wartime purchasing, speculative

---

16. The best study of wartime mobilization in a single state is Richard Buel, Jr., *Dear Liberty: Connecticut's Mobilization for the Revolutionary War* (Middletown,

farmers, inland traders, and profiteers of all sorts sprang up by the thousands to circulate these goods and paper money throughout the interior areas of America. By 1778, wrote Henry Laurens, "the demand for money" was no longer "confined to the capital towns and cities within a small circle of trading merchants, but spread over a surface of 1,600 miles in length, and 300 broad." The war and rapidly rising prices were creating a society in which, as one bitter commissary agent complained, "Every Man buys in order to sell again."[17] No event in the eighteenth century accelerated the capitalistic development of America more than did the Revolutionary war. It brought new producers and consumers into the market economy, it aroused latent acquisitive instincts everywhere, it stimulated inland trade as never before, and it prepared the way for the eventual momentous shift of the basis of American prosperity from external to internal commerce.

The paper money and the enormous amounts of debts that all these inland entrepreneurs, traders, shopkeepers, and market farmers thrived on were the consequences neither of poverty nor of anticommercial behavior. Debt, as we of all generations in American history ought to know, was already emerging as a symptom of expansion and enterprise. Farmers, traders, and others in these Revolutionary years borrowed money, just as they married earlier and had more children than ever before, because they thought the future was going to be even better than the present. Common people had been increasingly buying consumer goods since at least the middle of the eighteenth century, but the Revolutionary war now gave many more ordinary farmers, often for the first time in their lives, the financial ability to purchase luxury goods that previously had been the preserve of the gentry— everything from lace finery to china dishware. It was this prospect of raising their standard of living and increasing their "pleasures and diversions" that got farmers to work harder and produce "surpluses" during the war, and there is evidence that when the availability of these "luxury" goods diminished during the war the farmers' productivity and their "surpluses" diminished too.[18] For ages men had thought that industry and frugality among

---

Conn., 1980). For an insightful general assessment of the effects of mobilization, see Janet Ann Riesman, "The Origins of American Political Economy, 1690–1781" (Ph.D. diss., Brown University, 1983), 302–338.

17. Laurens quoted in Albert S. Bolles, *The Financial History of the United States from 1774 to 1789: Embracing the Period of the American Revolution*, 4th ed. (New York, 1896), 61–62 (I owe this citation to Janet Riesman); Carp, *To Starve the Army*, 106.

18. Nathanael Greene to Jacob Greene, after May 24, 1778, in Richard K. Showman ed., *The Papers of General Nathanael Greene* (Chapel Hill, N.C., 1976–), II, 404; Richard Buel, Jr., "Samson Shorn: The Impact of the Revolutionary War on Estimates of the Republic's Strength," in Ronald Hoffman and Peter J. Albert, eds.,

the common people went together. Now suddenly in America the industriousness of ordinary people seemed dependent not on the fear of poverty, but on the prospect of luxury.[19]

The economic troubles of the 1780s came from the ending of the war and government purchasing. Too many people had too many heightened expectations and were into the market and the consumption of luxuries too deeply to make any easy adjustments to peace. The collapse of internal markets and the drying up of paper money meant diminished incomes, overextended businesses, swollen inventories of imported manufactures, and debt-laden farmers and traders. The responses of people hurt by these developments were very comprehensible: they simply wanted to continue what they had done during the war. The stay laws and other debtor-relief legislation and the printing of paper money were not the demands of backward-looking and uncommercial people. They were the demands of people who had enjoyed buying, selling, and consuming and desired to do more of it. In order to have prosperity, argued one defender of paper money in 1786, it was not enough to have an industrious people and a fertile territory; money was essential too. And for many ordinary people in the 1780s money—in the absence of gold and silver coin—meant paper money issued by governments or government loan offices. "By anticipating the products of several years labor," farmers were able to borrow loan office certificates based on land in order "to accelerate improvements" and "so to augment industry and multiply the means of carrying it on" and thereby "enrich" both themselves and the state.[20]

Arms and Independence: The Military Character of the American Revolution (Charlottesville, Va., 1984), 157–160. On the growth of commercial farming in the middle of the 18th century, see especially Joyce Appleby, "Commercial Farming and the 'Agrarian Myth' in the Early Republic," *Journal of American History*, LXVIII (1982), 833–849. There is nothing on 18th-century America's increased importation of "luxuries" and "comforts" resembling Neil McKendrick *et al.*, *The Birth of a Consumer Society: The Commercialization of Eighteenth-Century England* (Bloomington, Ind., 1982). But see the articles of Carole Shammas, especially "The Domestic Environment in Early Modern England and America," *Journal of Social History*, XIV (1980), 3–24; Lois Green Carr and Lorena S. Walsh, "Inventories and the Analysis of Wealth and Consumption Patterns in St. Mary's County, Maryland, 1658–1777," *Historical Methods*, XIII (1980), 81–104; and Gloria L. Main, *Tobacco Colony: Life in Early Maryland, 1650–1720* (Princeton, N.J., 1982).

19. For examples of the new thinking about luxury as an inducement to industry, see Drew R. McCoy, *The Elusive Republic: Political Economy in Jeffersonian America* (Chapel Hill, N.C., 1980), 97.

20. [William Barton], *The True Interest of the United States, and Particularly of Pennsylvania Considered . . .* (Philadelphia, 1786), 12.

These calls for paper money in the 1780s were the calls of American business. The future of America's entrepreneurial activity and prosperity lay not with the hundreds of well-to-do creditor-merchants who dominated the overseas trade of the several ports along the Atlantic seaboard. Rather, it lay with the thousands upon thousands of ordinary traders, petty businessmen, aspiring artisans, and market farmers who were deep in debt and were buying and selling with each other all over America. For these people, unlike the overseas merchants who had their private bills of exchange, publicly created paper money was the only means "capable of answering all the *domestic* and *internal* purposes of a *circulating medium* in a nation" that lacked specie. The prosperity of a country, it was now argued, involved more than external commerce, more than having a surplus of exports over imports. "The *internal* commerce of the country must be promoted, by increasing its *real riches*," which were now rightly equated with the acquisitions, improvements, and entrepreneurial activity of ordinary people.[21]

There is no exaggerating the radical significance of this heightened awareness among Americans of the importance of domestic trade. Hitherto most Americans had thought of internal trade, as William Smith of New York put it in the 1750s, as publicly worthless—a mere passing of wealth around the community from hand to hand. Such exchanging, said Smith, "tho' it may enrich an Individual," meant that "others must be poorer, in an exact proportion to his Gains; but the collective Body of the People not at all."[22] Such was the traditional zero-sum mercantilist mentality that was now being challenged by the increased entrepreneurial activity of thousands of ordinary people. Farmers "in a new and unimproved country," it was now said, "have continual uses for money, to stock and improve their farms" or, as Madison noted, to "extend their consumption as far as credit can be obtained." And they now wanted more money than could be gotten by the old-fashioned means of applying "to a monied man for a loan from his private fortune." Consequently these farmers and other small-time entrepreneurs in state after state up and down the continent were electing representatives to their legislatures who could supply them with paper money, paper money which, as the preamble to a 1785 Pennsylvania statute establishing a loan office stated, was designed "to promote and establish the interests of internal commerce, agriculture and mechanc arts."[23] Not the defects of the Articles of Con-

21. *Ibid.*, 4, 25–26.
22. [William Smith], *The Independent Reflector . . . by William Livingston and Others*, ed. Milton M. Klein (Cambridge, Mass., 1963), 106. See J. E. Crowley, *This Sheba, Self: The Conceptualization of Economic Life in Eighteenth-Century America* (Baltimore, 1974), 38–39, 44, 49, 87, 97–99.
23. *Remarks on a Pamphlet, Entitled, "Considerations on the Bank of North-America"*

federation, but this promotion of entrepreneurial interests by ordinary people—their endless buying and selling, their bottomless passion for luxurious consumption—was what really frightened the Federalists.

The Federalists in the 1780s had a glimpse of what America was to become—a scrambling business society dominated by the pecuniary interests of ordinary people—and they did not like what they saw. This premonition of America's future lay behind their sense of crisis and their horrified hyperbolic rhetoric. The wholesale pursuits of private interest and private luxury were, they thought, undermining America's capacity for republican government. They designed the Constitution in order to save American republicanism from the deadly effects of these private pursuits of happiness.

III

The founders did not intend the new Constitution to change the character of the American people. They were not naive utopians; they were, as we have often noted, realistic about human nature. They had little or no faith in the power of religion or of sumptuary or other such laws to get people to behave differently. To be sure, they believed in education, and some of them put great stock in what it might do in reforming and enlightening American people. But still they generally approached their task in the 1780s with a practical, unsentimental appreciation of the givenness of human beings. They knew they lived in an age of commerce and interests. Although some of the landed gentry like Jefferson might yearn wistfully at times for America to emulate China and "abandon the ocean altogether," most of the founders welcomed America's involvement in commerce, by which, however, they commonly meant overseas trade.[24] They believed in the importance of such commerce, saw it as a major agent in the refining and civilizing of people, and were generally eager to use the power of government to promote its growth. They knew too all about "interest," which Madison defined "in the popular sense" as the "immediate augmentation of property and wealth." They accepted the inevitability and the prevalence of "interest" and respected its power. "Interest," many of them said, "is the greatest tie one man can

---

(Philadelphia, 1785), 14; Madison to Monroe, Apr. 9, 1786, in Hutchinson *et al.*, eds., *Papers of Madison*, IX, 26; [Barton], *True Interest*, 20; Pa. Statute of 1785, cited in E.A.J. Johnson, *The Foundations of American Economic Freedom: Government and Enterprise in the Age of Washington* (Minneapolis, Minn., 1973), 43 n.

24. Jefferson, *Notes on the State of Virginia*, ed. William Peden (Chapel Hill, N.C., 1955), Query XXII, 175; Jefferson to G. K. van Hogendorp, Oct. 13, 1785, in Boyd *et al.*, eds., *Papers of Jefferson*, VIII, 633.

have on another." It was, they said, "the only binding cement" for states and peoples. Hamilton put it more bluntly: "He who pays is the master."[25]

Since 1776 they had learned that it was foolish to expect most people to sacrifice their private interests for the sake of the public welfare. For the Federalists there was little left of the revolutionary utopianism of Samuel Adams. Already by the 1780s, Adams's brand of republicanism seemed archaic and Adams himself a figure from another time and place. Soon people would be shaking their heads in wonderment that such a person as Adams should have ever existed in America. "Modern times," it was said, "have produced no character like his." He was "one of Plutarch's men," a character out of the classical past. He was a Harvard-educated gentleman who devoted himself to the public. He had neither personal ambition nor the desire for wealth. He refused to help his children and gloried in his poverty. He was without interests or even private passions. Among the Revolutionary leaders he was unique. No other leader took classical republican values quite as seriously as Adams did.[26]

In fact, the other Revolutionary leaders were very quick to expose the unreality and impracticality of Adams's kind of republican idealism. As early as 1778 Washington realized that the Revolution would never succeed if it depended on patriotism alone. "It must be aided by a prospect of interest or some reward."[27] All men could not be like Samuel Adams. It was too bad, but that was the way it was. Human beings were like that, and by the 1780s many of the younger Revolutionary leaders like Madison were willing to look at the reality of interests with a very cold eye. Madison's *Federalist* No. 10 was only the most famous and frank acknowledgment of the degree to which interests of various sorts had come to dominate American politics.

The founders thus were not dreamers who expected more from the people than they were capable of. We in fact honor the founding fathers for their realism, their down-to-earth acceptance of human nature. Perhaps this is part of our despairing effort to make them one with us, to close that terrifying gap that always seems to exist between them and us. Nevertheless, in

25. Madison to Monroe, Oct. 5, 1786, in Hutchinson *et al.*, eds., *Papers of Madison*, IX, 141; *Carlisle Gazette* (Pa.), Oct. 24, 1787, quoted in Herbert J. Storing, ed., *The Complete Anti-Federalist* (Chicago, 1981), II, 208; Washington to James Warren, Oct. 7, 1785, in Fitzpatrick, ed., *Writings of Washington*, XXVIII, 291; Hamilton, in Farrand, ed., *Records of the Federal Convention*, I, 378. On the nature and role of interests in 18th-century British politics, see Michael Kammen, *Empire and Interest: The American Colonies and the Politics of Mercantilism* (Philadelphia, 1970).

26. Pauline Maier, *The Old Revolutionaries: Political Lives in the Age of Samuel Adams* (New York, 1980), 3–50, quotation at 47.

27. Washington, quoted in Lester H. Cohen, *The Revolutionary Histories: Contemporary Narratives of the American Revolution* (Ithaca, N.Y., 1980), 273.

our hearts we know that they are not one with us, that they are separated from us, as they were separated from every subsequent generation of Americans, by an immense cultural chasm. They stood for a classical world that was rapidly dying, a world so different from what followed—and from our own—that an act of imagination is required to recover it in all its fullness. They believed in democracy, to be sure, but not our modern democracy; rather, they believed in a patrician-led classical democracy in which "virtue exemplified in government will diffuse its salutary influence through the society." For them government was not an arena for furthering the interests of groups and individuals, but a means of moral betterment. What modern American politician would say, as James Wilson said in the Philadelphia Convention, that "the cultivation and improvement of the human mind was the most noble object" of government? Even Jefferson, who of all the founders most forcefully led the way, though inadvertently, to a popular liberal future, could in 1787 urge a Virginia colleague: "Cherish . . . the spirit of our people, and keep alive their attention. Do not be too severe upon their errors, but reclaim them by enlightening them." All the founding fathers saw themselves as moral teachers.[28] However latently utilitarian, however potentially liberal, and however enthusiastically democratic the founders may have been, they were not modern men.

Despite their acceptance of the reality of interests and commerce, the Federalists had not yet abandoned what has been called the tradition of civic humanism—that host of values transmitted from antiquity that dominated the thinking of nearly all members of the elite in the eighteenth-century Anglo-American world. By the late eighteenth century this classical tradition was much attenuated and domesticated, tamed and eaten away by modern financial and commercial developments. But something remained, and the Federalists clung to it. Despite their disillusionment with political leadership in the states, the Federalists in 1787 had not yet lost hope that at least some individuals in the society might be worthy and virtuous enough to transcend their immediate material interests and devote themselves to the public good. They remained committed to the classical idea that political leadership was essentially one of character; "The whole art of government," said Jefferson, "consists of being honest."[29] Central to this ideal of leadership was the quality of *disinterestedness*—the term the Federalists most used as a synonym

28. Joseph Lathrop (1786), in Hyneman and Lutz, eds., *American Political Writing*, I, 660; Wilson, in Farrand, ed., *Records of the Federal Convention*, I, 605; Jefferson to Edward Carrington, Jan. 16, 1787, in Boyd *et al.*, eds., *Papers of Jefferson*, XI, 49. See also Ralph Ketcham, *Presidents above Party: The First American Presidency, 1789–1829* (Chapel Hill, N.C., 1984).

29. Jefferson, "Summary View of the Rights of British America" (1774), in Boyd *et al.*, eds., *Papers of Jefferson*, I, 134.

for the classic conception of civic virtue: it better conveyed the increasing threats from interests that virtue now faced.

Dr. Johnson defined *disinterested* as being "superior to regard of private advantage; not influenced by private profit"; and that was what the founding fathers meant by the term.[30] We today have lost most of this older meaning. Even educated people now use *disinterested* as a synonym for *uninterested*, meaning indifferent or unconcerned. It is almost as if we cannot quite conceive of the characteristic that disinterestedness describes: we cannot quite imagine someone who is capable of rising above a pecuniary interest and being unselfish and unbiased where an interest might be present. This is simply another measure of how far we have traveled from the eighteenth century.

This eighteenth-century concept of disinterestedness was not confined either to Commonwealthmen or to the country tradition (which makes our current preoccupation with these strains of thought misleading). Nor did one have to be an American or a republican to believe in disinterestedness and the other classical values that accompanied it. Virtue or disinterestedness, like the concept of honor, lay at the heart of all prescriptions for political leadership in the eighteenth-century Anglo-American world. Throughout the century Englishmen of all political persuasions—Whigs and Tories both—struggled to find the ideal disinterested political leader amid the rising and swirling currents of financial and commercial interests that threatened to engulf their societies. Nothing more enhanced William Pitt's reputation as the great patriot than his pointed refusal in 1746 to profit from the perquisites of the traditionally lucrative office of paymaster of the forces. Pitt was living proof for the English-speaking world of the possibility of disinterestedness—that a man could be a governmental leader and yet remain free of corruption.[31]

This classical ideal of disinterestedness was based on independence and liberty. Only autonomous individuals, free of interested ties and paid by no masters, were capable of such virtue. Jefferson and other republican idealists might continue to hope that ordinary yeoman farmers in America might be independent and free enough of pecuniary temptations and interests to be virtuous. But others knew better, and if they did not, then the experience of the Revolutionary war soon opened their eyes. Washington realized almost at the outset that no common soldier could be expected to be "influenced

---

30. Johnson, *A Dictionary of the English Language* . . . (London, 1755); Charles Royster, *A Revolutionary People at War: The Continental Army and American Character, 1775-1783* (Chapel Hill, N.C., 1979), 22-23.

31. John Brewer, *Party Ideology and Popular Politics at the Accession of George III* (Cambridge, 1976), 97.

by any other principles than those of Interest." And even among the officer corps there were only a "few . . . who act upon Principles of disinterestedness," and they were "comparatively speaking, no more than a drop in the Ocean."[32]

Perhaps it was as Adam Smith warned: as society became more commercialized and civilized and labor more divided, ordinary people gradually lost their ability to make any just judgments about the varied interests and occupations of their country; and only "those few, who, being attached to no particular occupation themselves, have leisure and inclination to examine the occupations of other people." Perhaps then in America, as well as in Britain, only a few were free and independent enough to stand above the scramblings of the marketplace. As "Cato" had written, only "a very small Part of Mankind have Capacities large enough to judge of the Whole of Things." Only a few were liberally educated and cosmopolitan enough to have the breadth of perspective to comprehend all the different interests, and only a few were dispassionate and unbiased enough to adjudicate among these different interests and promote the public rather than a private good. Virtue, it was said as early as 1778, "can only dwell in superior minds, elevated above private interest and selfish views." Even Jefferson at one point admitted that only those few "whom nature has endowed with genius and virtue" could "be rendered by liberal education worthy to receive, and able to guard the sacred rights and liberties of their fellow citizens."[33] In other words, the Federalists were saying that perhaps only from among the tiny proportion of the society the eighteenth century designated as "gentlemen" could be found men capable of disinterested political leadership.

This age-old distinction between gentlemen and others in the society had a vital meaning for the Revolutionary generation that we have totally lost. It was a horizontal cleavage that divided the social hierarchy into two unequal parts almost as sharply as the distinction between officers and soldiers

32. Washington to John Hancock, Sept. 24, 1776, in Fitzpatrick, ed., *Writings of Washington*, VI, 107–108.

33. Adam Smith, *An Inquiry into the Nature and Causes of the Wealth of Nations*, ed. R. H. Campbell and A. S. Skinner (Oxford, 1976) (V.i.f. 50–51), II, 781–783; [John Trenchard and Thomas Gordon], *Cato's Letters; or, Essays on Liberty, Civil and Religious, and Other Important Subjects*, 5th ed. (London, 1748), III, 193; Phillips Payson, "A Sermon Preached before the Honorable Council . . . at Boston, May 27, 1778," in John Wingate Thornton, ed., *The Pulpit of the American Revolution . . .* (Boston, 1860), 337; Jefferson, "A Bill for the More General Diffusion of Education" (1779), in Boyd *et al.*, eds., *Papers of Jefferson*, II, 527. On the 18th-century British developments out of which "Cato," Smith, and others wrote, see the illuminating discussion in John Barrell, *English Literature in History, 1730–80: An Equal, Wide Survey* (London, 1983), 17–50.

divided the army; indeed, the military division was related to the larger social one. Ideally the liberality for which gentlemen were known connoted freedom—freedom from material want, freedom from the caprice of others, freedom from ignorance, and freedom from manual labor. The gentleman's distinctiveness came from being independent in a world of dependencies, learned in a world only partially literate, and leisured in a world of workers.[34] Just as gentlemen were expected to staff the officer corps of the Continental army (and expected also to provide for their own rations, clothing, and equipment on salaries that were less than half those of their British counterparts), so were independent gentlemen of leisure and education expected to supply the necessary disinterested leadership for government.[35] Since such well-to-do gentry were "exempted from the lower and less honourable employments," wrote the philosopher Francis Hutcheson, they were "rather more than others obliged to an active life in some service to mankind. The publick has this claim upon them." Governmental service, in other words, was thought to be a personal sacrifice, required of certain gentlemen because of their talents, independence, and social preeminence.[36]

In eighteenth-century America it had never been easy for gentlemen to make this personal sacrifice for the public, and it became especially difficult during the Revolution. Which is why many of the Revolutionary leaders, especially those of "small fortunes" who served in the Congress, continually complained of the burdens of office and repeatedly begged to be relieved from these burdens in order to pursue their private interests. Periodic temporary retirement from the cares and commotions of office to one's country estate for refuge and rest was acceptable classical behavior. But too often America's political leaders, especially in the North, had to retire not to relaxation in the solitude and leisure of a rural retreat, but to the making of money in the busyness and bustle of a city law practice.[37]

34. The best discussion of the distinctiveness of the gentry in colonial America is Rhys Isaac, *The Transformation of Virginia, 1740–1790* (Chapel Hill, N.C., 1982), esp. 131–132.

35. Royster, *Revolutionary People at War*, 86–95; John B. B. Trussell, Jr., *Birthplace of an Army: A Study of the Valley Forge Encampment* (Harrisburg, Pa., 1976), 86.

36. Francis Hutcheson, *A System of Moral Philosophy in Three Books . . .* (London, 1755), II, 113. "Let not your Love of Philosophical Amusements have more than its due Weight with you," Benjamin Franklin admonished Cadwallader Colden at mid-century. Public service was far more important. In fact, said Franklin, even "the finest" of Newton's "Discoveries" could not have excused his neglect of serving the commonwealth if the public had needed him (Franklin to Colden, Oct. 11, 1750, in Leonard W. Labaree *et al.*, eds., *The Papers of Benjamin Franklin* [New Haven, Conn., 1959–], IV, 68).

37. Jack N. Rakove, *The Beginnings of National Politics: An Interpretative History of the Continental Congress* (New York, 1979), 216–239, quotation by William Fleming

In short, America's would-be gentlemen had a great deal of trouble in maintaining the desired classical independence and freedom from the marketplace. There were not many American gentry who were capable of living idly off the rents of tenants as the English landed aristocracy did. Of course, there were large numbers of the southern planter gentry whose leisure was based on the labor of their slaves, and these planters obviously came closest in America to fitting the classical ideal of the free and independent gentleman. But some southern planters kept taverns on the side, and many others were not as removed from the day-to-day management of their estates as their counterparts among the English landed gentry. Their overseers were not comparable to the stewards of the English gentry; thus the planters, despite their aristocratic poses, were often very busy, commercially involved men. Their livelihoods were tied directly to the vicissitudes of international trade, and they had always had an uneasy sense of being dependent on the market to an extent that the English landed aristocracy, despite its commitment to enterprising projects and improvements, never really felt. Still, the great southern planters at least approached the classical image of disinterested gentlemanly leadership, and they knew it and made the most of it throughout their history.[38]

In northern American society such independent gentlemen standing above the interests of the marketplace were harder to find, but the ideal remained strong. In ancient Rome, wrote James Wilson, magistrates and army officers were always gentleman farmers, always willing to step down "from the elevation of office" and reassume "with contentment and with pleasure, the peaceful labours of a rural and independent life." John Dickinson's pose in 1767 as a "Pennsylvania Farmer" is incomprehensible except within this classical tradition. Dickinson, the wealthy Philadelphia lawyer, wanted to assure his readers of his gentlemanly disinterestedness by informing them at the outset that he was a farmer "contented" and "undisturbed by wordly hopes or fears."[39] Prominent merchants dealing in international trade brought wealth into the society and were thus valuable members of the community, but their status as independent gentlemen was always tainted

---

to Jefferson, May 10, 1779, at 237; George Athan Billias, *Elbridge Gerry, Founding Father and Republican Statesman* (New York, 1976), 138–139.

38. See William R. Taylor, *Cavalier and Yankee: The Old South and American National Character* (New York, 1961).

39. Wilson, "On the History of Property," in Robert Green McCloskey, ed., *The Works of James Wilson* (Cambridge, Mass., 1967), II, 716; Dickinson, "Letters of a Farmer in Pennsylvania" (1768), in Paul Leicester Ford, ed., *The Writings of John Dickinson*, Vol. I, *Political Writings, 1764–1774* (Pennsylvania Historical Society, *Memoirs*, XIV [Philadelphia, 1895]), 307 (hereafter cited as Ford, ed., *Writings of Dickinson*).

by their concern for personal profit.[40] Perhaps only a classical education that made "ancient manners familiar," as Richard Jackson once told Benjamin Franklin, could "produce a reconciliation between disinterestedness and commerce; a thing we often see, but almost always in men of a liberal education." Yet no matter how educated merchants were or how much leisure they managed for themselves, while they remained merchants they could never quite acquire the character of genteel disinterestedness essential for full acceptance as political leaders, and that is why most colonial merchants were not active in public life.[41]

John Hancock and Henry Laurens knew this, and during the imperial crisis each shed his mercantile business and sought to ennoble himself. Hancock spent lavishly, bought every imaginable luxury, and patronized everyone. He went through a fortune, but he did become the single most popular and powerful figure in Massachusetts politics during the last quarter or so of the eighteenth century. Laurens especially was aware of the bad image buying and selling had among southern planters. In 1764 he advised two impoverished but aspiring gentry immigrants heading for the backcountry to establish themselves as planters before attempting to open a store. For them to enter immediately into "any retail Trade in those parts," he said, "would be mean, would Lessen them in the esteem of people whose respect they must endeavour to attract." Only after they were "set down in a Creditable manner as Planters" might they "carry on the Sale of many specie of European and West Indian goods to some advantage and with a good grace." In this same year, 1764, Laurens himself began to curtail his merchant operations. By the time of the Revolution he had become enough of an aristocrat that he was able to sneer at all those merchants who were still

40. "We have found by experience, that no dependence can be had upon *merchants*, either at *home*, or in *America*," Charles Chauncy told Richard Price in 1774, "so many of them are so mercenary as to find within themselves a readiness to become slaves themselves, as well as to be accessory to the slavery of others, if they imagine they may, by this means, serve their own private separate interest" (D.C. Thomas and Bernard Peach, eds., *The Correspondence of Richard Price* [Durham, N.C., 1983], I, 170). For Adam Smith's view that the interest of merchants and indeed of all who lived by profit was "always in some respects different from, and even opposite to, that of the publick," see Smith, *Wealth of Nations*, ed. Campbell and Skinner, (I.xi.p.10) I, 267.

41. Jackson to Franklin, June 17, 1755, in Labaree *et al.*, eds., *Papers of Franklin*, VI, 82. On the colonial merchants' "detachment from political activity," see Thomas M. Doerflinger, "Philadelphia Merchants and the Logic of Moderation, 1760–1775," *William and Mary Quarterly*, 3d Ser., XL (1983), 212–213; and Edward Countryman, *A People in Revolution: The American Revolution and Political Society in New York, 1760–1790* (Baltimore, 1981), 113.

busy making money. "How hard it is," he had the gall to say in 1779, "for a rich, or covetous man to enter heartily into the kingdom of patriotism."[42]

For mechanics and others who worked with their hands, being a disinterested gentleman was impossible. Only when wealthy Benjamin Franklin retired from his printing business, at the age of forty-two, did "the Publick," as he wrote in his *Autobiography*, "now considering me as a Man of Leisure," lay hold of him and bring him into an increasing number of important public offices. Other artisans and petty traders who had wealth and political ambitions, such as Roger Sherman of Connecticut, also found that retirement from business was a prerequisite for high public office.[43]

Members of the learned professions were usually considered gentlemen, particularly if they were liberally educated. But were they disinterested? Were they free of the marketplace? Were they capable of virtuous public service? Hamilton for one argued strongly that, unlike merchants, mechanics, or farmers, "the learned professions . . . truly form no distinct interest in society"; thus they "will feel a neutrality to the rivalships between the different branches of industry" and will be most likely to be "an impartial arbiter" between the diverse interests of the society. But others had doubts. William Barton thought "a few individuals in a nation may be actuated by such exalted sentiments of public virtue, . . . but these instances must be rare." Certainly many thought lawyers did not stand above the fray. In fact, said Barton, "professional men of every description are necessarily, as such, obliged to pursue their immediate advantage."[44]

42. William M. Fowler, Jr., *The Baron of Beacon Hill: A Biography of John Hancock* (Boston, 1980); Charles W. Akers, *The Divine Politician: Samuel Cooper and the American Revolution in Boston* (Boston, 1982), 121, 128, 130, 141, 176, 311; Laurens to Richard Oswald, July 7, 1764, in Philip M. Hamer *et al.*, eds., *The Papers of Henry Laurens* (Columbia, S.C., 1968–), IV, 338 (see also Rachel N. Klein, "Ordering the Backcountry: The South Carolina Regulation," *WMQ*, 3d Ser., XXXVIII [1981], 667); David Duncan Wallace, *The Life of Henry Laurens* . . . (New York, 1915), 69–70, quotation at 335. In the 1780s Elbridge Gerry likewise retired from mercantile business and "set himself up as a country squire" (Billias, *Gerry*, 135–136).

43. Leonard W. Labaree *et al.*, eds., *The Autobiography of Benjamin Franklin* (New Haven, Conn., 1964), 196; Christopher Collier, *Roger Sherman's Connecticut: Yankee Politics and the American Revolution* (Middletown, Conn., 1971), 14, 21–22.

44. Jacob E. Cooke, ed., *The Federalist* (Middletown, Conn., 1961), No. 35; [Barton], *True Interest*, 27. For arguments in pre-Revolutionary Virginia whether lawyers were practicing "a grovelling, mercenary trade" or not, see Roeber, *Faithful Magistrates and Republican Lawyers*, 156–157. Some conceded that lawyers were members of one of the "three genteel Professions," but that they were guilty of more "petit Larceny" than doctors and clergymen. Madison was not convinced of the disin-

Everywhere, men struggled to find a way of reconciling this classical tradition of disinterested public leadership with the private demands of making
a living. "A Man expends his Fortune in political Pursuits," wrote Gouverneur Morris in an introspective unfinished essay. Did he do this out of "personal Consideration" or out of a desire to promote the public good? If he
did it to promote the public good, "was he justifiable in sacrificing to it the
Subsistence of his Family? These are important Questions; but," said Morris, "there remains one more," and that one question of Morris's threatened
to undermine the whole classical tradition: "Would not as much Good have
followed from an industrious Attention to his own Affairs?" Hamilton, for
one, could not agree. Although he knew that most people were selfish
scavengers, incapable of noble and disinterested acts, he did not want to be
one of them. Thus he refused to make speculative killings in land or banking
"because," as he put it in one of his sardonic moods, "there must be some
public fools who sacrifice private to public interest at the certainty of ingrati-
tude and obloquy—because my *vanity* whispers I ought to be one of those
fools and ought to keep myself in a situation the best calculated to render
service." Hamilton clung as long and as hard to this classical conception of
leadership as anyone in post-Revolutionary America.[45]

Washington too felt the force of the classical ideal and throughout his life
was compulsive about his disinterestedness. Because he had not gone to
college and acquired a liberal education, he always felt he had to live literally
by the book. He was continually anxious that he not be thought too ambitious or self-seeking; above all, he did not want to be thought greedy or
"interested." He refused to accept a salary for any of his public services, and
he was scrupulous in avoiding any private financial benefits from his governmental positions.

Perhaps nothing more clearly reveals Washington's obsession with these
classical republican values than his agonized response in the winter of 1784–
1785 to the Virginia Assembly's gift of 150 shares in the James River and

---

terestedness of lawyers (*ibid.*, 157, 147; Ketcham, *Madison*, 145). On the efforts
of some 19th-century thinkers to make professional communities the repositories
of disinterestedness against the selfishness and interestedness of businessmen, see
Thomas L. Haskell, "Professionalism *versus* Capitalism: R. H. Tawney, Emile Durk-
heim, and C. S. Peirce on the Disinterestedness of Professional Communities,"
in Thomas L. Haskell, ed., *The Authority of Experts: Studies in History and Theory*
(Bloomington, Ind., 1984), 180–225.

45. Morris, "Political Enquiries," in Willi Paul Adams, ed., " 'The Spirit of Com-
merce, Requires that Property Be Sacred': Gouverneur Morris and the American
Revolution," *Amerikastudien / American Studies*, XXI (1976), 329; Hamilton to
Robert Troup, Apr. 13, 1795, in Harold C. Syrett *et al.*, eds., *The Papers of Alexander
Hamilton* (New York, 1961–1979), XVIII, 329.

Potomac canal companies. Acceptance of the shares seemed clearly impossible. The shares might be "considered in the same light as a pension," he said. He would be thought "a dependant," and his reputation for virtue would be compromised. At the same time, however, Washington believed passionately in what the canal companies were doing; indeed, he had long dreamed of making a fortune from such canals. He thought the shares might constitute "the foundation of the *greatest* and most *certain* income" that anyone could expect from a speculative venture. Besides, he did not want to show "disrespect" to his countrymen or to appear "ostentatiously disinterested" by refusing the gift of the shares.[46]

What should he do? Few decisions in Washington's career called for such handwringing as this one did. He sought the advice of nearly everyone he knew. Letters went out to Jefferson, to Governor Patrick Henry, to William Grayson, to Benjamin Harrison, to George William Fairfax, to Nathanael Greene, to Henry Knox, even to Lafayette—all seeking "the best information and advice" on the disposition of the shares. "How would this matter be viewed then by the eyes of the world[?]" he asked. Would not his reputation for virtue be tarnished? Would not accepting the shares "deprive me of the principal thing which is laudable in my conduct?"—that is, his disinterestedness.

The story would be comic if Washington had not been so deadly earnest. He understated the situation when he told his correspondents that his mind was "not a little agitated" by the problem. In letter after letter he expressed real anguish. This was no ordinary display of scruples such as government officials today show over a conflict of interest: in 1784–1785 Washington was not even holding public office.[47]

These values, this need for disinterestedness in public officials, were very much on the minds of the founding fathers at the Philadelphia Convention, especially James Madison's. Madison was a tough-minded thinker, not given to illusions. He knew that there were "clashing interests" everywhere and that they were doing great harm to state legislative politics. But he had not

46. Washington to Benjamin Harrison, Jan. 22, 1785, to George William Fairfax, Feb. 27, 1785, in Fitzpatrick, ed., *Writings of Washington*, XXVIII, 36, 85.

47. Washington to Benjamin Harrison, Jan. 22, 1785, to William Grayson, Jan. 22, 1785, to Lafayette, Feb. 15, 1785, to Jefferson, Feb. 25, 1785, to George William Fairfax, Feb. 27, 1785, to Gov. Patrick Henry, Feb. 27, 1785, to Henry Knox, Feb. 28, 1785, June 18, 1785, to Nathanael Greene, May 20, 1785, in Fitzpatrick, ed., *Writings of Washington*, XXVIII, 36, 37, 72, 80–81, 85, 89–91, 92–93, 167, 146. The only friend whose advice on the disposition of the canal shares Washington did not solicit was Robert Morris, perhaps because he feared that Morris might tell him to keep them. Instead he confined his letter to Morris to describing the commercial opportunities of the canals. To Morris, Feb. 1, 1785, *ibid.*, 48–55.

yet given up hope that it might be possible to put into government, at the national if not at the state level, some "proper guardians of the public weal," men of "the most attractive merit, and most diffusive and established characters." We have too often mistaken Madison for some sort of prophet of a modern interest-group theory of politics. But Madison was not a forerunner of twentieth-century political scientists such as Arthur Bentley, David Truman, or Robert Dahl. Despite his hardheaded appreciation of the multiplicity of interests in American society, he did not offer America a pluralist conception of politics. He did not see public policy or the common good emerging naturally from the give-and-take of hosts of competing interests. Instead he hoped that these clashing interests and parties in an enlarged national republic would neutralize themselves and thereby allow liberally educated, rational men, "whose enlightened views and virtuous sentiments render them superior to local prejudices, and to schemes of injustice," to promote the public good in a disinterested manner. Madison, in other words, was not at all as modern as we make him out to be.[48] He did not expect the new national government to be an integrator and harmonizer of the different interests in the society; instead he expected it to be a "disinterested and dispassionate umpire in disputes between different passions and interests in the State." Madison even suggested that the national government might play the same superpolitical, neutral role that the British king had been supposed to play in the empire.[49]

The Federalists' plans for the Constitution, in other words, rested on their belief that there were some disinterested gentlemen left in America to act as neutral umpires. In this sense the Constitution became a grand—and perhaps in retrospect a final desperate—effort to realize the great hope of the Revolution: the possibility of virtuous politics. The Constitution thus looked backward as much as it looked forward. Despite the Federalists' youthful energy, originality, and vision, they still clung to the classical tradition of civic humanism and its patrician code of disinterested public leadership. They stood for a moral and social order that was radically different

---

48. Cooke, ed., *The Federalist*, No. 10; Gordon S. Wood, "Democracy and the Constitution," in Robert A. Goldwin and William A. Schambra, eds., *How Democratic Is the Constitution?* (Washington, D.C., 1980), 11–12. On the tendency to misread Madison, see Robert J. Morgan, "Madison's Theory of Representation in the Tenth Federalist," *Journal of Politics*, XXXVI (1974), 852–885; and Paul F. Bourke, "The Pluralist Reading of James Madison's Tenth *Federalist*," *Perspectives in American History*, IX (1975), 271–295.

49. Madison to Washington, Apr. 16, 1787, to Edmund Randolph, Apr. 8, 1787, in Hutchinson *et al.*, eds., *Papers of Madison*, IX, 384, 370; John Zvesper, "The Madisonian Systems," *Western Political Quarterly*, XXXVII (1984), 244–247.

from the popular, individualistic, and acquisitive world they saw emerging in the 1780s.

IV

The Antifederalists, of course, saw it all very differently. Instead of seeing enlightened patriots simply making a Constitution to promote the national good, they saw groups of interested men trying to foist an aristocracy onto republican America. And they said so, just as the Federalists had feared, in pamphlets, newspapers, and the debates in ratifying conventions. Fear of aristocracy did become the principal shibboleth and rallying cry of the opponents of the Constitution. Already during the 1780s the classical demand that government should be run by rich, leisured gentlemen who served "without fee or reward" was being met by increasing contempt: "Enormous wealth," it was said even in aristocratic South Carolina, "is seldom the associate of *pure* and *disinterested virtue*."[50] The Antifederalists brought this popular contempt to a head and refused to accept the claim that the Federalists were truly disinterested patriots. In fact, many of them had trouble seeing anyone at all as free from interests. If either side in the debate therefore stood for the liberal, pluralistic, interest-ridden future of American politics, it was the Antifederalists. They, not the Federalists, were the real modern men. They emerged from the confusion of the polemics with an understanding of American society that was far more hardheaded, realistic, and prophetic than even James Madison's.

There were, of course, many different Antifederalist spokesmen, a fact that complicates any analysis of the opposition to the Constitution. Yet some of the prominent Antifederalist leaders, such as Elbridge Gerry, George Mason, and Richard Henry Lee, scarcely represented, either socially or emotionally, the main thrust of Antifederalism. Such aristocratic leaders were socially indistinguishable from the Federalist spokesmen and often were as fearful of the excesses of democracy in the state legislatures as the Federalists. Far more representative of the paper money interests of the 1780s and the populist opposition to the "aristocracy" of the Federalists was someone like William Findley—that pugnacious Scotch-Irishman from western Pennsylvania. Gerry, Mason, and Lee did not really point the way to the liberal, interest-ridden democracy of nineteenth-century America, but Findley did. Until we understand the likes of William Findley, we won't

50. Jerome J. Nadelhaft, "'The Snarls of Invidious Animals': The Democratization of Revolutionary South Carolina," in Ronald Hoffman and Peter J. Albert, eds., *Sovereign States in an Age of Uncertainty* (Charlottesville, Va., 1981), 77.

understand either Antifederalism or the subsequent democratic history of America.

Findley came to the colonies from northern Ireland in 1763, at age twenty-two, in one of those great waves of eighteenth-century emigration from the northern parts of the British islands that so frightened Dr. Johnson. After trying his hand at weaving, the craft to which he had been apprenticed, Findley became a schoolmaster and then a farmer—until he was caught up in the Revolutionary movement, moved through the ranks to a militia captaincy, and became a political officeholder in Pennsylvania. Findley was the very prototype of a later professional politician and was as much a product of the Revolution as were the more illustrious patriots like John Adams or James Madison. He had no lineage to speak of, he went to no college, and he possessed no great wealth. He was completely self-taught and self-made, but not in the manner of a Benjamin Franklin who acquired the cosmopolitan attributes of a gentleman: Findley's origins showed, and conspicuously so. In his middling aspirations, middling achievements, and middling resentments, he represented far more accurately what America was becoming than did cosmopolitan gentlemen like Franklin and Adams.[51]

By the middle eighties this red-faced Irishman with his flamboyant white hat was becoming one of the most articulate spokesmen for those debtor–paper money interests that lay behind the political turbulence and democratic excesses of the period. As a representative from the West in the Pennsylvania state legislature, he embodied that rough, upstart, individualistic society that eastern squires like George Clymer hated and feared. In the western counties around Pittsburgh, gentry like Clymer could see only avarice, ignorance, and suspicion and a thin, weak society where there were "no private or publick associations for common good, every Man standing single."[52] Findley never much liked Clymer, but he reserved his deepest antagonism for two others of the Pennsylvania gentry—Hugh Henry Brackenridge and Robert Morris.

Findley's political conflicts with these two men in the Pennsylvania legislature in the 1780s foreshadowed and, indeed, epitomized the Antifederalists' struggle with the Federalists. It is perhaps not too much to say that Findley came to see the Constitution as a device designed by gentry like Brackenridge and Morris to keep men like himself out of the important affairs of government. This was especially galling to Findley because he

51. On Findley, see his letter to Gov. William Plumer of New Hampshire, Feb. 27, 1812, "William Findley of Westmoreland, Pa.," *PMHB*, V (1881), 440–450; and Russell J. Ferguson, *Early Western Pennsylvania Politics* (Pittsburgh, Pa., 1938), 39–40.

52. Grundfest, *Clymer*, 141.

could see no justification for the arrogance and assumed superiority of such men. Brackenridge and Morris were in reality, he believed, no different from him, and during the 1780s he meant to prove it.

Hugh Henry Brackenridge, born in 1748, was seven years younger than Findley. He was a Princeton graduate who in 1781 moved to western Pennsylvania because he thought the wilds of Pittsburgh offered greater opportunities for advancement than crowded Philadelphia. As the only college-educated gentleman in the area, he saw himself as an oasis of cultivation in the midst of a desert. He wanted to be "among the first to bring the press to the west of the mountains," so he helped establish a newspaper in Pittsburgh for which he wrote poetry, bagatelles, and other things.[53] He was pretty full of himself, and he never missed an opportunity to sprinkle his prose with Latin quotations and to show off his learning. This young, ambitious Princeton graduate with aristocratic pretensions was, in fact, just the sort of person who would send someone like William Findley climbing the walls.

William Findley was already a member of the state legislature in 1786 when Brackenridge decided that he too would like to be a legislator. Brackenridge ran for election and won by promising his western constituents that he would look after their particular interests, especially in favoring the use of state certificates of paper money in buying land. But then his troubles began. In Philadelphia he inevitably fell in with the well-to-do crowd around Robert Morris and James Wilson, who had cosmopolitan tastes more to his liking. Under the influence of Morris, Brackenridge voted against the state certificates he had promised to support and identified himself with the eastern establishment. He actually had the nerve to write in the *Pittsburgh Gazette* that the "eastern members" of the assembly had singled him out among all the "Huns, Goths and Vandals" who usually came over the mountains to legislate in Philadelphia and had complimented him for his "liberality." But it was a dinner party at Chief Justice Thomas McKean's house in December 1786, at which both he and Findley were guests, that really did him in. One guest suggested that Robert Morris's support for the Bank of North America seemed mainly for his own personal benefit rather than for the people's. To this Brackenridge responded loudly, "The people are fools; if they would let Mr. Morris alone, he would make Pennsylvania a great people, but they will not suffer him to do it."[54]

Most American political leaders already knew better than to call the people fools, at least aloud, and Findley saw his chance to bring Brackenridge down a peg or two. He wrote a devastating account of Brackenridge's state-

53. Claude Milton Newlin, *The Life and Writings of Hugh Henry Brackenridge* (Princeton, N.J., 1932), 71.

54. *Ibid.*, 80–81, 78; Ferguson, *Early Western Pennsylvania*, 66–69.

ment in the *Pittsburgh Gazette* and accused him of betraying the people's trust by his vote against the state certificates. It was all right, said Findley sarcastically, for a representative to change his mind if he had not solicited or expected the office, "which is the case generally with modest, disinterested men." But for someone like Brackenridge who had openly sought the office and had made campaign promises—for him to change his vote could only arouse the "indignation" and the "contempt" of the people. Brackenridge may have professed "the greatest acquired abilities, and most shining imagination," but he was in fact a self-seeking and self-interested person who did not have the public good at heart.

Brackenridge vainly tried to reply. At first he sought to justify his change of vote on the classical humanist grounds that the people could not know about the "complex, intricate and involved" problems and interests involved in legislation. "The people at home know each man his own wishes and wants." Only an educated elite in the assembly could see the problems of finance whole; it required "the height of ability to be able to distinguish clearly the interests of a state." But was Brackenridge himself a member of this disinterested elite? Did he really stand above the various interests of the state? He admitted under Findley's assault that he had a "strong *interest* to prompt me to *offer* myself" for election, but his private interest was the same interest with that of the western country where he lived. "My object was to advance the country, and thereby advance myself."[55]

It was a frank and honest but strained answer, a desperate effort by Brackenridge to reconcile the presumed traditional disinterestedness of a political leader with his obvious personal ambition. The more he protested, the worse his situation became, and he never recovered from Findley's attack. The two men crossed swords again in the election of delegates to the state ratifying convention in 1788, and Brackenridge as an avowed Federalist lost to the Antifederalist Findley. Brackenridge then abandoned politics for the time being and turned his disillusionment with the vagaries of American democracy into his comic masterpiece, *Modern Chivalry*.

Findley sent Brackenridge scurrying out of politics into literature by attacking his pretensions as a virtuous gentlemanly leader. He attacked Robert Morris in a similar way, with far more ruinous consequences for Morris. Findley and Morris first tangled while they were both members of the Pennsylvania legislature in the 1780s. During several days of intense debate in 1786 over the rechartering of the Bank of North America, Findley mercilessly stripped away the mask of superior classical disinterestedness

---

55. Newlin, *Brackenridge*, 79–80, 83–84; Ferguson, *Early Western Pennsylvania*, 70–72.

that Morris had sought to wear. This fascinating wide-ranging debate—the only important one we have recorded of state legislative proceedings in the 1780s—centered on the role of interest in public affairs.

Findley was the leader of the legislative representatives who opposed the rechartering of the bank. He and others like John Smilie from western Pennsylvania were precisely the sorts of legislators whom gentry like Madison had accused throughout the 1780s of being illiberal, narrow-minded, and interested in their support of debtor farmers and paper money. Now they had an opportunity to get back at their accusers, and they made the most of it. Day after day they hammered home one basic point: the supporters of the bank were themselves interested men. They were directors or stockholders in the bank, and therefore they had no right in supporting the rechartering of the bank to pose as disinterested gentlemen promoting the public good. The advocates of the bank "feel interested in it personally." Their defense of the bank, said Findley, who quickly emerged as the principal and most vitriolic critic of the bank's supporters, revealed "the manner in which disappointed avarice chagrins an interested mind."

Morris and his fellow supporters of the bank were embarrassed by these charges that they had a selfish interest in the bank's charter. At first, in George Clymer's committee report on the advisability of rechartering the bank, they took the overbearing line that the proponents of the bank in the general community "included the most respectable characters amongst us," men who knew about the world and the nature of banks. But as the charges of their selfishness mounted, the supporters of the bank became more and more defensive. They insisted they were men of "independent fortune and situations" and were therefore "above influence or terror" by the bank. Under the relentless criticism by Findley and others, however, they one by one grew silent, until their defense was left almost entirely in the hands of Robert Morris, who had a personal, emotional involvement in this debate that went well beyond his concern for the bank.[56]

Morris, as the wealthiest merchant in Pennsylvania and perhaps in all of North America, had heard it all before. The charges of always being privately interested had been the plague of his public career. No matter that his "Exertions" in supplying and financing the Revolution were "as disinterested and pure as ever were made by Mortal Man," no matter how much he sacrificed for the sake of the public, the charges of using public office for personal gain kept arising to torment him. No prominent Revolutionary

56. Mathew Carey, ed., *Debates and Proceedings of the General Assembly of Pennsylvania on the Memorials Praying a Repeal or Suspension of the Law Annulling the Charter of the Bank* (Philadelphia, 1786), 19, 64, 10, 30.

leader had ever been subjected to such "unmeritted abuse," such bitter and vituperative accusations of selfishness, as he had.[57]

Now in 1786 he had to hear it all over again: that his support of the bank came solely from his personal interest in it. What could he do? He acknowledged that he was a shareholder in the bank, but he tried to argue that the bank was in the interest of all citizens in the state. How could he prove that he was not self-interested? Perhaps if he sold his bank stock? If he did, he assured his fellow legislators that he would be just as concerned with the bank's charter. At one point he gave up and said he would leave the issue of his self-interestedness to the members of the house to determine. But he could not leave it alone, and was soon back on his feet. Members have said "my information is not to be trusted, because I am interested in the bank: but surely," he pleaded, "I am more deeply interested in the state." He hoped, "notwithstanding the insinuation made, that it will never be supposed I would sacrifice the interest and welfare of the state to any interest I can possibly hold in the bank." Why couldn't his arguments for the bank be taken on their merits, apart from their source? he asked. Let them "be considered, not as coming from parties interested, but abstractedly as to their force and solidity."

Such nervous arguments were symptoms of his mounting frustration, and he finally exploded in anger and defiance. Once more he stated categorically: "I am not stimulated by the consideration of private interest, to stand forth in defence of the bank." If people supposed that he needed this bank, they were "grossly mistaken." He was bigger than the bank. If the bank should be destroyed, he on his "own capital, credit, and resources" would create another one; and even his enemies ("and God knows I seem to have enough of them") would have to deal with him, if only "for the sake of their own interest and convenience."[58]

It was an excruciating experience for Morris. At one point in the debate he expressed his desire to retire from office and become a private citizen, "which suits both my inclination and affairs much better than to be in public life, for which I do not find myself very well qualified." But the lure of the public arena and what it represented in the traditional aristocratic terms of civic honor were too great for him, and instead he retired once and for all from his merchant business and like Hancock and Laurens before him sought to ennoble himself. In the late eighties and early nineties, he shifted all his entrepreneurial activities into the acquisition of speculative land—

57. Morris to Washington, May 29, 1781, E. James Ferguson *et al.*, eds., *The Papers of Robert Morris, 1781-1784* (Pittsburgh, Pa., 1973–), I, 96; Ellis Paxson Oberholtzer, *Robert Morris, Patriot and Financier* (New York, 1903), 52-56, 70-71.
58. Carey, ed., *Debates*, 33, 79-80, 98 (quotations on 80, 98).

something that seemed more respectable for an aristocrat than trade. He acquired a coat of arms, patronized artists, and hired L'Enfant to build him a huge, marble palace in Philadelphia. He surrounded himself with the finest furniture, tapestry, silver, and wines and made his home the center of America's social life. Like a good aristocrat, he maintained, recalled Samuel Breck, "a profuse, incessant and elegant hospitality" and displayed "a luxury . . . that was to be found nowhere else in America." When he became a United States senator in 1789, he—to the astonishment of listeners—began paying himself "compliments on his manner and conduct in life," in particular "his disregard of money." How else would a real aristocrat behave? [59]

For Morris to disregard money was not only astonishing, however; it was fatal. We know what happened, and it is a poignant, even tragic story. All his aristocratic dreams came to nothing; the marble palace on Chestnut Street went unfinished; his dinner parties ceased; his carriages were seized; and he ended in debtors' prison. That Morris should have behaved as he did says something about the continuing power of the classical aristocratic ideal of disinterestedness in post-Revolutionary America. It also says something about the popular power of William Findley, for it was Findley, more than anyone else in the debate over the bank, who had hounded Morris into renouncing his interests in commerce.

Findley in the debate knew he had Morris's number and bore in on it. "The human soul," Findley said, "is affected by wealth, in almost all its faculties. It is affected by its present interest, by its expectations, and by its fears." All this was too much for Morris, and he angrily turned on Findley. "If wealth be so obnoxious, I ask this gentleman why is he so eager in the pursuit of it?" If Morris expected a denial from Findley, he did not get it. For Findley's understanding of Morris's motives was really based on an understanding of his own. Did he love wealth and pursue it as Morris did? "Doubtless I do," said Findley. "I love and pursue it—not as an end, but as a means of enjoying happiness and independence," though he was quick to point out that he had wealth "not in any proportion to the degree" Morris had. Not that this made Morris in any way superior to Findley. Indeed, the central point stressed by Findley and the other western opponents of the bank was that Morris and his patrician Philadelphia crowd were no different from them, were no more respectable than they were. Such would-be aristocrats simply had "more money than their neighbours." In America, said

59. *Ibid.*, 81; Oberholtzer, *Morris*, 285–286, 297–299, 301–303; Eleanor Young, *Forgotten Patriot: Robert Morris* (New York, 1950), 170; Barbara Ann Chernow, *Robert Morris, Land Speculator, 1790–1801* (New York, 1978); H. E. Scudder, ed., *Recollections of Samuel Breck* . . . (Philadelphia, 1877), 203; *The Journal of William Maclay* (New York, 1927 [orig. pub. 1890]), 132.

Findley, "no man has a greater claim of special privilege for his £100,000 than I have for my £5." That was what American equality meant.

Morris, like all aspiring aristocrats in an egalitarian society, tried to stress that social distinctions were not based on wealth alone. "Surely," he said in desperate disbelief, "persons possessed of knowledge, judgment, information, integrity, and having extensive connections, are not to be classed with persons void of reputation or character." But Morris's claims of superiority were meaningless as long as he and his friends were seen to be interested men, and on that point Findley had him. Findley and his western legislative colleagues had no desire to establish any claims of their own to disinterestedness. In fact they wanted to hear no more spurious patrician talk of virtue and disinterestedness. They had no objection to Morris's and the other stockholders' being interested in the bank's rechartering: "Any others in their situation . . . would do as they did." Morris and other legislators, said Findley, "have a right to advocate their own cause, on the floor of this house." But then they could not protest when others realize "that it is their own cause they are advocating; and to give credit to their opinions, and to think of their votes accordingly." In fact, said Findley, such open promotion of interests meant an end to the archaic idea that representatives should simply stand and not run for election. When a candidate for the legislature "has a cause of his own to advocate, interest will dictate the propriety of canvassing for a seat." Who has ever put the case for special-interest elective politics any better?[60]

These were the arguments of democratic legislators in the 1780s who were sick and tired of being told by the aristocratic likes of James Madison that they were "Men of factious tempers" and "of local prejudices" and "advocates and parties to the causes which they determine." If they were interested men, so too were all legislators, including even those such as Morris and Brackenridge who were supposed to be liberal-thinking genteel men of "enlightened views and virtuous sentiments." "The citizens," Findley later wrote, by which he meant citizens like himself, "have learned to take a surer course of obtaining information respecting political characters," particularly those who pretended to disinterested civic service. They had especially learned how to inquire "into the local interests and circumstances" of such characters and to point out those with "pursuits or interests" that were "inconsistent with the equal administration of government." Findley had seen the gentry up close, so close in fact that all sense of the mystery that had hitherto surrounded aristocratic authority was lost.[61]

60. Carey, ed., *Debates*, 66, 87, 128, 21, 130, 38, 15, 72–73.

61. Cooke, ed., *The Federalist*, No. 10; [William Findley], *A Review of the Revenue System Adopted at the First Congress under the Federal Constitution* . . . (Philadelphia, 1794), 117.

The prevalence of interest and the impossibility of disinterestedness inevitably became a central argument of the Antifederalists in the debate over the Constitution. Precisely because the Constitution was designed to perpetuate the classical tradition of disinterested leadership in government, the Antifederalists felt compelled to challenge that tradition. There was, they said repeatedly, no disinterested gentlemanly elite that could feel "sympathetically the wants of the people" and speak for their "feelings, circumstances, and interests." Would-be patricians like James Wilson, declared William Findley, thought they were "born of a different race from the rest of the sons of men" and "able to conceive and perform great things." But despite their "lofty carriage," such gentry could not in fact see beyond "the pale of power and wordly grandeur." No one, said the Antifederalists, however elevated or educated, was free of the lures and interests of the marketplace. As for the leisured gentry who were "not . . . under the necessity of getting their bread by industry," far from being specially qualified for public leadership, they were in fact specially disqualified. Such men contributed nothing to the public good; their "idleness" rested on "other men's toil."[62]

But it was not just the classical tradition of leisured gentry leadership the Antifederalists challenged. Without realizing the full implications of what they were doing, they challenged too the whole social order the Federalists stood for. Society to the Antifederalists could no longer be a hierarchy of ranks or even a division into two unequal parts between gentlemen and commoners. Civic society should not in fact be graded by any criteria whatsoever. Society was best thought of as a heterogeneous mixture of "many different classes or orders of people, Merchants, Farmers, Planter Mechanics and Gentry or wealthy Men," all equal to one another. In this diverse egalitarian society, men from one class or interest could never be acquainted with the "*Situation* and Wants" of those from another. Lawyers and planters could never be "adequate judges of trademens concerns." Legislative representatives could not be just *for* the people; they actually had to be *of* the people. It was foolish to tell people that they ought to overlook local interests. Local interests were all there really were. "No man when he enters into society, does it from a view to promote the good of others, but he does it for his own good." Since all individuals and groups in the society were equally self-interested, the only "fair representation" in government, wrote the "Federal Farmer," ought to be one where "every order of men in the

---

62. Jonathan Elliot, ed., *The Debates in the Several State Conventions on the Adoption of the Federal Constitution* . . . (Philadelphia, 1896), II, 260, 13; [Findley], "Letter by an Officer of the Late Continental Army," *Independent Gazette* (Philadelphia), Nov. 6, 1787, in Storing, ed., *Complete Anti-Federalist*, III, 95; Ruth Bogin, *Abraham Clark and the Quest for Equality in the Revolutionary Era, 1774–1794* (East Brunswick, N.J., 1982), 32.

community . . . can have a share in it." Consequently any American government ought "to allow professional men, merchants, traders, farmers, mechanics, etc. to bring a just proportion of their best informed men respectively into the legislature." Only an explicit form of representation that allowed Germans, Baptists, artisans, farmers, and so on each to send delegates of its own kind into the political arena could embody the pluralistic particularism of the emerging society of the early Republic.[63]

Thus in 1787–1788 it was not the Federalists but the Antifederalists who were the real pluralists and the real prophets of the future of American politics. They not only foresaw but endorsed a government of jarring individuals and interests. Unlike the Federalists, however, they offered no disinterested umpires, no mechanisms at all for reconciling and harmonizing these clashing selfish interests. All they and their Republican successors had was the assumption, attributed in 1806 to Jefferson, "that the public good is best promoted by the exertion of each individual seeking his *own good* in his own way."[64]

As early as the first decade of the nineteenth century it seemed to many gentlemen, like Benjamin Latrobe, the noted architect and engineer, that William Findley and the Antifederalists had not really lost the struggle after all. "Our representatives to all our Legislative bodies, National, as well as of the states," Latrobe explained to Philip Mazzei in 1806, "are elected by the majority *sui similes*, that is, *unlearned*."

> For instance from Philadelphia and its environs we send to congress not *one* man of letters. One of them indeed is a lawyer but of no eminence, another a good Mathematician, but when elected he was a Clerk in a bank. The others are plain farmers. From the next county is sent a Blacksmith and from just over the river a Butcher. Our state legislature does not contain one individual of superior talents. The fact is, that superior talents actually excite distrust, and the experience of the world perhaps does not encourage the people to trust men of genius.[65]

This was not the world those "men of genius," the founding fathers, had wanted. To the extent therefore that the Constitution was designed

---

63. Philip A. Crowl, "Anti-Federalism in Maryland, 1787–88," *WMQ*, 3d Ser., IV (1947), 464; Richard Walsh, *Charleston's Sons of Liberty: A Study of the Artisans, 1763–1789* (Columbia, S.C., 1959), 132; [James Winthrop], "Letters of Agrippa," *Massachusetts Gazette*, Dec. 14, 1787, in Storing, ed., *Complete Anti-Federalist*, IV, 80; "Essentials of a Free Government," in Walter Hartwell Bennett, ed., *Letters from the Federal Farmer to the Republican* (University, Ala., 1978), 10.

64. Benjamin Latrobe to Philip Mazzei, Dec. 19, 1806, in Margherita Marchione *et al.*, eds., *Philip Mazzei: Selected Writings and Correspondence* (Prato, Italy, 1983), III, 439 (I owe this reference to Stanley J. Idzerda).

65. *Ibid.*

to control and transcend common ordinary men with their common, ordinary pecuniary interests, it was clearly something of a failure. In place of a classical republic led by a disinterested enlightened elite, Americans got a democratic marketplace of equally competing individuals with interests to promote. Tocqueville saw what happened clearly enough. "Americans are not a virtuous people," he wrote, "yet they are free." In America, unlike the classical republics, "it is not disinterestedness which is great, it is interest." Such a diverse, rootless, and restless people—what could possibly hold them together? "Interest. That is the secret. The private interest that breaks through at each moment, the interest that moreover, appears openly and even proclaims itself as a social theory." In America, said Tocqueville, "the period of disinterested patriotism is gone . . . forever."[66]

No wonder the founding fathers seem so remote, so far away from us. They really are.

POSTSCRIPT

Were the Antifederalists right? Was no one in government without interests? Perhaps Brackenridge and Morris had interests, but did other Federalists? Were the "men of intelligence and uprightness" and "enlightened views and virtuous sentiments" that Federalists like James Wilson and James Madison spoke of also interested? Were such liberally educated cosmopolitans really no different from the debtor farmers of western Pennsylvania? These were essentially Charles Beard's questions, and they are still good ones.[67]

66. James T. Schleifer, *The Making of Tocqueville's "Democracy in America"* (Chapel Hill, N.C., 1980), 242, 243; Tocqueville to Ernest de Chabrol, June 9, 1831, in Roger Boesch, ed., *Alexis de Tocqueville: Selected Letters on Politics and Society* (Berkeley, Calif. 1985), 38; Tocqueville, *Democracy in America*, ed. Phillips Bradley (New York, 1954), I, 243. It was not, of course, as simple as Tocqueville made it out to be. The ideal of disinterested politics did not disappear in the 19th century, and even today it lingers on here and there. It formed the basis for all the antiparty and mugwump reform movements and colored the thinking of many of the Progressives. For Theodore Roosevelt in 1894 "the first requisite in the citizen who wishes to share the work of our public life . . . is that he shall act disinterestedly and with a sincere purpose to serve the whole commonwealth" (Roosevelt, *American Ideals and Other Essays, Social and Political* [New York, 1897], 34 [I owe this reference to John Patrick Diggins]). Of course, at almost the same time, John Dewey was telling Americans that it was psychologically impossible for anyone to act disinterestedly. See John Patrick Diggins, *The Lost Soul of American Politics: Virtue, Self-Interest, and the Foundations of Liberalism* (New York, 1984), 341–343. See also Stephen Miller, *Special Interest Groups in American Politics* (New Brunswick, N.J., 1983).

67. Wilson, in Farrand, ed., *Records of the Federal Convention*, I, 154; Cooke, ed., *The Federalist*, No. 10. Vernon Parrington asked the same questions. If ordinary

Most Federalist leaders certainly saw themselves as different from the likes of William Findley, and to a large extent they were different. They certainly had wealth and property; otherwise they could not have been the leisured gentlemen they aspired to be. But what was the nature of that property? How did most of them make their incomes? The founding fathers' sources of income is not a subject we know much about. How, for example, did Franklin actually support his genteel living through all those years of retirement? Merchants lived off the profits of their overseas trade, and southern planters earned money by selling in transatlantic markets. Some gentry were landlords living off the earnings of tenants, and many others were professionals who earned money from fees. A few relied on the emoluments of government offices, though in the Revolutionary years this was not easy.

But with the exception of rents from property, most such direct sources of income were defiled by interest. That is, the income of most American gentlemen did not come without work and participation in commerce, as Adam Smith suggested it ought to for leaders to be truly disinterested. The "revenue" of the English landed aristocrats was unique, said Smith; their income from rents "costs them neither labour nor care, but comes to them as it were, of its own accord, and independent of any plan or project of their own." Thus would-be disinterested American public leaders struggled to find an equivalent, a reliable source of income that was not stained by marketplace exertion and interest. Many gentlemen of leisure found such a source in the interest from money they had lent out. It is not surprising that so many of the gentry used their wealth in this way. After all, what were the alternatives for investment in an underdeveloped society that lacked banks, corporations, and stock markets? Land, of course, was a traditional object of investment, but in America, as John Witherspoon pointed out in an important speech in the Continental Congress, rent-producing land could never allow for as stable a source of income as it did in England. In the New World, said Witherspoon, where land was more plentiful and cheaper than it was in the Old World, gentlemen seeking a steady income "would prefer money at interest to purchasing and holding real estate."[68]

The little evidence we have suggests that Witherspoon was correct. The

---

men were motivated by self-interest, as the Federalists believed, why would "this sovereign motive" abdicate "its rule among the rich and well born? . . . Do the wealthy betray no desire for greater power? Do the strong and powerful care more for good government than for class interests?" (*Main Currents in American Thought: An Interpretation of American Literature from the Beginnings to 1920* [New York, 1927], I, 302).

68. John Witherspoon, "Speech in Congress on Finances," *The Works of John Witherspoon* . . . (Edinburgh, 1805), IX, 133–134.

probate records of wealthy individuals show large proportions of their estates out on loan. In fact, it was often through such loans to friends and
neighbors that great men were able to build networks of dependents and
clients. In 1776 Cadwallader Colden was the creditor of seventy-three different people. All sorts of persons lent money, said John Adams: merchants,
professionals, widows, but especially "Men of fortune, who live upon their
income." Because earning interest from loans was considered more genteel
than most other moneymaking activities, John Dickinson reinforced the disinterestedness of his persona, the "Pennsylvania Farmer," by having him
living off "a little money at interest." When merchants and wealthy artisans
wanted to establish their status unequivocally as leisured gentlemen, they
withdrew from their businesses and, apart from investing in property, lent
their wealth out at interest. Franklin did it. So did Roger Sherman, John
Hancock, and Henry Laurens. By 1783 Hancock had more than twelve
thousand pounds owed him in bonds and notes. As soon as the trader Joseph
Dwight of Springfield, Massachusetts, had any profits, he began removing
them from his business and lending them out at interest. By the time of his
death in 1768 he had more than 60 percent of his assets out on loan.[69]

As Robert Morris pointed out, in the years before the Revolutionary war,
"monied men were fond of lending upon bond and mortgage: it was a fa-
vourite practice; was thought perfectly safe." Even many of the great planters
of the South earned more from such ancillary activities as lending money at
interest than they did from selling their staple crops. Charles Carroll of
Maryland had twenty-four thousand pounds on loan to his neighbors. A
large landowner in the Shenandoah Valley, James Patton, had 90 percent of
his total estate in the form of bonds, bills, and promissory notes due him. In
this context all the bonds and loan office certificates sold by the state and
congressional governments during the Revolution became just one more
object of investment for gentlemen looking for steady sources of income.[70]

69. Robert J. Taylor, *Western Massachusetts in the Revolution* (Providence, R.I.,
1954), 20; Robert A. East, *Business Enterprise in the American Revolutionary Era*
(New York, 1938), 20–22; Dickinson, "Letters of a Farmer," in Ford, ed., *Writings
of Dickinson*, 307; Fowler, *Baron of Beacon Hill*, 251; Margaret E. Martin, *Merchants
and Trade of the Connecticut River Valley, 1750–1820 (Smith College Studies in History*,
XXIV [Northampton, Mass., 1938–1939]), 159. See also Alice Hanson Jones,
Wealth of a Nation to Be: The American Colonies on the Eve of the Revolution (New York,
1980), 145–153.

70. Carey, ed., *Debates*, 96; Aubrey C. Land, "Economic Base and Social Structure: The Northern Chesapeake in the Eighteenth Century," *Journal of Economic
History*, XXV (1965), 650; Isaac, *Transformation of Virginia*, 133; East, *Business Enterprise*, 19; Robert D. Mitchell, *Commercialism and Frontier: Perspectives on the Early
Shenandoah Valley* (Charlottesville, Va., 1977), 116, 123.

For these sorts of creditors and investors, inflation caused by the excessive printing of paper money could have only devastating consequences. "A depreciating Currency," warned John Adams, "will ruin Us." Indeed, for all those local creditors who were at the same time urban merchants or southern planters dealing in overseas trade with transatlantic obligations, excessive paper currency was doubly harmful: they received cheapened money from their debtors but had to pay their overseas creditors in rising rates of exchange. Washington was both a planter and a banker. In the 1780s he was angry at what his debtors and the promoters of inflation through paper money emissions had done to him while he was away fighting the Revolution. Such scoundrels, he complained more than once, had "taken advantage of my absence and the tender laws, to discharge their debts with a shilling or six pence in the pound," while to those whom he owed money, he now had "to pay in specie at the real value." Rather than enter into litigation, "unless there is every reason to expect a decision in my favor," he reluctantly agreed to accept paper money in place of specie for his rents and debts, "however unjustly and rascally it has been imposed." No wonder then, said Robert Morris, that wealthy men, at least those who had survived the Revolution, had stopped taking up bonds and mortgages; they were "deterred from lending again by the dread of paper money and tender laws."[71]

We have always known that the skyrocketing inflation fueled by the excessive printing of paper money during these years was devastating to creditors, but we have not always appreciated precisely what this meant socially and morally. Credit was the principal sinew of the society and was absolutely essential for the carrying on of any form of commerce. Establishing one's creditworthiness in this personally organized society was nearly equivalent to establishing one's existence as a person, which is why letters of recommendation were so important. The relationships between creditors and debtors were not supposed to be merely impersonal legal contracts. Such engagements, even when they spanned continents and oceans, depended ultimately, it seemed, on personal faith and trust. Debts were thus thought by many to be more than legal obligations; they were moral bonds tying people together. That is why defaulting debtors were still thought to be more than unfortunate victims of bad times; they were moral failures, viola-

71. Adams to James Warren, Feb. 12, 1777, in Robert J. Taylor *et al.*, eds., *Papers of John Adams* (Cambridge, Mass., 1983), V, 83; Riesman, "Origins of American Political Economy," 135–136, 144; Norman K. Risjord, *Chesapeake Politics, 1781–1800* (New York, 1978), 124; Washington to Gov. George Clinton, Apr. 20, 1785, to Battaile Muse, Dec. 4, 1785, in Fitzpatrick, ed., *Writings of Washington*, XXVIII, 134, 341; Carey, ed., *Debates*, 96.

tors of a code of trust and friendship who deserved to be punished and imprisoned.[72]

It is not surprising therefore that many of those whom George Clymer called "honest gentry of intrinsic worth" tended to see all actions interfering with this relationship between creditor and debtor as morally abhorrent. Inflation artificially induced by Rhode Island's printing of paper money threatened, said a Boston gentleman, nothing less than "the first principles of society." Paper money, Madison told his fellow Virginia legislators, was unjust, pernicious, and unconstitutional. It was bad for commerce, it was bad for morality, and it was bad for society: it destroyed "confidence between man and man." Thus most Federalists who stood up for credit and the honest payment of debts did not see themselves as just another economic interest in a pluralistic society. They were defending righteousness itself. "On one side," said Theodore Sedgwick, "are men of talents, and of integrity, firmly determined to support public justice and private faith, and on the other there exists as firm a determination to institute tender laws, paper money, . . . and in short to establish iniquity by law." [73]

The Federal Constitution's abolition of the states' power to emit paper money was therefore welcomed by most gentry as the righting of a moral and social wrong. The wickedness of such inflationary state policies was so much taken for granted by the members of the convention that this prohibition of the states' authority in Article I, Section 10 of the Constitution was scarcely debated. Even a proposal to grant authority to the Federal Congress to emit bills of credit was thrown out by the convention, nine states to two. The truth is there were almost no real Antifederalists, such as William Findley, present in the convention to defend the states' paper money emissions of the 1780s. Of the delegates present, only eccentric Luther Martin spoke out against the prohibition of the states' emitting bills of credit. The Federalists morally controlled the debate over paper money in 1787–1788 and browbeat most potential defenders of it into silence. As

72. Roy A. Foulke, *The Sinews of American Commerce* (New York, 1941), 66–68, 74–75, 89; William E. Nelson, *Americanization of the Common Law: The Impact of Legal Change on Massachusetts Society, 1760–1830* (Cambridge, Mass., 1975), 44–45. For a sensitive analysis of the Virginia planters' etiquette of debt, see T. H. Breen, *Tobacco Culture: The Mentality of the Great Tidewater Planters on the Eve of the Revolution* (Princeton, N.J., 1985), esp. 93–106.

73. Grundfest, *Clymer*, 177; *Providence Gazette*, Aug. 5, 1786, quoted in David P. Szatmary, *Shays' Rebellion: The Making of an Agrarian Insurrection* (Amherst, Mass., 1980), 51; Madison, "Notes for Speech Opposing Paper Money" [Nov. 1, 1786], in Hutchinson *et al.*, eds., *Papers of Madison*, IX, 158–159; Taylor, *Western Massachusetts*, 166.

William R. Davie pointed out to the North Carolina ratifying convention, gentlemen in their speeches attached such dishonesty and shame to paper money that even "a member from Rhode Island" (which was defiantly excessive in emitting paper money) "could not have set his face against such language."[74] So dominant were classical values and so disturbing seemed the moral and social consequences of paper money that even those who defended paper emissions in the 1780s often did so in terms that conceded the Federalists' traditional argument against ordinary people's earning and spending money beyond their station.[75] Only in time, with the spread of paper-issuing banks and a new understanding of the economy, would Americans find the arguments to legitimate the position of men like William Findley.

Whatever the confusion of the Antifederalists, most Federalists believed they understood what their opponents were like. "Examine well the characters and circumstances of men who are averse to the new constitution," warned David Ramsay of South Carolina. Many of them may be debtors "who wish to defraud their creditors," and therefore, for some of them at least, Article I, Section 10 of the Constitution may be "the real ground of the opposition . . . , though they may artfully cover it with a splendid profession of zeal for state privileges and general liberty."[76] But even if this were not true, the Federalists at least knew that the end of the states' printing of paper money would be of "real service to the honest part of the community." If the new Constitution, said Benjamin Rush in 1788, "held forth no other advantages [than] that [of] a future exemption from paper money and tender laws, it would be eno' to recommend it to honest men." This was because "the man of wealth realized once more the safety of his bonds and rents against the inroads of paper money and tender laws."[77] That was putting it about as selfishly as it could be put.

74. Farrand, ed., *Records of the Federal Convention*, II, 310, III, 350.

75. Ruth Bogin, "New Jersey's True Policy: The Radical Republican Vision of Abraham Clark," *WMQ*, 3d Ser., XXXV (1978), 105.

76. David Ramsay, "An Address to the Freemen of South Carolina on the Subject of the Federal Constitution" (1787), in Paul Leicester Ford, ed., *Pamphlets on the Constitution of the United States* (Brooklyn, N.Y., 1888), 379–380. Madison thought that the Antifederalist pamphlets omitted "many of the true grounds of opposition" to the Constitution. "The articles relating to Treaties, to paper money, and to contracts, created more enemies than all the errors in the System positive and negative put together" (Madison to Jefferson, Oct. 17, 1788, in Boyd *et al.*, eds., *Papers of Jefferson*, XIV, 18).

77. Rush to Jeremy Belknap, Feb. 28, 1788, quoted in John P. Kaminski, "Democracy Run Rampant: Rhode Island in the Confederation," in James Kirby Martin, ed., *The Human Dimensions of Nation Making: Essays on Colonial and Revolutionary History*

Yet in the end it should not be put that way. To rest something as monumental as the formation of the Federal Constitution on such crude, narrow, and selfish motives was Beard's mistake, and it should not be repeated. The Federalists certainly had far more fundamental concerns at stake in 1787 than their personal credit and their social status. They were defending, not their personal interests (for they were often debtors as well as creditors), but rather a moral and social order that had been prescribed by the Revolution and the most enlightened thinking of the eighteenth century. So committed were they to these classical humanist values that they were scarcely capable of understanding, let alone admitting the legitimacy of, the acquisitive and enterprising world that paper money represented. They saw themselves, as sincerely and thoroughly as any generation in American history, as virtuous leaders dedicated to promoting the good of the nation. However strong and self-serving their underlying interests may have been, the Federalists always described their ideals and goals in the language of classical republican disinterestedness; and this language, these ideals and goals, repeated endlessly in private correspondence and public forums up and down the continent, inevitably controlled and shaped their behavior. Washington's agony over the canal shares and Morris's abandonment of his mercantile career are object lessons in the power of this culture to affect behavior. Self-interest that could not be publicly justified and explained was self-interest that could not be easily acted upon.

The founders thus gave future Americans more than a new Constitution. They passed on ideals and standards of political behavior that helped to contain and control the unruly materialistic passions unleashed by the democratic revolution of the early nineteenth century. Even today our aversion to corruption, our uneasiness over the too blatant promotion of special interests, and our yearning for examples of unselfish public service suggest that such ideals still have great moral power. Yet in the end we know that it was not the Federalists of 1787 who came to dominate American culture. Our wistful celebration of their heroic greatness, our persistent feelings that they were leaders the likes of whom we shall never see again in America, our ready acceptance of parties and interest-group politics—all tell us that it was William Findley and the Antifederalists who really belonged to the future. They, and not the Federalists, spoke for the emerging world of egalitarian democracy and the private pursuit of happiness.

(Madison, Wis., 1976), 267; Rush to Elias Boudinot, July 9, 1788, in Butterfield, ed., *Letters of Rush*, I, 471.

☆ ☆ ☆

PART II

Issues

☆ ☆ ☆ ☆ ☆

Shays's Rebellion and the Ratification of the Federal Constitution in Massachusetts

RICHARD D. BROWN

From the time that the Constitution was written, Shays's Rebellion has been regarded as a catalyst in the movement for the Constitution and for its ratification. Washington and Madison saw it that way, and historians from George Bancroft, John Fiske, and John Bach McMaster in the last century down to Forrest McDonald, Jackson Turner Main, and Gordon Wood in our own era have followed their lead. Emphases have varied, but there has been general agreement that the insurrection in Massachusetts significantly strengthened the Federalist movement.[1]

The evidence supporting this interpretation is already substantial, and more is in the offing.[2] The focus of most discussion, however, has been at the national level or on states where Massachusetts' turmoil furnished a

1. George Bancroft, *History of the Formation of the Constitution of the United States of America*, 2 vols. (New York, 1882); John Fiske, *The Critical Period of American History, 1783-1789* (Boston, 1888); John Bach McMaster, *A History of the People of the United States from the Revolution to the Civil War*, 8 vols. (New York, 1883-1913); Forrest McDonald, *We the People: The Economic Origins of the Constitution* (Chicago, 1958); Jackson Turner Main, *The Antifederalists: Critics of the Constitution, 1781-1787* (Chapel Hill, N.C., 1961); Gordon S. Wood, *The Creation of the American Republic, 1776-1787* (Chapel Hill, N.C., 1969); Robert A. Feer, "Shays's Rebellion and the Constitution: A Study in Causation," *New England Quarterly*, XLII (1969), 388-410.

2. Robert A. Becker, "'Combustibles in Every State': A Frame of Reference for Shays' Rebellion," paper given at annual meeting of the Organization of American Historians, Philadelphia, Apr. 3, 1982 (a revised version is planned for publication).

vivid exhibit to reinforce Federalist tendencies. Surprisingly, for Massachusetts itself, where the effects of Shays's Rebellion on the issue of the Constitution might have been expected to be most intense, comparatively little attention has been given to connections between the two. Samuel B. Harding's 1896 monograph on the Constitution in Massachusetts remains an important work; but with respect to Shays's Rebellion, he states only that it galvanized the Federalists, who were opposed by former Shaysites and their sympathizers. This connection between Antifederalism and the Shays movement was first made by Federalists in 1787 and has long been well known to scholars. It is most fully elaborated in Van Beck Hall's *Politics without Parties*; yet because Hall's chief objective was to show the correlation between local alignments in the early 1780s on fiscal issues and later votes in the ratifying convention, the political turmoil of 1786-1787, which Hall carefully analyzed, was diminished as a factor affecting the ratification of the Constitution.[3] Robert Feer, the author of a dissertation on the rebellion, denied its importance for ratification entirely, because, he said, people's orientation to state and national politics had already been fixed before 1786. An important monograph on the subject of Shays's Rebellion, by David P. Szatmary, differs and concludes by reinforcing the prevailing consensus that Federalists gained as a result of the insurrection and that the opposition displayed a "Shaysite orientation."[4]

The existence of such a broad and durable consensus among historians is unusual and reminds us that scholarship is not simply a succession of revisionist waves. The evidence, whether examined in the 1890s or the 1980s, supports this consensus. Yet it is possible that a fresh examination of the impact of Shays's Rebellion can enhance our understanding of the ratification of the Constitution in Massachusetts. For if it is clear that the insurrection strengthened the Federalists, it may also be true that it exercised a similar influence on Antifederalists. If it did, then perhaps it affected the polarization in Massachusetts politics more significantly than we have been prepared to recognize. These questions are worth pondering now that, two hundred years later, the legendary success of the Constitution has given it an aura of inevitability.

3. Samuel Bannister Harding, *The Contest over the Ratification of the Federal Constitution in the State of Massachusetts*, Harvard Historical Studies, II (New York, 1896); Van Beck Hall, *Politics without Parties: Massachusetts, 1780-1791* (Pittsburgh, Pa., 1972).

4. Robert Arnold Feer, "Shays's Rebellion" (Ph.D. diss., Harvard University, 1958); David P. Szatmary, *Shays' Rebellion: The Making of an Agrarian Insurrection* (Amherst, Mass., 1980), 131. See also Gordon S. Wood, "Democracy and the Constitution," in Robert A. Goldwin and William A. Schambra, eds., *How Democratic Is the Constitution?* (Washington, D.C., 1980), 1-17.

I

What came to be known as the Regulation by its friends and as the Rebellion by the government began with the stopping of courts by crowds, sometimes armed. They began at Taunton in Bristol County in June 1786, and then through the summer, courts responsible for the collection of debts were forcibly shut down in Berkshire, Hampshire, Middlesex, and Worcester counties. This aggressive politics out-of-doors, modeled on the resistance of 1774 and 1775, was complemented by county conventions of town delegates that passed resolutions calling for the redress of grievances and the reform of the Massachusetts constitution. During its summer and fall sessions, the General Court, guided by Governor James Bowdoin, chose not to accede to the principal demands, which centered on tax reduction and relief for debtors and also included ever-popular attacks on lawyers and the governor's salary. The leading Massachusetts public officials, who were drawn mostly from commercial centers, chose to ride out a storm which, after outbursts of political thunder and lightning, they believed would subside. When the months of October, November, and December 1786 showed that the intensity of the insurgent movement was growing and that armed men were prepared to take over Worcester, Hampshire, and Berkshire counties to enforce their demands, the Bowdoin administration shifted from a relatively passive to an active policy of suppression. The carrot of amnesty was offered to all who would lay down their arms and peaceably submit to government before January 1, 1787; simultaneously a stick was brandished in the form of an army raised in eastern Massachusetts and temporarily financed by Bowdoin's circle of wealthy commercial associates.

Though it is hard to tell where most inhabitants stood in late 1786, it is clear that in central and western Massachusetts there was considerable distaste for both parties to the conflict. Many sympathized with the Shaysite grievances and would not take arms as militiamen to suppress their neighbors, but they also deplored the insurgent attack on government and refused to join the rebellion. After months of organizing and agitation, the Shaysites mustered an army that was only a small fraction (perhaps 10 percent) of the minuteman force that had turned out in the powder alarm of September 1774.[5] When the new year began, it appeared that in many Massachusetts

5. Estimates of the size of the Shays army varied in 1786 and 1787, and no more reliable figures have come to light. The highest estimate came from Henry Knox, who supplied a figure of 12,000–15,000 rebel troops in letters to George Washington and others outside Massachusetts. But there is good reason to believe Knox inflated these numbers for political effect, since at the peak of its strength none of those who were close to the action ever gave an estimate higher than 2,500 men in arms. The fact that the government army raised to suppress the rebellion numbered

towns neither the Shaysites nor the government enjoyed broad, unqualified support.

This was the setting for the military conflicts of early 1787, when the Shaysites were decisively routed at Springfield (January 25) and Petersham (February 4) in Hampshire County and at Sheffield (February 27) in Berkshire. Though there were occasional guerrilla forays against a few retailers and progovernment figures in March and April and even an incident as late as June 1787, William Shepard's and Benjamin Lincoln's troops had shattered the rebellion. Its leaders fled the state, and the rank and file went home. What remained were the government's mopping-up operations. These included an occupying army ranging from one to two thousand strong, a series of laws proscribing leading rebels as well as their followers, and the visit to the three western counties of Worcester, Hampshire, and Berkshire of legal officers charged with enforcing the proscription laws.

During February, March, and April, Bowdoin and his associates were not in a compromising mood. Major General William Shepard, writing from Hampshire County in mid-February 1787, saw his task as "to rivet in their minds a compleat conviction of the force of government and the necessity of an entire submission to the laws." Fearing "assassination" and "secret plots," Shepard was prepared to sacrifice civil rights; and the General Court, following the administration's lead, acted decisively—formally declaring a rebellion and suspending the right to writs of habeas corpus.[6] Subsequently the legislature voted a Disqualifying Act that barred rebels from voting and from holding public offices, even such positions as schoolmaster and tavernkeeper. Robert Treat Paine, the attorney general, was sent west to prosecute offenders in the courts of the occupied counties, and he systematically began compiling a "Black List" to aid in the grim task of repression.[7]

Even as this policy was being set in motion, a few insiders questioned it.

4,400 men gives further credence to the 2,500 estimate. In the false Powder Alarm of Sept. 1–2, 1774, some 40,000 minutemen were reported on the march for Boston, and more than 3,000 collected at Cambridge within a few hours of the rumored attack on Boston. Measured against such an immediate, broadly based response, the numbers in the Shays army seem small. Forrest McDonald, *E Pluribus Unum: The Formation of the American Republic, 1776–1790* (Boston, 1965), 150, 290 n; Szatmary, *Shays' Rebellion*, 100–102; Richard D. Brown, *Revolutionary Politics in Massachusetts: The Boston Committee of Correspondence and the Towns, 1772–1774* (Cambridge, Mass., 1970), 226–227.

6. William Shepard to James Bowdoin, Westfield, Feb. 18, 20, 1787, in *The Bowdoin and Temple Papers*, Pt. II (Massachusetts Historical Society, *Collections*, 7th Ser., VI [Boston, 1907]), 142, 143, 147 (hereafter cited as *Bowdoin and Temple Papers*).

7. Robert Treat Paine Papers, Vol. XXIII, "*Blacklist* County of Hampshire," n.d., Massachusetts Historical Society, Boston.

General Benjamin Lincoln, who more than anyone else had been a scourge to Shays's army, wrote to Bowdoin a few days after Shepard's militant counsel, explaining that in Berkshire "our goals are now full" and that, except "the most aggravatedly guilty," neither he nor the sheriff would make further arrests. Indeed, in the interest of the general good, Lincoln wanted permission to free all Shaysites and their sympathizers in Berkshire, believing "those characters who have been committed are not the most dangerous."[8] Three weeks later, in a letter to Henry Knox, Lincoln wrote an eloquent defense of a generous, lenient policy that would welcome the rebels into the electoral process. It was not only expedient, he said; it was a matter of republican principle.[9] Though sworn to carry out administration policy, Lincoln did his best to mitigate its force; and when the General Court created a commission empowered to pardon Shaysite sympathizers, Lincoln headed it, ultimately extending pardons to 790 men who were not covered by the Disqualifying Act.[10]

By this time the sense that government repression was too severe was growing.[11] Even those who recognized the necessity of forcibly suppressing the rebellion regarded this mopping-up phase as misguided or worse because it violated the common sense of the social compact in their communities. Here the testimony of two orthodox Hampshire clergymen, officials who were at least nominally friends of the administration, is revealing. One, Joseph Lathrop, was minister of the First Parish in West Springfield, and on December 14, 1786, just before the crisis was forced, he had preached a sermon from Isaiah 1:19, 20: "If ye be willing and obedient, ye shall eat the good of the land: but if ye refuse and rebel, ye shall be devoured with a sword; for the mouth of the Lord hath spoken it." His message, in a town which on that very day General Shepard estimated contained more rebels (sixty) than any other in Hampshire County, was obedience to what Lathrop described as a legitimate government.[12] This government, however, must not be haughty or inflexible. Now, with so many suffering distress: "Government, at such a time, ought to adjust their demands to the common ability;

8. Benjamin Lincoln to James Bowdoin, Pittsfield, Feb. 22, 1787, in *Bowdoin and Temple Papers*, Pt. II, 157.

9. Discussed and quoted in Feer, "Shays's Rebellion," 395–398. The original document of Mar. 14, 1787, is in the Henry Knox Papers, MHS.

10. Robert J. Taylor, *Western Massachusetts in the Revolution* (Providence, R.I., 1954), 164.

11. *Ibid.*, 163.

12. Joseph Lathrop, *A Sermon, Preached in the First Parish in West-Springfield, December 14, 1786, Being the Day Appointed by Authority for a Publick Thanksgiving* (Springfield, Mass., 1787), esp. 5; "Maj. Shepard's Estimate of the No. of Insurgents in Hampshire, Dec. 14, 1786," in *Bowdoin and Temple Papers*, Pt. II, 116–117.

. . . for *they* bear a part of the burthens with others. . . . *Bear ye one another's burthens,* says the law of Christ. The law of reason says the same." As Lathrop explained the social compact, "No community ought to leave her prudent and industrious members to struggle in vain under an insupportable load." Lathrop warned that "drawing the sword" against government was wrong, and at the same time he encouraged expectations of a generous, responsive, paternal government authority.[13]

Across the river in Springfield, where General Shepard reported there were no rebels and where the minister of the First Parish, Bezaleel Howard, had earlier boasted that "not a single man from my parish attended" the closing of the court in Northampton, expectations regarding the government were similar.[14] Here the Reverend Mr. Howard, who like his colleague Lathrop condemned the insurgents, expressed outrage at the unjust and partisan conduct of the administration after Shays had been beaten. According to Howard, the act declaring the rebellion, which tainted as a traitor anyone who had aided an insurgent, had opened a Pandora's box of tyranny:

> The Magistrates, officers, and soldiers of Goverment took the advantage to Call fourth whom they would, from whatever place they were, and to vent all the spite, malice, and spleen, their jealousies and ill will, in their confinement in the public Goals . . . many of them Innocent, others more or less Guilty. The Gun and Bayonet was now the only standard of authority. . . . Such a state of anarchy and Confusion, Dispotism and Tyranny succeeded the Dispersion of Shays troops.
> . . . To be a soldier was sufficient to Invest him with power to drag whomsoever they would from their beds at midnight and commit them to Goal untill a partiall Examination could be had.[15]

But it was not only the soldiers or local partisans who where to blame. When a court was convened at Great Barrington to try the rebels of Berkshire,

> [Robert Treat] Paine, the States attorney, Exerted all his Malevolence and Malice on this occasion. And as the Complection of the time now is, but very little Testimony is Necessary towards the Conviction of any one that had in smallest degree assisted or supposd to have assisted or only countenanced. And as Every man more or less has them who are

---

13. Lathrop, *A Sermon, Preached*, 15, 23.

14. Bezaleel Howard to Nathan Howard, Esq., Sept. 16, 1786, Manuscript Collection, Springfield Public Library, Springfield, Mass.

15. Richard D. Brown, "Shays's Rebellion and Its Aftermath: A View from Springfield, Massachusetts, 1787," *William and Mary Quarterly*, 3d Ser., XL (1983), 609–610.

unfriendly about him, who gladly lay hold of such opportunities, witneses were very E[a]sily procured.

Indeed, Howard pointed out, numbers of innocent people were so afraid that others might denounce them that they sought pardons in advance from the commission Lincoln headed.[16]

What Howard saw happening was less the suppression of a rebellion—that had already collapsed—than the arbitrary, partisan use of power to punish those who had not been active on behalf of the government. In his view the Disqualifying Act was being used to keep Bowdoin (and his friends who speculated in soldiers' notes) in power. Thus the elections of the spring 1787 were critical. Though Howard was no Shaysite and had always urged submission to government, he argued that this government was vicious and deserved to be turned out of office. The potency of the backlash against the Bowdoin government is evident in Howard's description of the recently concluded election:

> By that severe and Tyranical [Disqualifying] act they Intended at one blow to Intirely cut of[f] all opposition to Bowdoin, and if they could asperse the Character of Hancock and thus diminish his popularity with the people, this secret and Important Business would be Compleat. This they Indeavored to perform by Sly Insinuation, malicious Whispers, and by downright falshoods, not only in the public paper, but also in all the towns where people of this character dwelt.
>
> But their Malovolant and spitfull treatment of Hancock, the cruelty of the disqualifiing act, the Suspension of the Habeus Corpus act, and the consequences thence arising, all Conspird to overthrow their favourite plan, and they had in the Conclusion an Entire Contrary Effect from what thos[e] Imps of Hypocrisy and oppresion designd they should have. Who could wonder to see them chop fallen when news came that Hancock had 3/4 of the votes?[17]

Howard, whose office required a nonpartisan facade, was privately articulating a view that was shared in much of Massachusetts. From Milton, James Warren wrote of the government's measures: "The People were Irritated, not softened and conciliated. . . . And for fear that Capt. Shays should destroy the Constitution they violated it themselves." Warren went on to rail at all the legislation Howard cited, and concluded, "It is certain a General discontent and disapprobation prevails in the Country, and has shewn itself in the late Elections." A Connecticut visitor, traveling in Berkshire and

16. *Ibid.*, 611.
17. *Ibid.*, 614–615.

Hampshire in June, found "the majority of the populace have been disaffected to Governmental measures."[18]

So in the gubernatorial election of 1787 Bowdoin lost. Though Bowdoin garnered more votes than he had in his successful race the previous year, he was swamped in 1787 by John Hancock, who polled 75 percent of a total vote that was three times larger than the turnout of 1786.[19] Because John Hancock was always so popular and always won by wide margins, the meaning of his victory is less clear-cut than the size of the turnout itself and the fact that the number of towns sending delegates to the General Court jumped by 60, from 168 (1786) to 228, the highest number in a decade.[20] Although hundreds of men in the western counties were disqualified from voting because of pro-Shays activities, the mobilization of voters set a record for a statewide election.[21] In the absence of other variables, it is clear that the rebellion and the actions of the government had generated a wave of interest in politics that had not been seen since the early years of the Revolution.

The actions of the new legislature were not Shaysite, the demands of the insurgents were not enacted, and a bill providing a general indemnity for

18. Warren to John Adams, May 18, 1787, in *Warren-Adams Letters: Being Chiefly a Correspondence among John Adams, Samuel Adams, and James Warren*, Vol. II, *1778–1814* (MHS, *Colls.*, LXXIII [Boston, 1925]), 292; Barnabas Bidwell to David Daggett, Tyringham, Mass., June 16, 1787, in "Selections from Letters Received by David Daggett, 1786–1802," American Antiquarian Society, *Proceedings*, N.S., IV (1885–1887), 368–369. James Madison was concerned by Shaysites' turning to state elections, as Alfred F. Young notes in "Conservatives, the Constitution, and the 'Spirit of Accommodation,'" in Goldwin and Schambra, eds., *How Democratic*, 117–147, esp. 128.

19. Hall, *Politics without Parties*, 237; see also William M. Fowler, Jr., "The Massachusetts Election of 1785: A Triumph of Virtue," Essex Institute, *Historical Collections*, CXI (1975), 290–304, data on 301, 304.

20. Compiled from legislative lists in *Acts and Laws of the Commonwealth of Massachusetts, 1780–1797*, 11 vols. (Boston, 1890–1897). Members of the legislature are listed at the beginning of each annual set of laws—1786: IV, 266–270; 1787: IV, 664–667. In some cases members who arrived after the first legislative session are not listed, and so the numbers given may understate attendance slightly. For the relevant years before 1780 the legislative lists are found in *The Acts and Resolves, Public and Private, of the Province of the Massachusetts Bay*, 21 vols. (Boston, 1869–1922), XIX, XX, XXI. Lists of towns for these years are found in the tax lists in Vols. IV and V of the same series.

Although 168 towns sent delegates in 1786, the actual number of delegates was 190, since some towns sent more than one.

21. Fowler, "The Massachusetts Election," Essex Institute, *Hist. Colls.*, CXI (1975), 304; Hall, *Politics without Parties*, 238, table 52.

rebels was defeated.[22] Yet the new legislature was decidedly more conciliatory than its predecessor and moved in rapid stages to end all punishment of Shaysites and to allow the immediate restoration of their civil rights. Though the evidence is not conclusive, the electoral mobilization of 1787 and the behavior of the new General Court embodied a reaction against the Bowdoin administration, and a backlash against its repressive policies after the Shaysites were defeated.

II

Massachusetts, of course, possessed a long-standing east-west sectional division that stretched from the colonial era into the nineteenth century, and the backlash against the repression intensified it and helped stimulate the great mobilization in the spring elections. Indeed, the rebellion and its suppression were important in determining the political climate for some time. As an early historian of Berkshire County wrote four years after Shays's death: "Too much, however, had been said and done, to permit the feelings of the people at once to become altogether friendly. Unhappy jealousies remained in neighborhoods and towns."[23] It was in this setting that the new United States Constitution was introduced in September 1787 with the vigorous and vocal support of Bowdoin and the eastern Massachusetts political elite.

The actual contest over ratification has been thoroughly treated by Samuel B. Harding and, from a different perspective, Van Beck Hall, so only a few points need to be underlined here. First, it should be noted that before the ratifying convention the battle was waged in the newspapers, over the terms of the ratification process—whether to submit the document directly to the towns for approval or to hold a special convention—and then over the actual delegates to the convention. The Federalists, scholars agree, organized a systematic effort that extended through all these aspects of the contest. During this period the letters of Federalists reveal that Shays's Rebellion helped them to mobilize their friends, though there is also evidence

22. Hall, *Politics without Parties*, 246–247; John Stetson Barry, *The History of Massachusetts*, Vol. III, *The Commonwealth Period* (Boston, 1857), 257, reports the vote against a general indemnity was 120 to 94.

23. David Dudley Field, ed., *A History of the County of Berkshire, Massachusetts* (Pittsfield, Mass., 1829), 140. Josiah Gilbert Holland, in *History of Western Massachusetts* (Springfield, Mass., 1855), said: "It sowed also the seeds of bitterness. It broke the chain of family affection" (I, 299).

that "the disaster of the spring 1787 elections," when they had lost control of the General Court, gave additional impetus to their political organizing and newsprint oratory.[24] Their attempts to suppress Antifederalist rhetoric and, in Federalist George R. Minot's words, "to *pack* a Convention whose sense would be different from that of the people" reveal that, as commercial and cosmopolitan as Massachusetts was and with as many well-placed Federalists as it had, ratification was an uphill struggle.[25]

This is the crux of the issue. Why was the Constitution in trouble in Massachusetts, a state customarily dominated by leaders from maritime towns and the regions where commercial agriculture flourished? If the Federalists were well organized and if Shays's Rebellion was useful to them —as was the case—why then were the comparatively unorganized Antifederalists in a majority in the convention when it met in January 1788? It is here that the ruling interpretation of Shays's Rebellion and the Constitution is inadequate for Massachusetts.

What needs to be grafted on to our understanding is the realization that in 1787 the aftermath of Shays's Rebellion—the repression and the state election that followed—mobilized participation in Massachusetts politics on an extensive scale and energized Antifederalists, though not in the same organized way as the Federalists.[26] Ever since the colonial era the types of leaders who would become Federalists had dominated Massachusetts politics. Drawn from commercially oriented eastern and Connecticut Valley towns, often linked by college, commercial, and kinship ties, they attended the General Court regularly and developed the experience required for leadership.[27] What the elections of 1787 witnessed, both in the spring and in the fall contests for the ratifying convention, was a larger representation from smaller, more purely agricultural towns than ever before. This mobilization of country representatives threatened to swamp the Constitution in a wave of antigovernment, antilawyer, antiestablishment reaction that was less related to the particular contents of the document itself than to the power and privilege its leading advocates symbolized.

24. Hall, *Politics without Parties*, 265.

25. Quoted in Main, *Antifederalists*, 202.

26. This was noted by Robert A. East, "The Massachusetts Conservatives in the Critical Period," in Richard B. Morris, ed., *The Era of the American Revolution: Studies Inscribed to Evarts Boutell Greene* (1939; rpt., New York, 1965), 366.

27. Robert Zemsky, *Merchants, Farmers, and River Gods: An Essay on Eighteenth-Century American Politics* (Boston, 1971); Stephen E. Patterson, "The Roots of Massachusetts Federalism: Conservative Politics and Political Culture before 1787," in Ronald Hoffman and Peter J. Albert, eds., *Sovereign States in an Age of Uncertainty* (Charlottesville, Va., 1981), 31–61; Hall, *Politics without Parties*.

Never before, it appears, had so many voters voted. Never before had so many country delegates turned out at once. From 190 representatives in the 1786 General Court, the number climbed to 266 in 1787, and then to 364 at the ratifying convention. Both Federalists and Antifederalists gained from the increased turnout, but the latter gained more. Ninety-nine towns were represented at the convention in 1787 that had not participated in the 1786 General Court, a 52 percent increase. Collectively these towns supplied thirty-six votes in favor of ratification and sixty-three against it.[28] Clearly the reaction against the Bowdoin government threatened to defeat the Constitution when the delegates met on January 9, 1788.

"The Convention now sitting here is the largest and most complete representation that ever was made of the State of Massachusetts," a spectator noted. "Men of all professions, of all ranks, and of all characters, good, bad, and indifferent, compose it," he said, and "the numbers against the Constitution are great." Samuel Nasson, a merchant from Sanford in York County, Maine, who was to emerge as an Antifederalist leader, believed that his side had a forty-eight-vote majority when the convention opened, and even Federalists conceded privately that they appeared to be trailing.[29] In their assessments of the convention they gave no hint that Shays's Rebellion had been in any way helpful to their cause. As the Federalist delegate Benjamin

28. The figures have been compiled from the legislative lists in the sources cited in n. 20 above, and from the ratifying convention delegates listed in *Debates and Proceedings in the Convention of the Commonwealth of Massachusetts, Held in the Year 1788, and Which Finally Ratified the Constitution of the United States* (Boston, 1856). Jackson T. Main, noting that more than 50 towns did not send delegates, implies that there was a weak Antifederalist turnout (*Antifederalists*, 209). Actually, according to Harding (*Contest over the Ratification*, 48), only 46 towns (14% of the 318 eligible) failed to send delegates, and 31 were thinly settled Maine frontier towns which in most cases had *never* sent a delegate to any state meeting, and which would not do so for years to come. Main argues that "two-thirds" of the missing towns "would probably have been Antifederal" (p. 209). This is uncertain. The Maine towns that did attend split their votes, 25 for the Constitution, 26 opposed. Because of a system of representation where apportionment was based on townships rather than population, the great mobilization of 1787 gave rural Antifederalists a major advantage over Federalists, whose strength lay in the more densely settled parts of the state. Because voter turnout records are so fragmentary, no quantitative estimate can be made. Presumably, the high level of town participation reflected high voter participation. Certainly this had been true in the spring 1787 elections.

29. Jeremy Belknap, "Minutes of the debates in the Massachusetts Convention which met in Boston in January 1788, for ratifying the Federal Constitution," in Charles Deane, "Report on the Belknap Donation," MHS, *Proceedings*, III (Boston, 1855–1858), 296 n; Harding, *Contest over the Ratification*, 67.

Lincoln observed: "We find ourselves exceedingly embarassed by the temper which raged the last winter in some of the counties. Many of the insurgents are in the Convention; even some of Shays's officers. A great proportion of these men are high in the opposition."[30] The repression of Shaysism strengthened Antifederalism.

After two weeks of debate, in which the Federalists had avoided any test votes for fear of defeat and had systematically expounded the Constitution sentence by sentence, Rufus King, one of the state's delegates to the Philadelphia Convention and now a delegate from Newburyport, offered a telling analysis of the political dynamics of the convention:

> The Opposition complain that the Lawyers, Judges, Clergymen, Merchants and men of Education are all in Favor of the constitution; and that for this reason they appear to be able to make the worst, appear the better cause.... Notwithstanding the superiority of Talents in favor of the constitution, yet the same infatuation, which prevailed not many months since in several Counties of this State, and which emboldened them to take arms agt. the Government seems to have an uncontroulable authority over a numerous part of our Convention. Their Objections are not directed against any part of the constitution, but their Opposition seems to arise from an Opinion, that is immoveable, that some injury is plotted against them, that the System is the production of the Rich, and ambitious; that *they* discern its operation, and that the consequence will be, the establishment of two Orders in the Society, one comprehending the Opulent and Great, the other the poor and illiterate.
>
> The extraordinary union in favor of the Constitution in this State, of the wealthy and sensible part of it, is a confirmation of their Opinion; and every Exertion hitherto made to eradicate it has been in vain.[31]

Because of the extreme polarization that Shays's Rebellion and its suppression had created, the Federalists' best tools, polished argument and the deference that accompanied high status, lost their customary power. "'A good thing don't need praising,'" one Antifederalist maintained, "but, sir, it takes the best men in the state to gloss this constitution."[32] To such asser-

30. Lincoln to George Washington, Boston, Feb. 3, 1788, *Debates and Proceedings*, 405.

31. King to James Madison, Boston, Jan. 27, 1788, in William T. Hutchinson *et al.*, eds., *The Papers of James Madison*, X (Chicago, 1977), 436–437. King seems to be thinking of the speeches of Benjamin Randall of Sharon (who spoke on Jan. 18) and Amos Singletary of Sutton (who spoke on Jan. 25).

32. Benjamin Randall of Sharon, Jan. 18, 1788, in *Debates, Resolutions, and Other*

tions there could be no rebuttal. Since Bowdoin and the political and religious establishment supported the Constitution, those delegates who felt, as one of them put it, "that had the last administration continued one year longer, our liberties would have been lost" could not be persuaded or cajoled.[33] Suspicion, always a legitimate part of the Whig outlook, ran rampant among those whom the state government had alienated.

In the end, however, the Federalists narrowly carried the convention. Their debating skills won a few votes, and several Antifederalists went home as the proceedings dragged on. But it was their compromise maneuver, in which the previously noncommittal convention president, John Hancock, came out in favor of the Constitution with amendments, that was decisive. Perhaps twenty delegates who had been leaning toward rejection now followed Hancock into the Federalist camp when it was agreed that the convention would recommend amendments to protect against certain abuses of federal power.[34] Whatever Hancock's antipathy to the Bowdoin set, the governor was aware that the mechanics and merchants of maritime Massachusetts wanted the Constitution; and his own credit with inland Massachusetts was good because he had proved a conciliatory governor who pardoned Shaysites and who voluntarily reduced his own salary—an important symbolic act. Now, by agreeing with the Antifederalists that the Constitution was indeed flawed and by adopting a number of their criticisms in proposed amendments, Hancock and his associates found a face-saving way to swing the convention to ratify the Constitution. The vote was 187 in favor, 168 opposed, a margin of 19 votes. Without any commanding leaders, without clever parliamentary maneuvers or brilliant debaters, without any statewide organization, the Antifederalists were just barely defeated.

Proceedings of the Convention of the Commonwealth of Massachusetts, Convened at Boston, on the 9th of January, 1788... (Boston, 1808), 67.

33. Samuel Thompson of Topsham, Maine, *ibid.*, 39. Ebenezer Peirce of Partridgefield in Maine asserted that in passing the Disqualifying Act "we then did not keep strictly to our own constitution" (*ibid.*, 109).

34. Main, *Antifederalists*, 206; Harding, *Contest over the Ratification*, 88–89.

No fully satisfactory explanation of Hancock's conduct is available. Among contemporary insiders there was talk that Federalists had promised Hancock the United States presidency in exchange for his support. This seems dubious at best; and Hancock would have been remarkably naive to have supposed that anyone could deliver on such a promise. More likely, Hancock was fence-sitting so as to make sure he came down on the winning side. He must also have been aware that Samuel Adams's initial inclination to oppose ratification had been altered by a visit from proratification Boston tradesmen. Hancock's own career as a merchant may have influenced his perspective, as altruistic and political calculations may have as well.

"Considering the great disorders, which took place in this State the last winter, and considering the great influence that the spirit which then reigned has had since," Benjamin Lincoln reflected, "and, considering, also, that when we came together a very decided majority of the Convention were against adopting the Constitution," he believed, "we have got through the business pretty well."[35] As always, Lincoln was a realist; and, with Federalists and Antifederalists alike, he quickly moved to close the wound on the body politic and draw a curtain over the scar that remained. When the voting was finished, generous speeches came from both sides, and a great ball was given in Boston to which all delegates were invited. Harmony was an old Massachusetts ideal, and though there might be an undertone of cant, the act of closing ranks in a display of patriotism served everyone's interest. People would not immediately forget the hard words and actions of 1786 and 1787, but in public they could pretend to, and in time reality would catch up. The fact that the economy brightened in 1788 and 1789 helped, as did the national government's system of assuming state debts and refinancing them with impost duties. As a result, though east-west divisions were never entirely erased, the battle over the Constitution represented the end of a pattern of polarization dividing Massachusetts, not the beginning of the Federalist-Jeffersonian split.[36]

In the context of the 1790s Daniel Shays, condemned to die for treason during the height of the repression, quickly became an object of pathos. When the Salem clergyman William Bentley visited the Reverend Bezaleel Howard in Springfield in August 1793, Howard showed his guest "the place where Col. Sheppard stationed his regiment when he fired upon Shay's and the ground over which he [Shays] so precipitately retreated." Already it had become a historic site for tourists. Shays himself was becoming a legendary figure: "There is a general opinion of the true courage of this unhappy man," Bentley reported, and, indeed, it was said that at Deerfield "about 10 days before our arrival he was openly begging from house and after several days gained eleven dollars from such as had favored his party."[37] Shays was no longer a threat to anyone; he was merely a beggar. By this time the Federalist historian George Richards Minot had already published *A*

---

35. Lincoln to George Washington, Boston, Feb. 9, 1788, *Debates and Proceedings*, 409. For clarity the order of Lincoln's phrases is slightly altered; the meaning is unchanged.

36. Hall, *Politics without Parties*, 286–287, 292, 321. See also Oscar Handlin and Mary F. Handlin, "Radicals and Conservatives in Massachusetts after Independence," *NEQ*, XVII (1944), 343–355; Sidney Kaplan, "Veteran Officers and Politics in Massachusetts," *WMQ*, 3d Ser., IX (1952), 29–57.

37. *The Diary of William Bentley* . . . , II (1907; rpt., Gloucester, Mass., 1962), 58.

History of the Insurrections, which described the Shaysites with sympathy as well as condescension.[38] The rebellion was being integrated into the Federalist history of republican success. The fact that the Shays movement and its repression had mobilized a wave of Antifederalism that had nearly blocked the ratification of the Constitution in the crucial state of Massachusetts was conveniently forgotten.

Today, however, as we consider the seemingly inevitable Constitution of 1787, it is worth remembering that, though Shays's Rebellion assisted its creation and its ratification in some states, in Massachusetts the heavy-handed repression of the rebellion created a nearly disastrous backlash against the Constitution. The apparently vindictive and insensitive way in which the central government in Boston had disfranchised and prosecuted the Shaysites after their surrender awakened all the traditional Whig fears and suspicions about the dangers of a powerful, distant government. The multitude of inland farmers had not been Shaysites, but in light of what they had witnessed recently, any national government—even one as limited as that proposed in the Constitution—provoked an anxiety and antipathy that very nearly sank the ratification movement. And had the Constitution failed to win Massachusetts' support, it would probably have been doomed in Virginia and New York. Under these conditions the Constitution would have become just another failed reform—a well-intended, brilliantly conceived and crafted dead letter.

38. George Richards Minot, *A History of the Insurrections, in Massachusetts, in the Year 1786, and the Rebellion Consequent Thereon* (Worcester, Mass., 1788).

☆ ☆ ☆ ☆ ☆

Money, Credit, and Federalist Political Economy

JANET A. RIESMAN

Article I, Section 10: No State shall . . . coin Money; emit Bills of Credit; make anything but gold and silver Coin a Tender in payment of Debts; pass any Bill of Attainder, ex post facto Law, or Law impairing the Obligation of Contracts . . .

I

It is well known that members of the Constitutional Convention disapproved of the state paper emissions of 1785 and 1786, but the reasons for their disapproval and for the sweeping provisions incorporated in Article I, Section 10, of the Federal Constitution are obscure. Those provisions can be understood only as the culmination of a decade-long, at times acrimonious debate about how to retire the debt spawned during the American Revolutionary war.

The debate was acrimonious for many reasons. The American war debt piled up with speed—and debt had always been an anathema to whiggish believers in independence. Depreciating securities appeared to encourage behavior ill becoming the virtuous citizens of a republic and thereby threatened to unhinge the very fabric of society. Americans came to fear that their debt might destroy the Republic before it ever became firmly established. By 1787, the reality of their difficulties made the hopes and expectations of 1775 and 1776 distant indeed.

In the first years of the Revolution, Americans had shared extravagant hopes for their Republic. Then, they not only intended to create a new form of government, a republic, but they also were confident of being able to demonstrate to the world that republics could achieve for each citizen a level of prosperity and happiness unparalleled in history. This faith was rooted in Americans' astonishment both over their prosperity and over the rapid rise in their population beginning around 1750. Benjamin Franklin and J. Hector St. John de Crèvecoeur had been among the first to claim that America was different from Europe because it was more fertile and offered unparalleled opportunities for the ordinary person to prosper, to marry young, and to have children blessed at birth with republican prosperity.[1] This sense of extraordinary potential endured through the Revolutionary crisis and was a favorite subject for sermons and exhortations. During the quarrel with Britain, Samuel Williams, an obscure Congregational minister from Bradford, Massachusetts, reminded his parishioners: America "bids the fairest of any to promote *the perfection and happiness of mankind.* . . . Our soil is adapted to the most useful kinds of produce; and our situation is not unfriendly to commerce." On the eve of the Constitutional Convention, Hugh Williamson, North Carolina's delegate to the Continental Congress, predicted that Americans stood at the crossroads of history and, with the proper frame of government, would swiftly become the "most flourishing, independent and happy" country on earth.[2]

Yet, if anything seemed to cloud the attainment of just the sort of prosperity that Americans dreamed of, it was debt. A country saddled with enormous public debt was surely on the brink of ruin. It was debt that in most American eyes gnawed at the heart of the English constitution, and it was the frightening possibility of contracting a huge public debt that lurked

1. For an analysis of eighteenth-century concepts of happiness and prosperity, see Janet A. Riesman, "The Origins of American Political Economy, 1690-1781" (Ph.D. diss., Brown University, 1983), 1-15; on Americans' perceptions of their land's internal fertility, see 223-293. Benjamin Franklin, "Observations concerning the Increase of Mankind . . . ," in Leonard W. Labaree *et al.,* eds., *The Papers of Benjamin Franklin* (New Haven, Conn., 1961-), IV, 227-234; J. Hector St. John de Crèvecoeur, "What Is an American?" in *Letters from an American Farmer* (1782; New York, Signet ed., 1963), 60-99; Alexander Hamilton, *A Full Vindication of the Measures of the Congress* . . . , in Harold C. Syrett *et al.,* eds., *The Papers of Alexander Hamilton* (New York, 1961-), I, 45-78. See also Edward Wigglesworth, *Calculations on American Population* . . . (Boston, 1775), 1-2.

2. Samuel Williams, *A Discourse on the Love of Our Country* . . . (Salem, Mass., 1775), 22-23; [Hugh Williamson], *Letters from Sylvius to the Freemen Inhabitants of the United States* . . . (New York, 1787), 2. For other examples of such sentiments, see Ezra Stiles, *The United States Elevated to Glory and Honor* . . . (New Haven, Conn., 1783), in John Wingate Thornton, ed., *The Pulpit of the American Revolution; or, The Political Sermons of the Period of 1776* (Boston, 1860), 403-440, 458-459, 472; and [Benjamin Thurston], *Address to the Public, Containing Some Remarks on the Present Political State of the American Republicks* . . . (Exeter, N.H., [1786]), 32, 35. Samuel Wales's sermon, *The Dangers of Our National Prosperity; and the Way to Avoid Them* (Hartford, Conn., 1785), is a particularly poignant expression of the dashed hopes of the "critical period"; see esp. 11-19.

dangerously behind any plans for war. This was the irony and danger of the Revolution. Would the act of fighting the war create a debt that would undermine the very republican liberties being fought for?

In 1776 American whigs believed wholeheartedly that the Revolution could be won in short order and that debt could thereby be avoided. No one wanted even to contemplate the unhappy possibility that the first burden the young Republic would face after the battles ceased would be an insurmountable public debt. So the Revolutionaries began the war confident that the provisions of what has subsequently been labeled "currency finance" would adequately provide the country with the money to pay soldiers and buy supplies. But circumstances conspired differently: Americans did not have the sources of British specie, credit, and patronage on which they depended so heavily during the French and Indian War, and the War for Independence lasted longer than most anticipated—not a few months, but seven years. The only thing to do, it seemed, was, in the colorful words of E. James Ferguson, to stuff "the maw of . . . Revolution with paper money" and to lean on the states, the only bodies with the power to tax, to drain the worthless stuff out of circulation. Nevertheless, the debt grew rapidly. By 1779, the Continental Congress had emitted at least $226,200,000 in paper bills, yet only $12,897,575 had been redeemed in taxes. While the Congress fretted constantly about the difficulties of getting the states to meet their quotas, the states were in the same predicament. Some $209,524,776 had been emitted by state governments, but only a small fraction of that amount had been redeemed. Thus the United States was some $450,000,000 in debt with little hope of easily and expediently retiring it.[3]

3. The congressional figures are from E. James Ferguson, *The Power of the Purse: A History of American Public Finance, 1776-1790* (Chapel Hill, N.C., 1961), 28-35. If one includes state credits for specie payments and goods valued in specie, then the states' payments to Congress total a bit more— $13,840,912. The state figures are from Byron W. Holt, "Continental Currency," *Sound Currency*, V (1898), 109-111. Holt suggests that the amounts actually issued exceeded those authorized. Some bills were counterfeited, of course; but the Treasury Department, under pressure of demand from the Commissary Department, may have issued more bills than were requisitioned by Congress. Thus, Holt's older work raises the possibility that $350,000,000 may be a more exact figure than Ferguson's $226,200,000. Holt was unable to determine the amount of emissions made by the states during the 1770s, because nearly half the state treasury records from the early years of the war are missing as well as those from the years believed to have witnessed the most extensive printing of state paper money—1778 and 1779. If records from several states known to have made substantial emissions (Massachusetts, Maryland, Delaware, and the Carolinas) were complete, the recorded emissions would no doubt be much higher than Holt's estimate. In fact, a complete set of records would likely show that the

It was unsettling enough to be saddled with such a huge debt in such a short time, but before the Revolutionaries could even begin to analyze the scope of debt, the social impact of the consequent inflation commanded their attention. The very presence of large quantities of paper money in circulation tempted people to speculate in depreciating currencies and in goods needed by the army. Before the first year of Revolution was over, many once virtuous citizens, so it seemed, were alarmingly on their way to becoming sharpers and swindlers of the worst sort. The speed with which such transformations occurred amazed everyone from members of Congress to country parsons in scattered towns and villages. "Publicola," a writer in the *Connecticut Journal*, feared famine at the hands of extortioners; another writer, in New Jersey, claimed that poor farmers left their fields unattended and went off to fight while others "bask[ed] in the sunshine of monopoly, forestalling and extortion"; yet another correspondent in Boston decried the "greediness of avaricious . . . sharpers, forestallers, [and] mushroom traders . . . all of whom have been, and still are, outdoing one another in raising the price of everything."[4]

The better sort who presumed leadership in the Revolutionary crisis were most frightened by these developments. It was difficult for such gentlemen to condone the bustling, market-oriented shrewdness of new traders and market farmers, for there still was plenty of weighty, learned tradition that held that shuffling goods in the domestic market and making a profit on price differentials did not create real wealth, but was merely speculative, self-serving, and nonproductive. Noah Webster's reflections on the fruits of this new sort of speculative wholesaling and retailing were among the most disillusioned. "The first visible effect of an augmentation of the medium and the consequent fluctuation of value," he wrote, "was, a host of jockeys, who

---

amount of state paper money in circulation by the 1780s far exceeded that of continental money. At the least, it can be reasonably estimated that, by the early 1780s, four hundred to five hundred million dollars in both state and continental bills had entered circulation and that the bulk of these bills remained unredeemed. Thomas Paine also addressed the debate about how to finance the Revolutionary war; see [Thomas Paine], *Common Sense*, 3d ed. (Philadelphia, Feb. 14, 1776), in Philip S. Foner, ed., *The Complete Writings of Thomas Paine* (New York, 1945), I, 31–39.

4. "Senex Consilium," *Hartford Courant*, Apr. 17, 1775; *Connecticut Journal*, Nov. 26, 1777; and "S.M.," *Boston Gazette*, Apr. 6, Dec. 21, 1778, cited in Ralph Harlow, "Economic Conditions in Massachusetts during the American Revolution," Colonial Society of Massachusetts, *Transactions*, XX (1918), 176. For other examples of such opinions, see "To the Public," *Norwich Packet*, Oct. 14–21, 1776; "Moses and the Prophets," *Continental Journal*, Feb. 13, 1777; a jeremiad by a writer in Newburyport, Mass., *Continental Journal*, Feb. 20, 1777; "Publicola," *Connecticut Journal*, Mar. 5, 1777; *New Jersey Gazette*, June 10, 1779.

followed a species of itinerant commerce; and subsisted upon . . . the difference in the value of the currency, in different places." He calculated that twenty thousand or so had "left honest callings, and applied themselves to this knavish traffic." He worried that "a sudden augmentation of currency" had "flattered people with the prospect of accumulating property without labor."[5]

Despite the universal outcry in newspapers, private letters, and sermons about the disintegration of republican behavior and the rapidly collapsing dream of a happy land of prosperous republicans, there was no agreement concerning what actions should be taken to rescue the Republic. The rising prices of nearly every commodity requested by the army meant that wheelbarrows of money would soon be needed to meet exorbitant costs. Clearly the tenets of "currency finance" were no longer appropriate. Those in the Continental Congress who eventually became nationalists realized that they could not afford drastically to curtail the supply of money when money was constantly needed to pay troops and buy huge quantities of food, clothing, and ammunition. Some other theory of finance was called for—one that would ensure a constant and undisturbed flow of stable money.

Given the difficulties posed by fighting a long and arduous war with strained resources, gentlemen in Congress were predisposed to believe that some way had to be found to determine just how much money was necessary for the needs of trade during wartime. Thus, by the late fall of 1776, John Adams, John Sergeant, Benjamin Rush, and others were persuaded by the theory, common in Britain in the 1750s and 1760s, that money—especially paper forms of money—ought to be held in balance with the needs of trade in order to circulate at par. That theory—an Enlightenment version of the quantity theory—had been espoused by George Berkeley and Josiah Tucker and later modified by David Hume and Robert Wallace. These English and Scottish writers believed that the economic world was quite simple and could readily be explained if all economic phenomena were thought of as determined by a delicate balance between goods at market and money in circulation. Prices, in particular, were set by this ratio. If there was too much money in circulation in relation to goods, prices rose; if the quantity of money was less than the goods at market, prices fell. With prices rising rapidly during the Revolution, many gentlemen in and out of Congress quickly came to believe that these ideas contained the solution to their country's current ills. "The value of money" was maintained, said Pelatiah Webster, a prominent financial theorist in Philadelphia, by "the proportion be-

5. Quoted in Albert Bolles, *The Financial History of the United States from 1774 to 1789...*, 4th ed. (1896; rpt., New York, 1971), 210.

tween the medium of trade and the objects of trade."[6] But in the 1770s, there was so much money in circulation that money had lost value and thrown all trade out of balance. All Congress needed to do, it seemed, in order to restore the balance between money and goods, was to insist that the states diligently retire their quotas of debt. Only then would it be possible to reduce the quantity of money to the precise levels appropriate for the needs of war, and only then would the dangerous inflation be halted.

Still, no one knew exactly how much money ought to be removed by taxation from circulation, how great the needs of trade actually were, or how to measure them. The careful balance could be restored only by gradual adjustment and constant monitoring; those persuaded by this point of view knew that they would recognize a healthy economy when they saw one. The evidence of a restored equilibrium would be unmistakable: monopolizing and hoarding—having been rendered ineffective—would disappear, and trade would proceed with smooth regularity. "When the value of money is fixed and can be kept so," Pelatiah Webster advised, "it is in the *most perfect state* its nature is capable of, and does, in the *most perfect manner*, answer all the purposes and uses which are desired or expected from it."[7] As a result, traders would come to trust the value of the money they received in trade, and men would no longer put up their prices as a hedge against depreciation.

Yet, as inflation continued in 1779 and 1780, these views collapsed rapidly. Taxation efforts continually failed, and demands for money escalated; prices showed no signs of diminishing. Perhaps most frightening was the growing awareness among gentlemen of pockets of deep alienation among the people. Popular conventions, which met with increasing frequency to set prices at pre-Revolutionary levels, declined to invite gentlemen to their proceedings. In cities like Philadelphia and Boston and outlying market towns like Lancaster, Pennsylvania, independent artisans and craftsmen became startlingly obstreperous about protecting their profits and ignored the entreaties for lower prices from local customers and from hardpressed army commissariats. Many in the Continental Congress disapproved heartily of price-fixing, which they believed would cause greater hoarding and disruption of the market.[8] What seemed clearest, as the country sank

6. Pelatiah Webster, "An Essay on Free Trade and Finance" (July 1779), in Pelatiah Webster, *Political Essays on the Nature and Operation of Money, Public Finances, and Other Subjects* . . . (Philadelphia, [1791]), 14. For a more extensive discussion of the quantity theory, see Riesman, "Origins of American Political Economy," 23-87, 350-367.

7. Pelatiah Webster, "A Third Essay on Free Trade and Finance" (Jan. 8, 1780), in Webster, *Political Essays*, 53.

8. The best account of the movement to fix wages and prices is Richard B. Morris,

into the despair of late 1779, was that the quantity theory was not the panacea it once seemed. So rapidly were ideas about the economy changing in the crucible of the Revolution that, whereas the quantity theory held sway in England for nearly twenty-five years, in America it lasted only three years —from the fall of 1776 to the fall of 1779. "The quantity of money in circulation is certainly a chief cause of its decline," Hamilton wrote late in December 1779, "but we find it is depreciated more than five times as much as it ought to be by this rule." Since it had depreciated at a rate that was not proportionate to the amount of money placed in circulation, it followed that the quantity of money, in and of itself, was not the only factor affecting the rate of depreciation or the value of money in circulation. There must, concluded Hamilton, be other causes at work that explained the collapse of America's paper currency.[9]

Government and Labor in Early America, 2d ed. (Boston, 1981), 92-135. See also William Graham Sumner, *The Financier and the Finances of the American Revolution* (New York, 1891), I, 51-85; Ralph Volney Harlow, "Aspects of Revolutionary Finance, 1775-1783," *American Historical Review*, XXXV (1929-1930), esp. 57-59; Anne Bezanson, "Inflation and Controls, Pennsylvania, 1774-1779," *Journal of Economic History*, VIII (1948), Supplement, esp. 15-17. The proceedings of the various state conventions have been collected and published in the appendix of Charles J. Hoadly *et al.*, eds., *The Public Records of the State of Connecticut, [1776-1803]* (Hartford, Conn., 1894-), I; see 585-620. Benjamin Rush, James Wilson, John Witherspoon, and John Adams all disdained price regulations. See Edmund C. Burnett, ed., *Letters of Members of the Continental Congress* (Washington, D.C., 1921-1936), II, 250-252; John Adams to Abigail Adams, Feb. 7, 1777, John Adams to James Warren, Feb. 12, 1777, II, 237, 248-249; John Witherspoon to William Churchill Houston, Jan. 27, 1778, III, 57. On popular attitudes about prices and trade, see Eric Foner, *Tom Paine and Revolutionary America* (New York, 1976), 172-182; John K. Alexander, "The Fort Wilson Incident of 1779: A Case Study of the Revolutionary Crowd," *William and Mary Quarterly*, 3d Ser., XXXI (1974), 589-612; "Mobility," "A Hint," *Pennsylvania Packet*, Dec. 8, 1778; *At a General Meeting of the Citizens of Philadelphia* (Philadelphia, [1779]), broadside for May 25, 1779; Bolles, *Financial History*, I, 163-164; and Jerome H. Wood, Jr., *Conestoga Crossroads: Lancaster, Pennsylvania, 1730-1790* (Harrisburg, Pa., 1979), 144-156.

9. Alexander Hamilton to ———, [Dec. 1779-Mar. 1780?], in Syrett *et al.*, eds., *Papers of Hamilton*, II, 242. See also *Considerations on the Subject of Finance* [Philadelphia, 1779], 4-5. Writing in 1786, John Witherspoon recalled the "opinion often expressed during the war, that depreciation must have been owing to other causes than the quantity, because it was greater than . . . natural depreciation" ("Essays on Money," in John Witherspoon, *The Works of John Witherspoon, D.D.* [Edinburgh, 1805], IX, 33). [Gouverneur Morris], *Letters on Appreciation* [Philadelphia, 1780], 2, 18-20, disagreed with Hamilton's interpretation and worried that various schemes favored in 1779 and 1780 would artificially appreciate paper currency.

In the fall of 1779 and the spring of 1780, many of the leading minds in the Continental Congress returned to the traditional opinion that specie was critical to value and, in turn, to the health of circulation and so ultimately a key ingredient in the long-range prosperity of the young Republic. Americans began to recognize that—in their fascination with the quantity theory—they had forgotten that specie, as Locke once argued, possessed intrinsic value and, as the source of value, must of necessity be the only basis for a currency. James Madison argued this position in one of the most remarkable economic treatises of the new decade. Yet, when Madison and others of like mind considered specie, they did so in a new light. They combined modern insights about the market gained from the experience of topsy-turvy conditions in the late 1770s with a reassertion of faith in specie. The result was a peculiarly Enlightenment, progressive vision of the economy—indeed the first American political economy.

II

In a rigorous and analytical essay written in the winter of 1779–1780, before he entered Congress for the first time, James Madison wrought a complex vision of specie that summed up older thinking and carried it forward into the 1780s. Madison argued that depreciation arose from a single cause: lack of confidence in a government's ability to redeem its paper currencies in specie. Madison asserted that previous writers had been wrong to dismiss the fact that specie commanded special importance as a source of value; to ignore that fact in creating a financial plan was folly. His analysis of why specie was critical demonstrated a subtle perception of aggregate market forces that surpassed both in complexity and profundity the observations of his contemporaries.

Madison began his essay "Money" by assuming that specie would be used wherever it bought the most, since it had "universal value." Specie never allowed itself to be devalued in trade; it always tended to "assimilate itself" to those countries or regions where its value in exchange was greatest. Madison then proceeded to demonstrate that both prices and inflation could not be accounted for by the quantity theory. That theory did not even hold true for specie. The value of specie, Madison explained, always had to be considered in relation to a complex set of variables, at the center of which was demand—something that had not been the focus of previous concern among members of Congress. When a country's prices were very high, Madison continued, the reason for the high prices was that demand for goods in that country outran the supply. Even if that land had a high quantity of specie, people would not in effect devalue their specie and "waste it" by buying in a land where "extravagant prices" prevailed. Instead, people would spend it where it bought the most and would take their money elsewhere. If, on the converse, a country's prices were very low, Madison then reasoned, that was simply because the number of goods outran the demand. Even if that country had a small quantity of specie, the value of the specie would not thereby appreciate in trade. Because specie was always spent where it was most valued, its value was always determined by worldwide demand. The natural and inexorable logic that determined people's market behavior operated to keep the value of specie constant and, in fact, helped to reaffirm that value over and over again. Since the level of prices in the market did not affect the value of specie, and since the value of specie was not in turn affected by the level of prices, Madison concluded that the quantity of specie did not explain or was not related to specie's value and that other explanations for the level of prices must be sought.

Once he had established that crucial point, Madison then proceeded with the core of his argument as it pertained to America's dilemma in 1779 and 1780. He asserted that the value of paper money depended only on one thing—the length of time that elapsed between its emission and its redemption in specie. He attributed the country's ills to popular lack of confidence in the government's ability to redeem its paper currency. With so much paper in circulation, it was easy to see why some attributed its loss of value solely to the excess quantities of it in circulation. But Madison was not persuaded. The quantity of money in circulation, he agreed, contributed to money's loss of value, but not in the way most people supposed. Madison aimed to demonstrate that reductions of the quantity of money would trigger an economic process that few had understood or envisioned. Once paper money began to be redeemed, prices of goods would fall. With lower prices for goods, specie would buy more in America and so would return to the country, giving strength and confidence to every obligation and contract. Large numbers of emissions, however, only added to the burden of currency that the government was expected to redeem. As the amount became greater, the length of time required to redeem it became greater. People had lost confidence that the government would ever have the strength to redeem it, and paper money came to be seen as representing nothing but an empty or illusory promise. That was the reason, Madison concluded, that it had depreciated.[10]

Although Madison provided a highly abstract and theoretical vision of

10. James Madison, "Money," [Sept. 1779–Mar. 1780], in William T. Hutchinson *et al.*, eds., *The Papers of James Madison* (Chicago, Charlottesville, 1962–), I, 302–310. This essay was later published in Philip Freneau's *National Gazette* (Philadelphia), Dec. 19, 22, 1791.

how specie behaved in the market, others contributed more practical suggestions about how to use direct infusions of hard currency to restore public credit immediately. Several writers—among them Gouverneur Morris, Alexander Hamilton, and the anonymous Pennsylvania essayist "Aristides"—warned, however, against using specie either to redeem old Continental bills or to purchase supplies. Pouring specie into circulation for such purposes, they argued, might create a monstrous speculation in supplies or in depreciated bills. If paper bills appreciated sharply and artificially, they would be hoarded and cease to circulate. Still deprived of a currency, the country would continue to suffer from inflation, and large quantities of paper money would be needed to meet the high expense of war.[11] It was these fears of jerking the economy into too rapid a recovery by pouring specie into circulation that led financially sophisticated thinkers in Congress to argue that specie now must be used differently. Specie had to be as a rock—stable, eternal, and always present. From this new understanding arose the fascination in Congress in the 1780s with banking. Between 1779 and 1781, Hamilton, Philadelphia lawyer William Barton, Robert Morris, Thomas Paine, Robert Livingston, a congressional committee headed by Timothy Matlack, and a host of anonymous writers urged the establishment of a national bank on a fund of specie. A financial system, they argued, ought to be created that used specie to build public confidence. A plan that tended to dissipate specie into the hands of speculators and monopolizers would neither improve the financial state of the country nor help the country pay off its growing public debt.[12]

11. Alexander Hamilton to ———, [Dec. 1779-Mar. 1780?], in Syrett *et al.*, eds., *Papers of Hamilton*, II, 240-242; Alexander Hamilton to James Duane, Sept. 3, 1780, *ibid.*, II, 412-417; "Aristides," "A Plan," *Philadelphia Packet*, Jan. 4, 1780; "Proceedings and Observations of the Committee of Finance, November 1780," in Burnett, ed., *Letters of Members of Congress*, V, 469-470.

12. Alexander Hamilton to ———, [Dec. 1779-Mar. 1780?], in Syrett *et al.*, eds., *Papers of Hamilton*, II, 242-251; William Barton, *Observations on the Nature and Use of Paper-Credit* . . . (Philadelphia, 1781), 22, 24-40; [Thomas Paine], *American Crisis*, IX (June 9, 1780), in Foner, ed., *Writings of Paine*, I, 169-170; Robert Morris, "Plan for Establishing a National Bank, with Observations," May 17, 1781, in E. James Ferguson and John Catanzariti, eds., *The Papers of Robert Morris, 1781-1784* (Pittsburgh, Pa., 1973-), I, 66-74. See also the following correspondence in Burnett, ed., *Letters of Members of Congress*, V: Elbridge Gerry to Robert Morris, June 11, 1780, 205-206; Robert R. Livingston to Philip Schuyler, June 16, 1780, 220; James Madison to Thomas Jefferson, June 23, 1780, 235; Ezekial Cornell to the Governor of Rhode Island (William Greene), June 27, 1780, 239; John Witherspoon to the Governor of New Jersey (William Livingston), Dec. 16, 1780, 487; John Sullivan to George Washington, Jan. 29, 1781, 548; and Jesse Root to the

Members of the Committee on Finance in Congress had, at times, radical expectations about the way specie might be used by the bank. Having warned that specie thrown into circulation would "Soon make its way to nations . . . which hold the Ballance of Trade against us," they argued that a bank could act like a "vortex for Drawing all the money" together. Contrary to Madison, who, in fact, consistently opposed the idea of the bank, the committee was convinced that specie should not become part of the circulating medium, but should be used in a new way to uphold a constantly circulating paper currency. Following this logic, they insisted that specie should never be used to redeem bills, buy supplies, or settle foreign debts. It should rarely, if ever, be paid out to anyone. Instead, it should be kept inviolate as an everlasting emblem of public credit. The circulating currency of the country should consist primarily of bank notes, personal notes, and the Continental currency, whose value would be resurrected by the establishment of the bank and guaranteed by the specie it held in its vaults.[13]

In its understanding of how a bank might use specie, the committee rested its plans on fabricating an illusion of confidence. It intended that bank notes and, indeed, the country's entire circulating currency ought to be redeemable in specie. The members presumed that anyone could present the currency of the country to the bank for immediate payment in specie. Since they also supposed these demands would occur only a handful of times, they assumed the bank's specie resources would remain undisturbed. It was on this acute sense of the laws of probability that they based their faith in an instrumental use of specie. When one or two people tested the character and integrity of the bank by demanding immediate redemption of its notes and the bank in turn dutifully fulfilled its obligation, news of its solidity would travel fast.

Once the bank had passed this test, bank supporters argued, it was unlikely that many more people would take the initiative to redeem the notes. Interest payments on the notes of March 1780 (issued when the Congress repudiated all the old Continental bills for new ones at a ratio of forty

---

Governor of Connecticut (Jonathan Trumbull), Jan. 8, 29, 1781, 520-521, 547. See also Burnett, ed., *Letters of Members of Congress*, V, 464-472, for the deliberations of the Matlack Committee, "Proceedings and Observations of the Committee of Finance." John Mathews, John Sullivan, Theodorick Bland, and Abraham Clark, delegates to the Continental Congress and members of the committee, all made recommendations for a bank.

13. "Proceedings and Observations of the Committee of Finance," in Burnett, ed., *Letters of Members of Congress*, V, 469-470. Madison voted against the bank; see Worthington Chauncey Ford *et al.*, eds., *Journals of the Continental Congress* (Washington, D.C., 1904-1937), XX, 546-547.

to one) would induce people to hang on to their money. Investors would tend not to redeem many notes; if they did, they would lose all subsequent interest payments. The bank need not worry about making a promise to redeem notes on demand, because there would be no advantage in surrendering them. Thus the interest payments would work to keep the notes in circulation and so discourage abrupt demands for redemption in specie. In this fashion, the interest payments themselves would also help protect the specie reserves of the bank.[14]

Those in Congress who drafted plans for the bank hoped to establish a fund of specie by inviting stockholders to deposit their coin or plate in the bank. Once the specie had been collected, bank notes would be issued on the basis of this specie fund. The priority of the bank would be to lend money to Congress. Since Congress would be guaranteed a direct source of money from the bank, it would no longer be necessary for Congress to print its own unsecured paper money to support the war. And, since the notes could always be redeemed with specie on demand, once the notes entered the stream of circulation, they would not depreciate. Thus, the difficulties of financing the war experienced in the 1770s would be avoided. In the absence of depreciation, prices would remain steady, monopolies would disappear, and trade would become free and vigorous. No uncontrolled and frightening escalation of prices would take place, and Congress would never again be compelled to flood the country with cash just to keep abreast of rising costs of war. Furthermore, the Congress would be forever absolved of its once complete and abject dependence on the willingness or unwillingness of the states to enact rigorous taxation in order to support the credit of congressional emissions.

The second, perhaps more extensive, task for the bank was to endow the money already in circulation with enough credit to enable it to pass in trade once again. Those who expected the most from the bank hoped even that

---

14. Hamilton to ———, [Dec. 1779-Mar. 1780?], in Syrett *et al.*, eds., *Papers of Hamilton*, II, 247; and Hamilton to Duane, Sept. 3, 1780, II, 415. Of all his contemporaries, Hamilton made the most exacting analysis of banking; see Alexander Hamilton to Robert Morris, Apr. 30, 1781, *ibid.*, 621-631, esp. 623-624. For similar opinions, see Robert Morris to Benjamin Franklin, July 13, 1781, and Robert Morris to John Jay, July 13, 1781, in Ferguson and Catanzariti, eds., *Papers of Robert Morris*, I, 283, 288; Barton, *Observations on Paper-Credit*, 22-25. On the congressional measure of Mar. 18, 1780, designed to revalue Continental currency at 40 to 1 (and thus to acknowledge the reality of depreciation), see Ferguson, *Power of the Purse*, 51-56. For further discussion of the bank and its distinctive difference from the Bank of England, see Riesman, "Origins of American Political Economy," 389-433, and the sources cited therein.

the credit of Continental currency repudiated at forty to one would be revived. Hamilton, in fact, made specific proposals for reestablishing the worth of those old notes. They could be used to purchase the new bank notes, which, Hamilton said, ought to bear an interest of 2 percent payable in specie and be fully redeemable in specie at the end of three years. The possibility of exchanging old notes for new ones that paid 2 percent interest and were redeemable in specie would revive even the most depreciated currency and make it a viable medium once again. Although not everyone had the high hopes Hamilton did of resurrecting the old Continental currency, most expected that the bank would, at least, support the new emissions authorized on March 18, 1780. The Bank of North America expected to take responsibility for guaranteeing the interest payments and the redemption on demand in specie of these new bills. Again, it was believed that the illusion of solidity and credit was as good as credit itself. Therefore, the mere promise to redeem any of these notes—even though few people demanded redemption—would make them readily acceptable in trade. There would be no need to retire them from circulation.[15]

These proposals appear quite simple, and the logic behind them appears quite straightforward. But, in fact, they represented a revolutionary departure from old ways of thinking about paper money. The circulation of all these notes was not seen as dependent upon the promise of eventually withdrawing all of them from circulation by taxation or redeeming them sooner or later with specie. Indeed, Morris and others who founded the bank had no intention of ever extinguishing all emissions. Because the currency was supported by imaginative and overlapping plans—all designed to foster confidence—it would be able to stay in circulation indefinitely. There was no longer any need to guarantee that paper currency would be retired in order to give each individual note credit. Redemptions were, in effect, only for show—to reassure people of the integrity of the bank. What was more, the bank also established credit without relying specifically on the tenets of the quantity theory. The idea, so often expressed even late in the 1770s, that withdrawal of excess quantities of money would raise the value of the money remaining in circulation, was overthrown. Value depended upon careful management of the bank, not upon money's relation in the market to the "needs of trade"—the favorite but ill-defined formula of the quantity theorists.

Those who conceived the bank, however, intended to do more than ame-

15. Robert Morris to the Public, May 28, 1781, in Ferguson and Catanzariti, eds., *Papers of Robert Morris*, I, 84–86; Alexander Hamilton to Robert Morris, Apr. 30, 1781, in Syrett *et al.*, eds., *Papers of Hamilton*, II, 627–630.

liorate the financial woes of the 1770s. It is a measure of their utopian hopes for prosperity in the young Republic that they conceived of the bank as the engine that would revolutionize the old colonial economy, preserve it from the excesses of the 1770s—from speculation and the sale and resale of goods needed by the army—and foster the sort of productivity eighteenth-century political economists dreamed of. It was this vision of the extraordinary potential of the internal resources of America that made their plan so revolutionary.

It would be a mistake to consider the Bank of North America just an updated version of a simple colonial silver bank, cautiously restraining its paper issues to conform to the value of its stock in hand. Instead, as it gained the confidence of the people, the new bank intended to expand the circulation of its notes more and more rapidly. Specie would become the pump that would activate the productive energies of the whole country. When begun in the 1780s, it was hoped that the care with which the bank was planned would command respect and that its notes would be trusted immediately. Then the bank would build upon that initial trust to revive industriousness and reinvigorate internal exchange. As the energy and productiveness of the country improved, the bank's opportunities to acquire specie would be enhanced. Since it would be more attractive for an investor to lend his specie for interest to the bank than to retain it in his own hands, he would willingly seek to deposit whatever specie he received in the bank. Morris and others also anticipated that additional specie might be acquired from abroad—either from loans or from a newly resumed overseas trade. With new sources of specie, the bank's stock would begin to grow; as a consequence, confidence in that institution would be reaffirmed. As the bank's specie stock expanded, the bank would issue more notes. Since new notes would be entirely backed by specie, they would command as much respect as the initial issues and pass at par. Because they would circulate as readily as the first issues, they would boost the extent of internal trade. As those notes spread throughout the country, internal trade would expand, and the process of growth would repeat itself. Again, merchants who acquired specie in trade would promptly offer that specie to the bank for investment. And again the bank's specie fund would be increased and new notes issued.

Those who favored the bank expected that this process would recur, and, as it did, the reputation of the bank would be firmly established. At some point in the future, when the bank's reputation was secure and the process of growth predictable and steady, the notes could be issued in tandem or even faster than the bank accumulated stock. Once "the Capital" was "put in Motion," said Morris, "the Benefits" that flowed from the bank would be so great that no one would object to "Encreasing the Capital." In other words, there was no reason to limit the number of notes that could be emitted.[16]

Nothing like this had ever been suggested before. Perpetual circulation was to be maintained without taxation, without retirement, and without any fixed limit on the numbers of bills that could be printed. If the plan were successful, America would have its first permanent circulating medium —a medium which would foster the expansion of the Republic's internal prosperity.

III

Robert Morris and other supporters of the bank hoped that it would become a permanent addition to the country's institutions. They anticipated that it would "Continue as long as the United States, and . . . become as usefull to Commerce and Agriculture in the days of Peace" as it would be "to Government During the War."[17] To ensure the permanency of the bank, Morris set to work to give it additional sources of support and to solidify the country's finances. After the bank was chartered, he moved forward on several fronts to make arrangements that would provide the government and the bank with revenues. During 1782, he attempted to reorganize tax collection throughout the country. He dispensed with the old Treasury Board which had managed the finances of the war effort, and he asked the states for new revenues of eight million dollars payable in quarterly installments. He insisted that the states lay taxes to meet these new demands; and, to ensure that they did, he installed tax receivers from among his friends in each state.[18] He also drew up plans for an impost—a 5 percent duty on

16. Robert Morris, "Plan for Establishing a National Bank," May 17, 1781, in Ferguson and Catanzariti, eds., *Papers of Robert Morris*, I, 70; Morris, "Circular on the National Bank," June 11, 1781, *ibid.*, 142–143 (quotation); Morris, "Queries and Answers on the National Bank," July 21, 1781, *ibid.*, 359–362. See also Sumner, *Financier and Finances*, II, 21–27; Clarence L. Ver Steeg, *Robert Morris, Revolutionary Financier, with an Analysis of His Earlier Career* (Philadelphia, 1954), 84–96; Bolles, *Financial History*, I, 292–296; Janet Wilson, "The Bank of North America and Pennsylvania Politics: 1781–1787," *Pennsylvania Magazine of History and Biography*, LXVI (1942), 3–28; Ferguson, *Power of the Purse*, esp. 146–158; Thomas M. Doerflinger, *A Vigorous Spirit of Enterprise: Merchants and Economic Development in Revolutionary Philadelphia* (Chapel Hill, N.C., 1986), 296–310.

17. Robert Morris, "Circular on the Bank," June 11, 1781, in Ferguson and Catanziriti, eds., *Papers of Robert Morris*, I, 143.

18. Ver Steeg, *Robert Morris*, 99–101. Among the friends whom Morris handpicked were Alexander Hamilton for New York, William Houston for New Jersey,

the value of "all goods, wares, and merchandise of foreign growth and manufactures"—which he urged the states to adopt in August 1781.[19] All these measures were designed to enable the bank to meet its interest payments to both stockholders and those who held interest-bearing notes and to enable the government to collect enough funds to return its loans from the bank.

Yet after 1781, Morris was never able to realize his plans as fully as he hoped. He was startled by the hostility that greeted his recommended taxes and the impost. State men suspicious of the growing power of the Continental Congress were convinced that Morris and his associates were bent on undermining state sovereignty. In Rhode Island, David Howell, an ardent defender of local liberties, so persuasively articulated the dangers of an impost to those concerned about protecting the states from outside incursions that legislators in Virginia and New York became alarmed and helped bring the controversial measure to an end. At the height of the Newburgh conspiracy in 1783, Morris became concerned enough about the consequences of the government's inability to pay its debts that he attempted to revive the impost plan, but again it was roundly defeated by increasingly powerful antinationalist groups.[20]

Having weathered the defeat of the impost, Morris cast about for other resources to guarantee the bank a revenue. His faith in America's potential for prosperity was tremendous and was in no way clouded by the country's

---

John Swanwick for Pennsylvania (after David Rittenhouse turned the post down), and George Olney for Rhode Island.

19. Robert Morris to the President of Congress (Thomas McKean), Aug. 6, 28, 1781, in Ferguson and Catanzariti, eds., *Papers of Robert Morris*, II, 25, 124–135, esp. 133. The original act was laid before the Continental Congress on Feb. 3, 1781. See Ver Steeg, *Robert Morris*, 98 (quotation); Ford *et al.*, eds., *Journals of the Continental Congress*, XIX, 112–113. See also Bolles, *Financial History*, 292–297; Ferguson, *Power of the Purse*, esp. 146–158. "Tullius," *Three Letters Addressed to the Public* . . . (Philadelphia, 1783), 23–28, emphatically supported the impost.

20. [David Howell], *Thoughts on the Five Per Cent* (Providence, R.I., 1782), 3–12. In 1782 Robert Morris dispatched Thomas Paine to Rhode Island to defend the integrity of the bank's purposes against Howell's aspersions; see Harry H. Clark, ed., *Six New Letters of Thomas Paine* (Madison, Wis., 1939). See also Ferguson, *Power of the Purse*, 146–168; Bolles, *Financial History*, 292–297. The best account of the battle in Rhode Island over the impost is Irwin H. Polishook, *Rhode Island and the Union, 1774–1795* (Evanston, Ill., 1969), 53–80. But see also John Paul Kaminski, "Paper Politics: The Northern State Loan-Offices during the Confederation, 1783–1790" (Ph.D. diss., University of Wisconsin, 1972), the only work directly concerned with the paper money quarrels of an entire region of the country; for Rhode Island, see 220–280.

current difficulties. He never doubted that the nation was brimming with the dynamic energy of enterprising men like himself, and he saw his task as finding just the right plan to call them into action. In order fully to tap their energies and to counter the forces that seemed to tear apart his proposals, Morris began in the summer of 1782 to develop a plan to enable the bank to make direct loans to leading applicants. The customers for these loans, he hoped, would be the very public creditors who now continually grumbled that the Continental Congress's word was worthless and that its certificates and money were mere scraps of paper. Funding the debt, Morris was convinced, would cause even the most confirmed skeptics to become confident in Continental currency once again and to trust the government's intention to fulfill its obligations.[21]

Morris's rather remarkable optimism is best understood in light of the assumptions that informed his thinking. Like many of his contemporaries, he was fascinated by the financial writings of Richard Price, the radical English Whig, who, in 1772, formulated a plan to retire England's enormous public debt. Price claimed to have discovered the principle of compound interest and proposed using it to accomplish what no English minister in the eighteenth century seemed willing or able to do: extinguish England's controversial and embarrassing debt. Price urged the English government to assume all its old debt issues and reissue them in the form of ordinary interest-bearing stock certificates. Then Price instructed the government to collect taxes and place them in a sinking fund, which could be lent out on short-term interest every year. Because the sinking fund always earned interest and because that interest each year was added anew to the fund, the fund grew geometrically—in other words, at a compound rate. In contrast, the interest paid to stockholders on the public debt was not a compound interest and did not grow geometrically every year. The difference between the interest earned from loans on the sinking fund and the interest paid to holders of the public debt would guarantee a surplus revenue for the government each year. From this growing surplus, greater and greater amounts of the debt could be retired. In time, Price insisted, England's entire debt could be eliminated.[22]

21. Robert Morris to the President of Congress (John Hanson), July 29, 1782, in Ferguson and Catanzariti, eds., *Papers of Robert Morris*, VI, 36-84.

22. Richard Price, *Observations on Reversionary Payments* . . . (London, 1771), and *An Appeal to the Public, on the Subject of the National Debt* (London, 1772). An important caveat in Price's scheme—meant as a rebuke to Sir Robert Walpole—was his instruction that the sinking fund be kept inviolate and not used by government as a supplement or replacement for tax revenues. The best source on America's fascination with Price is Donald F. Swanson, *The Origins of Hamilton's Fiscal Policies*, Uni-

Morris believed his new loan plan would work in a similar way. He intended to collect the current debt of the Continental government and reissue it as loans. The loans would be offered at 6 percent interest payable in ten years and distributed through state loan offices. Then the interest collected on the loans would be gradually used to pay off public creditors.

But that was only half of his plan. The other half revealed his assumptions about the sociology of the economy and demonstrated his enormous faith in America's potential. Funding the debt, he believed, would draw the most enterprising and energetic men to the center of the Republic's effort to promote prosperity. Income on the loaned debt would do more than provide a revenue to pay off old obligations. It would encourage public creditors who had long been "deprived of those Funds . . . necessary to the full Exercise of their Skill and Industry" to return to their various endeavors. With their new confidence that their money would be returned to them, they would willingly borrow from the government to begin new projects. Thus, Morris, like Price, recognized the different earning powers of various funds and how to put that insight to use to support public credit. Lending money would actually help restore the government's finances and pay the debt. "By distributing Property into those hands which could render it most productive," wrote Morris, "the Revenue would be increased, while the original Stock continued the Same." [23]

Once the loan plan was in operation, Morris predicted, the country would miraculously use the process of paying off its debt to advantage. He was convinced that the profits to be made from new investments undertaken by enterprising men would be so great that agriculture and commerce as a whole would be rapidly reinvigorated. The benefits of his plan would spread

---

versity of Florida Monographs: Social Sciences, No. 17 (Gainesville, Fla., 1963). Another 18th-century writer who thought extensively about Price's views on sinking funds was the Englishman Samuel Gale. See his *Essay II: On the Nature and Principles of Publick Credit* (St. Augustine, East-Florida, 1786), 1–50. The essay was probably written in 1783 and demonstrates the complexity of thinking in the 1780s about funding plans.

23. Ferguson and Catanzariti, eds., *Papers of Robert Morris*, VI, 63. For examples of increasing discontent among public creditors, see *To the Citizens of America, Who Are Creditors of the United States* [Philadelphia, 1782], broadside; "A Shorter Catechism," *New York Packet*, Feb. 5, 1784, quoted in John Bach McMaster, *A History of the People of the United States . . .* , I (1883; New York, 1938), 137–138; Ferguson, *Power of the Purse*, 149–150; Ver Steeg, *Robert Morris*, 166–170. The loan offices, which would distribute the new certificates, were created in the late 1770s to issue loan office certificates designed, at the time, to help siphon off excess currency from circulation and carry out the prescriptions of the quantity theory.

prosperity to all corners of the land. As profits for investors increased, sales at domestic markets would rise, and farmers and laborers would benefit from the new buying and selling. The pervasive prosperity would also help generate steady revenues for the bank and the government. In good times, Morris observed, people were willing to pay their taxes punctually, since in general the tax burden seemed lighter. Attitudes toward taxes affected attitudes toward government; with an easier tax burden, Morris anticipated that the quarrels and contentions of the late 1770s and early 1780s would cease. Public happiness would return, and the war debt would be retired; the country would at last achieve solvency, and the potential for prosperous contentment that was so much a part of Revolutionary hopes and ideology would become a reality.[24]

Morris's proposals were shaped by his keen sense of social hierarchy. He clearly believed that only gentlemen like himself could manage public affairs and fashion market processes. Although time and time again he defended the purity of his republicanism and the sincerity of his concern for the public good, his faith that the aristocracy of wealth was more farseeing and thus better able to improve the prosperity of the entire country was surely what most irritated his opponents. In the democratic political climate of the 1780s, many people scornfully dismissed his public intentions and hopes as the gloss of a man so wealthy and so aristocratic as to be very much out of place in a republic.[25] After watching his recommendations for funding the debt bitterly criticized and voted down by the states, Morris realized that he could not restore the finances of the country through the Office of the Superintendent of Finance, and he resigned. He was replaced by a Treasury Board that did virtually nothing.[26]

From 1784 to 1785 the rising prosperity of the country seemed to stem the urgency of solving the debt crisis. Yet gentlemen watched what to them were alarming signs of the final throes of a country gone mad over luxury

24. Ferguson and Catanzariti, eds., *Papers of Robert Morris*, VI, 56–60, 63.

25. Gordon S. Wood, "Interests and Disinterestedness in the Making of the Constitution" (above, this volume); Ferguson and Catanzariti, eds., *Papers of Robert Morris*, VI, 61. Morris spoke of the "meritorious and oppressed Body of Men, who are Creditors of the Public." Gouverneur Morris shared the same hierarchical view of credit and creditors. "You know, gentlemen," he told the Pennsylvania Assembly in 1785, "that your merchants cannot give credit unless they get credit; and you know how important credit is to frontier inhabitants" and to "those of the more settled country." See Gouverneur Morris, "An Address on the Bank of North America," in Jared Sparks, *The Life of Gouverneur Morris, with Selections from His Correspondence and Miscellaneous Papers* . . . (Boston, 1832), III, 439.

26. Ferguson, *Power of the Purse*, 170–176; Ver Steeg, *Robert Morris*, 172–186; Bolles, *Financial History*, I, 328–334.

items. Deep into the countryside went cartloads of fancy goods, which, one observer lamented, "are moths to our purses and rob us of that cash, which ought to be advanced for the payment of our debts." By 1786, it seemed, something in the nature of a social upheaval was under way: ordinary artisans and farmers were reported to be on a stunning shopping spree. There were constant complaints, in newspapers, pamphlets, and journals, about people buying hats, laces, silks, gauze, chintz sheets, china, rum, tea, and madeira and particularly about the social climbing which seemed to infect Americans everywhere. It appeared to gentlemen that everyone now wanted to be genteel. Men and women alike seemed obsessed with their outward appearance and with the dress and demeanor of their children. It was this "costly itch," as one commentator called the remarkable buying, that fueled the enormous importation of goods from Britain and that led suddenly insolvent spenders to cry out for paper money. The new consumerism thus confirmed elite distrust of paper money. Gentility, they reminded one another in satirical pieces in magazines and newspapers, could not be purchased at market, and luxuries from abroad made the debt of the country greater than ever.[27]

The structure of the bank itself, and Morris's pressure to collect revenues, only aggravated pressure on credit and further incited the wrath of popular,

27. "A Citizen of New-York," *The Commercial Conduct of the United States of America, Considered* . . . (New York, 1786), 1–19; see esp. 5–7 for sardonic remarks on social mobility (quotations on 6). See also [Thurston], *Address to the Public* . . . , 14, 20–21; "A Farmer," "The Cause of, and Cure for, Hard Times," *American Museum,* I (1787), 11–13; [Williamson], *Letters from Sylvius,* 16–17. One of the most remarkable findings of recent work on Shays's Rebellion is that the mobs and popular actions were directed not only against the courts where debts were settled but also against retailers. In almost every town in the Connecticut Valley—Springfield, West Springfield, Northampton, Hatfield, Westfield, Sunderland, and Deerfield— the leading shopkeepers were attacked by mobs composed in part of their debtors. These local retailers surely had tempted local people with just the sorts of consumer goods that were mentioned time and time again in pamphlets and newspaper articles, and they became an obvious target in the midst of widespread frustration over debt. See David P. Szatmary, *Shays' Rebellion: The Making of an Agrarian Insurrection* (Amherst, Mass., 1980), 100–104. Richard Buel, Jr., "Samson Shorn: The Impact of the Revolutionary War on Estimates of the Republic's Strength," in Ronald Hoffman and Peter J. Albert, eds., *Arms and Independence: The Military Character of the American Revolution* (Charlottesville, Va., 1984), 141–165. Buel analyzes the roots of consumerism among ordinary farmers; he suggests that they produced grain and other commodities in order to buy the manufactured foreign imports they could not acquire at home. When international trade collapsed during the Revolution, they refused to produce. But, once foreign trade was restored in the mid-1780s, demand soared among their ranks in particular (157–160).

local groups. Consumer spending forced merchants to borrow more frequently from the Bank of North America (and from merchant banks in
Massachusetts and New York). Since the British dumped many goods in
Philadelphia, the Bank of North America was flooded with demands for
money and cautiously began suspending loans in order to discourage more
and more unknown traders from borrowing. But the demands never ceased.
In the absence of sufficient bank credit, the pressure on private borrowing
became intense. As the growth of private debt mushroomed, several developments placed the Morrisites in a politically embarrassing position. Ordinary
people—especially those determined to continue an antinationalist, anticen-
trist form of republican government—charged that the Bank of North
America had become too exclusive. They insisted that it be less concerned
with the intricacies of finance on the national level and instead provide credit
to a wider group of merchants and master craftsmen, and they challenged
its constitutionality and legitimacy. The bank, they pointed out, had been
chartered by Congress, which had no power to create corporations. Furthermore, to the dismay of nationalists in Congress, pressure to pay debts in-
curred in the spiraling new consumerism increased the demands in every
state for paper money.

In refuting charges that the bank was meant to serve only the private interests of a closed group of wealthy merchants, Morris began to lay out the
assumptions of what would become, by the 1790s, an essentially Federalist
view of public finance. He reiterated his faith that gentlemen at the center of
affairs, with reputations that transcended local politics, ought to assume
ultimate responsibility for maintaining the public credit of the loosely allied
states. The bank itself was the key mechanism that helped make such management possible. Viewed from this perspective, attacks on the bank were
terrifying because they undermined the central control that the Morrisites
deemed necessary to check the disruptive power of local interests and protect the country from the dangers of further debt. This controlling energy
of the bank was extended through its right to lend as it saw fit, to conserve
specie resources, and to give aid to government. Partisans of the bank
assumed it upheld the entire circulation of the country by adroit, selective
encouragement or discouragement of groups of merchants and traders. It
was this overarching view that helps explain Morris's blindness to charges
that the bank was a monopoly favoring some over others. Morris claimed
that the bank was completely democratic and open to all.[28]

28. For antinationalists' attacks on the bank, see *Cool Thoughts on the Subject of the
Bank* [Philadelphia, 1786], 1–16; *Remarks on a Pamphlet, Entitled, "Considerations on
the Bank of North-America"* (Philadelphia, 1785), 3–16. Defenders of the bank included Thomas Paine, "Dissertations on Government; the Affairs of the Bank; and
Paper Money," in Foner, ed., *Writings of Paine*, II, 367–414; Gouverneur Morris,

Under sharp criticism from his nemesis, the irascible William Findley of Pennsylvania, who campaigned against the renewal of the bank's charter, Morris made clear why he and other gentlemen despised unsecured paper money. In rebutting Findley's demand for loan office paper, Morris began to condone and even to encourage the establishment of loan offices to extend credit to farmers. But this shift of position can be attributed only to the pressure he felt to demonstrate that he was an open-minded equalitarian and wanted credit extended to all. Morris gave his blessing to county loan offices only if they were founded on specie alone. He did not trust farmers to use unsecured loan office paper to establish long-term investments.[29] In his view, paper money enabled goods to be bought and sold quickly. But because no one would want to accept paper for long-term, valuable considerations, it served only the purposes of speculation and consumption, not productivity. Because of the insubstantial, transient nature of unsecured, circulating paper, few would be able to restrain their spending. The productive backbone of the country—the nation's farmers—would quickly be caught up in the dizzying world of quick trading. Therefore, Morris and others in Congress were convinced that paper money would perpetuate an essentially nonproductive economy, not one likely to grow substantially.[30]

"Address to the Assembly," in Sparks, ed., *Life of Gouverneur Morris*, III, 437–465; Pelatiah Webster, "An Essay on Credit in which the Doctrine of Banks is Considered . . . ," Feb. 10, 1786, in Webster, *Political Essays*, 427–464. James Wilson, "Considerations on the Bank of North America" (Philadelphia, 1785), in Robert Green McCloskey, ed., *The Works of James Wilson* (Cambridge, Mass., 1967), II, 824–840. For an example of the sorts of attacks to which men like Morris and Wilson were subjected in the 1780s, see William Findley, *Address from an Officer of the Late Continental Army* [Philadelphia, 1787], 4–5. In his *Thoughts concerning the Bank of North America* . . . (Philadelphia, 1787), Tench Coxe pleaded with adamant defenders of the Bank of North America to reorganize that institution to meet some of the antinationalists' most persistent criticisms (1–14). For a detailed account of the quarrel over the bank, see George David Rappaport, "The Sources and Early Development of the Hostility to Banks in Early American Thought" (Ph.D. diss., New York University, 1970). For the quarrel over the bank, see Mathew Carey, ed., *Debates and Proceedings of the General Assembly of Pennsylvania* . . . (Philadelphia, 1786); Morris's belated recommendations for a loan office are on 37–38 and are similar to the concurrent recommendations for a loan office by John Witherspoon, an ardent foe of unsecured paper money; see Witherspoon, "Essay on Money," *Works of Witherspoon*, IX, 51–52.

29. Morris was even ready to put his own money into a loan office as long as that office was faithfully operated on a specie fund. "If the country gentlemen are willing," he promised, "I will freely join in the creation of a capital in hard cash, for the establishment of a loan office" (Carey, ed., *Debates and Proceedings*, 37).

30. *Ibid.*, 80–81. Other articulate opponents of paper money were Witherspoon,

Such views made the shock and horror over increasing demands for paper money inevitable. Gentlemen were distressed in 1786 when legislatures in New Hampshire, Massachusetts, Rhode Island, New York, New Jersey, and Maryland passed paper money acts and when the Rhode Island legislature passed a strict tender or force act requiring everyone to accept paper money at face value.[31] Moreover, when the issue of tender laws was tried in the Rhode Island courts, in *Trevett* v. *Weeden*, it appeared to members of the Continental Congress that the Rhode Island legislature feared the power of the courts, did not trust the jurors whom the court appointed, and, indeed, objected to the fundamental right of trial by jury. Similar popular complaints about the courts in Pennsylvania convinced nationalists that the rage of debtors for paper money was likely to overturn the entire system of justice, based on centuries of English tradition.[32]

The sense of impending doom mounted late in 1786. Members of the Continental Congress worried that, if events in the states ran out of control, redistribution of property would become a reality and social life as gentlemen had known it would disappear. When Henry Knox told Washington in November 1786 that some people in Massachusetts believed "the property of the United States, has been protected from confiscation of Britain by joint exertions of *all* and therefore ought to be the *common property* of all,"

"Essay on Money," *Works of Witherspoon*, IX, 43–65; James Madison, "Outline for Speech Opposing Paper Money," ca. Nov. 1, 1786, in Hutchinson *et al.*, eds., *Papers of Madison*, IX, 156–158, and "Notes for a Speech on Paper Money," ca. Nov. 1, 1786, *ibid.*, 158–160; "Nestor," "Thoughts on Paper Money," *Pennsylvania Packet*, July 21, 1786; [Williamson], *Letters from Sylvius*, 1–34, esp. 33–34; and [Alexander Contee Hanson], *Remarks on the Proposed Plan of an Emission of Paper . . .* (Annapolis, Md., [1787]), 16–43.

31. One of the best accounts of the paper money crisis is McMaster, *History of the United States*, I, 283–355. See also Kaminski, "Paper Politics," 50–219; Szatmary, *Shays' Rebellion*, 39–55, 124–134; Jere R. Daniell, *Experiment in Republicanism: New Hampshire Politics and the American Revolution, 1741–1794* (Cambridge, Mass., 1970), 183–205; Robert J. Taylor, *Western Massachusetts in the Revolution* (Providence, R.I., 1954), 128–177.

32. James M. Varnum, *The Case, Trevett against Weeden* (Providence, R.I., 1787), 2; Carey, ed., *Debates and Proceedings*, 12. In the course of the debates over the Bank of North America, William Robinson, Jr., a representative to the Assembly in Pennsylvania who voted with the Morrisites, reminded his colleagues that "the constitution says, 'that in controversies respecting property, the party shall have trial by jury.' But the late house," he continued, "stepped between the president and directors of the bank, and their rights, and deprived them of the legal mode of trial. . . . Let no man say, that tyranny cannot exist in a large assembly. It may become a many-headed hydra, as fond of power as individuals." Carey, ed., *Debates and Proceedings*, 12.

Washington could only agree with him that many in the state legislatures were "determined to annihilate all debts public and private, and have Agrarian Laws, which are easily effected by . . . paper Money." To Washington and other gentlemen, demands for paper money did indeed seem like demands for agrarian laws. Force laws, which were increasingly passed in tandem with acts to emit paper currency, obliged people to exchange their property for any paper proffered in the market. If ordinary people could acquire enough paper and oblige the wealthier in society to accept paper in trade, under penalty of law, they could effectively force a redistribution of all property. Thus, demands for paper seemed to possess sinister, leveling implications that frightened the genteel part of society. Would demands for equality of rights swiftly be transformed into demands for the equality of property, the abolition of private rights, and the redistribution of all wealth? Well-to-do gentlemen who sat in Congress believed so.[33]

The disinclination and inability of state governments to pay their shares of the debt, with the seeming likelihood of Rhode Island's experience being repeated in other states, troubled nationalists in the Continental Congress. In Providence and Newport, one observer reported, "half the shops" were "shut," and "little or no business" was done. "The corners of the streets" were "crowded with paper money politicians of opposed ideas, chatting like magpies."[34] If governments were taken over by "paper money politicians," men like Knox, Washington, Morris, Madison, and Hamilton assumed that any substantial growth of prosperity would be impossible and political harmony would be destroyed. The only way to prevent those calamities was for greater powers to be vested in Congress.

For all these reasons, a new constitution and a national government seemed attractive. There seemed no other answer to the financial problems of collecting revenue and establishing a currency than to form a more effective government. The anonymous New Yorker who wrote *Honesty Shewed to Be True Policy; or, A General Impost Considered and Defended* realized this fact as early as the fall of 1786. The country's financial problems, he said, would not begin to be solved until some "superintending power . . . and a revenue" were established. Congress's "powers are not . . . enough to . . . cement us," he concluded. A constitution could ensure national control of finances. It might even mandate direct taxes, remove the privilege to emit paper money

33. George Washington to James Madison, Nov. 5, 1786, in Hutchinson *et al.*, eds., *Papers of Madison*, IX, 161–162. For other expressions in 1786 of fear concerning agrarian laws, see the touchy interchange between Robert Morris and William Findley in Carey, ed., *Debates and Proceedings*, 66, 87, 117, 122.

34. Cited in a note to a letter from James Madison to Ambrose Madison, Aug. 7, 1786, in Hutchinson *et al.*, eds., *Papers of Madison*, IX, 90.

from the states, and place it in the hands of a national government. Some even dared to hope a powerful central government might act to prohibit paper money.[35]

So great was the antipathy toward paper money, by the summer of 1787, that members of the Constitutional Convention were ready to take extraordinary measures both to make sure that unsecured currency would never be printed again and to prevent state expenses from mushrooming to heights comparable to those during the Revolution. In May, some members considered elevating to the federal level the power to emit money, traditionally held by the states, but by July that proposal was no longer acceptable. Paper money emitted by any government seemed an anathema, so that enumerated "power" was struck from Section 8. If the federal government did not enjoy a mandate to print a national paper currency, then it hardly seemed appropriate to allow the states that right. Therefore, James Wilson moved that the new Constitution prohibit such emissions altogether. When Edmund Randolph, George Mason, John Langdon, and John Francis Mercer warned that such a radical measure might bind the hands of the state legislatures in time of war, Wilson, Roger Sherman, and Oliver Ellsworth replied that the current "crisis" provided an irretrievable opportunity for "crushing paper money" once and for all.[36] They had no trouble persuading their colleagues to agree to add to Article I, Section 10, the directive that the states not "emit bills of credit, nor make anything but gold and silver coin a tender in payment of debts."[37] Thus, no paper money would ever again be printed by the states. But by making such a radical prohibition against paper money and by declining to mandate federal emissions, the delegates made the problem of solving the financial problems of the new nation all the more difficult and intricate.

35. *Honesty Shewed to Be True Policy; or, A General Impost Considered and Defended by a Plain Politician* (New York, 1786), 10-12. For the expectations of the benefits of a national constitution, see *A Plan for Payment of the National Debt by Means of a National Bank* (New York, 1787); *Honesty Shewed to Be True Policy*, 10-12; [Thurston], *Address to the Public*, 24-36; Stephen Higginson to Henry Knox, Nov. 12, 1786, in J. Franklin Jameson, ed., *The Letters of Stephen Higginson, 1783-1804*, in *Annual Report of the American Historical Association*, I (1896), 741-742, and cited by Hutchinson *et al.*, eds., *Papers of Madison*. XI, 155 n.

36. Max Farrand, ed., *The Records of the Federal Convention of 1787*, rev. ed. (New Haven, Conn., 1966), I, 26, 135-136, 173, 243, 292, II, 142-144, 167-169, 182, 187, 308-310, 374-375, 435, 439 (quotation), 444, III, 598. Adrienne Koch, ed., *Notes of Debates in the Federal Convention of 1787 Reported by James Madison* (1966; New York, 1969), 166-171, 477-481 (quotation on 479), 487, 497-509, 541-544. The Pinckney plan's recommendation for nationally emitted currency may be found in Farrand, ed., *Records*, III, 598.

37. Koch, ed., *Notes of Debates*, 541-542; Farrand, ed., *Records*, II, 444.

Therefore, a Committee of Detail was enjoined on August 18, 1787, to consider several unresolved problems of the convention—among them a method "to secure payment of the public debt."[38] As the committee began to deliberate, it seemed clear that the only way to meet the debt was for the government to find new revenues. The convention had already debated the issue of direct taxes. Indeed, at first it seemed that one great benefit of a new constitution was the power to act directly on each citizen. Taxes passed by a national legislature would have made imposts unnecessary and would have met the Antifederalists' charge that imposts were inherently undemocratic. New direct taxes, imposed by a national legislature, would have answered critics like David Howell of Rhode Island and Abraham Yates of New York who believed that all revenues a government collected should be subject to constant popular review and approval. But the effort to prescribe direct taxes quickly became entangled with the quarrel over slavery and with the impasse concerning apportionment of taxes. The best the Constitution could do was to describe the conditions under which direct taxes might be assessed. Article I, Section 9, permitted them only if a census or some apportionment guaranteed fair disposition of the burden; the Constitution then failed to provide any outright mandate for the government to begin collecting taxes on every head.

So it was that in the summer of 1787, which was filled with remarkable accomplishments, there was no resolution of the pressing problems of what to do about the huge public debt. If the country was ever going to have a revenue to assist it in retiring the debt, it was evident that some other plan would be needed. The Committee of Detail finally recommended that a "Secretary of Commerce and Finance" be appointed once the Constitution had gone into effect, "to prepare and report plans of revenue and . . . regulation of expenditure."[39] The answer to the problems of the debt, which had dogged members of Congress throughout the Revolutionary era, was thus left, with hope, to the new national congress.

Even as the ratification process got under way, the enormous challenge of solving the crisis over the public debt set the best Federalist minds to work.[40]

38. Farrand, ed., *Records*, II, 326.

39. *Ibid.*, 321–322, 343, 374–375; Koch, ed., *Notes of Debates*, 477–481, 487, 497–509, 541–544. See also Jacob E. Cooke, "The Compromise of 1790," *WMQ*, 3d Ser., XXVII (1970), 523–545; Norman K. Risjord, "The Compromise of 1790: New Evidence on the Dinner Table Bargain," *WMQ*, 3d Ser., XXXIII (1976), 309–314. There was considerable discussion of assumption at the Constitutional Convention, but no consensus was reached on the matter. See Farrand, ed., *Records*, II, 400, 412–414, 656, III, 628; Koch, ed., *Notes of Debates*, 528–530.

40. In 1787, probably before the Constitution was submitted to the states, the anonymous New York author of *A Plan for Payment of the National Debt by Means of a*

Upon reading the Constitution while in France in 1789, Gouverneur Morris expressed fear that the states, flatly prohibited from collecting imposts, would lose revenues and begin to increase the burden of taxation on their own peoples. He warned that any such extra burden would do little to recommend the Constitution among local and state interests. So Morris urged his friends back home to take a truly radical step: the new nation ought to assume the states' debts, so that the tax burden upon states could be reduced. The federal government, he suggested in a pamphlet entitled *Observations on the Finances of the United States in 1789*, would then owe the states whatever portion of their Revolutionary indebtedness remained unpaid. Thus, Morris explained, the federal government rather than the recalcitrant state governments would become the debtor, and would pay 6 percent interest to the states. With responsibility fully on the newly energized national government, capable of raising the necessary revenues, the likelihood of the debt's being retired would actually increase. In order to collect revenues to pay the entire debt, Morris then recommended that the federal government levy taxes on "legal proceedings in the nation's courts," on the post office, and on one-twentieth the value of all produce at the point of delivery (a sort of sales tax). These revenues would then be gathered in a sinking fund. As in Richard Price's plan, the revenues in the fund would be lent out for interest; as the interest compounded, the federal government would be able to pay off the state debts.[41]

There was not much distance between Gouverneur Morris's proposals and Alexander Hamilton's a year later. When the *First* and *Second Reports on Public Credit* are read against the background of public discussion of the debt from 1787 to 1790, it is clear that Hamilton was very much a man of the late eighteenth century in his fascination with the intricacies of annuities, tontines, and compound interest as tools to expand state revenues. Like Gouverneur Morris and others, he viewed assumption of the states' debts as a powerful remedy for the country's financial dilemma. And like Robert Morris, he declared his intention to fund the debt. Hamilton proposed

---

National Bank, 3–13, urged the abolition of paper money and the transformation of one of the state-chartered banks—the Bank of New York—into a national bank. Basing his plan on an annuity program modeled on Richard Price's widely admired proposals, he recommended that shares be issued to a large number of people from a broad social spectrum, apportioned according to their wealth and rank. Perhaps because the plan called for the expansion of a state-chartered bank, an action likely to provoke popular criticism, it was never adopted; yet it reflected the thinking of others, like Gouverneur Morris and Alexander Hamilton.

41. Gouverneur Morris, *Observations on the Finances of the United States in 1789*, in Sparks, *Life of Morris*, III, 469–478 (quotation on 475).

several ways for the people to share in the debt. He offered to exchange at par old depreciated paper for new certificates and recommended that the government promise to pay 4 percent per annum to holders. In order to gain time, however, the government declined to say exactly when it would pay off these shares. Hamilton also invited enrollment in annuity or tontine schemes based on projected life expectancy. For a small investment at a young age, a person could anticipate receiving a generous sum later in life or at death. Or one could take a chance in a sort of lottery—a tontine—on being the last of a group of survivors and so earn the right to collect at an advanced age the last and largest remaining share of the certificates. Such a variety of plans would attract large numbers of people and bind as many to the government's interest as possible.

The greatest novelty of Hamilton's plan, however, lay in his remarkable efforts to ensure sufficient revenues to pay off the debt, which—contrary to charges leveled against him—he definitely intended to extinguish. Hamilton wanted no part of a perpetual debt, and he made arrangements to provide the country with adequate revenues. Given the mandate of Article I, Section 8, he planned to raise as much as he could by stringent and specific imposts. He recommended a sinking fund, which would be set in motion by revenues from the post office.[42] But it was in the Bank of the United States that Hamilton placed his greatest hopes for extinguishing the debt. Hamilton expected that the government would lend shares of debt to launch the bank. By means of these shares (a portion of which were to be in specie), the bank could be capitalized quickly and begin making loans. By lending the same money over and over, the bank would create a revenue for itself which would be used to pay interest to stockholders including the government, the largest stockholder in the bank. The government would then use the interest on its shares in the bank to extinguish the public debt.[43]

Hamilton's plan represented an extraordinary elaboration of earlier plans for funding the debt. Although his recommendations were similar to what had been attempted or suggested by the two Morrises and by many in their circle, they outdid all previous schemes in the complexity of their interlocking and overlapping provisions. Hamilton was also the first to assume that the federal government had the right to create corporations—indeed, federal corporations—and he justified the act of creating the bank by boldly

42. Alexander Hamilton, "Report Relative to a Provision for the Support of Public Credit," Jan. 9, 1790, in Syrett *et al.*, eds., *Papers of Hamilton*, VI, 65–110, esp. 90–110.

43. Alexander Hamilton, "Second Report on the Further Provision Necessary for Establishing Public Credit (Report on a National Bank)," Dec. 13, 1790, *ibid.*, VII, 305–342, esp. 337–342.

asserting that the power to incorporate was inherent in the sovereignty of the people as vested in their federal government.[44]

Yet the very act of creating a national bank raised many questions. As the bank was debated, it became clear that not all Americans shared the Federalists' understanding of the instrumental use of corporations. Hamilton's opponents balked at the idea that government should manage the economy through a single institution and criticized the funding program from the start. As Hamilton's financial proposals went into operation and as the bank became a reality, critics of Federalist political economy became increasingly numerous and outspoken.

IV

These critics drew on a body of writings by antinationalists that dated from the mid-1780s. Although the intellectual initiative in the eighties lay with Robert Morris, Hamilton, and their allies, some antinationalists had already begun to develop an economic vision of their own. A few may simply have been anticommercial and determined to perpetuate a subsistence, precapitalist world, but many were forward-looking ideologues who espoused alternative conceptions of money and commerce.[45] The brilliance and creativity of theorists like Hamilton and the Morrises should not be allowed to obscure the emergence of other strains of commercial thinking in the era of the Constitution. In time, the innovative ideas about money put forth by antinationalists would become increasingly influential outside the world of high public finance centered in the capital of the new federal government.

44. Alexander Hamilton, "Opinion on the Constitutionality of an Act to Establish a Bank" [Feb. 23, 1791], *ibid.*, VIII, 98.

45. Unlike most Antifederalists, Richard Henry Lee and Patrick Henry were among the most outspoken critics of paper money. By contrast, the Shaysites favored paper money and focused their anger on shopkeepers with whom they evidently had long done business. These distinctions are not convincingly accounted for by the current consensus about Antifederalists and Shaysites, which is cogently summed up by David Szatmary's argument, in *Shays' Rebellion*, that "Massachusetts antifederalism represented an attempt to save a subsistence-oriented way of life from the penetrating edge of commercial society" (120). "Mercantile" might be a more appropriate word here than "commercial," for it appears that some Antifederalists had their own commercial vision. Support for this point of view is provided by Wood, in part iii of "Interests and Disinterestedness in the Making of the Constitution" (above, this volume); and Buel, "Samson Shorn," in Hoffman and Albert, eds., *Arms and Independence*, 157–160. The argument in the pages that follow will be elaborated in my book-length study of the commercial revolution in America, 1690–1830 (in progress).

During the 1780s, some antinationalists began to see paper money in a new light—as perfectly legitimate and more likely to promote prosperity than banks and elaborate funding schemes. They saw Robert Morris and his friends as bent on the creation of a perpetual revenue and a perpetual debt without popular approval. Conjuring up a vision of placemen and tax-gatherers swarming the countryside and gathering imposts and duties to support wealthy men in high places, antinationalists readily assumed that, once Morris's plans were enacted, there would be no end to the public debt and to the consequent strain on the people. Never dreaming that Morris admired him too, they lauded Richard Price's scheme as a properly republican means of reordering the nation's finances. They also developed a rationale for paper money that brimmed with as much hope for commercial prosperity as did Morris's writings on funding.[46]

One of the most revealing confrontations between the antinationalists and Morris and his supporters occurred in 1786 during the debates in the

46. Antifederalist political economy has been largely unexplored, but the sources are rich. The classic defense of local interests against the imposition of a congressional impost is Howell, *Thoughts on the Five Per Cent*, 3–12. Jonathan Parsons, *A Consideration of Some Unconstitutional Measures* . . . (Newburyport, Mass., 1784), charged that the impost was "money TAKEN" without his "*consent*" (13). Timothy Davis suggested solving the debt crisis by dividing all citizens into groups according to their income and allowing each one to pay a portion of the debt according to one's ability; such a plan, he asserted, would avoid the need for a national government to strengthen taxing powers (*Thoughts on Taxation* . . . [New York, 1784], 22). Abraham Yates praised William Blackstone, Richard Price, and Jacques Necker for their insight that the national debt had ruined England, and he quoted Price, Beccaria, and Montesquieu extensively in his continuing and constant warnings that Congress might enact an impost plan (*Political Papers, Addressed to the Advocates for a Congressional Revenue* . . . [New York, 1786], 3–20, esp. 6, 11, 17). In the midst of the debate over the Constitution, the "Federal Farmer" warned that, under the Constitution, state legislatures would lose vital control over their own finances and the people would be forced to suffer hosts of obnoxious taxgatherers ("Letters from the Federal Farmer to the Republican," No. XVII, Jan. 23, 1788, in Herbert J. Storing, ed., *The Complete Anti-Federalist* [Chicago, 1981], II, 332). And, like many Antifederalists, Luther Martin feared that the constitutional prohibition on paper money was so stringent that it would destroy the prosperity of the country ("The Genuine Information Delivered to the Legislature of the State of Maryland . . . " [1788], in Storing, ed., *Complete Anti-Federalist*, II, 30). Finally, just as Hamilton was preparing his *Reports*, the anonymous author of *Considerations on the Nature of a Funded Debt* . . . (New York, 1790) frenetically denounced any attempt to fund the debt on a national level and warned that such measures were far too extreme a solution (3–13). A general account of Antifederalist political economy may be found in Jackson Turner Main, *The Antifederalists: Critics of the Constitution, 1781–1788* (Chapel Hill, N.C., 1961), 72–118.

Pennsylvania Assembly over rechartering the Bank of North America as a state corporation. This dramatic exchange pitted William Findley, the state representative from Westmoreland County, against Robert Morris himself. Here was a perfect opportunity for alternative views of money—however lacking in respectability from the perspective of the Morrisites—to be aired. Findley spoke warmly of previous emissions of paper, which he said were "constantly productive." It was remarkable testimony to the credit of paper, according to Findley, that it circulated even while supporters of the bank decried its value, refused to accept it in trade, and tried to unload it as soon as possible. Its brisk circulation was the best evidence of its usefulness. Indeed, it was the backbone of commerce. It "brightens our prospects of prosperous days," said Findley. "The public creditor has been relieved by it. The moneyless farmer has with it paid his taxes, which had accumulated for years past." It even "brought into circulation . . . hard money," since paper built confidence in the future of trade. "The uses which keep it in circulation, are abundant. Therefore it cannot fail of holding its credit."[47]

Findley's premise that paper money invigorated rather than destroyed commerce was given even more forceful theoretical justification by William Barton in his incisive pamphlet of 1786, *The True Interest of the United States, and Particularly of Pennsylvania, Considered*. Barton himself appears to have been a nationalist, but his way of thinking about money seems an extension of Findley's reasoning.[48] By 1786 Barton was disillusioned with the bank; it

47. Carey, ed., *Debates and Proceedings*, esp. 42-43, 65, 70-71 (quotations), 80-81, 97-98.

48. William Barton, *The True Interest of the United States, and Particularly of Pennsylvania, Considered* . . . (Philadelphia,1786), 30. Barton's political sentiments are difficult to fathom. He supported the bank in 1781 and argued that banking was not incompatible with republicanism (*Observations on Paper-Credit* . . . , 39-40). However, he also appears to have supported the Constitution and was one of the first to connect commercial prosperity with national government: "A power must necessarily be lodged *somewhere*, for adjusting the commercial, as well as the political, interests of the several States in the Union, to *one general scale*; and, according to the principles on which our foederal Constitution is framed, this power ought to be vested in the SUPREME HEAD OF THE UNION, in order to establish the commerce of the United States on the solid basis of *national* system" (*True Interest*, 30). For insightful comments that suggest that Barton's sympathies lay with forward-looking, commercially minded Antifederal supporters of paper money, see Wood, "Interests and Disinterestedness in the Making of the Constitution," part ii (above, this volume). Barton's ideas were not unlike the less analytical but equally progressive vision of George Logan, (*Letters Addressed to the Yeomanry* . . . [Philadelphia, 1791], esp. 3-45). For insightful comments on Logan, see Joyce Appleby, "Commercial Farming and the 'Agrarian Myth' in the Early Republic," *Journal of American History*, LXVIII (1981-1982), 846.

had become too mercantile and exclusive. Instead, to replace the bank, he championed the establishment of loan offices which, unlike Morris's, would not be grounded on specie. The funds dispensed by Barton's loan offices would be secured solely upon land, which he considered a much more substantial resource than specie.

Though once a supporter of the bank, Barton now questioned the assumptions upon which it had been established and perpetuated. In so doing, he invoked the Scottish agriculturalist James Anderson's *Observations on Increasing National Industry* and James Steuart's *Inquiry into the Principles of Political Oeconomy*, along with the *Commentaries* of Sir William Blackstone, to support his argument that coined specie was a commodity with its own market price. "Gold and silver coin," he observed, "derives not its intrinsic value from performing the office of *money*: but possesses it as a *commodity*." Like any commodity, such as wood, leather, or paper, it also had intrinsic value. But that intrinsic value was always altered by market value, which Barton called "alienation." What, in fact, was far more valuable than specie was the "abundance of the productions of nature"—that is, the farm produce needed by all people. Since Barton believed that a country's cattle, cloth, butter, and milk, not its gold and silver, represented real riches, there was no particular reason for money, which was merely a symbol, to be made of gold and silver. Paper could easily suffice.[49]

Barton also undermined the old quantity theory and carried Madison's argument of 1780 to a more sophisticated level. The value of specie did not depend only on its relationship to goods at market in a particular country, but depended also on a highly complex market relationship with goods in markets all over the world. Those countries that possessed the richest internal resources would prove to be the richest countries with the strongest position in the international market. Since specie was a commodity, it tended to depreciate where there was an abundance of it; but paper, which represented nothing in particular, maintained its value as a medium of exchange. It was a single, stable, and absolute measure in a whirling sea of constantly changing interrelationships and therefore was a perfectly legitimate form of money.

Barton's vision blended two points of view: that, on the one hand, of commercial men who wanted more liberal credit and who saw paper money as a catalyst for prosperity, and the perspective, on the other hand, of those in the North who would soon ally themselves with the Jeffersonians and oppose the mercantile, aristocratic vision of Hamiltonian Federalism. Barton's outlook provides the first glimpse of a new sort of political economy that—despite the success of the Constitution—would give Antifederalist

49. Barton, *True Interest*, 3–5, 9.

commercial ideas continuing vitality for decades beyond ratification. For it was the Antifederalists even more than the Federalists who saw wealth as based primarily on the internal productivity of the country. And it was this idea that by the nineteenth century became the key in America to under-standing value and wealth. Nineteenth-century Americans envisioned their great internal resources—their land, their capacity for labor, and the energy of their people—as sufficiently solid to support the credit of their bank notes. The multiplication of so many banks and bank notes was possible by the 1830s, not because the United States had great resources of specie, but because Americans believed that bank credit was in fact based on the pro-ductive potential of manufacturing, turnpike, and canal companies, all of which were engaged in tapping the true wealth of the land.[50]

Central to these views of credit was a new view of money. Money came to be seen as a bundle of components that were all affected in varying ways by market forces. Barton captured this vision in the midst of making his argu-ment for a large system of loan offices based on the credit of land. Many things, he explained, had to be considered in defining the wealth of a nation: "the extent and productiveness of its lands, the number and industry of its inhabitants, and the plenty and intrinsic value of its natural produce." Each of these could vary in relation to one another and thereby affect the value of goods. Paper money was no more than a measure of the relative position of the value of one good versus another.[51] It was ideas such as these that helped undo the eighteenth-century world where specie had overriding significance as a repository of value. Only then could an economic world arise wherein, to use Joseph Schumpeter's words, "all the essential phenomena of eco-nomic life are capable of being described in terms of goods and services, of decisions about them, and of relations between them," and where "money enters the picture only in the modest role of a technical device that has been adopted in order to facilitate transactions."[52]

The nationalists like Pelatiah Webster, Robert Morris, James Madison, and Alexander Hamilton had themselves begun to put forth this new con-cept of money even in the 1780s. They had moved way beyond the colonial assumption that specie alone was wealth. They were the first in America to take seriously the notion that specie could be used instrumentally to protect paper notes from depreciation and so ensure the steady expansion of the

50. These points will be fully treated in my book-length study referred to in note 45 above.

51. Barton, *True Interest*, 7.

52. Joseph A. Schumpeter, *History of Economic Analysis*, ed. Elizabeth Boody Schumpeter (New York, 1954), 277. Schumpeter called this sort of thinking "Real Analysis," although he was not particularly happy about the term.

internal productivity of the country. They invented a new means of supporting paper currency that took account of the deep internal resources of the new Republic. In doing so, they imparted to American economic life a utopian dimension and a faith in limitless possibilities.

But it was their opponents, the Antifederalists, who took these radical ideas one step further and fully saw their democratic implications. They insisted that corporations, like the Bank of North America and the Bank of the United States, be stripped of privilege and that economic life be equally open to all. When William Findley and William Barton argued against the Bank of North America, they saw that the security of the forms of money the nation used was far less important to the future than the Federalists supposed. For the Antifederalists, true wealth was grounded upon the contribution of the energies and labor of all citizens to the prosperity of the Republic. For these men, and for others who in the nineteenth century would extend the logic of that insight, money was nothing more than a measure of production and exchange generated by the real internal wealth of America.

Thus, Federalists and Antifederalists together fashioned theories from the crucible of the Revolutionary crisis over public finance that, in the end, would promote the development of a vibrant business culture in the century following. Indeed, without the momentous shift which their views represented, that democratic, freewheeling, bustling society would not have been possible.

☆ ☆ ☆ ☆ ☆
The Practicable Sphere of a Republic
James Madison, the Constitutional Convention, and the Emergence of Revolutionary Federalism

LANCE BANNING

James Madison made three distinctive contributions to the writing of the Constitution. Together, these distinguished him as first among the framers. He was primarily responsible for the preliminary resolutions that served throughout the summer of 1787 as the outline for reform, proposals that initiated the Constitutional Convention's transformation of the old Confederation into a republican government of national extent. In the early weeks of the deliberations, he persuasively explained why lesser changes would not work, an enterprise in which he was impressively assisted but never overshadowed by a handful of like-minded men. And most distinctively of all, he repeatedly insisted that the meeting could not limit its attention to the crisis of the Union, but must also come to terms with the vices of democratic government as these had been revealed in the Revolutionary states. Constitutional reform, he argued, would also have to overcome a crisis of republican convictions, both by placing limitations on the states and by creating a greater republic free from the structural errors of the state constitutions and capable of restoring the damaged reputation of democratic rule. With the latter plea particularly, he led the Constitutional Convention

The author wishes to express his gratitude to Gordon S. Wood, E. Wayne Carp, and especially Drew McCoy for valuable comments on earlier versions of this essay. He also wishes to acknowledge a University of Kentucky Research Professorship, which made it possible to devote a year to full-time research and writing.

to a thorough reconsideration of the proper governmental structure of a sound republic. Meanwhile, with his famous argument that private rights are safer in a large than in a small republic, he helped instill a faith that the emerging Constitution might accomplish all the ends he had in mind.

All three of Madison's distinctive contributions are well and widely understood. All three, it should be noted, came early in the course of the proceedings. Madison was first among the framers, by general agreement of historians and his peers, in part because he came to Philadelphia the best prepared. Of all the delegates, he seemed to have the most precise and comprehensive knowledge of American affairs, together with a masterful ability to place the country's situation in historical and philosophical perspective. He had thought things through to a degree that no one else had done, and it was therefore his ideas that set the course, his suggestions to which other delegates initially responded. Throughout the summer, he would speak as often and impressively as any. He would serve on most of the convention's key committees. But he was not responsible for any of the famous compromises or for any of the late additions that reshaped the resolutions of May 29 into the document completed on September 17. He earned his reputation as the father of the Constitution principally because of what he did toward the beginning of the work—then, and after the adjournment, by which time his own ideas had been significantly remolded.[1]

This essay focuses on that remolding. For we have seldom asked how Madison was influenced *by* the framing of the Constitution—not, at least, without presuming that he must have been severely disappointed. Historians are well aware that the convention thoroughly revised the resolutions of May 29 and that the finished plan reflected great defeats as well as stunning triumphs for Madison's original proposals. They have carefully assessed his victories and disappointments. But they have yet to recognize how much he *learned*, how greatly he was *changed* by his participation in the framing. Thus, a closer look at the Virginian's preparations for the meeting and an effort to approach the making of the Constitution as an episode in the development of his ideas can cast new light on the convention, on Madison's original assumptions, and on the most important framer's understanding of the finished Constitution. When we turn the ordinary questions inside out, I hope to show, we find that we have yet to reach a balanced understanding of the great Virginian's founding vision, which was influenced by the shap-

---

1. Two of many excellent attempts to measure Madison's contributions against those of his colleagues are particularly helpful on this point: Clinton Rossiter, *1787: The Grand Convention* (New York, 1966), 247–252; and Harold S. Schultz, "James Madison: Father of the Constitution?" *Quarterly Journal of the Library of Congress,* XXXVII (1980), 215–222.

ing of the Constitution more profoundly—and in different ways—than has before been seen.

The Constitutional Convention, as Madison eventually explained, proposed a form of government that had no precedent in history. Neither wholly national nor purely federal, this novel scheme divided political responsibilities between concurrent and interlocking state and central governments, each of which would act directly on the individuals composing the political societies from which they rose. The people of the thirteen states could be conceived as granting portions of their sovereign power to different parts of both the state and general governments while reserving certain rights, together with the ultimate authority to alter or abolish any of these governments, for themselves. The structure thus established, Madison maintained, could make the central government effective without endangering the people or the states. It offered an entirely democratic solution to the characteristic problems of democracy.[2]

This solution to the nation's problems was significantly different from the one that Madison envisioned when the great convention opened. It differed even more, though this has not been noticed, from the proposals he supported midway through the work. He stubbornly resisted some of its essential features through most of the proceedings and worried when the gathering adjourned that they would vitiate the system.[3] And yet his numbers of *The Federalist* did not defend a system that he privately regarded as severely flawed, as seems to be the dominant impression. Rather, these impressive essays, building on ideas that first occurred in course of the convention and representing his more settled views, confessed his reconciliation to decisions he had earlier opposed and outlined a position he defended through the rest of his career.

I

Shortly after its deliberations opened, the Constitutional Convention entered on an argument that polarized its members for at least the next six weeks. With Madison and James Wilson of Pennsylvania at their head, the

2. See Madison's numbers of *The Federalist*, ed. Jacob E. Cooke (Middletown, Conn., 1961); and Gordon S. Wood, *The Creation of the American Republic, 1776–1787* (Chapel Hill, N.C., 1969), chaps. 13, 15. All references to *The Federalist* are to Cooke's edition.

3. "I hazard an opinion . . . that the *plan* . . . will neither effectually *answer* its *national object* nor prevent the local *mischiefs* which every where *excite disgusts*." Madison to Thomas Jefferson, Sept. 16, 1787, in William T. Hutchinson *et al.*, eds., *The Papers of James Madison* (Chicago, Charlottesville, 1962–), X, 163–164.

members from the larger states confronted delegates from smaller states on the provision in the resolutions of May 29 for proportional representation in both branches of the national legislature. No part of the debates is better known. Small-state delegates insisted on the equal vote that every state had always had in Congress. Madison and Wilson attempted to convince the smaller states that differences among the large ones would guarantee security against a coalition of the giants, pleading with opponents to surrender a demand for a concession plainly incompatible with larger federal powers and majority control. The confrontation, as has been repeatedly remarked, pitted large-state nationalists against delegates who worried that the smaller states would be completely dominated in a great republic. The latter soon were reinforced by others who insisted that the states as states *should* retain a role in the general government, that states as well as individuals *should* be represented in order to preserve a federal harmony and enable the states to protect their own share of power in a mixed regime.[4]

In this phase of the convention, Madison completed the initial, most neglected phase of a significant rethinking of his suppositions. He had come to Philadelphia convinced that no extension of the central government's authority could overcome the crisis of the Union if the execution of congressional decisions continued to depend on intermediary actions by the states. The fundamental flaw of the Confederation, he believed, lay in its structure. States were necessary instruments of federal action, but they were not amenable to federal commands. The articles of union took the form of a "political constitution," but the general government lacked independent means to carry out the tasks with which it was entrusted. It was thus as ineffectual in practice as the states would be if every citizen were free to follow or ignore their laws.[5] This insight was the starting point for the Virginia Resolutions, which sought to free the general government from secondary, state decisions capable of baffling all its measures. It was Madison's first major contribution to the framing.

When the Constitutional Convention opened, nonetheless, the most im-

---

4. For the latter argument, see particularly the speeches of John Dickinson, George Mason, Roger Sherman, and others on June 6 and 7, in Max Farrand, ed., *The Records of the Federal Convention of 1787*, rev. ed., 4 vols. (New Haven, Conn., 1937), I, 133, 136–137, 155. See also Dickinson's "Letters of Fabius," *ibid.*, III, 304.

5. "Vices of the Political System of the United States" (Apr. 1787), in Hutchinson *et al.*, eds., *Papers of Madison*, IX, 345–358. My arguments concerning Madison's preconvention thoughts and original intentions are based throughout primarily on this memorandum, the "Notes on Ancient and Modern Confederacies," and letters to Jefferson (Mar. 19, 1787), Edmund Randolph (Apr. 8, 1787), and George Washington (Apr. 16, 1787), all in vol. IX.

portant architect of the Virginia Plan had not yet formed a clear conception of fully concurrent governments, all possessing all the means required to carry out their tasks.[6] Although he insisted on the need to end the states' capacity to intervene between the making and the execution of federal decisions, he did not yet see how they could be denied all agency in executing federal commands, nor did he see how it was possible to keep the lesser legislatures from "molesting" one another or infringing private rights unless the general government could act directly on the states.[7] On the eve of the convention, Madison had written of his hope that "positive" additions to the powers of the general government—authority to regulate and tax the country's trade, together with at least a partial power of direct taxation— would render it unnecessary, *for the most part*, for Congress to compel the states.[8] He evidently still imagined, then, that on occasion the central government would still rely upon the states for requisitions or for other actions necessary to enforce its laws. And he was equally concerned to vest the central government with power to defend itself, the private rights of citizens, and peaceful relationships between the states from independent state decisions. Accordingly, while the Virginia Resolutions sought to solve the federal problem partly by removing the state governments from their direct and equal role in *making* federal decisions—by placing a republican regime on top of a confederation of republics—they also sought to guarantee the faithful execution of the central government's decisions by *compelling* the confederated states to follow federal directives, either by a federal veto on their laws or by a federal power of coercion.

As deliberations started, to put this point another way, Madison had not entirely freed himself from the assumption that the Union would remain confederal in several major respects. He had not yet firmly grasped the concept that would rapidly become the key to the convention's ultimate solution to the problem he defined. Although his thinking had been moving him in this direction (and although the resolutions of May 29 led the entire convention toward the same conclusion), the concept that the central government should act exclusively upon the people, not upon the states, is nowhere to be found in the Virginian's preconvention writings.

Language of this sort was introduced to the convention on May 30, when Gouverneur Morris contrasted a "national" government with one "merely federal" and George Mason distinguished a government acting on individuals from one acting on states. Madison, suggestively, was not as quick as

6. Wood remarks this in *Creation of the American Republic*, 525.

7. See especially the letter to Jefferson, in Hutchinson *et al.*, eds., *Papers of Madison*, IX, 318.

8. To Washington, *ibid.*, 385.

others to adopt this language, which soon was heard on every side. He even pointed out that there were instances in which the present government acted directly on individuals. It seems apparent, nevertheless, that he was soon profoundly influenced by the concept.[9] It obviously strengthened and improved his earlier analysis of the Confederation's ills. It rendered more explicit what was probably the most important thrust of the Virginia Resolutions, a thrust which he had neither followed to its logical conclusion nor separated from proposals based on different ideas.

Madison had started his analysis of the Confederation's weaknesses — the point is critical to understanding the development and content of his thought — by probing the relationship between the general government and states, conscious of the need to make the central government genuinely "sovereign" in its sphere, preoccupied with the ability of the provincial governments to frustrate federal measures. This is why he had referred to rendering the states "subordinately useful," why many of the resolutions of May 29 were meant to make the states obedient to federal commands.[10] As May turned into June, however, it became increasingly apparent that the concept of a central government that would compel obedience directly from the people, if more consistently applied, might become the central premise of reform. Day by day, the delegates could see more clearly that immediate connection with the people could permit the general government to wield effective power without relying on or trying to coerce the states.

As the battle with the smaller states approached its climax, Madison's attraction to this concept grew. As the arguments of his opponents began to sway some minds and as his allies clarified their own desires, he could imagine more concretely what he wished for, and he rebutted small-state fears with rising passion. On June 29, remarking that the states must sometimes be regarded as "political societies" and sometimes only as "districts of

9. Speech of June 28, in Farrand, ed., *Records*, I, 449. Unless otherwise noted, all quotations from the convention are from Madison's notes of the debates.

As early as May 31, Madison spoke of abandoning the coercive power, referring as he had in the letter to Washington to the impracticability of applying force "to people collectively and not individually" (*ibid.*, 54). Again, I recognize that the distinction made in the convention on May 30 was one that Madison had narrowly approached and even helped his colleagues seize. My point is simply that the other delegates helped him to complete the thought and move it further toward the center of his mind.

10. The precise dating of the memorandum on confederacies is subject to dispute, but it was almost certainly the earliest step in Madison's attempt to think his way toward the Virginia Plan. The reference to rendering the states "subordinately useful," which is frequently misunderstood, is in the letter to Randolph, in Hutchinson *et al.*, eds., *Papers of Madison*, IX, 369.

individual citizens," William Samuel Johnson suggested that the thirteen collectivities should be represented in each of these two ways in the two different branches of the legislature. Madison agreed with Johnson "that the mixed nature of the Govt. ought to be kept in view," but he denied that this required an equal representation of the states in either house. Oliver Ellsworth then developed Johnson's point:

> We were partly national; partly federal. The proportional representation in the first branch was conformable to the national principle and would secure the large States agst. the small. An equality of voices was conformable to the federal principle and was necessary to secure the Small States agst. the large. He trusted that on this middle ground a compromise would take place.[11]

Madison replied to Ellsworth on July 14 in his final plea before the crucial vote that carried the famous compromise:

> It had been said that the Governt. would . . . be partly federal, partly national; that altho' in the latter respect the Representatives of the people ought to be in proportion to the people: yet in the former it ought to be according to the number of States. If there was any solidity in this distinction he was ready to abide by it.

But there now seemed no solidity in the distinction as applied to the emerging system. Madison "called for a single instance in which the Genl. Govt. was not to operate on the people individually. The practicability of making laws, with coercive sanctions, for the States as political bodies, had been exploded on all hands."[12] Accepting the distinction now between a "national" government, which would act on individuals, and a "federal" government, which would act on states, Madison revealed that he had come to think of the new system as wholly "national" in its structure and operations. The system he envisioned and defended on July 14 was not the plan he had originally proposed.

This phase of the convention, though, is also highly likely to mislead us. Through these weeks, as nearly every major study has repeated, Madison appears as the magnificent titan of a "nationalist assault."[13] During these debates, he showed almost no fear of central power. Quickly read, some of his comments and proposals may suggest that he was willing to pursue consolidation of authority nearly to the point of turning states into the

11. Farrand, ed., *Records*, I, 461, 468.
12. *Ibid.*, II, 8-9.
13. So described in the title of chap. 9 of Rossiter's *1787*.

counties of a great republic, and analysts have sometimes said that his de-sires seem very similar to Alexander Hamilton's at this point in the work. But this opinion disregards the qualifying phrases or the context of his speeches. It reflects inadequate attention to the way his thinking had de-veloped before the confrontation with the smaller states began. And it pro-duces a misleading view of how he changed as a result of his defeat.

Madison did lead a nationalist offensive at the Constitutional Convention —provided that we use this word as delegates themselves employed it for purposes of this particular debate.[14] He entered the convention seeking national supremacy: complete, unchallengeable authority for the general government over matters of general concern. By July 14, he had come to think that national supremacy should be secured by the creation of a great republic which would rise directly from the people and possess all means required to act directly on the people to enforce its laws. He saw more clearly now than he had seen at the beginning of deliberations how the states could be removed from their intermediary role between the general government and people. He therefore struggled to the last to prevent the Connecticut Compromise. He had become a more consistent nationalist, in this respect, than he had been when the proceedings started.

Even on July 16, however, Madison can be legitimately described as a determined "nationalist" only in his quest for a structure and mode of opera-tion that would make the general government effective and supreme *within its proper sphere*, which he consistently conceived as relatively small. He was not a "nationalist" in his conception of the duties or responsibilities that should be placed in federal hands. On this issue he remained, as he had always been, a moderate. Indeed, if he had not been so accustomed and committed to a basically conventional conception of state and federal duties, he would not have concentrated so intently and so long on ways to keep the states from baffling federal measures, from intervening in the federal sphere.

After the convention, Madison repeatedly insisted that the Constitution should be seen less as a grant of new authority than as a means of rendering

14. During his retirement, Madison himself had more than one occasion to con-demn the error of supposing "that the term, *national*" as applied "in the early stage of the Convention . . . was equivalent to *unlimited* or consolidated." It was used, he wrote, "in contradistinction to . . . a *federal* Government," which operated through requisitions and rested on the sanction of the state legislatures. The emerging sys-tem, "being a novelty and a compound, had no technical terms or phrases appro-priate to it." "Old terms" had to be used "in new senses, explained by the context or by the facts of the case." To Andrew Stevenson, Mar. 25, 1826, in Farrand, ed., *Records*, III, 473–474; to N. P. Trist, Dec. 1831, in Gaillard Hunt, ed., *The Writings of James Madison*, 9 vols. (New York, 1900–1910), IX, 475–477.

effective the powers that the central government had always had.[15] Usually dismissed as an expedient response to Antifederalist objections, these statements might instead remind us of the reasoning behind the resolutions of May 29, which tells us much about the limits of their author's plans. In the writings that record his path to the convention, Madison consistently devoted very little space to powers he desired to shift from state to federal hands, for there was little that was new or controversial in what he was proposing on this subject.[16] Apart from power over trade, as he conceived it, the present constitution granted Congress positive authority to do most of the things a general government should do—even power to require the states to raise the revenues it needed.[17] The fundamental difficulty, then, was not a radically mistaken definition of the proper scope of federal responsibilities. It was the inability of the existing government to carry out the tasks that most informed Americans believed to be its proper business.[18] As he thought his way to the Virginia Plan, Madison concerned himself from the beginning, not with redivision of responsibilities between the general government and states, but with the structural and operational deficiencies of the existing system. He wanted an *effective* central government, not a vastly swollen one. In fact, he wanted a reform that would impinge on state authority only when the clear necessities of union or the fundamental liberties intended by the Revolution appeared to be endangered.[19]

15. *Federalist* No. 45, p. 314; Jonathan Elliot, ed., *The Debates in the Several State Conventions on the Adoption of the Federal Constitution* . . . , 5 vols. (Washington, D.C., 1888), III, 259.

16. The central government, he wrote in his first thoughts on reform, should have the "power of regulating trade and [power over] sundry other matters in which uniformity is proper." It should have—his second effort to express it—"compleat authority in all cases where uniform measures are necessary. As in trade &c. &c." *Et cetera*: for this was simply not his principal preoccupation. Madison to Jefferson, to Randolph, in Hutchinson *et al.*, eds., *Papers of Madison*, IX, 318, 370.

17. Revenue requisitions are "a law to the States" as state acts are laws to individuals (speech in the Confederation Congress, Feb. 21, 1783, *ibid.*, VI, 271).

18. "However ample the federal powers may be made, or however Clearly their boundaries may be delineated, on paper, they will be easily and continually baffled by the . . . States" unless supported by additional reforms that will make the general government "clearly paramount" to the state legislatures and capable of acting without their "intervention" (Madison to Jefferson, *ibid.*, IX, 318).

19. The obvious exception might appear to be his fierce commitment to a federal power to veto all state laws. (For an argument that Madison's support for this unwieldy and intrusive power demonstrates consolidationist desires, see Charles F. Hobson, "The Negative on State Laws: James Madison, the Constitution, and the Crisis of Republican Government," *William and Mary Quarterly*, 3d Ser., XXXVI

Early in his preconvention thinking Madison explained to Edmund Randolph that the alternatives before the country extended, theoretically, from total independence for the thirteen states to their complete consolidation into a single, national republic. He rejected both of these extremes in favor of a "middle ground" that would provide for national supremacy where common measures were required but leave the states' authority in force where they were not.[20] He sought this "middle ground," not just because he thought a more complete consolidation could not be achieved, but because he never doubted that a fragmentation of the Union *or* excessive concentration of authority in federal hands would eventually betray the Revolution.

How did he define "excessive?" The simplest answer is that he did not attempt to frame a rigid rule that might be universally applied, and we should not attempt to do so for him. Yet if we fail to understand how firmly he rejected any option other than the "middle ground," we will mistake his purposes, misread his words, and end with an imperfect grasp of what he taught and what he learned at the Constitutional Convention. At Philadelphia, the need to win a point was sometimes incompatible with an articulation of all of a member's thoughts. Speakers might suppress one set of fears because a different set was temporarily foremost in their minds. During the convention, Madison was fierce in his determination to create a general government that would suffice for all the nation's common needs, so fixed in this intention that we readily forget those early references to "middle

---

[1979], 215–235.) Yet Madison repeatedly identified the federal negative as a "defensive power," an instrument for overturning legislation incompatible with federal measures, harmony between the states, or private rights. Thinking of the veto as a better tool than judicial review for assuring state compliance with federal laws—and as the *only* tool with which the federal government could act directly to defeat injustices against minorities—he was, indeed, most stubbornly committed to the power and deeply disappointed when it was refused. But as a "negative," of course, the veto could not have been employed to make positive decisions for the states, and Madison consistently distinguished it from "positive" additions to the Union's powers. In developmental context, the idea for such a power flowed precisely from his habit of assuming that the individual legislatures would continue to conduct most of the people's business and from his wish for a device that would secure the supremacy of the general government over matters of general concern at *minimal* expense to the autonomy of the individual states, which would continue to possess most of the power. Suggestively, Madison defended the proposal in his preconvention letters as "the least . . . abridgement of the State Sovereignties" consistent with their union, as "the least possible encroachment on the State jurisdictions." Madison to Randolph, to Washington, in Hutchinson *et al.*, eds., *Papers of Madison*, IX, 370, 383.

20. Hutchinson *et al.*, eds., *Papers of Madison*, IX, 369. The same phrase reappears in the letter to Washington, *ibid.*, 383.

ground." But when he entered the convention, the powers he designed to transfer from the states to the general government were relatively few, the need for such a transfer generally conceded even by opponents of his plan. The battle with the smaller states was not essentially a contest over *how much* power should be placed in federal hands.[21]

The resolutions of May 29 suggested that the national legislature be empowered with the legislative rights already vested in the general Congress by the Articles of Confederation, together with the right to legislate "in all cases to which the separate States are incompetent, or in which the harmony of the United States may be interrupted by the exercise of individual Legislation." "It can not be supposed that these descriptive phrases were to be left in their indefinite extent to Legislative discretion," Madison later warned. "A selection and definition of the cases embraced by them was to be the task of the Convention. If there could be any doubt that this was intended, and so understood by the Convention, it would be removed by the course of [the subsequent] proceedings."[22]

Clearly, Madison himself had no intention of confiding plenary authority to the new government. Two days after the Virginia Plan was introduced, he said that he preferred enumeration of the general government's authorities, although he might accept a general grant of power if a workable enumeration could not be achieved.[23] The context shows that he was principally concerned to keep the gathering from getting sidetracked into a debate about the proper reach of federal powers. Later in the course of the proceedings, Madison would act as one of the convention's most consistent advocates of strict, though full, enumeration. Early on, he feared that a debate about specific powers could distract the meeting from a more impor-

---

21. Before the meeting started, Madison identified two specific "positive powers" that should be transferred to the Congress: regulation of the country's trade and power to collect at least some sorts of internal taxes as well as duties on imports and exports. The New Jersey Plan would have granted powers to regulate trade and to impose a stamp tax, postal duties, and an impost. A large majority of states had ratified amendments to the Articles approving an impost and a partial federal authority to regulate commerce.

22. Farrand, ed., *Records*, I, 21; Madison to John Tyler, 1833, *ibid.*, III, 526–527. See also Hunt, *Writings of Madison*, IX, 176–177, 475, including: "The general terms or phrases used in the introductory propositions . . . were never meant to be inserted in their loose form in the text of the Constitution. Like resolutions preliminary to legal enactments it was understood by all, that they were to be reduced by proper limitations and specifications, into the form in which they were to be final and operative."

23. Farrand, ed., *Records*, I, 53. A general grant might still, of course, have been a limited one.

tant issue: how to make the central government effective. But this does not suggest that he was unconcerned to keep it safe.[24]

Madison did nothing—at any point in the convention—that is inconsistent with the view that he imagined, and consistently attempted to secure, a new central government whose authority would be autonomous, unchallengeable, but also strictly limited to matters that the individual states could not effectively handle on their own. The very speeches in which he was most insistent on the evils of state intervention in the federal sphere also indicate in passing that he sought a "mixed" regime, that he intended to "preserve the State rights, as carefully as the trials by jury."[25] The advocates of compromise explicitly conceded that neither he nor Wilson wanted to remold the states as counties of a single, consolidated republic.[26] They knew how

24. On Aug. 18, Madison moved to refer a long list of additional grants of enumerated powers to the Committee of Detail. On Sept. 14, Benjamin Franklin wished to add a congressional power to cut canals, and Madison urged extending this to permit congressional creation of corporations. These actions, like the federal negative, have usually been seen as powerful evidence of the reach of his "nationalism" at this point. I believe that, carefully considered, they are in fact among the clearest indications of its limits. The powers he proposed to add in August were far from extensive. Several of them—power over a seat of national government, to dispose of western lands, to organize western governments, and so forth—were so obviously required that I believe his motion makes it clear that he wished to leave as little to implication as possible. His motion of Sept. 14 may be understood in similar terms. In moving for a power of incorporation, he probably had internal improvements and perhaps another national bank primarily in mind. Suggestively, Rufus King argued that the grant was unnecessary, probably hinting that it was already implicit. Similarly, Gouverneur Morris suggested that the power to create a university, another of Madison's desires, would be covered by the power over a seat of government. See Farrand, ed., *Records*, II, 324–325, 615. These maneuvers may be profitably considered in conjunction with Madison's remark in *Federalist* No. 41, p. 270, that every omission from the Constitution of grants of necessary powers would have become a ground for "necessary usurpations of power, every precedent of which is a germ of unnecessary and multiplied repetitions." See also *Federalist* No. 42, p. 280.

25. Farrand, ed., *Records*, I, 490.

26. On June 21, Dr. Johnson said that Hamilton "boldly and decisively contended for an abolition of the state governments," but that Wilson and Madison "wished to leave the States in possession of a considerable, tho' a subordinate jurisdiction" (*ibid.*, I, 355). A more suggestive incident occurred in the Virginia ratifying convention. Speaking on June 19, George Mason said that certain clauses of the Constitution were *intended* to prepare the way for gradual subversion of the powers of the states. In an uncharacteristic breach of parliamentary decorum, Madison immediately broke in, demanding "an unequivocal explanation" of an insinuation that all the signers of the Constitution had preferred a consolidated national system. Mason

central to the contemporary mind—and certainly to Madison's—was the distinction between a government to be created by a written constitution and a fully national regime. Many of them understood that, from the first, the architect of the Virginia Plan assumed that federal powers would be strictly limited to those to be defined by the convention and the people.[27]

II

More than one mistake has followed from a failure to distinguish Madison's determination to secure a general government whose authority would be *effective* or *complete* from his opinion of the *quantity of power*, the nature of the duties, that ought to be confided to federal hands. Thus, most interpretations of the framer's conduct follow Irving Brant, his great biographer, in seeing his defeat on the apportionment of the Senate as possibly the most important watershed in Madison's political career.[28] The small-state victory, in this interpretation, initiated a retreat from an expansive view of federal powers which started in the second half of the convention, gathered new momentum during Washington's administration, and culminated in the

----

insisted that many members of the convention *had* desired consolidation, but that Madison had "expressed himself against it" in a private conversation. Madison declared himself satisfied," and Mason completed his speech (Elliot, ed., *Debates in the State Conventions*, III, 517-530). Hugh Blair Grigsby, whose *History of the Virginia Federal Convention of 1788* . . . , 2 vols. (Virginia Historical Society, *Collections*, IX-X [Richmond, 1890-1891], was based in part on oral information, was being overly dramatic when he wrote that Madison "demanded reparation in a tone that menaced an immediate call to the field" (I, 97), but there can be no doubt that the framer sharply resented Mason's insinuation.

27. For an argument that Madison was a consistent strict constructionist throughout the 1780s, see Lance Banning, "James Madison and the Nationalists, 1780-1783," *WMQ*, 3d Ser., XL (1983), 227-255. There and in "The Hamiltonian Madison: A Reconsideration," *Virginia Magazine of History and Biography*, XCII (1984), 3-28, I suggest that recognition of his scrupulous respect for written constitutions is indispensable to reinterpretation of his conduct through the founding. Shortly before this essay was to go to the compositor, I encountered Michael P. Zuckert, "Federalism and the Founding: Toward a Reinterpretation of the Constitutional Convention," *Review of Politics*, XLVIII (Spring 1986), 166-210. Developed independently, this article makes several similar points about the limits of Madison's nationalism during the convention.

28. Irving Brant, *James Madison*, 6 vols. (Indianapolis, Ind., 1941-1961), III, chaps. 1-12, is the fullest and probably most influential discussion of Madison at the convention.

Virginia Resolutions of 1798.[29] The dominant impression of the founder's whole career is gravely marred by an analysis that does not keep in mind the difference between his concept of the *way* in which the new regime should work and his opinion of the work it ought to do.

The small-state triumph on July 16 did, indeed, throw everything into confusion. When Madison and others failed to bring a caucus of the larger states to risk continuing the confrontation, every previous decision in convention had to be thought through again.[30] Few delegates were more alarmed than Madison himself. Nevertheless, a reconsideration of his course through the rest of the meeting will suggest that the Virginian turned in quite a different direction than is usually believed.

Madison did not "reverse his course" in consequence of the decision of July 16. He did not become "less nationalistic" than he had been during the weeks when it appeared that the convention might approve proportional representation in both branches of the legislature. It is true that he had warned that the concession to the smaller states could rob the new regime of "every effectual prerogative," making it "as impotent and short lived as the old."[31] Here, however, he predicted the effect that compromise might have on other members from the larger states, not the course he would himself pursue.

Madison had sought from the beginning to make the general government's authority complete within a sphere of limited responsibilities. He remained intent on this objective. He continued to support a federal negative on all state legislation. Unlike other southerners, he continued to support a federal power to levy export taxes. He opposed insertion of provisions requiring more than a majority of Congress for passage of commercial legislation or limiting the Senate's role in money bills. Near the close of the convention, he moved to add additional specifics to the enumerated powers of Congress. A thorough search does not identify a single power that he wanted to withhold from the general government after July 16 but would have granted had the large states won proportional representation in both branches. Madison did not retreat on the issue of the quantum of authority

29. Ralph Ketcham, *James Madison: A Biography* (New York, 1971), 215, remarks that Madison's nationalism "reached its peak" in the weeks before the compromise. Irving Brant, *The Fourth President: A Life of James Madison* (Indianapolis, Ind., 1970), 170–174, argues that the Connecticut Compromise "affected at once his attitude toward federal powers."

30. See Randolph's remarks of July 16, Farrand, ed., *Records*, II, 17.

31. July 7, *ibid.*, I, 551. Brant and others have seen these comments as foreshadowing a change of Madison's position.

that should be vested in the general government. He had never assumed a more advanced position from which he found it necessary to withdraw.

The compromise did have significant effects on the Virginian, but it worked a different sort of change than has been thought. The concession to smaller states did not significantly affect his vision of the proper scope of federal power. It did almost immediately affect his view of how this power should be shared by the various parts of the new government.[32]

At the start of the convention, Madison had plainly seen the indirectly elected upper house as the branch best suited to control the passions of the people, to secure a place for wisdom and stability in the great republic, and to guard against the mutability, injustices, and multiplicity of laws that he identified as major weaknesses of democratic rule. When the proceedings opened, the role that he envisioned for the upper house contrasted sharply with his evident uncertainty, his Revolutionary fears, about the character and powers of a national executive. He planned to place enormous powers in the Senate and offered only very sketchy hints about the nature of the new executive.[33]

The decision of July 16 struck Madison as inconsistent with the rule of the majority, a barrier to the pursuit of general interests and a potential peril to the South. By this time, moreover, he was forcefully impressed by Wilson's argument that executive responsibility could be secured only by concentrating the executive authority in the hands of a single man. Together, these considerations moved him noticeably toward strengthening the executive at the expense of the Senate. This was the most obvious and most immediate effect of the Great Compromise.[34]

32. This accords with Harold S. Schultz, *James Madison* (New York, 1970), 67–68, 73–74.

33. Madison's preconvention letters all indicate that he had yet to form any clear ideas about a proper executive. The Virginia Plan did not even decide whether the executive was to be a single person, and Madison recorded himself as entering the first day's debate on the subject only to suggest that a prior decision on executive powers might help decide the question (Farrand, ed., *Records*, I, 66–67). Rufus King's notes (*ibid.*, 70) have Madison expressing a fear that large executive powers could produce "the Evils of elective Monarchies" and favoring an executive council from whose advice the head of the executive could depart only at his peril. Pierce's notes (*ibid.*, 74) accord with King's.

34. Farrand, ed., *Records*, II, 80–81, 392. All of Madison's biographers have noted this effect, but it is also worth remarking that Madison retained a considerable suspicion of a strong executive. As late as Sept. 7, he supported a move to revive an executive council. He insisted on a provision for impeachment of the executive, urged that the judiciary be associated in the veto process, opposed an absolute veto, and moved to permit conclusion of treaties of peace without executive consent.

A second consequence, unnoticed in the standard literature, was fully as important. By July 14, Madison had come to be completely dedicated to the prospect that the great republic might be made completely national in its structure and operations. The compromise wrecked his desires. He and all the delegates were forced to readjust their thinking to accord with the decision that the general government would *not* be wholly national in structure, that the Senate would still represent the states. Madison, in fact, was among the first to make the point explicit. "The principle of [the great] compromise . . . required," he said, "that there shd. be a concurrence of two authorities, in one of which the people, in the other the states, should be represented." [35] On August 31, he even moved a complex ratification formula which would require the consent of both a majority of people and a majority of states. He was attempting, now, to form a concrete and consistent image of a system "partly national and partly federal" in structure.

Madison said nothing during the convention to suggest that he approved of this sort of hybrid. He only pointed to the logical consequences of a decision he had disagreed with and used them to advance particular objectives. Even at the close of the convention, he was not completely reconciled to the reintroduction of state agency into the federal system.[36] Still, there obviously echoed in his mind the earlier insistence of John Dickinson, George Mason, Roger Sherman, and others that it was *proper* for the states to be directly represented in the federal government, if only to protect their share of power in a mixed regime. For when he came to write *The Federalist*, he persuasively defended just this point of view. He still objected to an *equal* representation of the states, but now supported their participation as political societies in the workings of the new regime.[37] The system he defended in *The Federalist* was only partly national; and by the time of the Virginia state convention, he was saying, "If the general government were wholly independent of the governments of the particular states, then, indeed, usurpations might be expected to the fullest extent." But as the central government "derives its authority from [the state] governments, and from the same source from which their authority is derived," no usurpations need be feared. Far from threatening a gradual absorption of the proper powers of the states, adoption of the Constitution would "increase the security of liberty more than any government that ever was," since in America the powers ordinarily confided to a single government—and sometimes even to a single

35. *Ibid.*, 80–81.

36. There can be no doubt that his prediction that the system would not meet his objects (see n. 3 above) resulted mainly from his discontent about the Senate and his disappointment with the convention's refusal to adopt the federal veto on state laws.

37. See, particularly, *The Federalist* Nos. 39, 45, 62.

branch—would be entrusted to two sets of governments, each of which would watch the other at the same time as its several branches served as an internal check against abuse.[38]

What had caused this change of mind? Antifederalist attacks on the convention's work? *The Federalist* was obviously written to defend the Constitution from its critics, and criticism surely forced its advocates to rationalize the work of the convention, leading them to see advantages in clauses they had not especially regarded or had even disapproved.[39] That Madison responded partly to the Antifederalist critiques seems all the likelier in light of a developmental study of the framing, which challenges a very common, deep, and usually unrecognized assumption that Madison and other framers entered the convention with their thoughts essentially in order, struggled with opponents holding different ideas, and compromised no more than they were forced to. Studies of the Constitutional Convention seldom make a full allowance for truly fundamental changes of mind. Yet even the ingenious experience the same fluidity of shifting, jarring, dawning thoughts that we ourselves experience in any group endeavor. The Constitutional Convention was a learning process, an interchange of thoughts, for every member present.[40] Early in the work, the course of the deliberations forced the major author of the Virginia Resolutions to begin rethinking his original proposals. From then until adjournment, like every other delegate, he listened to his colleagues, was influenced by their thoughts, and struggled constantly to readjust his thinking to a plan whose shape was changing day by day. These changes outraced even Madison's ability to fully comprehend what was emerging. Not until he wrote *The Federalist* did he attempt a systematic rationalization of the summer's work, and his defense of the completed Constitution articulated understandings he achieved only in the course of the deliberations or even after they were through.

For Madison, moreover, Antifederalist criticisms of the Constitution were more than merely arguments that he was obligated to rebut. They were worries worthy of consideration, worries to which he himself was not immune. Like most supporters of the Constitution, he condemned most Antifederalists as men of little intellect and impure motives, but he did not

38. Elliot, ed., *Debates in the State Conventions*, III, 96, 408–409.
39. Wood, *Creation of the American Republic*, 526–532.
40. Note Madison's own undated, late-life recognition that there were few members "who did not change in the progress of discussions the opinions on important points which they carried into the Convention . . . Few who, at the close of the Convention, were not ready to admit this change as the enlightening effect of the discussions" (Farrand, ed., *Records*, III, 455). For other explicit statements that his views changed during the convention, see *ibid.*, 497, 517, 521, 537.

regard all doubters in this way. Edmund Randolph and George Mason, for example, were colleagues he esteemed, colleagues he had listened to and learned from through the Philadelphia summer, colleagues whose anxieties and hopes he shared to a significant degree. Indeed, when we recall the limitations of his wishes during the convention, when we recognize that he was never simply on a single side of its divisions, it follows that the framing of the Constitution almost certainly affected Madison in one way modern scholarship has overlooked. It heightened his awareness of undemocratic and consolidationist opinion among his fellow framers. It taught him that among his allies in the battle with the smaller states were some who wished to carry centralization to objectionable extremes and some who were in-clined to treat the document completed in convention more flexibly than he considered safe. As he reflected on the course of the proceedings and antici-pated the important role that many of the framers would continue to per-form, he may have recognized that his opponents of the summer had been right to seek additional assurance that the general government would stay within its proper bounds.[41]

The evidence for this effect, a critic might assert, is tenuous at best. Madi-son said nothing, then or later, that would indisputably confirm that he was seriously disturbed by the opinions of his allies. There may be some tan-talizing hints that this was so. But there is no specific statement that would unimpeachably confirm it.[42]

41. I find suggestive a remark in a letter from Randolph: "I confess to you without reserve, that I feel great distrust of some of those, who will certainly be influential agents in the [new] government, and whom I suspect to be capable of making a wicked use of its defects. . . . I reverence Hamilton, because he was honest and open in his views," but "the management in some stages of the convention created a disgustful apprehension of the views of some particular characters" (Sept. 3, 1788, in Hutchinson *et al.*, eds., *Papers of Madison*, XI, 246–247).

42. Several of the most important hints are mentioned in the text and notes below. Explanation of some others would require a fuller study of proceedings in conven-tion than can be provided in this space. But see n. 24 (above) for one important difference between Madison and two of his large-state allies. And note the biting wit with which he countered Morris's desire to leave the legislature free to apportion representation — condemning such implicit confidence in rulers, especially from one so strongly persuaded of "the political depravity of men" (Farrand, ed., *Records*, I, 584). Madison repeatedly objected to permitting legislative discretion in any case in which the legislators might have an interest distinct from the people's (e.g., *ibid.*, II, 249–250). My conviction that he came to be increasingly concerned about the views of higher-flying nationalists depends to a significant degree on many indications of this sort that his extremist stand on making the central government effective was counterbalanced by a fear of making it too vigorous or freeing it too much from

But why should Madison have armed the doubters, either during the convention or as he worked to win approval of the Constitution? Perhaps we need not be surprised that his surviving writings do not prove beyond all doubt that he was worried by the centralizing, antidemocratic sentiments expressed in the convention.[43] The fact is that he did defend provisions he had earlier resisted, not only in *The Federalist* but through the rest of his career. And he defended them in language very similar to what he heard from his opponents during the convention. Perhaps he actually accorded his opponents' fears more plausibility than he admitted at the time. The records of proceedings leave no doubt that, on a spectrum which would take into account all issues faced by the convention, Madison stood almost equidistant from Hamilton and Randolph, from Mason and Gouverneur Morris. If we are open to the possibility that, standing in between, he was affected and occasionally alarmed by what he heard from both extremes, new insights will result; the framer's thought and conduct will appear less puzzling. The proof that Madison was privately alarmed by some of those who joined him in the battle with the smaller states cannot be found, so far as I can tell, in an explicit statement. But it is there, despite the absence of this sort of confirmation. It is present in the obvious progression of his thought. What did he desire at the beginning of the great convention? What did he defend when it was through? What happened in between?

Madison approached the Constitutional Convention persuaded that continuation of America's republican experiment required "concessions" from the states of part of their autonomy, "concessions" from the people sufficient to restrain the governing majority's eventual ability to have its way with additional security for private rights and long-term needs. But as he said to Thomas Jefferson, he wanted to concede *no more* to governmental vigor and stability than was consistent with the Revolution.[44] And he ended the convention knowing that his own intentions and his own evolving understanding of the Constitution were inconsistent with the hopes of several of his large-state allies. Madison intended to invigorate the Union in order to protect the Revolution from persistent public debts, swollen military

---

popular control. On issues that involved the latter question, he was on the moderate to democratic side in the convention.

43. Moreover, in the late-life writings, Madison was plainly trying both to serve as a dispassionate historian of the convention and to protect the Constitution from new threats. Concerned for the collective reputation of the framers, he spoke no ill of his dead colleagues and conscientiously attempted to give even Hamilton and Morris their full due. All of Madison's surviving writings, for that matter, are surprisingly free of aspersions on his political opponents.

44. To Jefferson, in Hutchinson *et al.*, eds., *Papers of Madison*, IX, 318.

forces, overpowerful executives, disillusionment with popular control, and majority contempt for constitutional protection of minority rights.[45] He searched for ways that all of this might be accomplished at minimal expense to the residual autonomy of the people in their several states. He consistently assumed that the new Constitution granted to the central government only the specific powers listed. Other framers wanted to invigorate the Union for very different ends, and only a minority shared Madison's consistent, scrupulous respect for constitutional restraints.[46]

If we think of the convention as an incident in the Virginian's education, it seems entirely likely that his numbers of *The Federalist* were written in response to friends as well as foes. They answered those who sought *more* governmental energy than he considered proper as well as those who feared the Constitution. They answered even his collaborator in the series. This is not to say that Madison already thought of Hamilton as dangerous to the Republic. The evidence does not permit us even to insist that he was consciously conducting a debate with his coauthor, though it is clear that he was less than fully comfortable with the alliance.[47] One thing, nonetheless, seems absolutely certain. For Madison, these essays represented more than an attempt to erect a theoretical justification of what the convention had done. They were also part of a continuing attempt to comprehend and publicly define a new political phenomenon, a novel instrument of government to which their author felt obliged to make a personal, emotional commit-

45. Madison developed this concern most fully in his speech in convention on June 29 (Farrand, ed., *Records*, I, 464–465) and in *The Federalist* No. 41. But the argument that only an effective union could preserve the states from standing armies, overpowerful executives, swollen taxes, persistent public debts, and other consequences inconsistent with republican liberty was outlined in a speech to the Virginia legislature as early as Nov. 1785 (Hutchinson *et al.*, eds., *Papers of Madison*, VIII, 431–432; see also IX, 286, 294–295, 299, 318, 371).

46. It is seldom noted, but a fact, that Hamilton's speech of June 29, in which he insisted that "no Governt. could give us tranquility and happiness at home, which did not possess sufficient stability and strength to make us respectable abroad" (Farrand, ed., *Records*, I, 467), immediately followed and was in part a *response to* Madison's most impassioned warning of the perils of overly energetic government.

47. When he informed Jefferson of the authorship of *The Federalist*, Madison declared that the authors "*are not mutually answerable* for *all the ideas of each other*" (Hutchinson *et al.*, eds., *Papers of Madison*, XI, 227). For a stronger statement—more suspect because it came later in life—see Elizabeth Fleet, ed., "Madison's 'Detached Memoranda,'" *WMQ*, 3d Ser., III (1946), 565. For another contemporary admission that some Federalists carried their alarm with the American majority too far, see Madison to Philip Mazzei, Dec. 10, 1788, in Hutchinson *et al.*, eds., *Papers of Madison*, XI, 389.

ment.[48] They were part of an extended effort to revise his own ideas in light of the experience of the summer, to adjust his thought to the decisions of the Federal Convention, and thus to reassure himself as well as others that the Constitution would fulfill the Revolution. As he wrote these essays, Madison was consciously distilling from the lessons of the framing a new constitutional philosophy. That philosophy cannot be fully understood without a grasp of *all* the ways that he was changed by the convention and the plan that it proposed. *The Federalist*, in turn, illuminates his conduct through the framing.

III

Two related emphases of modern scholarship have left us with a poorly balanced understanding of Madison's founding vision. In the first place, studies of the Constitutional Convention understandably and strongly emphasize his leadership of delegates determined to replace the old Confederation with a great republic. Although this draws attention properly to the Virginian's most important contribution, it discourages a due attention to the limits of his wishes, limits which suggest important differences within the nationalist coalition and alert us to a subtle struggle which engaged the framer no less than did the battle with the smaller states.

Studies that do not distinguish Madison's variety of nationalism, which was structural, or operational, in nature, from the views of radical proponents of a concentration of authority underestimate a critical dimension of the tensions present in the Constitutional Convention. Genuine consolidationists were present. Consolidation was a potent fear, as were the antidemocratic sentiments of several framers. Madison participated in these fears. He also consciously attempted to identify the novel system shaped by the decisions in convention and to readjust his thoughts to its demands. Much of this is missed in most examinations of his conduct, and all of it was instrumental to the shaping of *The Federalist*. Only in these essays did Madison begin to demonstrate how much he had been changed by the convention and the Constitution. Here he was most careful to articulate assumptions and concerns that had continuously shaped his conduct. Here he offered a philosophy remolded by the lessons he had learned.

This brings us to the second emphasis that interferes with a better understanding of Madison's position at the founding. An imprecise description of

48. "Whatever . . . the opinions entertained in forming the Constitution, it was the duty of all to support it in its true meaning as understood *by the Nation* at the time of its ratification. No one felt this obligation more than I have done." Madison to J. G. Jackson, Dec. 27, 1821, in Farrand, ed., *Records*, III, 450.

his stand in the convention suggests that he intended to confide more power to the central government than he ever really did. This suggestion then is reinforced by an excessive emphasis on *Federalist* No. 10. Undue concentration on this single essay, Madison's most careful presentation of the argument that private rights are safer in a large than in a small republic, strengthens the impression that he planned to safeguard liberty almost exclusively by means of an "extension of the sphere" and might, therefore, have actually preferred a greater concentration of authority in central hands than the convention finally approved.

Federalist No. 10 *is* indispensable to understanding the concerns and hopes that generated the Virginia Resolutions and inspired James Madison's defense of the completed Constitution. Agonized by his perception that the rule of state majorities appeared to be persistently at odds with private rights and long-term public needs, unable to relinquish either one of his commitments, Madison attempted to escape the trap by generalizing lessons drawn from his political experience, particularly from the experience of Virginia's recent struggle over tax support for teachers of religion.[49] Had a single sect been dominant in the Old Dominion, he believed, no considerations could have blocked this measure. The multiplicity of disagreeing sects had done what no appeal to principle and public good could have accomplished. From this and other lessons, aided possibly by David Hume, he leaped to the conclusion that the democratic way to counteract the self-destructive features of a democratic system was to enlarge the size of the republic. A large enough republic would encompass such a host of sects and factions that majorities would seldom find a common purpose inimical to private rights or long-term public needs. Its large election districts would encourage the selection of representatives less likely to abandon justice or the enduring public good for "temporary or partial considerations."[50] The legislature of a great republic might even have been trusted with the task of overseeing factional disputes within the states and intervening to protect minorities when factional majorities endangered private rights.

This train of reasoning was basically complete when Madison prepared the "Vices of the Political System of the United States." He pressed it through the Constitutional Convention. It became a cornerstone of his assertion that the Constitution promised a republican solution to the vices most endemic to republics. Taken by itself, however, the argument for an extension

---

49. I make this argument at greater length in "James Madison, the Statute for Religious Freedom, and the Crisis of Republican Convictions," paper delivered at the Bicentennial Conference on the Virginia Statute for Religious Freedom, Sept. 1985, Charlottesville, forthcoming in volume of proceedings from Cambridge University Press.

50. *Federalist* No. 10, p. 62.

of the sphere by no means offers a sure path to understanding Madison's entire position. Taken by itself, it leads most easily to serious distortion of his views.

This is true, particularly, if we disregard the qualifications that Madison was careful to insert in every presentation of his thesis. As he explained to Jefferson, the general government created by the Constitution might safely have been trusted even with a veto on state laws because its officers, impartial judges of contentions in the individual states, would at the same time have no interests separate from the interests of the body of the states and people.[51] Not just one, but two considerations had been present in the framer's mind throughout the shaping of the great republic. Vicious legislation, he believed, can issue either from the passions of an interested majority *or* from legislators who betray the needs of their constituents in order to pursue their personal interests and ambitions.[52] Enlargement of the size of the republic will impede formation of a factional majority, but this is only half of a solution to the problem of representative democracy. And it may increase the risk that representatives will not reflect the people's needs and will. "There is a mean," says *Federalist* No. 10, "on both sides of which inconveniencies will be found." Although small electorates may favor the selection of representatives so close to their constituents as to be unable or unwilling to pursue the general good, large electorates may choose men insufficiently "acquainted with all their local circumstances and lesser interests."[53] Extension of the sphere of the republic will therefore prove a truly democratic remedy for democratic ills "only . . . within a sphere of a mean extent." "In too extensive" a republic, Madison admitted, "a defensive concert may be rendered too difficult against the oppression of those entrusted with the administration."[54]

Majority excess had never seemed to Madison the only danger to republics —not even in the Revolutionary states. He was always equally concerned that rulers might betray the people, that power can corrupt, that men in power would attempt to free themselves from limitations in order to pursue distinct objectives of their own. He was therefore always careful to insist that framers of a constitution "must first enable the government to controul the governed; and . . . next . . . oblige it to controul itself."[55] One of these

51. Oct. 24, 1787, in Hutchinson *et al.*, eds., *Papers of Madison*, X, 214.

52. "Vices of the Political System," *ibid.*, IX, 354–357.

53. *The Federalist* No. 10, pp. 62–63.

54. Madison to Jefferson, Oct. 24, 1787, in Hutchinson *et al.*, eds., *Papers of Madison*, X, 214.

55. *The Federalist* No. 51, p. 349. See also "Vices of the Political System," in Hutchinson *et al.*, eds., *Papers of Madison*, IX, 357.

necessities was not more vital than the other, and dependence on the people for election did not seem to Madison a totally sufficient guarantee of the responsibility of rulers. Accordingly, his contributions to *The Federalist* were quite particular about the special sort of great republic he defended. Essay No. 10 is full of references to "well constructed" great republics, and Madison wrote two dozen other numbers to explain what "well constructed" means. Among the most important was essay No. 51, whose most suggestive passage reads:

> The larger the society, provided it lie within a practicable sphere, the more duly capable it will be of self-government. And happily for the *republican cause*, the practicable sphere may be carried to a very great extent, by a judicious modification and mixture of the *federal principle*.[56]

There are many keys to understanding Madison's participation in the making and defense of the new Constitution. One of the most helpful is to see the founding as a *process* in which Madison's initial preparations, the Philadelphia Convention, and the effort to secure adoption of the Constitution were passages of a single stream. Each passage helps explain the others and the whole. Through all its course, this view of his participation would suggest, Madison had been seeking "the practicable sphere of a republic," the "middle ground" between excessive localism (and the tyranny of unrestrained majorities) and undue concentration of authority in distant, unresponsive rulers. He found this "middle ground" only when he felt compelled to put in print a systematic effort to relate the Constitution to the principles of the Revolution, only as he reconstructed the collective reasoning of the convention, compared the Constitution to the hopes with which he had begun, and readjusted his ideas in light of the experience of the summer. He found it in the document itself: in the compound, partly federal features of the new regime.

Madison, in 1786, was a committed, troubled unionist, persuaded that the Union would not last without effective general government and that an end of union would eventually entail an end of American democracy. He concluded that the powers of the central government would have to be extended so that they would reach all of the nation's common business and that these powers must be rendered genuinely supreme. In the early weeks of the convention, intent upon this object, he became increasingly determined to remove the states entirely from their intermediary role between the general government and people, to make the central government wholly national in its structure and workings. Over his determined opposition, the convention nevertheless decided that the new regime would not be wholly

56. *The Federalist* No. 51, p. 353.

national in structure; and when the gathering adjourned, he was severely disappointed. But he was quickly forced by his assumption of a leading role in the ratification contest to think his way again through every step in the creation of the Constitution, and by the time he wrote *The Federalist*, he was beginning to believe that the convention had been right to reason that a certain agency for the states as states would help maintain the equilibrium he wanted.

This acceptance of a federal role for states as states—and not a reconsideration of the proper powers of the central government—was Madison's real reversal in the aftermath of the convention's most important compromise. It is best explained by recognizing that he learned from the convention only slightly less than he had taught. "The practicable sphere of a republic," he had always thought, would be that sphere which would be large enough that it might "break and control the violence of faction," but not *so* large that it would also break the democratic bond between the rulers and the ruled, the "communion of interests and sympathy of sentiments" which bind a representative to his constituents.[57] However much he worried over the excesses of majorities, however hard he fought for national control of national affairs, Madison had always been no less concerned to guard self-government against excessive concentration of authority in rulers unresponsive to the people. In 1787, he changed his mind repeatedly about the constitutional devices most likely to achieve the proper blend of power and responsibility, but he was dedicated first to last to a *republican* solution to the nation's ills. And he defined republics as governments in which the will of the majority might be restrained, but not indefinitely denied.

Revolutionary principles, for Madison, included *both* security for private rights *and* democratic rule. Democracy, in turn, depended on perpetuation of the Union. Pressed by circumstances, other members of his generation could be tempted to conclude that one or two of these three principles might have to be severely compromised in order to preserve the others. But Madison had something in his makeup that compelled him to rebel against this choice, and this rebellion was the crux of his distinctive contribution to the founding. The critical necessity, as he conceived it, was to build a structure that would best secure them all. Such a structure, he was soon prepared to hope, had actually emerged—and not by accident alone—from the collective reasoning of the convention. Carefully respected, he maintained, the Constitution might provide as much security for all the objects of the Revolution as the nation's ingenuity could offer. Liberty, democracy, and union might prove safer in a federal system of republics than in any simpler system.[58]

57. *Ibid.*, No. 10, p. 56, No. 57, p. 386.
58. *Ibid.*, No. 51, p. 351.

In a *federal* system of republics, Madison explained, the will of the majority would be refined and purified by passing it successively through different filters. Authority would be distributed among two sets of governmental branches, state and general. Within each set, the different branches would be chosen sometimes more and sometimes less directly by the people, which would guarantee a due concern for both their short- and long-term needs. State and national representatives would each be charged with the responsibilities that they were best equipped for. Both would be denied authority to act on matters poorly suited to their character or knowledge. State representatives would not participate in national decisions, which demanded less-constricted vision. Federal officials would not intervene in matters that required a more particular familiarity with local needs and situations.[59] Thus, the product of successive distillations of the people's will would be, withal, the people's will. No branch of any part of the compound republic would be able to successfully pursue an interest different from the well-considered interest of the people as a whole. The state and general governments would help to keep each other within the proper bounds. Future generations would continue to enjoy as much self-government as human nature would allow.

This was not the system Madison had started out to build. It was not the system he had advocated at the Constitutional Convention. And yet the finished Constitution did define the sort of "middle ground" that he had always wanted. It promised an effective blend of governmental energy and freedom. It might, at once, "perpetuate the Union, and redeem the honor of the Republican name."[60] Thus, "the practicable sphere of a republic," he announced, had finally been found. Identified by the collective wisdom of the Constitutional Convention, which he was not too proud to think might be superior to his alone, it rested in the partly national but also partly federal features of the large, compound republic. It is time for us to reassert the novelty of these distinctive features, and time to recognize that Madison's defense of the completed Constitution did not have a single theme, but two: that this new government was perfectly consistent with the principles of a republican revolution, and that the Federal Constitution did not establish and would not support a consolidated national government, which he considered inconsistent with the character and needs of what was still to be a genuinely revolutionary union.

---

59. *Ibid.*, No. 10, p. 63.

60. Madison to Edmund Pendleton, Feb. 24, 1787, in Hutchinson *et al.*, eds., *Papers of Madison*, IX, 295.

☆ ☆ ☆ ☆ ☆

Slavery and the Constitutional Convention
Making a Covenant with Death

PAUL FINKELMAN

For the nineteenth-century abolitionist William Lloyd Garrison, the Constitution was the result of a terrible bargain between freedom and slavery. The
American states were, in Garrison's words, united by a "covenant with
death" and "agreement with Hell." Garrison and his followers refused to
participate in American electoral politics, because to do so they would have
had to support this "covenant with death." Instead, under the slogan "No
Union with Slaveholders," the Garrisonian abolitionists repeatedly called
for an end to the nation. Their disunion sentiments were based in part on
the moral principle of avoiding the corruption of the proslavery Constitution. But their position was also pragmatic. Convinced that the legal protection of slavery in the Constitution made political activity futile, the Garrisonians thought only moral suasion could save America from its "covenant
with death."[1]

The Garrisonians did not necessarily see the Constitution as the result of
a deliberate conspiracy of evil men; rather, they understood it to be the
consequence of political give-and-take at the Convention of 1787. Thus, in
his aptly titled pamphlet *The Constitution: A Pro-Slavery Compact*, Wendell
Phillips analyzed "that 'compromise,' which was made between slavery and

The author wishes to thank Stanley N. Katz, James McPherson, John Murrin,
James Oakes, William M. Wiecek, and LeRoy Votto for their comments on an earlier
draft of this essay.

1. See William M. Wiecek, *The Sources of Antislavery Constitutionalism in America,
1760–1848* (Ithaca, N.Y., 1977), chap. 10; and James Brewer Stewart, *Holy Warriors:
The Abolitionists and American Slavery* (New York, 1976), 98–99, 158–159.

freedom, in 1787; granting to the slaveholder distinct privileges and protection for his slave property, in return for certain commercial concessions on his part toward the North." Phillips further argued that "the Nation at large were fully aware of this bargain at the time, and entered into it willingly and with open eyes."[2] Phillips's argument both exaggerated and understated the nature of the relationship between slavery and the Constitution. Certainly, some of those at the convention "entered into" the bargain with great reservations, and many at the ratifying conventions may indeed have had their eyes at least partially closed to the full extent of the "bargain." On the other hand, the bargain involved more than commerce and slavery; it concerned the very creation of the Union itself.

Other nineteenth-century antislavery thinkers disagreed with the Garrisonians. Salmon P. Chase, the most successful antislavery politician, fought a lifelong battle to convince his colleagues, and numerous jurists, that the Constitution was really opposed to slavery. Despite his creative attempts, Chase's efforts always failed.[3] The United States Supreme Court almost always protected slavery in the cases it heard.[4] Likewise, almost all American presidents and their cabinet officers protected slavery in foreign and domestic politics. Perhaps most frustrating to the political abolitionists was the fact that some of their most brilliant allies in the crusade against slavery—the Garrisonians—agreed with their enemies on the meaning of the Constitution. Thus, one Ohio Liberty Party man ruefully noted after reading Wendell Phillips's pamphlet on the Constitution: "Garrison, Phillips, and Quincy; Calhoun, Rhett, and McDuffie; all harmoniously laboring to prevent such a construction of the Constitution as would abolish slavery."[5]

A careful reading of the Constitution reveals that the Garrisonians were

2. [Wendell Phillips], *The Constitution A Pro-Slavery Compact; or, Selections from the Madison Papers, &c.*, 2d ed. (New York, 1845), v–vi.

3. Eric Foner, *Free Soil, Free Labor, Free Men: The Ideology of the Republican Party before the Civil War* (New York, 1970), chap. 3; Salmon P. Chase, *Reclamation of Fugitives from Service* (Cincinnati, Ohio, 1847). This was Chase's written brief in *Jones v. Van Zandt*, 5 Howard (U.S.) 215 (1847). Here Chase was unsuccessful in his attempt to persuade the Supreme Court to overturn the verdict against Van Zandt for helping a group of fugitive slaves claimed by Jones.

4. William M. Wiecek, "Slavery and Abolition before the United States Supreme Court, 1820–1860," *Journal of American History*, LXV (1978–1979), 34–59.

5. George Bradburn to Gerrit Smith, December 15, 1846, Gerrit Smith Papers, box 4, Syracuse University, Syracuse, New York. The Garrisonian analysis was not, of course, designed to give aid and comfort to defenders of slavery. The Garrisonians merely read the Constitution and the debates of the convention and analyzed what they found. Similarly, an acceptance of the Garrisonian view of the Constitution—that it was a document which explicitly protected the institution of slavery—is not an endorsement of the Garrisonian cure: a rejection of political activity and disunion.

right to believe that the national compact favored slavery. And a detailed examination of the Convention of 1787 explains how the Constitution evolved in this way. Both the text of the Constitution and the debates surrounding it help us understand that the "more perfect Union" created by this document was in fact fundamentally imperfect.

I

The word "slavery" appears in only one place in the Constitution—in the Thirteenth Amendment, where the institution is abolished. Throughout the main body of the Constitution, slaves are referred to as "other persons," "such persons," or in the singular as a "person held to Service or Labour." Northern delegates to the 1787 Convention believed the word "slave" would "stain" the Constitution. Southerners avoided the term because they did not want unnecessarily to antagonize their colleagues from the North. As long as they were assured of protection for their institution, the southerners at the convention were willing to do without the word "slave."[6]

Despite the circumlocution, slavery was given both explicit and implicit sanction throughout the Constitution. Provisions explicitly sanctioning slavery are found in five places.[7]

Art. I, Sec. 2. The three-fifths clause provided for counting three-fifths of all slaves for purposes of representation in Congress. This clause also provided that, if any "direct tax" was levied on the states, it could be imposed only proportionately, according to population, and that only three-fifths of all slaves would be counted in assessing what each state's contribution would be.

6. This issue is discussed by Staughton Lynd in his essay "The Abolitionist Critique of the Constitution," in Lynd, *Class Conflict, Slavery, and the United States Constitution: Ten Essays* (Indianapolis, Ind., 1967), 159–160. See also the first four paragraphs of part iv of this essay.

7. Curiously, Don Fehrenbacher finds that "only three [clauses of the Constitution] were directly and primarily concerned with the institution" of slavery. Fehrenbacher acknowledges only that other clauses "impinged upon slavery." Fehrenbacher also asserts that "the Constitution had some bias toward freedom but was essentially open-ended with respect to slavery." Fehrenbacher fails, however, to explain what part of the Constitution was profreedom, while at the same time ignoring many proslavery aspects of the Constitution. Don E. Fehrenbacher, *The Federal Government and Slavery* (Claremont, Calif., 1984), 3, 6. For an analysis of the Constitution closer to the one presented here, see Wiecek, *Sources of Antislavery Constitutionalism*. Wiecek lists 11 separate clauses in the Constitution that "directly or indirectly accommodated the peculiar institution," but makes no distinction between direct and indirect protections of slavery (62–63).

Art. I, Sec. 9, Par. 1. The slave importation clause prohibited Congress from banning the African slave trade before 1808, but did not require Congress to end the trade after that date.

Art. I, Sec. 9, Par. 4. This clause declared that any "capitation" or other "direct tax" imposed had to take into account the three-fifths clause. It ensured that, if a head tax were ever levied, slaves would be taxed at three-fifths the rate of whites. The "direct tax" portion of this clause was redundant, because that was provided for in the three-fifths clause.

Art. IV, Sec. 2, Par. 3. The fugitive slave clause prohibited the states from emancipating fugitive slaves and required that runaways be returned to their owners "on demand."

Art. V. This article prohibited any amendment of the slave importation or capitation clauses before 1808.

Taken together, these five constitutional provisions gave the South a strong claim to "special treatment" for its peculiar institution. The three-fifths clause also gave the South extra political muscle to support that claim.

The five clauses that directly protected slavery were supplemented by numerous other clauses of the Constitution. Some indirect protections, such as the prohibition on taxing exports, were included primarily to protect the interests of slaveholders. Others, such as the guarantee of federal support to "suppress Insurrections" and the creation of the electoral college, were written with slavery in mind, although they were also supported for reasons having nothing to do with slavery. Finally, some clauses, such as the restrictions on federal court jurisdiction, did not inherently favor slavery, but ultimately did protect slavery when interpreted by the courts or implemented by Congress after the adoption of the Constitution. These are the most prominent indirect protections of slavery:

Art. I, Sec. 8, Par. 15, empowering Congress to call "forth the Militia" to "suppress Insurrections," including slave rebellions.[8]

Art. I, Sec. 9, Par. 5, prohibiting taxes on exports and thus preventing an indirect tax on slavery by taxing the staple products of slave labor, such as tobacco, rice, and eventually cotton.

Art. I, Sec. 10, Par. 2, prohibiting states from taxing exports, thus preventing an indirect tax on the products of slave labor by a nonslaveholding state.[9]

---

8. Wendell Phillips considered this clause, and the one of Art. IV, Sec. 4, to be among the five key proslavery provisions of the Constitution (*The Constitution A Pro-Slavery Compact*, vi).

9. Although no slave state would have levied such a tax, a free state like New York, Massachusetts, or Pennsylvania might conceivably have taxed products produced in other states but exported through the harbors of New York, Boston, or Philadelphia.

Art. II, Sec. 1, Par. 2, providing for the indirect election of the president through an electoral college based on congressional representation. This provision incorporated the three-fifths clause into the electoral college and gave whites in slave states a disproportionate influence in the election of the president.

Art. III, Sec. 2, Par. 1, limiting federal diversity jurisdiction to "Citizens of different States" (rather than inhabitants). This ensured that slaves and, in some cases, free blacks would not have access to federal courts.[10]

Art. IV, Sec. 1, requiring that "Full Faith and Credit" be given to the laws and judicial proceedings of other states, thus obligating free states to recognize laws creating and protecting slavery.

Art. IV, Sec. 2, Par. 1, limiting the privileges and immunities clause to "citizens" and denying these protections to slaves and, in some cases, free blacks.

Art. IV, Sec. 2, Par. 2, providing for the return of fugitives from justice, thus requiring that free states return for trial whites and free blacks accused of aiding fugitive slaves or in some other way violating slave codes.

Art. IV, Sec. 4, guaranteeing that the United States government would protect states from "domestic Violence," including slave rebellions.

Art. V, requiring a three-fourths majority of the states to ratify the Constitution, thus ensuring that the slaveholding states would have a perpetual veto over any constitutional changes.[11]

Finally, the structure of the Constitution ensured against emancipation by the new federal government. Because the Constitution created a government of limited powers, Congress lacked the power to interfere in the domestic institutions of the states.[12] Thus, during the ratification debates

10. The proslavery implications of this clause did not become fully apparent until the Supreme Court issued its opinion in *Dred Scott* v. *Sandford*, 19 Howard 393 (1857).

11. Had all 15 slave states remained in the Union, they would to this day be able to prevent an amendment on any subject. In a 50-state union, it takes only 13 states to block any amendment.

12. Under various clauses of the Constitution the Congress might have protected, limited, or prohibited the interstate slave trade (Art. I, Sec. 8, Par. 3), slavery in the District of Columbia or on military bases (Art. I, Sec. 8, Par. 17), or slavery in the territories (Art. IV, Sec. 3, Par. 2). None of these clauses permitted Congress to touch slavery in the states. Some radical abolitionists argued that under the guarantee clause, Art. IV, Sec. 4, Congress had the right to end slavery in the states. See Wiecek, *Sources of Antislavery Constitutionalism*, 269–271. The delegates in Philadelphia did not debate these clauses with slavery in mind, although, as will be shown in this essay below (part iii), the commerce clause was accepted as part of a bargain over the African slave trade.

only the most fearful southern Antifederalists opposed the Constitution on the grounds that it threatened slavery.[13] Most southerners, even those who opposed the Constitution for other reasons, agreed with General Charles Cotesworth Pinckney of South Carolina, who told his state's house of representatives:

> We have a security that the general government can never emancipate them, for no such authority is granted; and it is admitted, on all hands, that the general government has no powers but what are expressly granted by the Constitution, and that all rights not expressed were reserved by the several states.[14]

The Constitution was not "essentially open-ended with respect to slavery," as one eminent scholar has argued.[15] Rather, it was a document that provided enormous protections for the peculiar institution of the South at very little cost to that region. At the Virginia ratifying convention Edmund Randolph denied that the Constitution posed any threat at all to slavery. He challenged opponents of the Constitution to answer, "*Where* is the part that has a tendency to *the abolition of slavery?*" He answered his own question asserting, "Were it right here to mention what passed in [the Philadelphia] convention . . . I might tell you *that the Southern States, even South Carolina herself, conceived this property to be secure*" and that "there was not a member of the Virginia delegation who had *the smallest suspicion of the abolition of slavery*." South Carolinians, who had already ratified the Constitution, would have agreed with Randolph. In summing up the entire Constitution, General Charles Cotesworth Pinckney, who had been one of the ablest defenders of slavery at the convention, proudly told the South Carolina House of Representatives: "In short, considering all circumstances, we have made the best terms for the security of this species of property it was in our power to make. We would have made better if we could; but on the whole, I do not think them bad."[16]

13. One such southerner was Patrick Henry, who used any argument he could find to oppose the Constitution. Henry asserted at the Virginia ratifying convention that, "among ten thousand *implied powers* which they may assume, they may, if we be engaged in war, liberate every one of your slaves if they please." Jonathan Elliot, ed., *The Debates in the Several State Conventions on the Adoption of the Federal Constitution* . . ., 2d ed. (Washington, D.C., 1836), III, 589. Ironically, the implied war powers of the president would be used to end slavery, but only after the South had renounced the Union.

14. Elliot, ed., *Debates*, IV, 286.

15. Fehrenbacher, *The Federal Government and Slavery*, 6 n. 2.

16. Elliot, ed., *Debates*, III, 598–599, IV, 285–286.

II

General Pinckney had good reason to be proud of his role in Philadelphia. Throughout the convention Pinckney and other delegates from the Deep South tenaciously fought to protect the interests of slaveholders. In these struggles they were usually successful.

At the beginning of the convention slavery did not seem to be a pressing issue. Rivalries between large and small states appeared to pose the greatest obstacle to a stronger Union. The nature of representation in Congress; the power of the national government to levy taxes, regulate commerce, and pay off the nation's debts; the role of the states under a new constitution; and the power of the executive were on the agenda. Yet, as these issues were debated, the importance of slavery—and the sectional differences it caused—became clear.[17] Throughout the summer of 1787 slavery would emerge to complicate almost every debate. Most important by far was the way slavery figured in the lengthy debate over representation.

On May 29, Governor Edmund Randolph of Virginia submitted the series of resolutions known as the Virginia Plan to the convention. In introducing these resolutions Randolph claimed they responded to the "crisis" of the nation "and the necessity of preventing the fulfilment of the prophecies of the American downfal." This plan would create an entirely new form of government in the United States. The power of the central government would be vastly enhanced at the expense of the states. The new Congress would have greater powers to tax, to secure the nation "against foreign invasion," to settle disagreements between states, and to regulate commerce.[18]

Randolph's plan called for a radical restructuring of the American government by making population the basis for representation in the national Congress. Under the Articles of Confederation, each state had one vote in Congress. By changing the basis of representation to population, Randolph's plan immediately created tensions between the large and small states at the convention. But Randolph's plan also raised the dilemma of whether slaves would be counted for the purposes of determining how many representatives each state would get in the new Congress. This dilemma of how to

17. It is perhaps an exaggeration to assert, as Staughton Lynd has done, that the "sectional conflict between North and South was the major tension in the Convention," simply because there were so many other "major" tensions; it is clear, however, that sectional conflicts and the place of slavery in the new nation caused as much tension as any other individual issue ("The Abolitionist Critique," in Lynd, *Class Conflict, Slavery, and the United States Constitution*, 160).

18. Max Farrand, ed., *The Records of the Federal Convention of 1787*, rev. ed. (New Haven, Conn., 1966), I, 18.

count slaves, or whether to count them at all, would trouble the delegates throughout the Constitutional Convention.

Randolph came from the most populous state in the nation, which had a vested interest in basing representation in the Congress on population. But how that population would be counted greatly affected the potential representation of Virginia and the rest of the South. The state's white population, as the 1790 census would reveal, was only slightly larger than Pennsylvania's. If representation were based solely on free persons, the North would overwhelm the South. But if slaves were counted equally with free persons, the Virginia delegation would be overwhelmingly larger than the delegation of any other state, and the South would have more members of Congress than the North. The Virginians also realized, however, that the northern states were unlikely to embrace enthusiastically a system of government that counted slaves for purposes of representation. Thus, Randolph's plan hedged the issue, declaring "that the rights of suffrage in the National Legislature ought to be proportioned to the Quotas of contribution, or to the number of free inhabitants, as the one or the other rule may seem best in different cases."[19] Randolph's avoidance of the term "slaves" by referring to "quotas of contribution" indicates the sensitivity of the subject.

Squabbling over slavery began in earnest the next day, May 30. James Madison moved to delete the term "free inhabitants" from the Randolph Plan because he felt the phrase "might occasion debates which would divert the Committee [of the whole] from the general question whether the principle of representation should be changed" from states to population.[20] Madison understood that any debate over the role of slavery in the Union at this time might destroy the convention before it got started. But his proposal would have left representation based solely on "quotas of contribution," and this was also unacceptable to most delegates. Madison himself agreed "that some better rule ought to be found." Alexander Hamilton then proposed that representation be based solely on the number of "free inhabitants" in each state. This proposal was too volatile to be debated so early in the convention, and it was quickly tabled. Other attempts at compromise failed. Finally, the Delaware delegates helped put a temporary end to this divisive debate by telling the convention that they "were restrained by their commission from assenting to any change on the rule of suffrage," and if the body endorsed any change in representation, they would be forced to

19. *Ibid.*, 20. In 1790 Virginia had a free population of 454,983. The next largest free populations were Pennsylvania, 430,630; Massachusetts, 378,693; and New York, 318,824. Virginia also had 292,627 slaves, whereas the entire North had only 40,089 slaves.

20. *Ibid.*, 36.

leave the convention. The issue was then postponed, and the convention adjourned for the day.[21]

Debate over representation continued intermittently for the next two weeks, but it was not until June 11 that the issue of slavery reemerged to complicate the debate. On that day the convention considered for the first time, and also approved provisionally, the three-fifths clause. Over the next three months the convention would, on a number of occasions, redebate and reconsider the three-fifths clause before finally adopting it.[22]

The evolution of the three-fifths clause during the convention shows that the clause was not essentially a compromise over taxation and representation, as traditional historians have implied.[23] Rather, it began as a compromise between those who wanted to count slaves fully for purposes of representation and those who did not want to count slaves at all. Thus, on this crucial question the slave states won a critical victory without making any important concessions.

On June 11 Roger Sherman of Connecticut proposed that representation be based on the "numbers of free inhabitants" in each state. John Rutledge and Pierce Butler of South Carolina objected and argued for representation according to "quotas of contribution," which had become a euphemism for counting slaves in a formula for representation.[24] James Wilson and Charles

21. *Ibid.*, 36–38. It seems likely that the Delaware delegation exaggerated the constraints on their commission in a shrewd attempt to avoid a potentially catastrophic debate over slavery and representation. When the convention did in fact adopt representation based on population, the Delaware delegates remained and did not threaten to leave.

22. Approval by the convention did not mean permanent adoption, for until June 20 the convention debated the proposed Constitution as a Committee of the Whole, which allowed for full discussion without binding the delegates to any final resolution of an issue. Anything approved by the convention as a Committee of the Whole would have to be voted on again when the convention was in regular session. Furthermore, under the standing rules of the convention, delegates were free to ask for a reconsideration of decisions on one day's notice. Finally, all clauses of the new Constitution were eventually sent to two drafting committees, the Committee of Detail and the Committee of Style. The reports of these committees were also subject to full debate and amendment by the entire convention.

23. Historians presenting the traditional view include Francis Newton Thorpe, *The Story of the Constitution of the United States* (New York, 1891), 131; Max Farrand, *The Framing of the Constitution of the United States* (New Haven, Conn., 1913), 108; Charles Warren, *The Making of the Constitution* (Boston, 1928), 288–294 (esp. 290–291), 584–586; Clinton Rossiter, *1787: The Grand Convention* (New York, 1966), 173, 188–189. These scholars, with the possible exception of Rossiter, argue that slavery was unimportant at the convention.

24. Farrand, ed., *Records*, I, 196. This motion by Sherman somewhat undermines the traditional notion of a split between the "small" and "large" states over represen-

Pinckney, the younger cousin of General Charles Cotesworth Pinckney, skillfully headed off the Rutledge-Butler proposal.

Wilson proposed, and Pinckney seconded, a motion that ultimately became the three-fifths clause of the Constitution. Here for the first time was an example of cooperation between the North and the South over slavery. Significantly, Wilson was known to oppose slavery and came from a state, Pennsylvania, which had already adopted a gradual emancipation scheme. Nevertheless, harmony at the convention was more important to Wilson than the place of slavery in the new nation. By teaming up, the nominally antislavery Pennsylvanian and the rabidly proslavery Carolinian may have hoped to undercut the antislavery sentiments of other northern delegates while also satisfying the demands of the proslavery delegates like Butler and Rutledge.

The delegates from most of the slave states accepted this proposal without protest. However, Elbridge Gerry of Massachusetts was unwilling to compromise. With some irony he protested, "Blacks are property, and are used to the southward as horses and cattle to the northward; and why should their representation be increased to the southward on account of the number of slaves, than horses or oxen to the north?" Gerry believed this would be an appropriate rule for taxation, but not for representation, because under it four southern voters would have more political power than ten northern voters. He also argued that this clause would degrade freemen in the North by equating them with slaves.[25] No other northerner opposed representation for slaves at this time, and the convention sitting as a Committee of the Whole voted in favor of the three-fifths clause.

Thus, with little debate the three-fifths clause was initially accepted as a basis for representation. The clause, which would give the South enormous political leverage in the nation, was accepted without any quid pro quo from the South. Application of the clause to taxation would not come until later in the convention. Indeed, there was no reason in mid-June to believe it would ever be applied to taxation. A brief history of the three-fifths ratio, prior to 1787, bears this out.

---

tation. Sherman, from the small state of Connecticut, was willing to accept population as a basis for representation in the lower house of the legislature, as long as slaves were not counted, and provided that there was equality in the upper house. A week earlier George Mason of Virginia had suggested the importance of sectionalism in a long speech arguing for an executive "vested in three persons, one chosen from the Northern, one from the Middle, and one from the Southern States" (112–113).

25. *Ibid.*, 201, 205–206, 208. Gerry's arguments must be pieced together from the various notes taken by Madison, Yates, and Paterson. It is perhaps significant that the best notes on Gerry's speech came from the two northerners, Yates and Paterson.

The ratio of three free persons to five slaves was first proposed in the Congress in 1783 as part of an overall program for the national government to raise revenue from the states. The ratio was controversial. Southerners thought it overvalued slaves, and northerners thought it undervalued them. Delegates from Virginia and South Carolina, the states with the greatest number of slaves, wanted taxation based on land values. The entire package allowing for taxation based on population only was initially rejected by the Congress and then later resurrected. It was then sent to the states as an amendment to the Articles of Confederation. The proposal never received the unanimous consent of the states and, therefore, never became part of the Articles of Confederation. Thus, there is little substance to the traditional view that the three-fifths clause "was a legacy from the Congress of 1783" or that "most northern delegates must have realized even before they arrived in Philadelphia that it would be the minimum price of southern acceptance of any new constitution."[26] The only useful legacy of the Congress of 1783 was the numerical ratio itself, which had been applied only to taxation and, as such, had been rejected by the entire nation.

The meaning of the three-fifths clause to the delegates in Philadelphia was clear in the report of the Committee of the Whole on June 13, which stated that representation would be "in proportion to the whole number of white and other free citizens and inhabitants, of every age, sex and condition, including those bound to servitude for a term of years and three fifths of all other persons not comprehended in the foregoing description, except Indians, not paying taxes in each State." The phrasing of the term "white and other free citizens and inhabitants" clearly implied that the "other persons" were neither white nor free.[27] By mid-June a majority in the convention had

26. Rossiter, *The Grand Convention*, 173; Donald L. Robinson, *Slavery in the Structure of American Politics, 1765–1820* (New York, 1971), 156–158. Max Farrand adopted a similar analysis in *The Framing of the Constitution*, arguing that "one finds references in contemporary writings to the 'Federal ratio,' as if it were well understood what was meant by that term" (108). It is probably true that many of the delegates at the convention accepted the ratio of three to five as a proper one for determining the value of slaves in society, but this does not mean that they agreed the ratio ought to be applied to representation. The debate over the three-fifths ratio in the Congress is found in Worthington Chauncey Ford *et al.*, eds., *Journals of the Continental Congress, 1774–1789* (Washington, D.C., 1904–1937), XXV, 948–952 (debates of Mar. 28 to Apr. 1, 1783); XXIV, 214–216, 223–224. The fact that no slave state at this time counted slaves for the allocation of representation in state legislatures underscores the weakness of the argument that slaves *had* to be counted for representation. See n. 35, below.

27. Farrand, ed., *Records*, I, 227. The final draft of the Constitution would omit the word "white," thus leading the antislavery radical Lysander Spooner to argue that the "other persons" referred to resident aliens. On its face Spooner's argument

accepted the principle that representation in the national Congress would be based on population and that three-fifths of the slave population would be added to the free population in determining representation. However, a minority of the delegates, led by those from New Jersey, were still unhappy with this plan.

On June 15 William Paterson introduced what is commonly known as the New Jersey Plan. The plan rejected congressional representation based on population and, instead, retained the system of representation then in force under the Articles of Confederation: that the states would have an equal number of delegates in the Congress. For the next fifteen days the convention debated, without any reference to slavery, whether representation in Congress would be based on population. In most of the votes on this issue the South (except Delaware) supported population-based representation. These votes were predicated on the assumption that the three-fifths clause, which had already been accepted, would be part of the basis of representation.[28]

By June 30 the convention was at a standstill. The states in favor of population-based representation had enough votes to adopt their scheme. But if they were unable to persuade the delegates from the smaller states to acquiesce on this point, the convention itself would fail. In the middle of this debate Madison offered a new mode of analysis for the delegates, contending

> that the States were divided into different interests not by their difference of size, but by other circumstances; the most material of which resulted partly from climate, but principally from their having or not having slaves. These two causes concurred in forming the great division

---

seems more polemical than serious. Whatever strength it had lay in the ambiguity of the wording of the Constitution, which avoided such terms as "slave," "white," and "black." The debates and drafts of the Constitution reveal the clear intent of the framers with regard to slavery. Lysander Spooner, *The Unconstitutionality of Slavery* (Boston, 1845), 94.

28. The southern states also expected to grow faster than the northern, and thus representation based on population would help them in the long run. But, even if whites did not move south, slaves could still be imported. Southerners, confident that a growing slave population would augment their representation in Congress, consistently supported population as the basis of that representation. Staughton Lynd makes this argument in "The Compromise of 1787," in Lynd, *Class Conflict, Slavery, and the United States Constitution.* Gunning Bedford of Delaware observed in the debates of June 30 that Georgia, "though a small State at present," was "actuated by the prospect of soon being a great one." Similarly, South Carolina was "actuated by present interest and future prospects," and North Carolina had "the same motives of present and future interest." Farrand, ed., *Records,* I, 491.

of interests in the U. States. It did not lie between the large and small States: it lay between the Northern and Southern. and if any defensive power were necessary, it ought to be mutually given to these two interests.[29]

So Madison proposed two branches of Congress, one in which slaves would be counted equally with free people and one in which slaves would not be counted at all. Under this arrangement, "the Southern Scale would have the advantage in one House, and the Northern in the other." This proposal was made despite Madison's reluctance to "urge any diversity of interests on an occasion when it is but too apt to arise of itself."[30]

Madison's proposal was ignored by the convention. He may have offered it simply to divert attention from the heated debate between the large and small states. If this was indeed his goal, he was not immediately successful. The small states, led by Delaware, continued to express fear that they would be swallowed up by larger states if representation in the Congress were based solely on population.[31]

Subsequent debates, however, reveal the validity of Madison's analysis that sectionalism—caused by slavery—was a major cause of division within the nation. Indeed, slavery continued to complicate the convention debates

29. Farrand, ed., *Records*, I, 486. The day before, June 29, Alexander Hamilton had made a similar observation. Hamilton, not surprisingly perhaps, saw the issue solely in economic terms. "The only considerable distinction of interests, lay between the carrying and non-carrying States, which divide instead of uniting the largest States" (466).

30. *Ibid.*, 486–487.

31. As if to directly refute Madison's sectional arguments, Delaware's Gunning Bedford argued that his state had little in common with "South Carolina, puffed up with the possession of her wealth and negroes," or Georgia and North Carolina. All three states had "an eye" on "future wealth and greatness," which was predicated on slavery, and thus they were "united with the great states" against the smaller states like Delaware (*ibid.*, 500 [Yates's notes]). Nevertheless, Delaware would remain a slave state until the adoption of the Thirteenth Amendment. New Jersey, which also opposed representation based on population, might also be considered a slave state. At this time New Jersey had taken no steps to end slavery. New Jersey would be the last northern state to pass a gradual emancipation statute, not doing so until 1804. See, generally, Arthur Zilversmit, *The First Emancipation: The Abolition of Slavery in the North* (Chicago, 1967). In the Virginia ratifying convention James Madison asserted that New York and New Jersey would "probably, oppose any attempts to annihilate this species of property" (Elliot, ed., *Debates*, III, 459). However, as William Paterson's subsequent antislavery statements suggest, the New Jersey delegates were even more offended by counting slaves for purposes of representation than they were fearful of population-based representation.

long after the division between large and small states had evaporated. On July 2, Charles Pinckney argued that there was "a solid distinction as to interest between the southern and northern states." Pinckney noted that the Carolinas and Georgia "in their Rice and Indigo had a peculiar interest which might be sacrificed" if they did not have sufficient power in any new Congress.[32] Immediately after this speech the convention agreed to a proposal by General Charles Cotesworth Pinckney that the entire question of representation be turned over to a committee of one delegate from each state. The convention then adjourned until July 5.

On the fifth the committee proposed what historians have since called the Great Compromise. Under this plan representation in the lower house of the legislature would be based on population, and in the upper house the states would have an equal vote. The three-fifths clause was a part of this proposal.[33]

On July 6 the convention once again approved the concept of representation based on population for the lower house of the Congress. A five-man committee was then formed to redraft the clause. In the absence of a census this committee would also have to recommend to the convention the number of representatives that each state would get in the First Congress. Before the convention adjourned for the day, Charles Pinckney again raised sectional issues connected to slavery, arguing that "blacks ought to stand on an equality with whites," but he "wd. . . . agree to the ratio settled by Congs."[34] The significance of Pinckney's argument here was twofold. First, in a debate that had nothing to do with slavery per se, Pinckney raised the issue, as if to warn the convention not to forget the special needs of the South. Second, Pinckney made it clear to the convention that he (and presumably other southerners) thought that the three-fifths rule for counting slaves was a great concession.

On July 9 the committee of five reported its recommendations. Gouverneur Morris, who was on the committee, admitted that the allocations in the report were "little more than a guess." A number of delegates were dissatisfied with these guesses, because in allocating representation in the First Congress the committee had taken into account "the number of blacks and whites." This action led William Paterson to register a protest—only the second so far in the convention—against the three-fifths clause. This was the beginning of a four-day debate over slavery and representation. Paterson asserted that he regarded

32. Farrand, ed., *Records*, I, 516 (from Yates's notes), 510 (from Madison's notes).
33. *Ibid.*, 526.
34. *Ibid.*, 542.

negroes slaves in no light but as property. They are no free agents, have no personal liberty, no faculty of acquiring property, but on the contrary are themselves property, and like other property entirely at the will of the Master.

Paterson pointedly asked, "Has a man in Virga. a number of votes in proportion to the number of his slaves?" He noted that slaves were not counted in allocating representation in southern state legislatures, and asked, "Why should they be represented in the Genl. Govt.[?]" Finally, Paterson argued that counting slaves for purposes of representation encouraged the slave trade.[35]

In response, Madison once again proposed that representation in one house of the legislature be based on total population and the other on only the free population. Pierce Butler again argued for wealth as a basis for representation. This proposal, of course, meant that slaves would be counted equally with whites. Rufus King of Massachusetts gave unexpected support to Butler by warning that the South would not unite with the rest of the country "unless some respect were paid to their superior wealth." Furthermore, King reminded his northern colleagues that, if they expected "preferential distinctions in Commerce," they should be willing to give up something. At least at this point in the convention, King was willing to accept the three-fifths ratio for representation.[36] Here was the beginning of a major compromise between the Deep South and the commercially oriented states of the North. At the moment, King and other northerners were offering the three-fifths clause to the South, but the South offered no concession in return.

The result of this debate was the appointment of yet another committee to come up with a new proposal for representation in the First Congress. This committee reported its deliberations the next day, July 10, and the convention debated them. Like the previous committee, this one had to cal-

35. *Ibid.*, 560–561. Paterson's animosity towards counting slaves is indicated in an analysis of state population reprinted *ibid.*, 572. Paterson tried to estimate the population of each state and the numbers of slaves that would augment representation. For the Deep South he noted, "In the lower States the acc[oun]ts are not to be depended on." Paterson was of course correct about the allocation of representation in the slave states. No slave state at this time based representation solely on population. In Virginia, for example, each county had two representatives in the lower house of the state legislature. In South Carolina the representatives per parish varied, but the allocations were not based on slave population. In 1808, when South Carolina did go to a population-based system, the representatives were allocated according to "the whole number of white inhabitants in the State."

36. *Ibid.*, 562.

culate representation in the First Congress without the benefit of a census. Not surprisingly, some delegates were unhappy with the allocation given their states. More important, though, was the sectional animosity that these allocations stimulated.

Almost immediately John Rutledge and Charles Cotesworth Pinckney of South Carolina moved to reduce New Hampshire's representatives from three to two. Although Rufus King had supported Butler in debate on the previous day, he now defended the committee's allocation, warning that the New England states would not accept any reduction in their representation. King also endorsed Madison's analysis of sectionalism, arguing that "a difference of interests did not lie where it had hitherto been discussed, between the great and small States; but between the Southern and Eastern." King nevertheless continued to seek compromise and explicitly recognized the need "for the security of the Southern" interests. For this reason he acquiesced in the three-fifths rule and was even willing to consider "a still greater security" for the South, although he admitted he did not know what that might be. He also asserted that "no principle would justify giving" the South "a majority" in Congress.[37]

Charles Cotesworth Pinckney responded that the South did not require "a majority of representatives, but [he] wished them to have something like an equality." Otherwise, a northern-dominated Congress would pass commercial regulations favorable to the North, and the southern states would "be nothing more than overseers for the Northern States." Hugh Williamson of North Carolina agreed, arguing that under the present system the North would get a majority in Congress which it would never relinquish, and thus "the Southn. Interest must be extremely endangered."[38]

Gouverneur Morris of Pennsylvania, who would soon emerge as the most vocal opponent of concessions for slavery, became the first delegate to challenge the assumption that the South was richer than the North and therefore deserved greater representation in Congress. He also argued that, in time of emergency, northerners would have to "spill their blood."[39] Madison's notes unfortunately do not contain the full text of Morris's statement. But the implications are clear. Northerners would have to "spill their blood" because there were more free people in the North than in the South and because slavery made the South an unreliable ally in wartime.

A series of attempts to reduce the representation of some northern states or increase the representation of southern states failed. The convention then adopted an allocation for representation in the First Congress by a vote of

37. *Ibid.*, 566.
38. *Ibid.*, 566–567.
39. *Ibid.*, 567.

nine to two. The negative votes did not come from the smallest states, but from the most southern, South Carolina and Georgia.[40] The delegates from these two states made their point: they must have protection for slavery, or they would oppose the Constitution.

The next day, July 11, the convention debated the provision for a census to determine future representation in Congress. Hugh Williamson of North Carolina amended the provision under consideration to explicitly include the three-fifths clause for counting slaves. Still dissatisfied with the three-fifths clause, Butler and Charles Cotesworth Pinckney of South Carolina "insisted that blacks be included in the rule of Representation, *equally* with the Whites," and moved to delete the three-fifths clause. Butler argued that "the labour of a slave in S. Carola. was as productive and valuable as that of a freeman in Massts.," and since the national government "was instituted principally for the protection of property," slaves should be counted fully for representation.[41] The Butler-Pinckney proposal was quickly defeated.

The defeat of the Butler-Pinckney resolution did not, however, end the debate over slavery and representation. A motion to require Congress to take a census of all "*free* inhabitants" passed on a slim six-to-four vote, with four slave states voting no. The motion to count three-fifths of all slaves then came up for direct debate. King and Gorham of Massachusetts expressed reservations, and Sherman of Connecticut urged conciliation.

James Wilson of Pennsylvania, who had initially proposed the three-fifths clause, now supported it on pragmatic grounds. Admitting he "did not well see on what principle the admission of blacks in the proportion of three-fifths could be explained," Wilson agreed that, if they were citizens, they should be counted equally with whites; and if they were property only, it was reasonable to ask, "Then why is not other property admitted into the computation?" But Wilson argued that these logical inconsistencies "must be overruled by the necessity of compromise." Gouverneur Morris, also of Pennsylvania, was not so willing to sacrifice principle. Having been "reduced to the dilemma of doing injustice to the Southern States or to human nature," Morris chose the former, asserting that he "could never agree to give such encouragement to the slave trade . . . by allowing them a representation for their negroes."[42] The three-fifths clause then failed, by a vote of four to six. However, this defeat was not the result of Morris's arguments in favor of principle: three slave states, including South Carolina, opposed the measure as well as three northern states.[43]

40. *Ibid.*, 568–570.
41. *Ibid.*, 580–581.
42. *Ibid.*, 586–588.
43. *Ibid.* South Carolina apparently opposed the three-fifths clause because the

The next day, July 12, the three-fifths clause was back on the floor, directly tied to taxation for the first time. The debate was the most divisive yet on the question of slavery. Six southerners, representing Virginia, North Carolina, and South Carolina, addressed the issue. Their collective demand was clear: either give the South substantial representation for its slave population, or the South would oppose the Constitution. William R. Davie of North Carolina, who until this point in the convention had sat patiently in virtual silence, declared "it was high time now to speak out." Davie warned that North Carolina would "never confederate" unless slaves were counted, at the very least, under a three-fifths ratio. Davie threatened that if some representation for slaves was not adopted, "the business [of the convention] was at an end."[44] Randolph, who had so far avoided the debates over slavery, "lamented that such a species of property existed," but nevertheless "urged strenuously that express security ought to be provided for including slaves in the ratio of Representation." Meanwhile, the South Carolinians, as might be expected, demanded full representation for slaves, declaring themselves willing, even eager, to be taxed fully for their slaves in return for full representation for their slaves.[45]

Only Gouverneur Morris was prepared to call Davie's bluff. Morris warned that Pennsylvania would "never agree to a representation of Negroes," but he also agreed that it was "vain for the Eastern states to insist on what the Southn States will never agree to." As much as Morris wished "to form a compact for the good of America," he seemed ready to risk failure on the issue of slave representation.[46] Although no other northern delegate was willing to join Morris on this issue, Oliver Ellsworth and William Samuel Johnson of Connecticut strongly supported southern interests, giving further evidence of the emerging compromise between New England and the South over slavery and commerce. After a heated debate, the three-fifths clause finally passed by a vote of six to two, with two states divided.[47]

---

state was holding out for full representation for slaves. Delaware may also have taken this position, although it is more likely that Delaware voted no here because Delaware was consistently opposed to any representation based on population. Maryland opposed the clause because of its current wording. Thus, even though the three-fifths clause had been defeated, it seemed that a majority in favor of it could be found.

44. *Ibid.*, 593.
45. *Ibid.*, 594.
46. *Ibid.*, 593.
47. *Ibid.*, 597. The two divided delegations were Massachusetts and South Carolina. In the former delegation some members apparently opposed this concession to the South. In the latter, some members apparently were holding out for full repre-

After more than a month and a half of anguished argument, the convention had finally resolved the issue of representation for what would become the House of Representatives. Throughout, slavery had constantly confused the issue and thwarted compromise. Sectional interests caused by slavery had emerged as a major threat to the Union. At this juncture in the convention the smaller states still feared the larger ones; however, the northern and southern states had also come to openly distrust each other. In the last debate over representation, General Charles Cotesworth Pinckney declared himself "alarmed" over statements about slavery by northern delegates.[48] His alarm would soon spread to other delegates from the South.

No sooner had the issue of representation been laid to rest than it reemerged as part of the debate over taxation. On July 13 Elbridge Gerry proposed that, until an actual census could be taken, taxation would be based on the initial representation in the House. This seemingly reasonable proposal set the stage for a partial reopening of the debate over representation.

Reviving an earlier proposal,[49] Hugh Williamson of North Carolina tried to cut New Hampshire's representation in the House of Representatives from three to two. Williamson argued that because New Hampshire had not yet sent any delegates to the convention, it was unfair to force the state to pay taxes on the basis of three representatives. This explanation fooled no one, and Williamson's maneuver failed. Next, Read of Delaware expressed the fear that Gerry's motion was a plot by the larger states to tax the smaller ones. This led Madison to reiterate his belief that "the difference of interest in the U. States lay not between the large and small, but the N. and Southn. States." Madison supported Gerry's motion "because it tended to moderate the views both of the opponents and advocates for rating very high, the negroes." After three votes Gerry's motion passed. The convention had deepened its commitment to the three-fifths clause, both for representation and for taxation.[50]

With the sense of the convention on this issue apparently clear, Randolph moved to bring language previously used in the working document into

---

sentation for slaves. In this debate Pierce Butler had argued for full representation for blacks (*ibid.*, 592). The two negative votes came from Delaware and New Jersey, states which had consistently opposed population-based representation.

48. *Ibid.*, 592.

49. See above, p. 203.

50. Farrand, ed., *Records*, I, 601–602. Gouverneur Morris would later argue that the application of the three-fifths clause to direct taxes was inserted "as a bridge to assist" the convention "over a certain gulph" caused by slavery. Once the convention had passed this point, Morris was ready to abandon direct taxation based on the three-fifths clause (*ibid.*, II, 106).

conformity with the three-fifths clause. Earlier in the convention the body had declared that representation would be based on "wealth." Randolph now proposed substituting the wording of the three-fifths clause for the word "wealth."[51] This opened the way for yet one more debate over the three-fifths clause. This debate revealed the deep animosities that had developed between some northern and southern delegates.

Gouverneur Morris began by mocking the attempt to replace the word "wealth" with the three-fifths clause. If slaves were "property," then "the word wealth was right, and striking it out would produce the very inconsistency which it was meant to get rid of." Morris then launched into a full-scale attack on southern demands. In the process he suggested that a peaceful end to the convention, and the Union itself, might be in order.[52] Morris asserted that, until this point in the convention, he had believed that the distinction between northern and southern states was "heretical." Somewhat disingenuously, he declared that he "still thought the [sectional] distinction groundless." But he saw that it was "persisted in; and that the Southn. Gentleman will not be satisfied unless they see the way open to their gaining a majority in the public Councils." The North naturally demanded "some defence" against this. Morris thus concluded:

> Either this distinction is fictitious or real: if fictitious let it be dismissed and let us proceed with due confidence. If it be real, instead of attempting to blend incompatible things, let us at once take a friendly leave of each other. There can be no end of demands for security if every particular interest is to be entitled to it.

Morris argued that the North had as much to fear from the South as the South had to fear from the North.[53]

South Carolina's Pierce Butler responded with equal candor: "The security the Southn. States want is that their negroes may not be taken from them which some gentlemen within or without doors, have a very good mind to do."[54] For the rest of the convention Butler and his southern colleagues would remain vigilant in protecting this interest.

By Saturday the fourteenth, sectional tempers had cooled. The convention now reconsidered the makeup of what would ultimately become the Senate. The small states again reiterated their fears that the large states would overwhelm them in a legislature based entirely on population. Delegates from New Jersey and Connecticut made it clear that they would not support the

51. *Ibid.*, I, 602–603.
52. *Ibid.*, 603–604.
53. *Ibid.*
54. *Ibid.*, 605.

emerging Constitution unless there was state equality in at least one branch of the legislature. Charles Pinckney once again proposed that representation in both houses of the legislature be based on population. In supporting this motion Madison again argued that "the real difference of interests lay, not between the large and small but between the N. and Southn. States. The institution of slavery and its consequences formed the line of discrimination." Madison seemed particularly worried that state equality would give the North a perpetual majority in one branch of the legislature.[55]

Over Madison's protests, the equality of the states in the Senate remained part of the Constitution. On the final vote on this issue, three of the four negative votes came from the South.[56] This vote indicated that Madison's sense of sectional division was at least as important as the division between large and small states.

On July 16, when debate resumed over the powers of Congress, Butler and Rutledge opposed giving Congress the power to legislate where the states were "incompetent." The southerners feared this "vague" and, therefore, dangerous power, and thus four slave states supported a futile attempt to recommit this clause. This debate illustrates that sectional fears, more than rivalries between large and small states, had emerged as a major problem for the convention. Butler and Rutledge, after all, were delegates from a state that thought of itself as "large." But they were fearful of what a Congress dominated by the North might do. Any vagueness in language might be used to harm slavery.[57]

The irony of the shifting sentiments of the Carolinians became clearer a day later, when Gunning Bedford offered compromise language for this clause. Bedford, of Delaware, had up to this time vociferously represented the needs, and fears, of his state. During the debates over representation he had emphatically told his fellow delegates, "*I do not, gentlemen, trust you.*"[58] Bedford was probably as jealous of state power, and as fearful of national power, as any man at the convention. Yet, on this issue he was not fearful and was willing to compromise, because even he saw nothing dangerous in the proposed clause, especially if it contained his compromise language. Bedford's amendment did not mollify the delegates from South Carolina

55. *Ibid.*, II, 9–10.

56. *Ibid.*, II, 13, 15. The negative votes were from Virginia, South Carolina, Georgia, and Pennsylvania.

57. *Ibid.*, 17. The recommittal vote ended in a tie (and thus lost). The only northern state to vote for it was Connecticut, which almost always voted with the Deep South on issues concerning slavery. The only Deep South state to oppose the recommital was North Carolina.

58. *Ibid.*, I, 500.

and Georgia, however, who remained opposed to allowing the national government to legislate for the *"general interest* of the Union."[59] These Deep South delegates no doubt suspected that such language might somehow be used to harm slavery. Legislating for the "general interest" of the Union, they feared, might some day threaten the particular interest of slavery.

III

The debates over structural features of the new central government were not as heated or as lengthy as those over the legislature. Nevertheless, slavery complicated these debates and partially affected their outcome.

The convention was deeply divided over how the nation's chief executive should be chosen. On July 17 the convention considered, and rejected by wide margins, election by the Congress, direct election by the people, and election by the state legislatures. Significantly, the most vocal opposition to election by the people came from three southerners: Charles Pinckney, George Mason, and Hugh Williamson. While Pinckney and Mason argued against the competence of the "people," Williamson was more open about the reasons for southern opposition. He noted Virginia would not be able to elect her leaders president because "her slaves will have no suffrage."[60] The same of course would be true for the rest of the South.

For James Madison the debate over the presidency was particularly difficult. Because he believed that "concepts of right and justice were paramount expressions of majority rule,"[61] Madison instinctively favored election of the president by the people. He told the convention that "the people at large" were "the fittest" to choose the president. But "one difficulty . . . of a serious nature" made election by the people impossible. Madison noted that the "right of suffrage was much more diffusive in the Northern than the Southern States; and the latter could have no influence in the election on the score of the Negroes." In order to guarantee that the nonvoting slaves could nevertheless influence the presidential election, Madison favored the crea-

59. *Ibid.*, II, 27.

60. *Ibid.*, 30–32. Roger Sherman, who virtually always voted with the South on important matters, also opposed direct election of the president.

61. Ralph Ketcham, *James Madison: A Biography* (New York, 1971), 181. Madison did not have unlimited faith in the people, as his essay "Vices of the Political System of the United States" indicates (186–189), and indeed, he has some sympathies for indirect election of officials because such a system limited the power of the people. However, this is not the position he took in the convention, where he argued for the theoretical value of direct election, and opposed it, at least in part because of slavery.

tion of the electoral college.[62] Under this system each state was given a number of electors equal to its total congressional and senatorial representation. This meant that the three-fifths clause would help determine the outcome of presidential elections.[63] Thus, the fundamentally antidemocratic electoral college developed, at least in part, to protect the interests of slavery.

By late July, then, the convention had hammered out what would be the basic outline of the Constitution. On July 23 the convention agreed to send the draft of the Constitution to a Committee of Detail. At this juncture General Charles Cotesworth Pinckney "reminded the Convention that if the Committee should fail to insert some security to the Southern States agst. an emancipation of slaves, and taxes on exports, he shd. be bound by duty to his State to vote agst. their Report."[64] This protest must have surprised the convention. In the previous nine days the subject of slavery had not been directly debated; and where it had come up at all, such as in the discussion of the election of the president, the South had had its way. Now, just as the work of many weeks was about to go to a committee for what

62. Farrand, ed., *Records*, II, 56–57. The acceptance of the electoral college based on the House of Representatives took place on July 20, the day after Madison's speech (64). On July 25 the convention reconsidered this vote. Once again Madison argued that the North would have an advantage in a popular election, although here Madison did not specifically mention slavery (111).

63. Ironically, this antidemocratic system which Madison ultimately supported would have a major impact on his later career. Thomas Jefferson's victory in the election of 1800, and Madison's elevation to the position of secretary of state and heir apparent, would be possible only because of the electoral votes the southern states gained on account of their slaves. This point is made by Lynd in "The Abolitionist Critique," in Lynd, *Class Conflict, Slavery, and the United States Constitution*, 178; and Robinson, *Slavery in the Structure of American Politics*, 405. Robinson also notes that many northerners believed the outcome of the 1812 election would have been different if it were not for the three-fifths clause. Curiously, however, neither Fehrenbacher, Wiecek, nor Donald Robinson discusses the creation of the electoral college as one of the compromises caused by slavery.

During the debates over the judiciary, Madison again used sectionalist arguments to further his position. Madison favored appointment of judges by the president and opposed the appointment of the judiciary by the Senate. He argued that the North would control the Senate, and this control, he asserted, would "throw the appointments entirely into the hands of the N[or]thern States, a perpetual ground of jealousy and discontent would be furnished to the Southern States." However, other southerners who feared a powerful executive discounted the sectional argument. Farrand, ed., *Records*, II, 81. See disagreement by Pinckney and Randolph, *ibid.*, and especially Mason, *ibid.*, 82–83.

64. Farrand, ed., *Records*, II, 95.

some may have hoped was a final redrafting, Pinckney raised new demands for the protection for slavery.

Pinckney's outburst provoked no immediate reaction. The convention remained in session for three more days, redebating how the executive should be chosen and numerous minor details. Finally, on July 26 the convention adjourned until August 6, to allow the Committee of Detail to put the convention's work into some coherent form. This five-man committee included two southerners, Rutledge and Randolph, while a third member, Oliver Ellsworth of Connecticut, came from a state which had consistently supported southern interests in the convention.

The report that emerged from the Committee of Detail contained a number of provisions aimed at the protection of slavery. The new Congress could not interfere with the African slave trade and would need a two-thirds majority to pass navigation acts. The new government would be obligated to protect the states from rebellions and insurrections. Although Clause IV provided for representation based on "the provisions herein after made," no such provisions were in fact in this draft. The three-fifths clause applied to "direct" taxes and "capitation" taxes, but not to representation. Taxation of both exports and imported slaves was also prohibited. With the exception of a clause allowing Congress to regulate commerce by a simple majority, the draft Constitution seemed to give the South everything it wanted.[65] The Committee of Detail appeared to have taken to heart Pinckney's demand for "some security to the Southern States."

On August 7 the convention began to debate the committee report. On the eighth yet another debate over the three-fifths clause took place. Hugh Williamson moved to clarify the status of this clause by replacing the phrase "the provisions herein after made" with a direct reference to the three-fifths provision. After the convention adopted Williamson's motion, Rufus King protested that counting slaves for representation "was a most grating circumstance," especially because the draft of the Constitution also prohibited Congress from banning the slave trade or even taxing the produce of slave labor. He thought that some provision ought to be made for ending the slave trade, but at minimum he argued that "either slaves should not be represented, or exports should be taxable."[66]

Roger Sherman, who would prove to be the Deep South's most vocal northern ally, agreed with King that the slave trade was "iniquitous" but

---

65. *Ibid.*, 177–189. All references to numbered sections are to those of the printed report, as reproduced *ibid.* That report goes up to Art. XXII because there are two articles numbered VI.

66. *Ibid.*, 220.

believed that this issue should not be raised in connection with the question of representation, which had "been Settled after much difficulty and deliberation." Madison, Ellsworth, and Sherman then tried to discuss other topics. But Gouverneur Morris would not let the slavery issue drop. He moved to insert the word "free" in front of the word "inhabitants" in the clause directing how representation would be determined. Believing that "much . . . would depend on this point," Morris said that he could "never . . . concur in upholding domestic slavery," which was "the curse of heaven on the States where it prevailed." Morris compared the "rich and noble cultivation" of the middle states with "the misery and poverty which overspread the barren wastes of Va. Maryd. and the other States having slaves" and concluded that counting slaves for representation

> when fairly explained comes to this: that the inhabitant of Georgia and S.C. who goes to the Coast of Africa, and in defiance of the most sacred laws of humanity tears away his fellow creatures from their dearest connections and damns them to the most cruel bondages, shall have more votes in a Govt. instituted for protection of the rights of mankind, than the Citizen of Pa or N. Jersey who views with a laudable horror, so nefarious a practice.

According to Morris, the draft Constitution compelled the North "to march their militia for the defence of the S. States; for their defence agst those very slaves of whom they complain." Furthermore, the government lacked the power to levy a tax on imported slaves or on the goods produced by them. Worst of all, counting slaves for representation encouraged the South to import more of them. Morris scoffed at the idea that there could ever be a direct tax, such as the three-fifths clause allowed, because it was "idle to suppose that the Genl Govt. can stretch its hand directly into the pockets of the people scattered over so vast a Country." Thus the South would get extra representation in Congress for its slaves and have to pay nothing in return. Morris declared he "would sooner submit himself to a tax for paying for all the Negroes in the U. States than saddle posterity with such a Constitution."[67]

For the first time in the convention, two northerners had denounced slavery in the same debate. A third, Jonathan Dayton of New Jersey, joined them by seconding Morris's motion. Curiously, the southerners did not respond in kind to these attacks. Sherman and Wilson urged calm, and Charles Pinckney merely indicated that he would reply "if the occasion were a proper one." The convention then overwhelmingly rejected Morris's

67. *Ibid.*, 220–223.

amendment.[68] For the South this debate, along with the vote that followed it, was a major victory. Many of the weaknesses of slavery had been exposed in the debate. The strongest case against the institution had been made. Yet, all the northern states except New Jersey voted with the South.

In the following week the convention managed to avoid rancorous debates over slavery, even though sectional distrust sometimes appeared.[69] This period of calm was broken on August 16, when the convention began another debate over the powers of Congress. In a routine discussion of the power of Congress to levy taxes and duties, George Mason raised the issue of the power of Congress to tax exports. In a part of the draft Constitution that had not yet been debated, Congress was specifically prohibited from taxing exports. Mason wanted to debate the issue out of order. He did not want to give Congress the right to levy any taxes unless a corresponding prohibition on export taxes was adopted. "He was unwilling to trust to its being done in a future article" and "professed his jealousy for the productions of the Southern or as he called them, the staple States." Mason was quickly reassured by Sherman and Rutledge that such a provision could be dealt with later. He could not, however, have been totally reassured when Gouverneur Morris declared that a prohibition on taxing exports was "radically objectionable." A number of other delegates then debated this issue. With the exception of Madison, all the southerners opposed taxing exports; all of the northerners (except those from Connecticut and Massachusetts) favored the idea.[70]

Although the question of taxing exports was postponed, this short debate gave hints of a developing compromise between New Englanders and delegates from the Deep South. In reassuring Mason, South Carolina's John Rutledge noted that he would vote for the commerce clause as it stood, but only "on condition that the subsequent part relating to negroes should also be agreed to."[71] Delegates from Connecticut and Massachusetts indicated

68. *Ibid.*, 223.

69. For example, North Carolina's Richard Spaight expressed fear that the capital would always remain in New York City, "especially if the Presidt. should be a Northern Man" (*ibid.*, 261). In debates over qualifications for officeholding, clear sectional differences emerged. Southerners usually favored property qualifications and strict residency, or even nativity qualifications. Northerners did not. Ellsworth of Connecticut argued that a meaningful property qualification in the South would preclude almost all northerners from holding office, and a fair qualification in the North would be meaningless in the South, where the delegates presumed there was more wealth (*ibid.*, 248–249, 267–272).

70. *Ibid.*, 305–308.

71. *Ibid.*, 306.

some support for Rutledge's position. What should perhaps be called the "dirty compromise" of the convention was taking shape. The South Carolina delegation would support the commerce clause if New England would support protection for the slave trade and a prohibition on export taxes. This compromise would develop during the next two weeks.

On August 21 the New England states joined the five slave states south of Delaware on three crucial votes. On the first vote all three New England states voted to prohibit taxes on exports. Before the vote Connecticut's Ellsworth argued that such products as "Tobo. rice and indigo" would be taxed and "a tax on these alone would be partial and unjust." Next, in a key five-to-six vote Connecticut joined the five slave states to defeat a proposal, made by James Madison, to allow taxes on exports by a two-thirds vote. On the final vote Massachusetts joined Connecticut, and the measure favored by the South passed, seven to four. In both votes the Virginia delegation was divided, three to two, with James Madison and George Washington in the minority.[72]

The convention then debated a motion by Luther Martin to allow an import tax on slaves. Martin represented Maryland, a slave state, but one with a surplus of slaves, a fact that helps explain his opposition to the African trade. Rutledge opposed Martin's motion with a two-pronged attack. He first told the convention that the "true question at present is whether the Southn. States shall or shall not be parties to the Union." The implied threat of secession was clear. He then told the northern delegates that, if they would "consult their interest," they would "not oppose the increase of Slaves which will increase the commodities of which they will become the carriers." Ellsworth of Connecticut agreed, refusing to debate the "morality or wisdom of slavery" and simply asserting that "what enriches a part enriches the whole." The alliance for profit between the Deep South and New England was now fully developed. Charles Pinckney then reaffirmed that South Carolina would "never receive the plan if it prohibits the slave trade."[73] Shrewdly, Pinckney equated a tax on imported slaves with a prohibition on the trade itself. On this note the convention retired for the day.

Roger Sherman opened debate the next day by adopting a familiar pose. He declared his personal disapproval of slavery but refused to condemn it in other parts of the nation. He then made three separate arguments why a prohibition of the slave trade was a bad idea. First, "the public good did not require" an end to the trade. Noting that the states already had the right to import slaves, Sherman saw no point in taking a right away from the states unnecessarily when "it was expedient to have as few objections as possible"

72. *Ibid.*, 360, 363–364.
73. *Ibid.*, 363–365.

to the new Constitution.[74] Here Sherman assumed that opposition to the Constitution because it prohibited the slave trade should be defused, but that opposition because it *allowed* the slave trade would be inconsequential. Sherman was prepared to appease the demands of slavery to bring about the Union, but he was willing to ignore the demands of those who opposed slavery. Second, Sherman observed that "the abolition of slavery seemed to be going on in the U.S." If left alone, the "good sense of the several States" would soon put an end to all slavery in the country.[75] In making this argument Sherman confused the abolition of the slave trade with the abolition of slavery itself.[76] Finally, revealing his priorities, Sherman urged the convention to hurry and finish its business, noting, no doubt, that they had been in session for almost three months.[77]

George Mason of Virginia responded with a fierce attack on the "infernal trafic" in slaves, which he blamed on "the avarice of British Merchants." Reflecting the sectional hostilities at the convention, Mason then "lamented" that his "Eastern brethren had from a lust of gain embarked in this nefarious traffic." Mason leveled some of the strongest criticism of slavery yet heard at the convention, declaring it an "evil" system which produced "the most pernicious effect on manners." In language similar to Jefferson's in the *Notes on the State of Virginia*, he declared that "every master of slaves is born a petty tyrant" and warned that slavery would "bring the judgment of heaven on a Country" and ultimately produce "national calamities." Despite this attack on the whole institution, Mason ended his speech by demanding only that the national government "have power to prevent the increase of slavery" by prohibiting the African trade.[78] Mason failed to say that Virginia, like

74. *Ibid.*, 369.

75. *Ibid.*, 369–370.

76. During the ratification process, proponents of the Constitution would similarly confuse the power to end "slavery" after 1808, which Congress lacked, with congressional power to end the African slave trade. James Wilson, for example, told the Pennsylvania ratifying convention that after "the lapse of a few years . . . Congress will have power to exterminate slavery from within our borders" (Elliot, ed., *Debates*, II, 484). Since Wilson attended all the debates over this clause, it is impossible to accept this statement as his understanding of the slave trade clause. More likely, he simply made this argument to win support for the Constitution. In New Hampshire a supporter of the Constitution also argued that the slave trade clause gave Congress the power to end slavery. He was quickly disabused of this notion by Joshua Atherton (*ibid.*, 207).

77. Farrand, ed., *Records*, II, 370.

78. *Ibid.*, 369–370. Thomas Jefferson, *Notes on the State of Virginia* (Paris, 1784), in Adrienne Koch and William Peden, eds., *The Life and Selected Writings of Thomas Jefferson* (New York, 1944), "Query XVIII," 277–278. Jefferson wrote there: "The

Maryland, had a surplus of slaves and did not need the African slave trade any longer. James McHenry more candidly wrote in his private notes: "That the population or increase of slaves in Virginia exceeded their calls for their services," and thus a prohibition of the slave trade "would be a monopoly" in Virginia's "favor." Under such conditions "Virginia etc would make their own terms for such [slaves] as they might sell."[79] The "etc" no doubt included McHenry's own state of Maryland.

Ellsworth answered Mason. Because "he had never owned a slave," Ellsworth declared he "could not judge of the effects of slavery on character." However, if slavery were as wrong as Mason had suggested, merely ending the trade was insufficient. Ellsworth, of course, knew that the Virginians opposed allowing the national government to abolish slavery. Therefore, since there were many slaves in Virginia and Maryland and fewer in the Deep South, any prohibition on the trade would be "unjust towards S. Carolina and Georgia." So Ellsworth urged the convention not to "intermeddle" in the affairs of other states.[80] The convention had now witnessed the unusual phenomenon of a New Englander defending slavery against the attacks of a Virginian.

The Carolinians were quite capable of defending their own institution. Charles Pinckney, citing ancient Rome and Greece, declared that slavery was "justified by the example of all the world." He warned that any prohibition of the slave trade would "produce serious objections to the Constitution which he wished to see adopted."[81] His cousin, General Pinckney, also declared his support for the Constitution, but noted that his "personal influence . . . would be of no avail towards obtaining the assent" of his home state. He believed Virginia's opposition to the trade was more pecuniary than moral. Virginia would "gain by stopping the importations" because "her slaves will rise in value, and she has more than she wants." Prohibiting the trade would force South Carolina and Georgia "to confederate" on "unequal terms." While Virginia might gain, the nation as a whole would not. More slaves would produce more goods, and that result would help not

---

whole commerce between master and slave is a perpetual exercise of the most boisterous passions, the most unremitting despotism on the one part, and degrading submissions on the other. Our children see this, and learn to imitiate it. . . . The parent storms, the child looks on, catches the lineaments of wrath, puts on the same airs in the circle of smaller slaves, gives a loose to the worst passions, and thus nursed, educated, and daily exercised in tyranny, cannot but be stamped by it with odious peculiarities." Jefferson's *Notes* was available in the United States by the time of the convention.

79. Farrand, ed., *Records*, II, 378 (McHenry's notes).
80. *Ibid.*, 370–371.
81. *Ibid.*, 371–375.

only the South but also states involved in "the carrying trade." Seeing the slave trade solely as an economic issue, Pinckney thought it "reasonable" that imported slaves be taxed. But a prohibition of the slave trade would be "an exclusion of S. Carola from the Union." As he had made clear at the beginning of his speech, "S. Carolina and Georgia cannot do without slaves." Rutledge and Butler added similar sentiments, as did Abraham Baldwin of Georgia and Williamson of North Carolina.[82]

The southerners were supported by the voices of New Englanders. Gerry of Massachusetts offered some conciliatory remarks, and Sherman, ever the ally of the South, declared that "it was better to let the S. States import slaves than to part with them, if they made that a sine qua non." However, in what may have been an attempt to give his remarks an antislavery tone, he argued that taxing imported slaves was morally wrong, because that "implied they were *property*."[83] This position undoubtedly pleased Sherman's southern allies, who did not want to pay taxes on any slaves they imported. This position also underscored the profound support that the Carolinians and Georgians found among some New Englanders.

The reasons for cooperation between New England and the Deep South on this issue were now clear. New Englanders, involved in the "carrying trade," would profit from transporting rice and other products produced by slave labor. And the South Carolinians seemed willing to support New England's demands for giving Congress power to regulate all commerce. In return, New Englanders would support the right of the Carolinas and Georgia to import the slaves they could not "do without."

On the other side of the issue only John Langdon of New Hampshire and John Dickinson of Delaware vigorously opposed allowing the slave trade to continue. Dickinson argued that the trade was "inadmissible on every principle of honor and safety." Furthermore, he was prepared to call the Carolinians' bluff on the question of Union, doubting the Deep South would reject the Constitution if the trade were prohibited. James Wilson was also skeptical of southern threats, but he did not offer any strong rebuttal. Nor did Rufus King, who only pointed out that prohibiting a tax on imported Africans was an "inequality that could not fail to strike the commercial sagacity of the Northn. and middle States."[84]

The most interesting contribution to this debate came from Gouverneur Morris of Pennsylvania, who had, up till now, been the most consistent

82. *Ibid.*, 371–375.

83. *Ibid.*

84. *Ibid.*, 372–373. Wilson's position here must be contrasted with the position he took in the state ratifying convention (see above, n. 76). Nathaniel Gorham of Massachusetts also registered his opposition to the slave trade, but only after the issue was recommitted.

opponent of slavery at the convention. This extremely wealthy man with many commercial interests suggested that the subject of navigation acts and the slave trade be sent to committee. "These things may form a bargain among the Northern and Southern States," he shrewdly noted. His suggestion was quickly accepted by the convention.[85]

Two days later, on August 25, the committee reported out a compromise proposal; on the twenty-sixth the convention began to debate it. The committee proposed that Congress be barred from prohibiting the African slave trade until 1800, but that in the meantime a reasonable tax could be levied on imported slaves. General C. C. Pinckney immediately proposed that the date be changed to 1808, which would be twenty years after the Constitution was ratified. Gorham of Massachusetts seconded this motion. Madison complained that this provision was "dishonorable to the National character" and to the Constitution and that "twenty years will produce all the mischief that can be apprehended from the liberty to import slaves." Nevertheless, the proposal was adopted by a seven-to-four vote. The yes votes came from three New England states, Maryland, and the three Deep South states.[86]

Gouverneur Morris, still resisting a continuation of the slave trade, then proposed that the clause specifically declare that the "importation of slaves" be limited to the Carolinas and Georgia. Morris wanted it known "that this part of the Constitution was a compliance with those States." This motion, which appears to have been proposed only to embarrass supporters of the trade, was withdrawn. By a seven-to-four vote the slave trade provision was then adopted. The three New England states once again joined Maryland and the Deep South to allow the slave trade to continue for twenty years.[87] Half of the "dirty compromise" was complete.

85. *Ibid.*, 374. McHenry's notes on this debate are quite revealing. Although not attributing remarks to any particular delegate, McHenry's notes make clear that part of the conflict between Virginia and the Deep South on the issue was economic. Virginia had surplus slaves to sell south, and the value of those slaves would be undermined by the African trade.

86. *Ibid.*, 414–415.

87. *Ibid.*, 415–416. The convention then changed the wording of the tax provision of the clause, limiting the tax on slaves to ten dollars. Walter Berns in "The Constitution and the Migration of Slaves," *Yale Law Journal*, LXXVIII (1968–1969), 198, argues that the term "migration" in the slave trade clause referred to the *interstate* slave trade, and that the term "importation" referred to the African slave trade. If this analysis were correct, then it would appear that the delegates from the Deep South were willing to allow Congress to prohibit the domestic slave trade as well as the African slave trade after 1808. This analysis defies all understanding of the convention. Berns, moreover, provides no evidence that *anyone* at the Constitutional Convention or in any of the state ratifying conventions believed this. As William Wiecek more correctly argues in *Sources of Antislavery Constitutionalism*, 75, the

On August 28 the convention debated what would become the privileges and immunities clause of the Constitution. Charles Cotesworth Pinckney "seemed to wish some provision should be included in favor of property in slaves," but he did not press the point, and the clause was adopted with only South Carolina voting no. Pinckney's concern was apparently over the right of masters to travel from state to state with their slaves. In fact, those states which had already passed gradual emancipation statutes, like Pennsylvania, had made provisions for slave transit. Perhaps for this reason, other southern delegates did not share Pinckney's concern. This seems to have been the only time during the convention when southerners perceived a threat to slavery, but were unable to muster the votes, or perhaps their own energies, to head it off.[88]

The convention immediately turned to the fugitives from justice clause. Butler and Charles Pinckney "moved 'to require fugitive slaves and servants to be delivered up like criminals.' " Both James Wilson and Roger Sherman protested this amendment, and "Mr. Butler withdrew his proposition in order that some particular provision might be made apart from this article."[89]

The next day, the debates over commerce, the slave trade, and fugitive slaves were all joined. The "dirty compromise" was complete. In a debate over the commerce clause Charles Pinckney, the younger and more impetuous of the two cousins, moved that a two-thirds majority be required for all commercial regulations. He argued that "the power of regulating commerce was a pure concession on the part of the S. States" and that therefore the two-thirds requirement was reasonable.[90]

General C. C. Pinckney agreed that "it was the true interest of the S. States to have no regulation of commerce." But, in one of the most revealing

term "migration" was "potentially a weapon in the hands of moderate abolitionists" of the mid-nineteenth century.

88. Farrand, ed., *Records*, II, 443. This problem is examined in Paul Finkelman, *An Imperfect Union: Slavery, Federalism, and Comity* (Chapel Hill, N.C., 1981).

89. Farrand, ed., *Records*, II, 443. James Hutson has found a draft of the fugitive slave clause in the Pierce Butler papers that is not in Butler's handwriting and concluded that this unknown "author would seem to challenge Butler for the dubious honor of being the father of the fugitive slave clause" ("Pierce Butler's Records of the Federal Constitutional Convention," *Quarterly Journal of the Library of Congress*, XXXVII [1980], 64, quote at 68). Butler was not one of the great minds of the convention, and it is certainly likely that he collaborated in drafting the provision with someone else, especially Charles Pinckney. In any event, Butler probably got the idea from the Northwest Ordinance, which was passed in July by the Congress sitting in New York. The ordinance contained the first national fugitive slave provision. It does seem likely, however, that Butler was the delegate who actually introduced, and pushed for, the fugitive slave provision at the convention.

90. Farrand, ed., *Records*, II, 449.

statements of the convention, he explained why he would vote to support a clause requiring only a simple majority for passage of commercial legislation. Pinckney said he took this position because of "their [the eastern states'] liberal conduct towards the views of South Carolina." The "views of South Carolina" concerned the slave trade. In the margins of his *Notes* Madison made this clear. Madison wrote that Pinckney

> meant the permission to import slaves. An understanding on the two subjects of *navigation* and *slavery*, had taken place between those parts of the Union, which explains the vote on the Motion depending, as well as the language of Genl. Pinkney and others.[91]

The debate that followed made clear the nature of the compromise. Butler, for example, declared that the interests of the southern and eastern states were "as different as the interests of Russia and Turkey." Nevertheless, he was "desirous of conciliating the affections of the East" and so opposed the two-thirds requirement. The Virginians, who had opposed the slave trade provisions, now supported the demand for a two-thirds requirement for commercial legislation. But they were in the minority. The motion went down to defeat, as South Carolina voted with the northern states. The commerce clause was then adopted without any recorded opposition.[92]

91. *Ibid.*, 449-452. Luther Martin, who opposed the Constitution, made the same point in his letter to the Maryland ratifying convention. He had been on the committee, suggested by Morris, (see above, pp. 217-218), and on the committee he "found the *eastern* States, notwithstanding their *aversion to slavery*, were very willing to indulge the southern States, at least with a temporary liberty to prosecute the *slave trade*, provided the southern States would in their turn gratify them, by laying no *restriction* on *navigation acts*; and after a very little time, the committee by a great majority, agreed on a report, by which the general government was to be prohibited from preventing the importation of slaves for a limited time, and the restrictive clause relative to navigation acts was to be omitted." Luther Martin, *The Genuine Information Delivered to the Legislature of the State of Maryland Relative to the Proceedings of the General Convention Lately Held at Philadelphia*, in Herbert J. Storing, ed., *The Complete Anti-Federalist* (Chicago, 1981), II, 60-61.

92. Farrand, ed., *Records*, II, 451-453. Other scholars have noted this compromise as well, but most have done so approvingly. Charles Warren believed that slavery was relatively insignificant in the making of the Constitution. Arguing that the morality of the slave trade was unimportant, he wrote that "historians have underestimated the importance of the concession made on commerce by the South." He approvingly quoted George Ticknor Curtis: "The just and candid voice of History has also to thank the Southern statemen who consented to this arrangement for having clothed a majority of the two Houses with a full commercial power." *The Making of the Constitution*, 585, 585 n, quoting Curtis, *History of the Origin, Formation, and Adoption of the Constitution of the United States* (Boston, 1854-1858), II, 306-307. Warren's analysis follows Max Farrand, "Compromises of the Constitu-

Immediately after this vote, Butler introduced the fugitive slave clause. Without debate or recorded vote, it too passed.[93] The last bargain over slavery had been made. The northerners who had opposed the fugitive slave provision only a day before were now silent.

The debates of late August reveal how willing the northern delegates— especially the New Englanders—were to support slavery and the demands of the Deep South. The slave trade clause was not adopted simply to "lure Georgia and South Carolina into the Union," as William W. Freehling has glibly argued.[94] Rather, the debates of August clearly show that the slave trade was actively supported by New Englanders to "lure" southern support for the commerce clause. The delegates from the Deep South did not need to be lured into the Union, because they were already deeply committed to the Constitution by the time the slave trade debate occurred. Moreover, the South had already won major concessions on the three-fifths clause and the prohibition on taxing exports. These were permanent features of the Constitution, unlike the slave trade provision, which would lapse in twenty years. Although some southerners talked of not joining the Union unless the slave trade were allowed, it seems unlikely they would have risked going it alone over a temporary right of importation. This prospect is even more unlikely because at the time of the convention none of these states was actively importing slaves from Africa. Thus, the argument that the slave trade provision was necessary to bring the Deep South into the Union rests on the assumption that those states would have rejected the Constitution over the right to import slaves in the future when they in fact were not currently importing them. Furthermore, even without constitutional protection for the slave trade, importations from Africa would have been legal until the Congress actually took the time, and mustered the votes, to prohibit them.

However one views the African trade, it is hard to see how anyone could assert that the fugitive slave clause was also a "lure." Added at the last possible moment, without any serious debate or discussion, this clause was a boon to the South without any quid pro quo for the North. On this vote the northern delegates seemed simply not to understand the import of the issue or were too tired to fight.

The August debates also reveal that the northern delegates could have had no illusions about the nature of the covenant they were forming with the

---

tion," in *Annual Report of the American Historical Association for the Year 1903* (Washington, D.C., 1904), I, 73–84. The historiography of this issue is discussed in Lynd, "The Abolitionist Critique," in Lynd, *Class Conflict, Slavery, and the United States Constitution*.

93. Farrand, ed., *Records*, II, 453–454.

94. William W. Freehling, "The Founding Fathers and Slavery," *American Historical Review*, LXXVII (1972), 81, quote at 84.

South. The northern delegates could not have forgotten General C. C. Pinckney's earlier assertion that "S. Carolina and Georgia cannot do without slaves." While the "Fathers" might have "liked to call [slavery] temporary," the evidence of the convention shows they should have known better.[95] Throughout the convention the delegates from the slave states made no attempt to hide the fact that they believed slavery would be a permanent part of their culture and society. No one who attended the Philadelphia Convention could have believed that slavery was "temporary" in the South.

With the adoption of the commerce clause and the fugitive slave clause, the issues of immediate concern to slaveowners seemed to be settled. However, on August 30 the debate over the domestic violence clause of what became Article IV of the Constitution led to renewed conflicts over slavery. Dickinson of Delaware attempted to delete the limitation that permitted the national government to intervene to prevent violence only "on the application" of a state legislature. This change would have allowed the national government, and not the states, to determine when intervention was necessary. The motion was easily defeated, with the five slave states voting no, apparently because they did not want the national government to interfere in their domestic affairs. However, on a vote to change the wording of the clause from "domestic violence" to "insurrections," the four slave states south of Virginia voted yes, but the motion lost five to six.[96] Fear of slave insurrections no doubt motivated the South to wish for explicit protection on this matter.

The convention now turned to the numerous proposals which had been tabled throughout the summer. North-South cooperation was quite evident through the next two weeks. Motions introduced by a delegate from one section were often seconded by one from the other. Although some patterns of sectional voting can be found in these debates, they are rare and may be more coincidental than significant.[97] Some sectional fears were raised, particularly by Mason of Virginia, but by this time he was clearly opposed to the whole Constitution.[98]

95. Farrand, ed., *Records*, II, 371, 373; Freehling, "The Founding Fathers," *AHR*, LXXVII (1972), 84.

96. Farrand, ed., *Records*, II, 466–467. The vote on the Dickinson motion was three to eight. The three yes votes came from the middle states, New Jersey, Pennsylvania, and Delaware. Delaware was also a slave state, and would remain one until the adoption of the Thirteenth Amendment in 1865. But, by this time in the convention, it was clear that Delaware did not think of itself as a slave state.

97. For example, in a vote to limit the president's treaty power, Maryland, South Carolina, and Georgia voted yes, and the other states present voted no (*ibid.*, II, 541).

98. *Ibid.*, 537–538, 541–542, 543. On Aug. 31 he had declared "that he would sooner chop off his right hand than put it to the Constitution" (*ibid.*, 479). Ulti-

The one exception to this pattern of sectional cooperation occurred on September 10, the last day of debate before the Constitution went to a final Committee of Style. John Rutledge of South Carolina noted his opposition to the amendment procedure because "the articles relating to slaves might be altered by the States not interested in that property and prejudiced against it." At Rutledge's insistence the convention added a clause forbidding any amendment of the slave trade provision and the capitation tax provision before 1808.[99] As they had throughout the convention, the delegates from the Deep South left almost nothing to chance in their zeal to protect slavery.

Emerging from the Committee of Style on September 14, the penultimate version of the Constitution produced further debate on issues relating to slavery and sectionalism. On September 15 an attempt to increase the representation of North Carolina in the First Congress failed, on a strictly sectional vote. Similarly, an attempt to change the clause on export taxes, to make it yet more favorable to the South, failed. Here, however, Maryland and South Carolina joined the North in defeating the measure.[100] The convention's last substantive action on slavery-related matters concerned the fugitive slave clause. The Committee of Detail had reported the clause with the language, "No person legally held to service or labour. . . ." The convention substituted the term "under the laws thereof" for the term "legally," "in compliance with the wish of some who thought the term [legal] equivocal, and favoring the idea that slavery was legal in a moral view."[101]

IV

This final compromise over the wording of the fugitive slave clause was an entirely appropriate way to end discussion of slavery at the convention. Throughout the convention the delegates had fought over the place of slavery in the Constitution. A few delegates had expressed moral qualms

---

mately, he would refuse to sign the Constitution. On Sept. 12 Mason would use sectional arguments in an attempt to create a stronger prohibition on states levying an export tax (*ibid.*, 588–589, 631).

99. *Ibid.*, 559–561.

100. *Ibid.*, 623–627.

101. *Ibid.*, 601–602, 628 (angle brackets in Farrand); there is no indication who requested this change. A similar change of wording was made in the three-fifths clause at the suggestion of Edmund Randolph, changing the word "servitude" to "service" for describing indentured whites. Randolph argued that the original term "being thought to express the condition of slaves" would be inappropriate, while the new term described "the obligations of free persons" (*ibid.*, 607). There was also a little more discussion about the amendment clause as it affected the slave trade, but nothing resulted from this (*ibid.*, 629).

over slavery, but most of the criticism had been political and economic. Northerners opposed representation for slavery because it would give the South a political advantage; Virginians opposed the slave trade, at least in part, because it would undermine the value of their excess slaves. The initial reaction to the fugitive slave clause typified this. When Pierce Butler and Charles Pinckney first proposed it, James Wilson complained, "This would oblige the Executive of the State to do it, at public expence."[102] The costs Wilson worried about were more financial than moral.

The word "slavery" was never mentioned in the Constitution, yet its presence was felt everywhere. The new wording of the fugitive slave clause was a characteristic example. Fugitive slaves were called "persons owing service or labour," and the word "legally" was omitted so as not to offend northern sensibilities. Northern delegates could return home asserting that the Constitution did not recognize the legality of slavery. In the most technical linguistic sense they were perhaps right. Southerners, on the other hand, could tell their neighbors, as General Charles Cotesworth Pinckney told his, "We have obtained a right to recover our slaves in whatever part of America they may take refuge, which is a right we had not before."[103]

Indeed, the slave states had obtained significant concessions at the convention. Through the three-fifths clause they gained extra representation in Congress. Through the electoral college their votes for president were far more potent than the votes of northerners. The prohibition on export taxes favored the products of slave labor. The slave trade clause guaranteed their right to import new slaves for at least twenty years. The domestic violence clause guaranteed them federal aid if they should need it to suppress a slave rebellion. The limited nature of federal power and the cumbersome amendment process guaranteed that, as long as they remained in the Union, their system of labor and race relations would remain free from national interference. On every issue at the convention, slaveowners had won major concessions from the rest of the nation, and with the exception of the commerce clause they had given up very little to win these concessions. The northern delegates had been eager for a stronger Union with a national court system and a unified commercial system. Although some had expressed concern over the justice or safety of slavery, in the end they were able to justify their compromises and ignore their qualms.

At the close of the convention two delegates, Elbridge Gerry of Massachusetts and George Mason of Virginia, explained why they could not sign the document they had worked so hard to help create. Both had a plethora of objections that included slavery-related issues. But their objections were

102. *Ibid.*, 443.
103. Elliot, ed., *Debates*, IV, 286.

not grounded in moral or philosophical opposition to slavery; rather, like the arguments of those delegates who ultimately supported the compromises over slavery, the objections of Gerry and Mason were practical and political. Gerry objected to the three-fifths clause because it gave the South too much political power, at the expense of New England. Mason opposed allowing the slave trade to continue, because "such importations render the United States weaker, more vulnerable, and less capable of defence."[104]

During the ratification struggles others would make more principled stands against the compromises over slavery. A New Yorker complained that the Constitution condoned "drenching the bowels of Africa in gore, for the sake of enslaving its free-born innocent inhabitants." In New Hampshire, Joshua Atherton opposed ratification because it would make all Americans "*consenters to*, and *partakers in*, the sin and guilt of this abominable traffic." A Virginian thought the slave trade provision was an "excellent clause this, in an Algerian constitution: but not so well calculated (I hope) for the latitude of America."[105]

It was more than just the slave trade that northern Antifederalists feared. Three opponents of the Constitution in Massachusetts noted that the Constitution bound the states together as a "whole" and "the states" were "under obligation . . . reciprocally to aid each other in defence and support of every thing to which they are entitled thereby, right or wrong." Thus, they might be called to suppress a slave revolt or in some other way defend the institution. They could not predict how slavery might entangle them in the future, but they did know that "this lust for slavery, [was] portentous of much evil in America, for the cry of innocent blood, . . . hath undoubtedly reached to the Heavens, to which that cry is always directed, and will draw down upon them vengeance adequate to the enormity of the crime."[106]

The events of 1861–1865 would prove the three Massachusetts Antifederalists of 1788 correct. Only after four years of unparalleled bloodshed could the Union be made more perfect, by finally expunging slavery from the Constitution.

104. Farrand, ed., *Records*, II, 633, 640.

105. *Letters from a Countryman from Dutchess County* (letter of Jan. 22, 1788), in Storing, ed., *The Complete Anti-Federalist*, VI, 62; Elliot, ed., *Debates*, II, 203. *Essays by Republicus* (essay of Mar. 12, 1788), in Storing, ed., *Complete Anti-Federalist*, V, 169.

106. Consider Arms, Malichi Maynard, and Samuel Field, *Reasons for Dissent*, in Storing, ed., *Complete Anti-Federalist*, IV, 262–263.

☆ ☆ ☆ ☆ ☆
James Madison and Visions of American Nationality in the Confederation Period
A Regional Perspective

DREW R. McCOY

On September 3, 1789, a scant six months after the inception of the new federal government he had labored so hard to create, Congressman James Madison was furious. For days he had listened with mounting frustration as his colleagues discussed what he considered a momentous issue. Finally he exploded. Baited by John Lawrence of New York, who had alluded to his prominent role at the Virginia ratifying convention of the previous year, Madison sent shock waves through the halls of the First Congress. "If a prophet had risen" in that convention "and brought the declarations and proceedings of this day" into view, he firmly announced, "Virginia might not have been a part of the union at this moment."[1]

Had Madison's outburst occurred a year or two later, it would hardly surprise us. But in the late summer of 1789 Alexander Hamilton had not even been nominated for his cabinet position, and the weighty controversies surrounding his fiscal system lay well ahead. The issue that unleashed Madison's ire was, on the surface, comparatively minor, even incidental — choosing a permanent location for the new federal government. Since the Virginian was contending strenuously for a site on the Potomac River, we might be tempted to dismiss his ardor as nothing more than an early example of

1. William T. Hutchinson *et al.*, eds., *The Papers of James Madison* (Chicago, Charlottesville, 1962-), XII, 372. Madison's statement, reported by some newspapers in slightly different and more extreme language, appears to have attracted considerable attention outside Congress as well. See Tench Coxe to Madison, Sept. 9, 1789, *ibid.*, 394–397, esp. n.1.

congressional solicitude for local interest. In fact, Madison saw far more at stake here than a potential boost to his own state's prosperity and influence. At issue, he believed, was the very success of the fragile experiment in republican nationalism established by the Constitution of 1787. Two days later, when he and other advocates of the Potomac site were reprimanded for failing to support postponement of the decision for a few months, Madison's response again conveyed his sharp anxiety. "As in fact we find a predetermined majority ready to dispose of us," he charged, "the sooner we know our destiny the better; for it can be of little consequence, if we are to be disposed of, whether we are disposed of in September or December."[2]

Since Madison was justly renowned for being even-tempered, his alarm and petulance are striking. They are more broadly significant as well, because they point toward an understanding of larger issues relating both to him and to post-Revolutionary political reform in general. Madison saw two causes—union and justice—as central to the capital controversy of 1789. He feared, above all, that selection of a site northeast of the Potomac would jeopardize the already tenuous loyalty of western Americans to the new government. "I am extremely alarmed for the Western Country," he noted privately at the time, having just seen "fresh and striking proofs of its ticklish situation."[3] He saw disunion as not only a real but an immediate danger, one that was substantially enhanced by eastern congressmen who, by fighting removal to the Potomac, made no secret of their contempt for "the country beyond the mountains." Rapid settlement of this vast transmontane region was inevitable: "If the calculation be just, that we double in twenty-five years, we shall speedily behold an astonishing mass of people on the western waters." The issue, Madison told his fellow congressmen, was simple. "Whether this great mass shall form a permanent part of the confederacy, or whether it shall be separated into an alien, a jealous and a hostile people," he warned on September 4, "may depend on the system of measures that is shortly to be taken."[4]

The cause of union was inseparable in Madison's mind from simple justice, and here he asked his colleagues once again to look to the future. Contending that the government should be placed as close as possible to the center of the Republic's population, he admitted that the current center was probably in Pennsylvania, closer to the Susquehanna River—the most popular alternative to the Potomac—than to his preferred site. But everyone

2. Joseph Gales, comp., *Debates and Proceedings in the Congress of the United States, 1789–1824* (Washington, D.C., 1834–1856), 1st Cong., 1st sess., I, 878.

3. Madison to Henry Lee, Oct. 4, 1789, in Hutchinson *et al.*, eds., *Papers of Madison*, XII, 426–427.

4. *Ibid.*, 377.

knew that this situation was bound to change quickly, even within the next few years. "On what do the measures and extent of population depend?" Madison asked. "They depend on the climate, on the soil, and the vacancy to be filled." Like money, population sought "those places where it least abounds, and has always the same tendency to equalize itself." Applied to the United States, the logic of this simple formula was unmistakable. Already large numbers of Americans were on the move "from the more crouded to the less crouded parts" of the Union. "The swarms do not come from the southern, but from the northern and eastern hives," Madison argued, which would "continue to be the case, until every part of America receives its due share of population." Who could deny, then, that future population growth would be most rapid in the vast, temperate, fertile, and largely unpeopled regions south and west of the Potomac? "If there be any event, on which we may calculate with certainty," Madison insisted, "I take it that the centre of population will continually advance in a south-western direction."[5]

This particular vision of population growth and diffusion was not novel in 1789, nor was it peculiar to the scholarly Madison. Many Americans in the 1780s, especially but not exclusively in the southern states, shared his beliefs. Their expectations, moreover, figured importantly in the creation and ratification of the Constitution. The process of political reform in the Confederation period had two distinct if related dimensions: one was centered on the familiar issue of distributing power between the state and federal governments, and the other on the less formal issue of distributing power among different regions of the Union. Contrary to the impression created by most scholarship on the Constitution—which has generally focused on the transfer of important powers from the state to the national level, abstract questions of sovereignty, and principled conflict between nationalists and "men of little faith"—the regional, or geopolitical, dimension of the movement deserves greater scrutiny and emphasis. Hence the following discussion focuses on the relationship between these apparent demographic trends and patterns, the formidable regional tensions and conflict that beset the Confederation in the 1780s, and the Constitution as a potential means of territorial integration.[6]

5. *Ibid.*, 378–379. See also Madison to George Washington, Aug. 11, 1788, *ibid.*, XI, 229, for an indication of how rapidly Madison expected the shift to occur and to affect the capital issue.

6. The reference to "men of little faith" is, of course, from the stimulating work of Cecelia M. Kenyon; see her famous essay "Men of Little Faith: The Anti-Federalists on the Nature of Representative Government," *William and Mary Quarterly*, 3d Ser., XII (1955), 3–43. Two conspicuous exceptions to the prevailing historiographical pattern are H. James Henderson, *Party Politics in the Continental Congress* (New York,

Approached from this perspective, the political history of the post-Revolutionary era is less a story of ideological controversy—whether rooted abstractly in an Atlantic republican tradition or more concretely in the different outlooks and interests of "agrarian-localist" and "commercial-cosmopolitan" Americans—than it is a reflection of the daunting challenge of fashioning political coherence from the recalcitrant materials of a regionally differentiated colonial past.[7] Even the most continental-minded Revolutionary Americans were acutely aware of the extent to which regional consciousness affected political behavior in the United States, for they could hardly overlook the overwhelmingly sectional pattern of factionalism in the federal Congress. Their struggle during the 1780s to accommodate the tensions arising from long-standing regional cleavages both acknowledged and challenged the maneuverings of others bent on furthering apparent sectional imperatives. Indeed, as an examination of the background to Madison's outburst of 1789 and, more briefly, of its aftermath will suggest, this relationship between the quest for territorial integration and the presence of chronic regional conflict informed many, if not most, of the major political developments of the last two decades of the eighteenth century.

To the extent that scholars have developed a regional perspective on these years, their analysis has often suffered from an anachronistic and misplaced emphasis on the single issue of slavery and its implications.[8] As we cannot

---

1974); and Joseph L. Davis, *Sectionalism in American Politics, 1774-1787* (Madison, Wis., 1977), both of which develop a regional approach. My analysis draws heavily on their insights and broad perspective. More recently, Peter S. Onuf has developed a fresh and provocative interpretation of the importance of regional perceptions in furthering national integration in the 1780s; see *The Origins of the Federal Republic: Jurisdictional Controversies in the United States, 1775-1787* (Philadelphia, 1983), esp. chaps. 7-9. See also the relevant sections of Donald L. Robinson, *Slavery in the Structure of American Politics, 1765-1820* (New York and London, 1971), esp. the conclusion on 443-446.

7. For a brief but suggestive discussion of parallels between the North American case and the experience of other former colonies struggling to achieve regional integration and national coherence, see H. James Henderson, "The Structure of Politics in the Continental Congress," in Stephen G. Kurtz and James H. Hutson, eds., *Essays on the American Revolution* (Chapel Hill, N.C., 1973), 157-196, esp. 170-174. For examples of the two more traditional approaches referred to in the text, see, of course, Gordon S. Wood, *The Creation of the American Republic, 1776-1787* (Chapel Hill, N.C., 1969); and Jackson Turner Main, *Political Parties before the Constitution* (Chapel Hill, N.C., 1973), esp. chaps. 12 and 13, with special attention to 357-358.

8. See especially chaps. 7 and 8 of Staughton Lynd, *Class Conflict, Slavery, and the United States Constitution* (Indianapolis, Ind., and New York, 1967). Lynd's essays

help knowing, of course, territorial integration was not permanently achieved in the United States for another three-quarters of a century, after a protracted political and military struggle focusing on that issue and at the terrible cost of more than half a million lives. But by then regional divisions and even the Republic itself had assumed substantially different forms, and we must endeavor first to view the 1780s, not from the tempting but distorting perspective of the Civil War, but rather from the vantage point of those who were by necessity ignorant of a future in which slavery determined sectional identities and became the dominant concern of national politics. Southern Federalists of the 1780s—who viewed regional matters in very different and more complex terms than did their antebellum descendants—certainly attempted to take the future into account; as Madison's case so richly suggests, their analysis of current demographic and economic developments generated projections that could shape their approach to political reform. If the Constitution was for them something much more than an ad hoc response to immediate issues and exigencies, however, the irony in their miscalculation is all the more striking. Indeed, in view of subsequent, largely unanticipated shifts in circumstance, it must be said of Madison and his colleagues that ratification took place under generally false expectations.

I

Why did Madison (and many other Americans in the 1780s) believe that population growth was favoring and would continue to favor the southern states? This perception was a quite reasonable inference from the facts and apparent trends of the moment. After 1763, migration to North America from Germany, Ulster, and elsewhere in Britain and Europe continued to be heavy, with much of it flowing directly to the southern backcountry, where colonial governments, most notably in Georgia and the Carolinas, encouraged and even subsidized settlement.[9] This flood of foreign immigra-

---

are valuable for their penetrating insights and creative energy, but their import is considerably vitiated by his mistaken insistence on linking all sectional or regional conflict to the underlying importance of slavery. For a less stark example of the all too familiar tendency to conceive of regional conflict, especially between the eastern and southern states, in terms of the fundamental distinctions created by slavery, see Edmund S. Morgan, "The Puritan Ethic and the American Revolution," in *The Challenge of the American Revolution* (New York, 1976), esp. 110–115.

9. Jack M. Sosin, *The Revolutionary Frontier, 1763–1783* (New York, 1967), chap. 2. For relevant discussions of demographic patterns in late 18th-century America, see J. Potter, "The Growth of Population in America, 1700–1860," in D. V. Glass

tion helped produce population leaps in several of the southern colonies that were truly dramatic, especially compared to other parts of British North America. In 1760, for example, the populations of New York and North Carolina had been roughly equal, but by 1780 the southern colony had jumped ahead by approximately sixty thousand people. A similar contrast can be drawn between South Carolina and New Jersey—here the southern colony opened a lead of nearly forty thousand souls—and in the youngest colony of Georgia the population increased by almost sixfold during this same twenty-year period.[10]

Patterns of internal migration during the 1770s and 1780s also confirmed prevailing perceptions. By far the most active frontier was in western Virginia (in what would shortly become the state of Kentucky) and the western Carolinas, where the first phase of a great migration to the trans-Allegheny West had just begun. The surge of settlement in the Kentucky-Tennessee area was nothing short of staggering; from only scattered settlements before the Revolution, the numbers there increased to more than one hundred thousand by the end of the 1780s. Moreover, there was ample evidence to support Madison's belief that many of the migrants to the southern frontiers came from the comparatively crowded states north and east of the Potomac. Pennsylvania had for quite some time been a distributing center to the South and West, sending significant numbers to the back-country of Maryland, Virginia, the Carolinas, and Kentucky.[11] Farther south, in territory that would revert to Spain at the conclusion of the War for Independence, the pace of settlement, while far less significant, had been notably brisk during the years just prior to the Revolution. For example,

---

and D.E.C. Eversley, eds., *Population in History: Essays in Historical Demography* (London, 1965), 631–679; Robert V. Wells, "Population and the American Revolution," in William M. Fowler, Jr., and Wallace Coyle, eds., *The American Revolution: Changing Perspectives* (Boston, 1979), 103–122; and Herman R. Friis, "A Series of Population Maps of the Colonies and the United States, 1625–1790," *Geographical Review*, XXX (1940), 463–470. See also, more generally, Ronald Hoffman *et al.*, eds., *An Uncivil War: The Southern Backcountry during the American Revolution* (Charlottesville, Va., 1985).

10. These population estimates are derived from the figures (for "White" and "Negro" combined) presented in United States Bureau of the Census, *Historical Statistics of the United States, Colonial Times to 1970* (Washington, D.C., 1975), Pt. II, 1168.

11. James T. Lemon, *The Best Poor Man's Country: A Geographical Study of Early Southeastern Pennsylvania* (Baltimore, 1972), 76, 86–87; and Wayland Fuller Dunaway, "Pennsylvania as an Early Distributing Center of Population," *Pennsylvania Magazine of History and Biography*, LV (1931), 134–169.

New Jerseyites had opened up settlement along the Mississippi River at Natchez in 1772, and Rufus Putnam and Phineas Lyman of Connecticut had led more than four hundred Yankee families to new homes in West Florida during the winter of 1773-1774.[12] Indeed, there may well have been during the 1780s a conspicuous, albeit temporary, rush of northern farmers to the many inviting regions of the southern interior.[13] It is hardly surprising, then, that Madison was far from alone among southerners in assuming that the balance of population and hence influence in the American confederacy were tilting unmistakably in their direction. Nor is it surprising that many, if not most, northerners agreed.[14]

We must not forget, in this connection, that before the 1790s internal migration was almost exclusively to lands south, not north, of the Ohio River. The latter region, the so-called Northwest Territory, has often dominated the attention of scholars of the post-Revolutionary West, but this emphasis can be terribly misleading. It obscures the fact that the area north of the Ohio was throughout the 1780s more a prospective than an actual frontier and, moreover, that the prospects for swift and extensive settlement there were ambiguous at best. Before the adoption of the Constitution, only an insignificant smattering of Americans had ventured into territory where large numbers of Amerindians, and even the British, still posed daunting obstacles to expansion.[15] Indeed, postwar expectations that the lands north of the Ohio would replicate the pattern south of the river and fill rapidly with settlers had been abruptly dashed. As early as 1785 it had become apparent to many members of Congress that only new policies and extraor-

12. Sosin, *Revolutionary Frontier*, 39. See also Edmund S. Morgan, "Conflict and Consensus in the American Revolution," in Kurtz and Hutson, eds., *Essays on the Revolution*, 297-303.

13. John Richard Alden, *The First South* (Baton Rouge, La., 1961), 74-75.

14. It is impossible, of course, to measure the precise extent of this broad inference in either region. But scholars of the 1780s, especially in recent years, appear to agree that Madison's expectations were in fact quite widely shared throughout the country. My own reading of the sources points in the same direction. See, for example, Robinson, *Slavery in American Politics*, esp. chap. 5; H. James Henderson, "The Structure of Politics in the Continental Congress," in Kurtz and Hutson, eds., *Essays on the American Revolution*, 189-191 (esp. n. 38); and, above all, Davis, *Sectionalism in American Politics*, esp. 67, 75, 117, and 121.

15. For broad context, see Frederick Jackson Turner, "Western State-Making in the Revolutionary Era," in Turner, *The Significance of Sections in American History* (1895, 1896), (New York, 1932), 86-138; Francis S. Philbrick, *The Rise of the West, 1754-1830* (New York, 1965), chaps. 4 and 5; and Malcolm J. Rohrbough, *The Trans-Appalachian Frontier: People, Societies, and Institutions, 1775-1850* (New York, 1978), chaps. 1-3.

dinary incentives could attract significant numbers of desirable settlers to the national domain. The result was the burst of creative legislation, culminating in the renowned Northwest Ordinance and the less-celebrated sale of territory to the Ohio Company in the summer of 1787, that has attracted so much scholarly attention.[16]

If congressmen in the 1780s talked a lot about the Northwest Territory and gradually formed successful plans for its eventual settlement and incorporation into the Union, they were also clearly frustrated by the repeated failures and delays that characterized the immediate postwar years. They were even capable of expressing serious doubt that migration to certain areas would ever be significant, no matter what the political incentives. During several journeys to the western country in the mid-1780s, for example, James Monroe of Virginia, an important member of congressional committees on western affairs, gained a striking impression of "a great part" of the region north of the Ohio River, especially the areas "near Lakes Michigan and Erie" and "upon the Mississippi and the Illinois." The first, he reported, was "miserably poor," and in the second he found stretching for miles nothing but barren, desolate plains that would "perhaps never contain a sufficient number of Inhabitants to entitle them to membership in the confederacy," at least not under the plan tentatively established by Congress in 1784.[17] That Monroe was referring to what would soon become parts of western Ohio, Indiana, Michigan, and Illinois may startle us — but not if we remember that even in New England, which would contribute so heavily to the peopling of this northwestern frontier, there was little evident interest in the area before the late 1780s. For any number of reasons, in short, few Americans anticipated the rapidity or the volume of subsequent migration to the Old Northwest.[18] No wonder, then, that the tendency everywhere in the 1780s was to view the West as overwhelmingly an extension of the South.

This perception was especially strong in Virginia, a state that provided an impressive coterie of Federalist leaders, for yet another reason. The dreams

16. For an excellent discussion of these matters, see Peter S. Onuf, "Expansion and Republicanism: The Disposition of Western Lands and Provisions for the Orderly Incorporation of New States," paper presented at the Johns Hopkins University conference "The American Revolution: The Unfinished Agenda," Mar. 29, 1985, forthcoming in volume from New York University Press.

17. James Monroe to Thomas Jefferson, Jan. 19, 1786, in Julian P. Boyd *et al.*, eds., *The Papers of Thomas Jefferson* (Princeton, N.J., 1950-), IX, 189.

18. See the discussion in Jack Ericson Eblen, *The First and Second United States Empires: Governors and Territorial Government, 1784–1912* (Pittsburgh, Pa., 1968), chap. 1.

of some Virginians in these years about the commonwealth's economic future knew few bounds. If promptly and prudently constructed, internal improvements—roads and especially canals—would not simply link the western frontier to the Atlantic Ocean by means of the Potomac and James rivers; they would, as George Washington put it, open "a field almost too extensive for imagination."[19] Washington was far from alone in his confidence that, if the proper canals were built, all the trade of the western waters, north and south of the Ohio River, would eventually be funneled through Virginia. "These works," Thomas Jefferson exulted, "will spread the feild of our commerce Westwardly and Southwardly beyond any thing ever yet done by man."[20] Certainly the Virginians were aware of alternative routes. They fretted that Pennsylvanians were busily planning their own canals; they recognized the Hudson River as a potential rival, forty years before the construction of the Erie Canal (though Jefferson expressed confidence that "nature . . . has declared in favour of the Patowmac"); and they could even view the great Mississippi as a competitor for some of the commonwealth's anticipated trade.[21] Indeed, for a brief time in the early 1780s some Virginians—including Washington, Monroe, Henry Lee, and perhaps even Jefferson—were so enthralled by this Potomac vision that they displayed surprisingly little interest in securing unrestricted American rights on the Mississippi. Their attitude changed, however, once they grasped the centrality of the river to western security and when they saw as well that, even if the bulk of western exports inevitably flowed south to market, European manufactures would still be most cheaply and efficiently imported from east to west via Virginia's prospective river and canal system.[22] For these Chesapeake visionaries, in sum, the course of American empire was moving steadily west and south, and they had little doubt that the hub of this magnificent Republic, with or without extensive settlement north of the Ohio River,

19. George Washington to James Madison, Nov. 17, 1788, in Hutchinson *et al.*, eds., *Papers of Madison*, XI, 350. For a brief but perceptive discussion of another prominent Virginian's infatuation with this vision, see Charles Royster, *Light-Horse Harry Lee and the Legacy of the American Revolution* (New York, 1981), esp. 70–74.

20. Jefferson to Madison, Dec. 8, 1784, in Boyd *et al.*, eds., *Papers of Jefferson*, VII, 558.

21. Jefferson to Washington, Mar. 15, 1784, *ibid.*, 26.

22. *Ibid.*, 25–27; Jefferson to Madison, Feb. 20, 1784, *ibid.*, VI, 548; Madison to Jefferson, Apr. 27, 1785, in Hutchinson *et al.*, eds., *Papers of Madison*, VIII, 265–270; and esp. Madison to George Nicholas, May 19, 1788, *ibid.*, XI, 50. Relevant secondary accounts include Davis, *Sectionalism in American Politics*, 118–121; Royster, *Light-Horse Harry Lee*, 70–74; and esp. Jay Kinney, "James Madison's Nationalist Persuasion: Virginia, Expansion, and the Alliance with Hamilton, 1780–1792" (undergraduate honors thesis, University of Texas at Austin, 1980), 38–40.

and with or without an open Mississippi, would be the venerable Old Dominion.

Many Americans in the 1780s made a number of key assumptions about regional divisions in the Republic that lent specific shape to this broad vision of imperial drift. Although confusion about the specific configuration of American regionalism was common, they generally saw the thirteen states that had made the Revolution as composed of at least two distinctive (and often hostile) regions—the "eastern" states of New England and the "southern" states from the Chesapeake south to Georgia. Fewer references were made to an intermediate and less cohesive region of "middle" states that included New York, New Jersey, and Pennsylvania, but this rough typology contained room for considerable variation and flexibility.[23] Commentators often confused "eastern" and "northern" and were particularly ambiguous about the position of the middle states in their regional alignments. Sometimes the eastern and middle states were lumped together to form a northern region, but not always. Pennsylvania, for instance, could be perceived as northern, southern, or neither, depending on the observer and his assumptions.[24] Indeed, before the Revolution the colonies had commonly been divided into only two categories, eastern and southern, with the latter including everything from New York south.[25] Moreover, as the ambiguous status of Pennsylvania amply suggests, when Americans drew the line be-

23. See Fulmer Mood, "The Origin, Evolution, and Application of the Sectional Concept, 1750-1900," in Merrill Jensen, ed., *Regionalism in America* (Madison and Milwaukee, Wis., 1965), esp. 25-26 and 38-46; and Alden, *First South*, chap. 1. In a provocative essay Robert J. Gough has offered significant insight into these issues; see "The Myth of the 'Middle Colonies': An Analysis of Regionalization in Early America," *PMHB*, CVII (1983), 393-419. Gough made a quantitative analysis of the geographical references made by delegates to the Continental and Confederation congresses, for instance, and discovered that they made about 47% of their geographical allusions to New England, 28% to the South, 17% to the North, and only 8% to the middle states. He noted as well that the delegates were sensitive to a fundamental North-South split but were inconsistent in placing states in specific sections (400).

24. See, for example, "Letter from Massachusetts and Letter from New York," *Connecticut Journal*, Oct. 17, 24, 31, 1787, in Merrill Jensen *et al.*, eds., *The Documentary History of the Ratification of the Constitution* (Madison, Wis., 1976-), III, 376, 384; James Iredell in the North Carolina ratifying convention, in Jonathan Elliot, ed., *The Debates in the Several State Conventions, on the Adoption of the Federal Constitution* ... (Washington, D.C., 1836), IV, 185-186; Charles Pinckney in the South Carolina ratifying convention, *ibid.*, 323-324; and David Ramsay, "An Address to the Freemen of South Carolina ... ," in Paul Leicester Ford, ed., *Pamphlets on the Constitution of the United States* ... (Brooklyn, N.Y., 1888), 375.

25. Alden, *First South*, 8.

tween North and South after the Revolution, the critical factor was not necessarily the presence or absence of large numbers of slaves. Since the process of abolition had not yet begun in New York and New Jersey in the 1780s, in fact, one might argue that the mythical line between slavery and freedom was not even all that clearly or firmly drawn.

It is true, of course, that perhaps the best-known statement of the North-South division from this period came from Madison, who bluntly asserted in the Constitutional Convention that "the institution of slavery and its consequences formed the line of discrimination."[26] It is not surprising that many scholars have rushed to congratulate Madison for his prescience, but their emphasis on a few memorable excerpts from his convention speeches has tended to simplify and distort the regional element in his thinking and, moreover, to exaggerate the broader significance of slavery in defining sectional identity and conflict. Indeed, slavery played something far less than a dominant role in shaping regional perceptions and controversy after the Revolution, especially compared to the post-1820 era from which scholars have too readily extrapolated.[27] Just as often in the Confederation period the distinction between North and South was perceived as one between the "carrying" and the "non-carrying," or "producing," states, in which case northern became virtually synonymous with commercial.[28] At the Constitutional Convention, for instance, Gouverneur Morris raised the specter of regional developments that would lead to a form of southern dominance in

26. July 14, 1787, in Hutchinson *et al.*, eds., *Papers of Madison*, X, 102. See also June 30, 1787, *ibid.*, 90. Madison drew this line between Pennsylvania and Maryland.

27. The Missouri Controversy of 1819, as Don E. Fehrenbacher has noted in this connection, marked a decisive departure in the history of southern sectionalism, since during the first quarter century of Independence "slavery, though defended vehemently at times, especially by representatives of South Carolina and Georgia, was not the primary subject of contention between North and South." See "The Missouri Controversy and the Sources of Southern Sectionalism," in Don E. Fehrenbacher, *The South and Three Sectional Crises* (Baton Rouge, La., 1980), 9–10. Fehrenbacher has a fuller and even more telling discussion of these issues in his magisterial book, *The Dred Scott Case: Its Significance in American Law and Politics* (New York, 1978), chap. 4.

28. See, for example, William Grayson in the Virginia ratifying convention, in Elliot, ed., *Debates*, III, 292, 340, and Alexander Hamilton in the Constitutional Convention, June 29, 1787, in Max Farrand, ed., *The Records of the Federal Convention of 1787*, rev. ed. (New Haven, Conn., 1937), I, 466, and in the New York ratifying convention, in Harold C. Syrett and Jacob E. Cooke, eds., *The Papers of Alexander Hamilton* (New York, 1961–), V, 22, 62.

which the "interior and landed" interest would run roughshod over the "maritime" interest. "It has been said that N.C., S.C., and Georgia only will in a little time have a majority of the people of America," he observed in reference to the commonly anticipated movement of population toward the Southwest that portended this "oppression of commerce."[29] Southern congressmen, in turn, could readily accede to Article VI of the Northwest Ordinance, which restricted slavery in the national domain, in part because they did not yet regard "free" and "southern" (or "pro-southern") territory as contradictory terms. What made an area potentially "southern" in 1787 was not so much the presence of slavery, in other words, but simply its location and prospective status as an agricultural or producing region—which distinguished it, especially, from New England.

Indeed, the eastern, or carrying, states of New England stood far enough apart from the rest of the Republic, in both fact and imagination, to dominate perceptions of regional alignments. They lacked what Pennsylvania had in grain, Virginia in wheat and tobacco, and the Carolinas in rice and cotton: locally produced agricultural commodities that sustained a dynamic export trade. Tied primarily to commerce, fisheries, and shipbuilding, the New England economy seemed anomalous in a fundamentally agrarian Republic. Moreover, the region's uniquely intense religious heritage, along with the overwhelmingly English background and character of its population, contributed to a high level of sectional cohesion and identity.[30] By 1790, few New Englanders, in the words of one scholar of the region, "doubted that they were morally superior, ethnically more distinctive, socially more integrated, and economically and politically more advanced than the inhabitants of any other part of the union."[31] And they were not alone in seeing themselves as fundamentally different. Southerners and New Englanders alike commonly thought in terms of serious distinctions and often conflict between these eastern states and the rest of the Union. A decade later, in 1798, with the New England–based Federalist party apparently in firm control of the national government, Thomas Jefferson lamented that southerners were "completely under the saddle of Massachusetts and Connecticut," who "ride

29. Farrand, ed., *Records*, I, 603–605.

30. There is a nice discussion of the basis for New England's separateness in Rudolph M. Bell, *Party and Faction in American Politics: The House of Representatives, 1789–1801* (Westport, Conn., 1973), chap. 2. For a penetrating discussion of the sources and consequences of New England regionalism, see James M. Banner, Jr., *To the Hartford Convention: The Federalists and the Origins of Party Politics in Massachusetts, 1789–1815* (New York, 1970), esp. chaps. 1, 3.

31. *Ibid.*, 84.

us very hard." He took comfort only in the thought that these New En-glanders were so different, in both character and circumstance, as to consti-tute the natural and generally impotent adversaries of all other Americans. "They are circumscribed within such narrow limits, and their population so full, that their numbers will ever be the minority," he reassured a fellow Virginian, smugly adding that "they are marked, like the Jews, with such a perversity of character, as to constitute, from that circumstance, the natural division of our parties."[32]

The intensity of Jefferson's contempt for New Englanders may well have been unusual, but his beliefs and expectations about population, geography, and the future were not. Compared to the South, indeed, New England was commonly identified as a densely or fully populated region with little poten-tial for further growth. Occasionally southerners attributed this congestion to the area's earlier settlement, curiously overlooking the age of Virginia and Maryland and apparently equating the South with Georgia and the back-country.[33] That New England had reached or was close to its population threshold was no mystery: it occupied such limited space. A glance at any map quickly revealed how small the region actually was, especially compared to the sprawling territory southwest of the Ohio and Potomac rivers. Befit-ting the customary emphasis on climate in the eighteenth century, more-over, many Americans were impressed by the fact that New Englanders had to contend with the effects of harsh winters and relatively poor soil, both of which, they assumed, limited population growth and generated strong in-centives for migration to more inviting territory. The inference, in short, was that Yankee farmers would need little prodding to desert the rocky soil of their native hills for the mild climate of the spacious, fertile domain that beckoned from the South. Many New Englanders sadly acknowledged the force of this logic and bemoaned the imminent depopulation of their home-land. Southerners confidently awaited increased settlement of their land. As Congressman Michael Jenifer Stone of Maryland boasted during the debate over locating the federal capital in 1789, "The increase of population to the Eastward is merely conditional; there is nothing to invite people to settle in the Northern parts of this continent, in preference to the Southern"; and "even if they were settled there," he concluded with a flourish, "every principle which encourages population would operate to induce them to emigrate to the Southern and Western parts." Stone insisted he was pro-pounding no idle or abstract theory. Challenging his fellow legislators to

32. Jefferson to John Taylor, June 1, 1798, in Paul Leicester Ford, ed., *The Writ-ings of Thomas Jefferson* (New York, 1896), VII, 263, 265.
33. See, for example, James Iredell in the North Carolina ratifying convention, in Elliot, ed., *Debates*, IV, 177.

compare the increase of population in Kentucky since the Revolution with the situation in "any part of the Eastern States," he tendered empirical proof that "men multiplied there beyond any thing known in America."[34]

II

This general context lends rich meaning to one of the pivotal episodes of the Confederation period, the famous negotiations between American Secretary for Foreign Affairs John Jay and the Spanish envoy to New York, Don Diego de Gardoqui. The relevant facts are familiar enough. After months of discussion the two diplomats initialed in 1786 a preliminary treaty between their governments that offered American merchants valuable trading privileges within the Spanish Empire. In return, Americans agreed to forbear the navigation of the Mississippi River for a period of twenty-five years. Although the negotiations occurred at a time when the southern states formed such a cohesive voting bloc in Congress that they were generally able to take the lead in shaping policy, in this case they did not, because a solid majority coalition of the eastern and middle states produced the necessary votes to sustain Jay's position, at least during the negotiations. There was little hope for final ratification of the controversial treaty, however, since the requisite votes of nine states (rather than a simple majority) in its favor were impossible to secure. Five southern states instantly objected to Jay's willingness to cede, even if only temporarily, American navigation rights in the West; and, more important, cracks soon appeared in the eastern-middle bloc of seven states that had initially voted to allow him to offer the concession. By the spring of 1787, as a concerted campaign (led by Madison) to woo some of the middle states delegates away from the easterners began to pay off, the negotiations effectively collapsed.[35]

Although Jay's daring initiative aborted, he precipitated a fierce controversy that is immensely significant, both for what it reveals about the intensity of regional conflict in the 1780s and for its profound effect on the Confederation Congress and on the subsequent movement for national political reform. On the simplest level, the controversy involved specific

34. Gales, comp., *Debates and Proceedings*, 1st Cong., 1st sess., I, 853–854.
35. Excellent discussions of the negotiations and their wide-ranging ramifications can be found in Henderson, *Party Politics in the Continental Congress*, chap. 14, and Davis, *Sectionalism in American Politics*, chaps. 7 and 8. Henderson has made a strong argument for a so-called southern ascendancy in Congress between 1784 and 1787; see *Party Politics*, chap. 13, and "Structure of Politics," in Kurtz and Hutson, eds., *Essays on the American Revolution*, 174, 186–188.

regional interests that are easily identified. New Englanders were searching anxiously for any possible boosts to their sagging commercial economy, and they had an especially keen eye for potentially lucrative markets for their fisheries in Spain. Southerners, on the other hand, were anxious to gain undisputed control of the Mississippi River in order to promote continued expansion west of the mountains, to assure the future prosperity of the region, and to protect the interests of southern land speculators in the West. From this perspective the treaty appeared to represent a temporary sacrifice of southern interests for the immediate advantage of northern interests. Angered by recent southern opposition to national commercial reform, and fearful as well that reckless adventurers in the West would push the United States into a disastrous and needless war with Spain, New Englanders saw the treaty and a general accommodation with Spain as perfectly sensible and justified. Speaking in Congress, Rufus King of Massachusetts characteristically emphasized "the distressed state of the Eastern States," noting that "they had an ungrateful soil and no staple but what they drew from the Sea." Refusing to treat with Spain on the proposed terms, he believed, was thus tantamount to "sacrificing the interest and happiness of a Million [in New England] to promote the views of speculating landjobbers [in the South]."[36] Southerners, in turn, angrily rejected as utterly unnecessary and unjust any such weighing and bartering of vital regional concerns.[37]

The Jay-Gardoqui episode contains several layers of meaning. Looming over this rather straightforward contest pitting one set of specific regional interests against another was a larger, more significant, and far less familiar controversy over nothing less than the future shape and character of the American republic. The French minister to the United States, Louis-Guillaume Otto, offered a penetrating and relevant analysis of the crisis in a September 1786 letter to his superiors in Paris. The position of the treaty's supporters, he wrote, was essentially defensive, for it arose from their fear that the western lands "would insensibly attract the most industrious inhabitants of the northern states, who would not hesitate an instant to exchange the arid rocks of Massachusetts and of New Hampshire for the smiling plains of the Ohio and the Mississippi." New Englanders also worried that a limited population spread so thinly over such an immense surface would "weaken the springs" of American government and threaten anarchy. From either point of view, it seemed appropriate to limit expansion, con-

36. Charles Thomson, Minutes of Proceedings, Aug. 16, 1786, in Edmund C. Burnett, ed., *Letters of Members of the Continental Congress* (Washington, D.C., 1936), VIII, 429.

37. In addition to the discussions in Henderson and Davis, see Robert A. East, "The Massachusetts Conservatives in the Critical Period," in Richard B. Morris, ed., *The Era of the American Revolution* (New York, 1939), 372–374.

solidate population and resources in the East, and strengthen the economy of the maritime states—all of which, Otto reported, were implicit goals of Jay's treaty.[38]

Southerners, according to the French diplomat, were just as self-interested but perhaps even less candid in averring their true motives. They condemned, of course, the blatant injustice of discouraging "the restless spirit of a people ever urged on by necessity, and eager to change home and climate." But when southerners disingenuously argued that occlusion of the Mississippi was objectionable primarily because it would cruelly throw westerners into the arms of the British, who could offer alternative routes to market along the Great Lakes and the St. Lawrence River, they were diverting attention from their principal concern and motive. In fact, the southern states were constantly maneuvering to advance their relative position in the Confederation and thus neglected no chance "of increasing the population and importance of the western territory, and of drawing thither by degrees the inhabitants of New England." By depriving New England gradually of industrious inhabitants and adding all the while to the population of the interior states, this movement would "doubly enfeeble" the powerful eastern states and permanently shift the balance of power toward the South and West. Thus Otto was hardly surprised by the intensity of the southern uproar against a treaty that threatened to undermine this strategy, in part by furnishing restless northerners with an alternative to emigration "by increasing their prosperity and the extension of their commerce."[39]

There is ample evidence that Otto's impressions offered acute insight into what was indeed a larger dimension of the crisis of 1786. Many northerners, including Jay himself, were openly troubled by a prevailing "rage for emigrating" that ostensibly threatened to depopulate and weaken the eastern states.[40] Rufus King advocated a temporary renunciation of the Mississippi precisely because it would stem this tide and stabilize an increasingly dangerous state of affairs. He noted as well that it would force unruly westerners, for the time being at least, to look east and forge strong commercial and cultural ties to the Atlantic states. This would be good for eastern merchants, but, more important, it offered the hope, however slim, that these frontier communities would not be lost altogether to either civilization or the Union.[41] Since the diplomatic initiative lay with Jay and this northern

38. Otto to Vergennes, Sept. 10, 1786, as printed in the appendix of George Bancroft, *History of the Formation of the Constitution of the United States of America* (New York, 1882), II, 390.

39. *Ibid.*, 391–393.

40. See Davis, *Sectionalism in American Politics*, 118.

41. Rufus King to Elbridge Gerry, June 4, 1786, and King to Jonathan Jackson, Sept. 3, 1786, in Burnett, ed., *Letters of Members of Congress*, VIII, 380–382, 458–460.

position, we find an essentially defensive and considerably more vehement position assumed by southerners. James Monroe and William Grayson, two of Virginia's delegates to Congress, saw the negotiations as a transparent ploy to abort the natural stream of development, currently in progress, that promised to revolutionize regional power relationships in the Union. As Timothy Bloodworth, a North Carolina congressman, pithily expressed this view in a report to his governor on Jay's activities, "It is wel known that the ballance of Power is now in the Eastern States, and they appear determined to keep it in that Direction."[42]

Monroe's analysis of the crisis was perhaps the most thorough, certainly the most vivid if not fantastic, and, since he hardly kept his thoughts to himself, probably the most influential southern response to the events of 1786. He did his best to alarm Madison, who was temporarily out of Congress, but saved his shrillest cries for the more receptive ears of Governor Patrick Henry. That there was "plotting" under way, Monroe reported, was beyond doubt, and it was a complex plot to boot. The salient purposes behind relinquishing the Mississippi were, after all, clear enough: to break up current settlements on the western waters, "prevent any in future, and thereby keep the States southward as they now are." Even if the western communities somehow managed to survive, they would surely be lost to the Confederation, since Spain would readily command the loyalty of those whose livelihood depended on use of the river. The scheme, then, was "to throw the weight of population [in the Republic] eastward and keep it there," and Monroe pointed to an interesting subplot, one that Grayson openly declaimed against in Congress.

One effect of the new state of affairs, Monroe told Henry, would be "to appreciate the vacant lands of New York and Massachusetts."[43] Occlusion of the Mississippi might devastate the Ohio and Mississippi river frontiers, but it would not deter, indeed it would encourage, settlement elsewhere; namely, in the vacant regions of New York, Vermont, and Maine. Southerners could reassure themselves that the soil and climate of these northern frontiers were hardly as inviting as those of the Southwest—Grayson observed in Congress, in this connection, that the treaty would only help New York "more speedily settle her waste land."[44] But should Jay manipulate the government to enhance their appeal, these northern regions, which were

42. Timothy Bloodworth to the Governor of North Carolina, Sept. 29, 1786, ibid., 474.

43. James Monroe to Patrick Henry, Aug. 12, 1786, ibid., 424-425.

44. Thomson, Minutes of Proceedings, Aug. 18, 1786, ibid., 438. For a discussion of the opening of these northern frontiers, see Sosin, Revolutionary Frontier, chap. 3.

already attracting their own share of population, would offer an alternative, however inferior in southern eyes, for land-hungry easterners on the move. Indeed, Monroe was well aware of the potential value of at least one northern frontier, the Mohawk Valley of upstate New York, where he and Madison had just recently speculated in land.[45] In expanse and long-term significance it could hardly rival the vast frontier of the trans-Appalachian Southwest; nevertheless, Virginians were doubtless aware of the potential for development in the broad region of the Hudson River and the Great Lakes that might challenge the significance of both the Potomac and Mississippi rivers. And this northern development depended largely, they believed, on a redirection, through contrived political means, of natural demographic and economic energy away from the Southwest.[46]

If that were not enough, Monroe saw a further, rather bizarre twist to the eastern plot that moved it squarely into the realm of conspiracy. A small group was scheming, he believed, "to break the Union." Jay and his cronies were already intriguing with "principal men" in several states to bring about, if necessary, a dismemberment of the Confederation at the Potomac. Monroe warned Madison and Henry that no time should be lost: southerners must spring into action to thwart the conspiracy by courting the favor and support of the middle states that now threatened to join the eastern states in a formidable and perhaps permanent northern bloc. Pennsylvania was the key, he argued; if a division of the Union could not be prevented, that state must be kept from joining "the eastern scale"—if necessary, he added ominously, by force.[47]

III

How many of Monroe's impressions corresponded to reality and how many were pure fantasy are not altogether clear.[48] We do not have to subscribe to

45. A nice summary of this matter may be found in Irving Brant, *James Madison: The Nationalist, 1780-1787* (Indianapolis, Ind., and New York, 1948), chap. 21.

46. As Brant correctly observes, Madison's stand on the Mississippi issue was to this extent in direct conflict with his personal economic interest. One effect of closing the river would undoubtedly have been to channel western commerce right through his lands on the Mohawk River.

47. Monroe to Madison, Sept. 3, 1786, in Hutchinson *et al.*, eds., *Papers of Madison*, IX, 113-114. See also Monroe to Madison, Aug. 14, 1786, *ibid.*, 104; and Monroe to Henry, Aug. 12, 1786, in Burnett, ed., *Letters of Members of Congress*, VIII, 424-425.

48. See the excellent brief discussion in an editorial note in Hutchinson *et al.*, eds., *Papers of Madison*, IX, 104-105 n. 3.

his specific belief in secessionist plots, however, to agree with Madison's observation six months later that "the existing Confederacy" was under such strain that it was indeed "tottering to its foundation." Writing in February 1787 from New York, where he was once again ensconced in Congress, Madison reported that the government under the Articles of Confederation verged on utter collapse and that a radical change of some kind was as imminent as it was inevitable. Monarchy was one grim specter, but it was more likely, he thought, that two or perhaps three regional confederacies would emerge from the ruins of the present, and now moribund, national framework.[49] If we view the constitutional revolution that followed as, at least in part, an effort to resolve what had become a profound crisis in regional integration, the connections to earlier events and perceptions are striking. Although many southerners continued to believe that the demographic potential of their region portended future dominance in the Union, some viewed the proposed Constitution as a likely means of subverting, rather than fulfilling, that vision. And among contrary-minded southern optimists who took the leap of faith and supported the Constitution, Madison's nationalist commitment was distinctive for its transcendence of narrow regional concerns.

Monroe, Grayson, and Henry led the Antifederalist charge in Virginia in no small part because they saw the Constitution as a blueprint for permanent northern, or more specifically eastern, domination of the Union. Their analysis in 1788 differed little from what it had been in 1786, except now they apparently believed that the eastern schemers, rather than fomenting disunion, planned to manipulate the Constitution to accomplish their regional goals. At the Virginia ratifying convention Grayson insisted that easterners still wanted to close the Mississippi and that they had plans to do so under the aegis of this new, more powerful federal government. The larger point, of course, was that New Englanders would never encourage or even permit the substantial migration to the Southwest that would compromise their position of influence in the Union. The controversy over the Mississippi was thus "a contest for dominion—for empire," Grayson argued; it involved the "great national contest" of "whether one part of the continent shall govern the other." The Virginian knew that "God and nature have intended, from the extent of territory and fertility of soil, that the weight of population should be on this side of the continent": but he also knew that "at present, for various reasons, it is on the other side." The northern states had "the majority" and would tenaciously "endeavor to re-

49. Madison to Edmund Randolph, Feb. 25, 1787, *ibid.*, 299. See also Madison to Edmund Pendleton, Feb. 24, 1787, *ibid.*, 294–295.

tain it." [50] If Virginians were foolhardy enough to ratify the Constitution, he concluded, they would watch helplessly as northerners bartered away the Mississippi, obstructed the admission of any new southern states to the Union, manipulated commerce to their own peculiar advantage, and—interestingly enough, in view of Madison's response to the debates over locating the capital in the First Congress—placed "the federal ten miles square wherever they please." [51]

Federalists in Virginia (and elsewhere in the South) had to refute all such charges point by point, often by debating in great detail the putative consequences of particular Constitutional provisions for such matters as regulating commerce and making treaties. They also countered with a series of more general arguments: that the balance of power in the Union was in fact moving inexorably from north to south and from east to west, that it would continue to do so after ratification, and that the Constitution contained, moreover, a specific provision for assuring the prompt ascendancy of a southern (or at least pro-southern) agrarian majority. From Virginia to Georgia supporters of the Constitution painted time and again the familiar portrait of differential rates of regional population growth. Occasionally this view was disputed; one Georgian, who was quickly and smugly contradicted, argued that the South was less favorable to population growth than the North, "nature itself being the great obstacle," while a South Carolinian charged that restless, land-hungry New Englanders would never migrate in the expected numbers to the unfamiliar heat and humidity of the Southwest. [52] But southern Federalists insisted, in the words of another South Carolinian, Edward Rutledge, that, if "gentlemen should carry their views into futurity, and not confine themselves to the narrow limits of a day," they would understand that all such fears of permanent northern dominance were "ill-founded." [53] As George Nicholas of Virginia noted, "We shall soon outnumber them in as great a degree as they do us at this time: therefore this government, which, I trust, will last to the remotest ages, will be very shortly in our favor." [54] How long would this happy transformation take? "In twenty years, there will probably be a great alteration," predicted James Iredell of

50. Elliot, ed., *Debates*, III, 365–366.

51. *Ibid.*, 292, 585. See also 352–353, for Henry's statement of the case, and 340, for Monroe's.

52. See "A Georgian," *Gazette of the State of Georgia*, Nov. 15, 1787, in Jensen *et al.*, eds., *Documentary History*, III, 237–238; "Demosthenes Minor," Nov. 22, 1787, *ibid.*, 244–245; and Rawlins Lowndes in the South Carolina legislature, in Elliot, ed., *Debates*, IV, 309.

53. Elliot, ed., *Debates*, IV, 276–277.

54. *Ibid.*, III, 102.

North Carolina.[55] Just as confident but with a somewhat less optimistic timetable was the South Carolinian David Ramsay. "In fifty years," he mused, "it is probable that the Southern States will have a great ascendancy over the Eastern."[56]

The key to this southern Federalist argument was the second section of the first article of the proposed Constitution, which pegged representation in the House of Representatives (and by extension in the electoral college) to a periodic reassessment of each state's population. This census, or enumeration, was meant, according to a North Carolinian, "for the salvation and benefit of the Southern States."[57] Since the regional balance of power in Congress would respond directly to demographic trends, "our influence in the general government will be constantly increasing."[58] This provision of the Constitution had indeed originated with southern delegates to the Philadelphia Convention, led by the Virginians Edmund Randolph and George Mason, who had been eager to secure the future from the interference of nervous easterners who would inevitably try to protect their eroding power. The Virginia delegates had admitted that "according to the present population of America, the Northn. part of it had a right to preponderate." But the salient point was that it would lose that right "when the reason no longer continued." Since "the nature of man" guaranteed that "those who have power in their hands" would never relinquish it voluntarily, they were unwilling to leave decisions about future apportionment in the hands of legislators who would be loath to acknowledge the new state of affairs. A formal mechanism for adjusting power to population, therefore, had to be made part of the fundamental law. "As soon as the Southern and Western popu-

55. *Ibid.*, IV, 178.

56. Ramsay, "An Address to the Freemen of South Carolina . . . ," in Ford, ed., *Pamphlets*, 375. It is worth noting, indeed, that the southern delegations to the Philadelphia Convention had overwhelmingly taken the large state position on the matter of proportional representation. That the delegates from Georgia, which actually had a quite small population, and North Carolina, which was middling in demographic size, would join Virginia (a bona fide large state) vividly confirms the power of southern expectations. Georgia's population of 1787 may have been small, but the state also laid claim to territory so vast that it almost surpassed the surface area of all the other states combined, excluding Virginia and North Carolina, both of which also had extensive western territory waiting to be peopled. See Henderson, *Party Politics in the Continental Congress*, 415, esp. n. 129. For interesting evidence of the predominantly regional configuration of "voting blocs" at the convention, see S. Sidney Ulmer, "Sub-group Formation in the Constitutional Convention," *Midwest Journal of Political Science*, X (1966), 288–303.

57. Elliot, ed., *Debates*, IV, 209.

58. Ramsay, "An Address," in Ford, ed., *Pamphlets*, 375.

lation should predominate, which must happen in a few years," Mason argued, "the power wd. be in the hands of the [northern] minority, and would never be yielded to the majority, unless provided for by the Constitution."[59] Indeed, southern delegates to the convention had to contend far more strenuously for representation by a census beyond the control of Congress than they did for a fractional representation of their slave populations, an issue that was, contrary to many historical accounts, much less controversial.[60]

Mason got the census provision he wanted, but in his case, ironically, it turned out not to be enough. When the Philadelphia Convention completed its work, he refused to sign the document, and at the Virginia convention he was a staunch Antifederalist. Mason still believed in the familiar demographic calculus, but he no longer thought the South could survive even the temporary northern ascendancy that the Constitution assured. When an adversary trumpeted the standard argument—that "though the Northern States had a most decided majority against us, yet the increase of population among us would, in the course of years, change it in our favor"—Mason sarcastically dismissed it as "a very sound argument indeed: that we should cheerfully burn ourselves to death in hope of a joyful and happy resurrection!"[61]

Pressed hard by pessimists like Mason, some southern Federalists made rather extravagant claims about when and how their region might expect to control the new government. No doubt the heady prospect of lording it over the high and mighty easterners held substantial appeal. In Madison's case, however, we find something more than this simple vision of southern hegemony. Although his nationalist commitment was deeply rooted in his background and experience as a Virginian, it also reflected a sensitive and sophisticated vision of regional balance, accommodation, and integration. In one interesting respect Madison advised his fellow southerners to stop dreaming about the future long enough to remember the lessons of the past: he flatly told them that they needed close ties to the rest of the Union in order to enhance their basic security. Militarily, the southern states were extraordinarily weak. The presence of large numbers of slaves was a key consideration, of course, but so too was geography. Penetrated by so many long, navigable rivers, they were highly vulnerable to invasion from the sea —who could forget, after all, the devastation wreaked by British troops

59. Farrand, ed., *Records*, I, 578, 586. See the entire debate on July 11 for the comments of both Virginians and of others.
60. Howard A. Ohline, "Republicanism and Slavery: Origins of the Three-Fifths Clause in the United States Constitution," *WMQ*, 3d Ser., XXVIII (1971), 563-584.
61. Elliot, ed., *Debates*, III, 267.

during the last years of the Revolution?—and thus direly needed the protection both of an efficient national government and of northern military and naval strength.[62] For this reason alone Madison seemed more willing to make concessions to legitimate northern interests, believing unlike Mason, for instance, that a simple majority vote on commercial policy in Congress was not a dangerous or unreasonable imposition on the southern states.[63]

The comparatively national character of Madison's vision, Chesapeake-based though it was, is reflected even better in his understanding of the West. As we have seen, he believed as fervently as most southerners that both people and power were marching steadily toward the Southwest and that the southern states had, in this sense, time on their side. As he noted to Jefferson a few months prior to the Philadelphia Convention, proposals for proportional representation in the national legislature should appeal to "the Eastern States by the actual superiority of their populousness, and to the Southern by their expected superiority."[64] At the convention, moreover, his description of current population movements, which he framed in terms of natural law, made his expectations of the future quite clear: "The people are constantly swarming," he asserted, "from the more to the less populous places—from Europe to Ama. from the Northn. and Middle parts of the U.S. to the Southern and Western."[65]

But unlike other Federalists south of the Potomac, Madison did not view the West as an exclusively southern sphere of influence, nor did he understand the future in terms of crude southern dominance. He dismissed, in this connection, the common Antifederalist argument that most northerners, especially New Englanders, were hostile to expansion and therefore eager to barter away the Mississippi. He emphasized instead that northerners were vitally interested in outlets for their surplus population and that their interest already extended far beyond the proximate frontiers of New York and northern New England. As he frequently reminded his adversaries, the trans-Allegheny region would inevitably be settled "from the north as well as from the south," which meant that its prosperity would add to, not detract from, "the strength and security of the union."[66] Every day brought fresh evidence

62. *Ibid.*, 251. See also Madison to Edmund Pendleton, Jan. 16, 1781, in Hutchinson *et al.*, eds., *Papers of Madison*, II, 286-287, for the source of Madison's perception. Others who made the same argument during the ratification debates included C. C. Pinckney of South Carolina; see Elliot, ed., *Debates*, IV, 283-284.

63. Madison in Constitutional Convention, Aug. 29, 1787, in Hutchinson *et al.*, eds., *Papers of Madison*, X, 158, and in Virginia ratifying convention, June 24, 1788, *ibid.*, XI, 176.

64. Madison to Jefferson, Mar. 19, 1787, *ibid.*, IX, 318-319.

65. July 11, 1787, *ibid.*, X, 99.

66. Madison in Virginia convention, June 12, 1788, *ibid.*, XI, 128. See also

of this eastern interest in settling and developing the western territories, and in this context, according to Madison, American rights on the Mississippi were ever more a national, rather than a narrowly regional, concern.

It is important to note that Madison was responding directly in 1788 to a recent series of events that lent some credence to his view. Following adoption of the Northwest Ordinance a year earlier, a group of New Englanders under the leadership of an Ipswich, Massachusetts, minister, Manasseh Cutler, had purchased from Congress a substantial chunk of territory north of the Ohio River and implemented plans for its immediate settlement. In April 1788 the Ohio Company founded the town of Marietta, the first legal settlement in the Old Northwest.[67] Madison was optimistic that if "due provisions" were made for "the safety and order" of communities such as Marietta, the ties between New England and the West would strengthen. He even went so far as to make the bold prediction that before long the Muskingum River would become "as well known, and inspire as much solicitude" in the eastern states as Kentucky now did in Virginia.[68] Perhaps some New Englanders were slowly getting the same idea. Cutler's closest ties in his promotional efforts were as much to Virginians, including Washington, as they were to other New Englanders, but he was not alone in seeing the possibility that, as Congressman Nathan Dane of Massachusetts, one of the chief architects of the Northwest Ordinance, put it, at least part of the region north of the Ohio would be inclined to adopt "Eastern politics."[69] Although it would be several decades before most New Englanders completely shed their knee-jerk fear of the West as an anti-eastern projection of the southern states, Madison envisioned and welcomed that day, because under those circumstances the Constitution might indeed serve, as he hoped, "to bind together the Western and Atlantic States."[70]

Madison's comments the next day, *ibid.*, 135–136; Madison to George Thompson, Jan. 29, 1789, *ibid.*, 437; and the parallel argument of George Nicholas, in Elliot, ed., *Debates*, III, 240.

67. Eblen, *First and Second Empires*, 45–47; Philbrick, *Rise of the West*, 124; Turner, "Significance of the Section" (1925), in Turner, *Significance of Sections*, 30–31; and William Parker Cutler and Julia Perkins Cutler, *Life, Journals, and Correspondence of Reverend Manasseh Cutler, L.L.D.* (Cincinnati, Ohio, 1888), 2 vols.

68. Madison to George Nicholas, May 17, 1788, in Hutchinson *et al.*, eds., *Papers of Madison*, XI, 46.

69. Cutler and Cutler, eds., *Life of Cutler*, I, 135–136; Dane to Rufus King, July 16, 1787, and Dane to King, Aug. 12, 1787, in Burnett, ed., *Letters of Members of Congress*, VIII, 621–622, 636. See also Massachusetts Delegates to the Governor of Massachusetts, May 27, 1788, *ibid.*, 740.

70. Madison to Nicholas, May 17, 1788, in Hutchinson *et al.*, eds., *Papers of Madison*, XI, 45. There is substantial evidence that the Northwest Ordinance was

Madison's vision was not so much one of a simple southern majority, then, as one of regional accommodation and an agricultural, hence republican majority. The distinction bears emphasis. As he imagined the American future, sustained population growth would ensure the prompt development of the vacant western lands—which alone gave hope, he believed, for a successful experiment in republican nationality. Since all of the original Atlantic states, north and south, would participate and share an interest in developing the West, territorial expansion offered a potentially powerful source of union and regional integration. Just as important, the exploitation of western territory would sustain the republican character of the new nation by dissipating the fearful effects of increasing population density and allowing the majority of Americans, for several generations at least, to possess land and the civic integrity it conferred.[71] Even in the eastern states, Madison hoped, the majority might remain, with the help of steady migration, safely agricultural.

As with most visions of future grandeur, however, Madison's had more than one catch. He firmly believed that, if the new government created by the Constitution were to further this national promise, it had to reflect and respond to the patterns of demographic change that he anticipated. Hence the central importance of selecting a just and appropriate site for the government. It is in this context, indeed, that we can best appreciate the background and significance of Madison's explosive indignation during the first session of Congress in September 1789.

---

indeed a major step toward regional accommodation both in relation to the western territories and in an even broader sense. As Peter S. Onuf has recently noted, by 1787 northerners were discovering "their own political and private, speculative reasons for favoring new states," while southerners remained confident that the creation of new states north of the Ohio, even if peopled largely by New Englanders, could serve their interests south of the river and ultimately strengthen their position in the Union. See Onuf, *Origins of the Federal Republic*, 169-171. For evidence that even the most regionally minded southerners took no apparent or vigorous exception to, and perhaps even welcomed, the New England character of the Northwest Ordinance and Cutler's settlers, see William Grayson to James Monroe, Aug. 8, 1787 and Oct. 22, 1787, in Burnett, ed., *Letters of Members of Congress*, VIII, 631-632 and 659. See also Edward Carrington to James Monroe, Aug. 7, 1787, and the Virginia Delegates to the Governor of Virginia, Nov. 3, 1787, *ibid.*, 631, 672-673. As Onuf perceptively suggests, the most important result of the Northwest Ordinance, whether supporting southerners actually intended it or not, was "to encourage expansionist sentiment in the North and to commit the United States as a whole to the creation of new states" (*Origins of the Federal Republic*, 171).

71. See Drew R. McCoy, *The Elusive Republic: Political Economy in Jeffersonian America* (Chapel Hill, N.C., 1980), chaps. 1-6.

IV

Madison had insisted as early as the Philadelphia Convention that "the necessity of a central residence of the Govt wd be much greater" under the new regime than under the Articles of Confederation. He cited a number of practical reasons: "The members of the [new] Govt wd. be more numerous. They would be taken more from the interior parts of the States: they wd. not, like members of [the present] Congs. come so often from the distant States by water." Even more important, the precarious nature of America's daring experiment in nationality meant that the new government, with its significantly expanded power and influence, had to be "in that position from which it could contemplate with the most equal eye, and sympathize most equally with, every part of the nation."[72] Madison believed, indeed, that the site of the government would significantly influence the substance and effects of national policy. "Those who are most adjacent to the seat of legislation," he observed, "will always possess advantages over others. An earlier knowledge of the laws; a greater influence in enacting them; better opportunities for anticipating them, and a thousand other circumstances, will give a superiority to those who are thus situated."[73] Viewed in this light, the Potomac site was doubtless all the more appealing for its "remoteness from the influence of any overgrown commercial city."[74] In order to serve the needs and vision of Madison's agricultural, republican majority, in sum, the federal government had to be placed in its proper and appropriate location.

At the Virginia ratifying convention Madison's Antifederalist adversaries, convinced that the new regime would serve very different interests, made some dire predictions about where the capital would in fact be placed. Although Madison doggedly refuted their accusations, it was not long before he had cause to wonder just who had been right. When the Confederation Congress in September 1788 fixed the new government's first meeting at New York, Madison despaired at this possible "proof of the preponderancy of the Eastern strength, and of a disposition to make an unfair use of it."[75] And the ensuing debate over a permanent location a year later aroused his

72. Madison in Constitutional Convention, Aug. 11, 1787, in Farrand, ed., *Records*, II, 261 (brackets in quotations from Farrand represent the angle brackets of his text).

73. Madison in Congress, Sept. 4, 1789, in Hutchinson *et al.*, eds., *Papers of Madison*, XII, 375.

74. Note on Congress's Place of Residence, ca. Oct. 14, 1783, *ibid.*, VII, 379.

75. Madison to Washington, Sept. 14, 1788, *ibid.*, XI, 255. See also Madison's letter to Edmund Randolph on the same day (253).

full-fledged anger and alarm because it appeared to confirm his worst suspicions: that his particular vision of regional integration was not widely shared in the new government, and that an eastern faction was prepared to exploit its temporary advantage to the hilt and seek long-term regional dominance under the forms of the Constitution. As Richard Bland Lee, his fellow congressman from Virginia, so tellingly lamented, the faith of all those "south of the Potomac" was being profoundly shaken, for they were being shown that "what had been predicted by the enemies to the Constitution had come to pass."[76]

Historians have understandably emphasized what would appear to be the more significant issues associated with Hamiltonian finance, but this early debate over locating the capital may well have been the single most divisive issue to confront all three sessions of the First Congress. It was instrumental, moreover, in forming what proved to be relatively stable sectional voting blocs in the new national legislature. The familiar pattern of regional polarization that had characterized the old congress quickly reappeared, triggered by the explosive capital issue and furthered by an equally acrimonious debate at the first session of the Second Congress over another relatively neglected regional issue, that of fixing the ratio of a state's population to its congressional representation.[77] This apportionment controversy, which arose from the constitutional requirement that Congress reassess within three years after its first meeting the vital matter of how many representatives each state would be granted, assumed an explicitly sectional character when the Senate produced a bill in early 1792 that many southerners objected to as highly partial to the eastern states. Secretary of State Jefferson, among others, blasted this Senate scheme as unjust and even unconstitutional, angrily noting that by taking "the fractions of some states to supply the deficiency of others" it effectively made "the people of Georgia the instrument of giving a member to New Hampshire." Crafty easterners, he concluded, were playing "a hazardous game." The new government already gave them so much, but they wanted more. How far, he wondered, would their arrogant greed and ambition push them?[78]

As Richard Buel, Jr., has noted, the timing of this bitter debate over representation, which unfolded during the early months of 1792, enhanced

76. Richard Bland Lee in Congress, Sept. 3, 1789, in Gales, comp., *Debates and Proceedings*, 1st Cong., 1st sess., I, 856.

77. See Mary P. Ryan, "Party Formation in the United States Congress, 1789 to 1796: A Quantitative Analysis," *WMQ*, 3d Ser., XXVIII (1971), 523–542, esp. 538; and H. James Henderson, "Quantitative Approaches to Party Formation in the United States Congress: A Comment," *ibid.*, XXX (1973), 307–323.

78. Thomas Jefferson to Archibald Stuart, Mar. 14, 1792, in Paul Leicester Ford, ed., *The Writings of Thomas Jefferson* (New York, 1895), V, 453–454.

its significance. The apportionment controversy coincided with increasingly strident attacks on Hamilton's fiscal programs, which were rapidly assuming in the minds of many southern Americans the shape of a full-fledged system.[79] Since opponents of those programs were counting on reapportionment to bolster southern strength and check Hamilton's influence in Congress, it is not surprising that their anger over the Senate's apportionment bill shaded imperceptibly into the more formal, ideological thrust of their mounting dissent. What we can see in Madison's sharp reaction to the 1789 debates over locating the capital, in short, is the earliest phase of the disillusionment that would soon energize the Republican insurgency of the 1790s. "Hamiltonianism" subsequently appeared to him, and indeed to many southerners, as in large part the logical extension of the familiar eastern particularism of the 1780s.

The regional dimension of this partisan insurgency is hard to miss. Southerners eventually got their capital on the Potomac, of course, but they continued to worry for several years after the so-called Compromise of 1790 that scheming easterners would renege on the commitment to move south. One historian has even suggested that opposition to Hamilton's Bank of the United States stemmed principally from the suspicion that the institution threatened implementation of the plan to bring the capital to the Potomac.[80] Although this specific fear proved unfounded, southerners confronted a regime in the early and mid-1790s that appeared to them to favor the interests of northern speculators and merchants over those of agriculture and the South. When Jefferson urged President Washington in early 1792 to serve a second term, it is revealing that he cited the need to keep disillusioned southerners loyal to the present Union until reapportionment inevitably enhanced their region's strength in the new political system.[81] And when, at about the same time, Madison began a series of seventeen essays attacking the drift of national policy, it is appropriate that he opened his assault on that regime with a spirited defense of westward expansion in an article entitled "Population and Emigration." Madison had not forgotten the anti-western machinations of at least some northerners during the Jay-Gardoqui crisis, and the optimistic assessment of northern intentions that he had voiced during the ratification debates had already been shaken. Now he was only one of many southerners who feared that Hamilton and his allies were bent on discouraging the westward flow of Americans in the

79. See Richard Buel, Jr., *Securing the Revolution: Ideology in American Politics, 1789–1815* (Ithaca, N.Y., 1972), 21–23.

80. See Kenneth R. Bowling, "The Bank Bill, the Capital City, and President Washington," *Capitol Studies*, I (1972), 59–71.

81. Jefferson to Washington, May 23, 1792, in Ford, ed., *Writings of Jefferson*, VI, 1–6.

interest of consolidating population and resources in the East. In the secretary's 1791 "Report on Manufactures," presented at the same session of Congress that saw the eruption of the apportionment controversy, his opponents found dramatic evidence of this alternative geopolitical economy, one that was, in fact, premised on strikingly different assumptions and expectations about population density and the American future.[82]

Madison's nationalist commitment had always differed substantially from the largely northern strain of Federalist nationalism that assumed dominance in the early 1790s. It was not until 1800, in a second revolution, however, that he and Jefferson were able to rally their agricultural majority, rescue the Constitution from its captors, and set matters on the course that he had charted in 1787.[83] As the only region of the country with a social and political elite that was self-consciously agricultural, the southern states provided appropriate initiative and leadership in the forging of this national majority. We might say that the Jeffersonians assumed control of the federal government when they successfully broadened their southern political base to include enough political outsiders and upwardly mobile insurgents from the middle states to outvote—with the indispensable aid of the three-fifths clause, some would soon charge—the New England-based Federalists.[84]

82. For elaboration see McCoy, *Elusive Republic*, chap. 6.

83. For an excellent discussion of the differences between Madison's and Hamilton's nationalist persuasions, see two articles by Lance Banning: "James Madison and the Nationalists, 1780–1783," *WMQ*, 3d Ser., XL (1983), 227–255, and "The Hamiltonian Madison: A Reconsideration," *Virginia Magazine of History and Biography*, XCII (1984), 3–28.

84. Perhaps a brief word on the three-fifths clause is in order. I have not examined this issue for the simple reason that it is not central to the story of regional conflict that is presented here. Historians who have tended to read the sectional conflict of the antebellum years back into the 18th century have, of course, made a great deal of the issue; for a valuable corrective to this essentially anachronistic emphasis on the three-fifths clause as a significant source of sectional conflict in 1787–1789, see Howard A. Ohline, "Republicanism and Slavery: Origins of the Three-Fifths Clause in the United States Constitution," *WMQ*, 3d Ser., XXVIII (1971), 563–584. Disgruntled New England Federalists in a sense originated this emphasis by pointing to the clause in the years after 1800 as a primary—and thoroughly unjust—source of the Republican ascendancy. As Ohline suggests, however, few northerners at the 1787 convention objected to the principle of counting slaves for the purposes of representation in a republican system of government, and there is little evidence that discussion of the three-fifths clause at the convention can be fitted into the North-South sectional model that has been so popular with historians.

I do not mean to suggest, of course, that the parties can be understood simply or solely as organizations that reflected and promoted different regional interests or even visions. As my own previous work amply suggests, the Jeffersonian movement

Madison characteristically preferred to view this phase of American history, in retrospect, as the triumph of a republican rather than a specifically regional majority. Nevertheless, his plea for that case underscored the regional character of political coalitions in the early Republic. In a letter written in November 1820, shortly after his retirement from public life, he complained that the present generation of Americans was unable or unwilling to understand properly its Revolutionary heritage. The past was too often ignored, misconstrued, or purposely distorted for partisan advantage. "Facts even the most easily traced, when not remembered, seem, in many instances, to be entirely misunderstood or misapplied," he grumbled, and nothing astounded him more "than the allegations issuing from so many sources against what is called the Southern ascendancy." This accusation—that the federal government had always been controlled by the southern states and had become their tool—was obviously false for the 1790s, he argued, and "if during subsequent periods the Southern opinions and views have generally prevailed in the National Councils, it is to be ascribed to the coinciding opinions and views entertained by such a portion of other sections as produced, in the aggregate, a majority of the nation. The ascendancy, therefore, was not a Southern, but a Republican one, as it was called and deemed by all, wherever residing, who contributed to it."[85]

Madison's statement suggests that he viewed the political developments of the first two decades of the nineteenth century as a vindication of his vision of 1787, and no doubt to an extent he did. Yet he just as clearly understood that in some respects he—and most southerners—had gravely miscalculated. Madison, at least, had foreseen New England's extensive involvement in the development of the West and correctly gauged the effects of the resulting familial and cultural ties on eastern attitudes. By 1820 even Rufus King—who in 1786 had been ready to write off all those who ventured west of the mountains as barbarians lost to the Union—had substantially revised his view of things western, in no small part, perhaps, because his own family was contributing to the massive exodus of New Englanders,

---

drew upon a resonant ideology whose appeal could and did cut across both regional and class lines. As H. James Henderson suggested some time ago, perhaps what we need is "a conceptual scheme that can account both for the sectional cast of the rivalry between Federalists and Republicans and for what seems to be a more class-oriented conflict in the North, particularly in the larger middle states and above all in Pennsylvania"; see "Quantitative Approaches to Party Formation," *WMQ*, 3d Ser., XXX (1973), 320. For a quite useful discussion of the regional dimension of party conflict in the post-Revolutionary years, see William J. Cooper, Jr., *Liberty and Slavery: Southern Politics to 1860* (New York, 1983), chaps. 4 and 5.

85. Madison to Tench Coxe, Nov. 4, 1820, in *Letters and Other Writings of James Madison* (Philadelphia, 1865), III, 185.

which Madison had anticipated, to the newly formed states of the Old Northwest.[86] But contrary to Madison's hopes, eastern involvement in western affairs, rather than automatically furthering regional accommodation, had the potential to exacerbate intersectional tensions and discord, as the explosive Missouri controversy of 1819–1821 so stunningly revealed.[87] Even more important, perhaps, the completion of the Erie Canal in the 1820s dashed any lingering vestiges of the Potomac vision that had danced in the heads of an entire generation of Virginians. Not long after Madison's death in 1836, in fact, many southerners seemed as fearful of a north-west commercial axis and political alliance as New Englanders had been of the south-west juggernaut a scant half a century earlier.[88] There was ample cause for anxiety. The sudden emergence in the late 1850s of a new Republican party, one that could capture the presidency without winning a single southern electoral vote, marked the realization of that ominous potential and underscored the essential flaw in the southern Federalist vision of the late 1780s.

Where Madison had gone astray with so many others, of course, was in assuming that population would grow much more quickly south and west of the Potomac-Ohio axis than it would in the older states and other regions to the north. As we have seen, support of the Constitution in the South was considerably strengthened by the common inference that a permanent southern, or at least prosouthern, majority would soon emerge in a government based on proportional representation. At the time the Constitution was adopted, population had indeed been growing more rapidly in the

86. For a discussion of King and the broader issue, see Robert H. Wiebe, *The Opening of American Society: From the Adoption of the Constitution to the Eve of Disunion* (New York, 1984), 136–137.

87. It is interesting that some of the same principals in the Mississippi crisis of 1786 were directly involved in the Missouri controversy. Monroe, now president of the government he had opposed as an Antifederalist, attributed to King, one of the leading spokesmen for restricting slavery in the West, the same anti-southern motives that had allegedly been behind Jay's abortive negotiations with Gardoqui more than thirty years earlier. Perhaps it was Monroe's vivid recollections of the Jay-Gardoqui controversy, which had not involved slavery in any way, that prompted him to dismiss in 1819 the significance (and even the sincerity) of the antislavery moralism in which easterners like King now couched their politics. See, for example, Monroe to Jefferson, Feb. 7, 1820, in Stanislaus Murray Hamilton, ed., *The Writings of James Monroe* (New York and London, 1898–1903), VI, 113–114.

88. See Turner, "Significance of the Section," in Turner, *Significance of Sections*, 29–30. For an interesting discussion of how slowly New England attitudes could adjust to changed circumstances, see Peter J. Parish, "Daniel Webster, New England, and the West," in *Journal of American History*, LIV (1967–1968), 524–549.

South than in the North for several decades. But as the census results as early as 1800 began to suggest, this trend was abruptly reversed. Granted, southerners proved partially correct about one aspect of the demographic picture, at least in the short run: the territory south of the Ohio River initially gained population somewhat more rapidly than the territory to the north. In 1820 the combined population of Ohio, Indiana, Illinois, and Michigan was approximately 800,000, while the comparable figure for Missouri, Kentucky, Tennessee, Alabama, Mississippi, Louisiana, and Arkansas surpassed 1,300,000. For the original thirteen states, however, southerners had been dead wrong; population grew so much more rapidly in the states north of the Potomac, especially in New York and Pennsylvania, that by 1820 the white population of the northern states and territories was already close to twice that of the southern states and territories.[89] Even before he had access to the 1820 census figures, Madison quietly conceded that the southern states had never had, and never would have, the demographic majority that had once been almost universally anticipated for them.[90]

Almost universally, but not quite: a few northerners, at least, were probably not caught by surprise. During the 1789 debate over locating the federal capital, Fisher Ames of Massachusetts had mocked the chorus of southern boasts that the balance of population in the Union was receding rapidly from his native New England. Southerners forgot, he argued, that both their oppressive climate and the presence of slavery actually discouraged population. Victims of blind arrogance, they compounded their error by failing to understand that "trade and manufactures will accumulate people in the Eastern states" at such an impressive rate that the gap between North and South would probably widen, rather than tilt in the other direction.[91] One of Madison's correspondents at the time, Tench Coxe of Philadelphia, had sounded the same bold and unorthodox note, albeit in far more sympathetic terms. Madison and others assumed, Coxe hinted, that simply because the territory south and west of the Potomac was larger in surface area, it would inevitably be more populous; but what they failed to take adequate cognizance of was the superior power of trade and manufactures—which did not require vast expanses of land, fertile soil, or a mild climate—to attract and retain population. Since the southern states were destined to

89. These figures are quoted from Lynd, *Class Conflict, Slavery, and the Constitution*, 174–177. They can be verified from the figures presented in U.S. Bureau of Census, *Historical Statistics of the United States*, Part I, 24–37.

90. Madison to Coxe, Nov. 4, 1820, in *Letters and Other Writings of Madison*, III, 185.

91. Ames in Congress, Sept. 4, 1789, in Gales, comp., *Debates and Proceedings*, 1st Cong., 1st sess., I, 869–870.

remain largely agricultural, Coxe concluded, they "will not be populated in proportion to territory when compared relatively with the Country North of Potowmack where the commercial hives already exist, and where manufacturing Scenes must yearly open and encrease."[92]

Coxe's commentary illuminates the implicit and essentially fallacious assumptions that supported southern expectations of future greatness in the years just after the Revolution. It underscores, moreover, the significance of Madison's assumption, contrary to Coxe's and Ames's: that Americans, if not unwisely restrained by the kinds of policies his opponents pursued, would actually flee the highest stages of modern commercial society, following the natural laws of population growth and diffusion away from commerce and manufacturing toward the less densely populated areas that offered a more comfortable subsistence in agriculture.[93] The Virginian not only assumed that this movement to the South and West would naturally occur; he regarded it as essential to the health and security of the Republic. Certainly there is no indication that Coxe persuaded him to change his mind. Gazing west from the front porch of Montpelier, his family estate in Orange County, Virginia, Madison looked across miles of lush greenery toward the mountains and the paradise that he knew lay beyond. No wonder he was reluctant to lend credence to what proved to be a far more incisive and sophisticated understanding of the demographic implications of economic development.

Perhaps the best measure of the Virginian's confidence in his projections had come at the 1787 convention, when he had objected to representation by states, rather than population, in the upper house of Congress in part because of "the perpetuity it would give to the preponderance of the Northn. agst. the Southn. Scale." He counted eight northern and five southern states; should his preferred proportional representation be applied to the Senate, he told the delegates, the North would still outnumber the South, "but not in the same degree, at this time; and every day would tend towards an equilibrium."[94] It proved fortunate indeed for the antebellum southern states that Madison did not get his way. That by the election of 1860 it no longer mattered offers the most telling commentary on the magnitude of his and the southern miscalculation of the late 1780s.

92. Coxe to Madison, Sept. 20, 1789, in Hutchinson *et al.*, eds., *Papers of Madison*, XII, 413.

93. For a fuller consideration of the background and context of Madison's vision, see McCoy, *Elusive Republic*.

94. Madison in Constitutional Convention, July 14, 1787, in Hutchinson *et al.*, eds., *Papers of Madison*, X, 102.

☆ ☆ ☆

PART III
Aftermath

☆ ☆ ☆ ☆ ☆

The Structure
of Politics at the
Accession of George
Washington

JACK N. RAKOVE

I. THE FILTRATION OF TALENT

In the summer of 1785, the Newburyport merchant Jonathan Jackson wrote
John Adams a long letter recording his thoughts on the political situation
of the United States. Having just completed an unsuccessful commercial
voyage to England, Jackson was in no mood to be optimistic, either about
his own affairs or the current state of politics. "As I went away so have I
returned," he noted, "tired of Politics and willing to leave them to any who
know how to manage them." But where were such men to be found? Certainly not in the existing federal Congress, where Jackson himself had once
briefly served.

> Congress as at present appointed never appeared to me competent to
> the Business—they have not sufficient Stability collectively or indi-
> vidually—there is not permanency enough in their Appointment to
> induce them generally to qualify themselves for their Employment—to
> take it up and follow it as a Business.

Nor was the Congress unique in this respect, for this instability in office was
a "capital *Defect* thro[ugh]out our appointments." To be effective, Jackson
argued, government had to be made "the Business of a few—and made their
Business both from Motives of Interest and of Ambition." The people in

The author wishes to acknowledge the support of Project '87 and the National
Endowment for the Humanities, and the assistance of Charlene Bangs Bickford and
Helen E. Veit of the Documentary History of the First Federal Congress project at
George Washington University. Richard Buel offered useful comments.

general erred by failing to require officials to give public business "their whole Attention[,] paying them properly for it and thereby creating a Responsibility in all Men put into Office." Notwithstanding his revealing tendency to think of government as a needlessly messy activity requiring a suitably businesslike approach to be set right, Jackson should not be dismissed as an early advocate of what would later become a stock theme in American politics. For no less enlightened a reformer than Benjamin Rush echoed this same point a year later in his famous essay decrying the common tendency "to confound the terms of *the American revolution* with those of *the late American war.*" "Government is a science," Rush declared, "and can never be perfect in America, until we encourage men to devote not only three years, but their whole lives to it." No wonder "so many men of abilities object to serving in Congress," Rush concluded; who would wish "to spend three years in acquiring a profession which their country immediately afterwards forbids them to follow"?[1]

Concerned as Jackson and Rush were with the problem of getting the right men into office, their remarks nicely illustrate one of the central themes in the modern interpretation of the making of the Constitution. The most forceful statement of this interpretation belongs to Gordon S. Wood. In his influential formulation, the division between Federalists and Antifederalists was a "quarrel . . . fundamentally . . . between aristocracy and democracy," a struggle of "the worthy against the licentious." Distressed by the character of the men who had come to dominate state politics in the 1780s, the Federalists sought, above all else, "to restore a proper share of political influence to those who through their social attributes commanded the respect of the people and who through their enlightenment and education knew the true policy of government." In part this task might be accomplished simply through the creation of a vigorous national government whose very existence would induce "Men of real Virtue, knowledge, and clear property" to return to "public life."[2] But to assure this result, James Madison concluded, something more was needed: "such a process of elections as will most certainly extract from the mass of the Society the purest

1. Jonathan Jackson to John Adams, Aug. 10, 1785, Adams Papers, microfilm, reel 365, Massachusetts Historical Society, Boston. Rush's essay originally appeared under the pen name Nestor in the *Independent Gazetteer* (Philadelphia), June 3, 1786; it is reprinted in Merrill Jensen *et al.*, eds., *The Documentary History of the Ratification of the Constitution* (Madison, Wis., 1976-), XIII, 46-49.

2. Gordon S. Wood, *The Creation of the American Republic, 1776-1787* (Chapel Hill, N.C., 1969) chap. 12, esp. 506-518 (quotations at 485, 508); Tench Coxe to William Tilghman, Feb. 8, 1787, William Tilghman Papers, box 2, Historical Society of Pennsylvania, Philadelphia.

and noblest characters which it contains; such as will at once feel most strongly the proper motives to pursue the end of their appointment, and be most capable to devise the proper means of attaining it."[3]

The fruit of this concern was the complex mechanism of elections and appointments, with its staggered terms of office and separate constituencies, that so many commentators now regard as the bane of the American political system. To be sure, the convention's electoral balancing act had multiple roots, reflecting not only the continual bargaining between small and large states but also the framers' desire to preserve the independence of each branch of the national government. Yet most Federalists probably agreed that the deeper purpose of the electoral process was to get better men into office and to enable them to exercise mature and independent political judgment. If this system worked as Madison hoped, even the House of Representatives, the one popularly elected branch of government, would be insulated from the populist forces whose influence was so manifest in the state politics of the 1780s.

This belief that the adoption of the Constitution would lead to the emergence of a more aristocratic national elite was not confined to Federalists alone; nor did one have to read *The Federalist* No. 10 to understand just how the new political system was meant to operate. In the New York ratification convention, for example, the moderate Antifederalist Melancton Smith offered an analysis of the electoral process that makes Madison's appear almost unsophisticated by comparison. Of course, "the influence of the great will generally enable them to succeed in elections," Smith predicted:

> It will be difficult to combine a district of [*sic*] country containing thirty or forty thousand inhabitants,—frame your election laws as you please,—in any other character, unless it be in one of conspicuous military, popular, civil, or legal talents. The great easily form associations; the poor and middling class form them with difficulty.

Moreover, Smith reasoned, "men in the middling class" would probably "not be so anxious to be chosen." How much influence could they expect to wield even if they were elected? Positions of real influence would naturally be occupied by their social betters, and this would "render the place of a

3. From Madison's memorandum on "Vices of the Political System of the United States," in William T. Hutchinson *et al.*, eds., *The Papers of James Madison* (Chicago, Charlottesville, 1962-), IX, 357. Compare the language in this first formulation of his theory of the extended republic with the tempered expression of *Federalist* No. 10, where Madison spoke more simply of his hope that "the suffrages of the people . . . will be more likely to centre on men who possess the most attractive merit, and the most diffusive and established characters" (*ibid.*, X, 268).

representative not a desirable one to sensible, substantial men, who have been used to walk in the plain and frugal paths of life."[4] Other Antifederalist writers pursued similar themes, arguing that ordinary citizens lacked the inherent capacity of the wealthy to "unite their efforts to procure men of their own rank to be elected."[5]

Both Federalist hopes and Antifederalist fears obviously rested on a certain arithmetical plausibility. No doubt it *was* reasonable to imagine that, within the large districts from which representatives would be chosen, reputation and merit would outweigh the pedestrian sources of influence that merely local politicians could exercise. In a lower house that would originally consist of a mere sixty-five representatives, one Antifederalist wrote, "the smallness of their number enhances the dignity of their *seats*; and none can expect to obtain a *seat*, except men of the most elevated station."[6] By the same token, what kind of men were state assemblies more likely to send to the federal Senate: undistinguished backbenchers, or those whose experience and education would best enable them to articulate their state's interests? Where the opposing commentators seemed to differ, then, was not over the character of those most likely to be elected, but over the issue of whether this process would tend rather to fulfill or to violate the underlying purposes of representation.

Yet given the central place that such expectations commanded in both Federalist and Antifederalist thought, it is certainly worth asking what correspondence they bore to the actual conduct of politics. What Madison and his fellow Federalists predicted about the likely character of national legislators was, after all, very much—and perhaps little more than—an act of faith. Who could say whether elections would actually produce the desired results, obviating what Madison described as "the vicious arts, by which elections are too often carried," and granting victory to those "whose en-

4. Melancton Smith, speech of June 21, 1788, in Jonathan Elliot, ed., *The Debates in the Several State Conventions on the Adoption of the Federal Constitution* . . ., 2d ed. (Philadelphia, 1901), II, 243–251. A similar sociology figures in the distinction between "democratical" and "aristocratical" classes that was offered in the *Additional Number of Letters from the Federal Farmer to the Republican*, reprinted in Herbert J. Storing, ed., *The Complete Anti-Federalist* (Chicago, 1981), II, 265–268 (Letter 7 [1787]).

5. Brutus, No. III, *New York Journal*, Nov. 15, 1787, reprinted in Jensen *et al.*, eds., *Documentary History of the Ratification of the Constitution*, XIV, 122–123; and see *Observations Leading to a Fair Examination, of the System of Government Proposed by the Late Convention . . . from the Federal Farmer to the Republican* (New York, 1787), *ibid.*, 31.

6. Impartial Examiner, *Virginia Independent Chronicle*, June 4, 1788, in Storing, ed., *Complete Anti-Federalist*, V, 192.

lightened views and virtuous sentiments render them superior to local prejudices"? What was to stop some local "demagogue" from capturing an election if two better-qualified candidates split the virtuous vote?[7]

More to the point, the Federalists could hardly be confident about the
nature of the appeal that public life in general would exert in the years to
come. Throughout the Revolutionary years, both the state legislatures and
the Continental Congress had suffered from a high rate of turnover in membership. Inexperience and inefficiency went hand in hand, and much of the
criticism that was being directed against *all* government by the 1780s could
be traced, as Jonathan Jackson had argued, to the difficulty of recruiting a
stable and capable corps of legislators.[8] But this turnover was not primarily
the result of the dissatisfaction of the voters with those whom they had
elected. It reflected instead the complaints of the *elected*, who too often
found the demands of public life more than they wished to bear for any
extended period and who chose to retire from office as soon as they grace-
fully could. For however much lip service Americans paid to the concept of
the virtuous republican who knew how to subordinate private interest to the
common good, remarkably few of them learned to prefer the duties of public
office to the contentments of private life. The exaltation of civic life that was
so central to the classical republican tradition never became dominant in
America even during the Revolution, when patriotic constraints were most
effective. In time of peace, its appeal was even further diminished. Cincinnatus could offer a fine model for the exceptional circumstances of war and
revolution—and even perhaps for the accession of the first president—but
not for assuring the sobriety of legislation and stability of administration
that Federalists so desired. Federalist hopes and Antifederalist fears were
equally problematic. Perhaps service in Congress would appeal not to the
"natural aristocracy" whose dominance Melancton Smith feared, but rather
to aspiring lawyers interested in a job that offered steady pay and escape
from the drudgery of debt collection. What the deliberations of 1787–1788
lacked, then, was a plausible or adequate explanation of the range of motives
that would lead men to seek office.

Rather than pursue our interpretations of the late 1780s into ever more
refined formulations of "the republican synthesis," we might better ask
just how well the passionately articulated expectations of 1787–1788 corresponded with the underlying circumstances of American politics. The idea
that the "filtration of talent" would serve to recruit a new and more distinguished political elite and to insulate the national government from the

---

7. *Federalist* No. 10, in Hutchinson *et al.*, eds., *Papers of Madison*, X, 268, 269.

8. See the discussion in Jack N. Rakove, *The Beginnings of National Politics: An
Interpretive History of the Continental Congress* (New York, 1979), 216–239.

populist excesses of the states is a proposition that certainly bears reconsideration. Without denying its central place in the debates over *ratification*
of the Constitution, its relation to the emerging structure of national politics can be questioned from at least three vantage points. First, one has to ask
whether the relevant provisions of the Constitution were in fact designed to
secure the results that Federalists desired and Antifederalists feared. Second,
it would be useful to examine these expectations in the light of what is
known about actual patterns of congressional officeholding after 1789. Just
as Madison's argument in *Federalist* No. 10 failed to anticipate the organization of political parties, it is possible that his electoral calculus bore
little resemblance to the operations of the political system. Finally, one has
to consider whether the kind of political restoration or retrenchment the
Federalists envisioned was itself still realistic at the close of the 1780s. Even
if the electoral system had operated to promote the candidacies of virtuous
men, one would have to ask how well members of Congress would be
able to act in the disinterested fashion that Madison and others apparently
intended.

II. FRAMERS AND FEDERALISTS:
A NEGLECTED DISTINCTION

It has been some time since historians have displayed conspicuous interest
in the actual drafting of the Constitution or the origins of particular
clauses. Modern political controversies have drawn renewed attention to a
few provisions—notably those involving war powers and impeachment. Yet
more than seventy years after Charles Beard offered *An Economic Interpretation of the Constitution*, historians still seem preoccupied with identifying the
political and social alignments that favored or opposed the creation of a
stronger national government.[9] Creditors and debtors have given way to

9. For examples of historical approaches to "original meaning" problems, see
Charles Lofgren, "War-Making under the Constitution: The Original Understanding," *Yale Law Journal*, LXXXI (1972), 672–702; Peter Charles Hoffer and N.E.H.
Hull, *Impeachment in America, 1635–1805* (New Haven, Conn., 1984); and Jack N.
Rakove, "Solving a Constitutional Puzzle: The Treatymaking Clause as a Case
Study," *Perspectives in American History*, N.S., I (1984), 233–281. It is worth noting
that 1913 saw the appearance not only of Beard's great work but also of Max Farrand's *Framing of the Constitution of the United States* (New Haven, Conn., 1913),
which grew out of the latter's editing of the convention's records. Although other
narrative accounts of the convention have been published since, it would be fair to
say that most scholars would turn first to Farrand's brief volume, which remains the
standard work.

cosmopolitans and localists and, more recently, to court and country. But the thrust of inquiry has changed less than one might suppose. Even in Gordon Wood's monumental study, the substance of the Constitution matters less than the way in which it symbolized the gulf between democratic and aristocratic forces within American society. Just as the framers of the Constitution tend to be submerged within the larger Federalist movement, so the specific concerns that operated within the convention often seem less important than the arguments that were made for and against ratification.

And not without reason. The concerns of framers and ratifiers *had* diverged. The struggle between large and small states that had so dominated the internal politics of the convention did not remain a pivotal issue after September 1787. Similarly, the principal result of the ratification debates was the acceptance of an idea that the framers had not taken seriously: that a bill of rights could somehow provide a valuable check against the excesses of power. Moreover, the intensity of the struggle over ratification left a body of writings and speeches whose rich detail contrasts sharply with the spare words of the Constitution and the elliptical character of the convention's debates as evidence of the fundamental divisions with the American polity. Yet for all this, the Constitution should not be viewed solely through the lens of *The Federalist* and other ratification commentaries. For, once the passions of 1788 had faded and the polemical literature they produced had fallen into an obscurity from which only modern scholarship has rescued it, the language of the Constitution retained its force. That was where contemporaries turned when constitutional disputes arose, as they did as early as June 1789, and that is where historians ought to begin as well.

Was the Constitution consciously framed to promote a filtration of talent? No doubt many Federalists supported it because they believed it would enable a better class of leaders—or simply a better class—to recover political power. But it is difficult to demonstrate that this was what either the Constitution itself mandated or the framers intended. The *formal* criteria for membership in Congress were certainly not set high: the attainment of age twenty-five and seven years of citizenship for the House, age thirty and nine years of citizenship for the Senate; and the additional requirement that a member, "when elected, be an Inhabitant of that State in [for] which he shall be chosen" are all that Article I asks. Nor did the framers seek to restrict the size of the electorate, in the way, for example, that the Whig oligarchy of early Georgian England had managed to.[10] Members of the House of Representatives were to be elected by the same voters who had been sending "demagogues" into the state legislatures.

10. J. H. Plumb, *The Origins of Political Stability: England, 1675–1725* (London, 1967), 102–103.

Moreover, when one tracks the various provisions that would regulate the process of selection through the convention, it is apparent that the course of debate led the framers *away* from the idea that the Constitution ought to erect significant barriers against entrance into public life. Perhaps the best evidence of this can be found in the fate of efforts to establish property qualifications for appointment to office. As late as July 26, the convention had asked the Committee of Detail to draft a provision "requiring certain qualifications of landed property and citizenship in the United States for the Executive, the Judiciary, and the Members of both branches of the Legislature." In its report of August 6, however, the committee merely proposed that the legislature should be empowered "to establish such uniform Qualifications of the Members of each House, with Regard to Property, as to the said Legislature shall seem expedient." When this provision was taken up on August 10, Charles Pinckney pointedly noted that the committee had departed from its instructions. He moved instead to insert a clause requiring legislators "to swear that they were respectively possessed of a clear unincumbered Estate," with a suitably descending scale of property for the two houses.[11]

The ensuing debate revealed that attempts to establish property qualifications were objectionable on both practical and theoretical grounds. Two committee members explained why their report had not met Pinckney's expectations. Fix the requirement too high, John Rutledge noted, and it would anger the people; fix it too low, and the qualifications would be made "nugatory." Moreover, Oliver Ellsworth added, it was impossible to establish a scale that would work equally well for different parts of the Union or for different periods in the history of the nation. These objections were so decisive that Pinckney's motion was rejected by a simple voice vote.

But that still left open the question whether the legislature ought to possess any discretionary power to establish conditions of membership. One problem was the difficulty of employing any criterion other than property. The more telling objection lay, however, against giving the legislature any discretion. As Hugh Williamson noted, such license could allow the lawyers who might well dominate the new congress to secure "future elections . . . to their own body." But if qualifications could not be fixed *constitutionally*, it seemed better to do away with them entirely. Otherwise, Madison warned, the legislature would be able "by degrees [to] subvert the Constitution." The entire clause was accordingly eliminated.[12]

---

11. Max Farrand, ed., *The Records of the Federal Convention of 1787*, 3 vols. (New Haven, Conn., 1911), II, 116–117, 121–126, 165, 248–249.

12. *Ibid.*, 248–250.

If the character of national legislators could not be regulated by imposing property requirements on the elected, could the same goal be achieved by limiting the suffrage? When the Committee of Detail proposed allowing the House of Representatives to be chosen by the same voters who elected the lower houses of the state legislatures, Gouverneur Morris and John Dickinson vigorously argued in favor of restricting the franchise to landed freeholders. But this proposal was also roundly rejected. The Constitution placed no restrictions on the right of suffrage.[13]

Nor can it be said that the framers seriously considered just how elections for the House of Representatives were to be conducted. In agreeing to vest Congress with a residual power to determine the manner of electing congressmen, they were clearly concerned with the possibility that the state legislatures would manipulate the electoral process. But what is more striking is the latitude within which the states were to be allowed to act. As Madison himself noted,

> Whether the electors should vote by ballot or vivâ voce, should assemble at this place or that place; should be divided into districts or all meet at one place, sh[oul]d all vote for all the representatives; or all in a district vote for a number allotted to the district; these and many other points would depend on the Legislatures, and might materially affect the appointments.[14]

Coming from one who presumably regarded the manner in which congressmen were to be elected as a critical element of the entire system—and who had once described voting by ballot as "the only radical cure for those arts of Electioneering which poison the very fountain of Liberty"—this was hardly a trivial concession. Indeed, nothing better illustrates the degree to which Madison's notion of the electoral virtues of the extended republic was simply a statement of faith. The indefinite character of his thinking on this subject was due in part to the greater priority he had been forced to place within the convention on the struggle to secure the principle of proportional representation; and it may also have reflected his disappointment that the Senate, the single branch of government on which he had originally fastened his deepest hopes, was to be elected by the state legislatures. In any event, there is no evidence that Madison had developed beyond generalities his notion of how representatives were to be elected. When in 1788 the states began adopting a variety of procedures for electing representatives—including not only district and statewide elections but also a hybrid in which electors voted state-

13. *Ibid.*, 201–210, 215–216, 225.
14. *Ibid.*, 240–241.

wide for members from particular districts—Madison informed Jefferson, "It is perhaps to be desired that various modes should be tried, as by that means only the best mode can be ascertained." [15]

Decisions on other provisions also worked to remove formal barriers against election to the legislature. Instead of requiring a congressman to be "resident" in his state for a fixed period of years, the convention agreed that he need only be an "inhabitant" of the state at the time of election.[16] When it came to deciding how legislators were to be paid, the convention did not presume that members of Congress would be independently wealthy. It authorized paying legislative salaries from the national treasury not merely to prevent the states from retaining undue influence over their representatives, but also from an expectation that newly admitted western states might balk at supporting an adequate representation if forced to defray legislative salaries from their own limited funds.[17]

Finally, and perhaps most revealingly, the convention relaxed the prohibition against the appointment of legislators to other offices. Of all the provisions relating to conditions of membership, this was the most sharply controverted, and it was not resolved—and then only by the narrowest margin—until September 3. The report of the Committee of Detail would have prevented legislators from accepting any federal office during the term of their election, with senators further barred from "holding any such office for one year afterwards." Supporters of these restrictions argued the conventional whiggish view that, without such restraints, the legislature would attract, as George Mason noted with typical irony, "those generous and benevolent characters who will do justice to each other's merit, by carving out offices and rewards" for their own profit. But the majority, who eventually restricted the prohibition only to offices that had been either "created" or whose "emoluments [had been] increased" during a legislator's term, were apparently swayed by equally candid arguments in favor of promoting ambition. James Wilson put the key point bluntly when he declared that "he was far from thinking the ambition which aspired to Offices of dignity and trust, an ignoble or culpable one." Thus while the narrow margin with which the diluted version of this clause was approved indicates that the framers had not reached a consensus, they would nevertheless have agreed

15. Madison to Caleb Wallace, Aug. 23, 1785; Madison to Jefferson, Oct. 8, 1788, in Hutchinson *et al.*, eds., *Papers of Madison*, VIII, 354, XI, 276.

16. *Ibid.*, II, 216–219. It should be noted that the convention did act to *increase* the period of citizenship required for both the House and Senate above that proposed by the Committee for Detail. See debates for Aug. 9 and 13, Farrand, ed., *Records*, II, 235–239, 268–273.

17. *Ibid.*, I, 371–375, II, 290–293.

that the revision was intended to encourage men to enter legislative service in part from forthright calculations of personal ambition. Whether the ambitions to be unleashed belonged to corruptible "office-hunters" or to "those whose talents" would "give weight to the Govern[men]t" remained to be seen.[18]

On balance, then, the principal concern of the framers was not to limit access to national office to those who were most conspicuously qualified to occupy it, but rather to open up the process of political recruitment in the hope that better men would be moved to enter public life and prove capable of achieving electoral success. For the new government to succeed in this respect, however, it would have to rely on the actual circumstances of political life rather than the formal requirements that the Constitution itself had failed to impose. Federalist desires could be realized only if the enlarged sphere of the extended republic worked to filter talent upward or if the simple prestige and power of the new government drew qualified men away from the privacy of their law offices, plantations, and countinghouses. Neither the formal provisions of the Constitution nor the heated debates of the ratification campaign could secure such results; they depended instead on other factors—personal as well as political—that no constitution could by itself legislate.

III. WHY MEN ENTERED CONGRESS—AND LEFT

If the adoption of the Constitution was thus meant to release new ambitions, the preservation of its intricate system of checks and balances would also depend, Madison argued in *Federalist* No. 51, on directing those ambitions toward appropriate ends. "Ambition must be made to counteract ambition," he wrote. "The interest of the man must be connected with the constitutional rights of the place."[19] Yet despite its apparent gritty realism, this celebrated statement was no less problematic than other early predictions about the likely operation of the Constitution.

For ambition could counteract ambition only if those elected made continuation in a particular office the object of their careers. The benefits of bringing more enlightened leaders into office would be lost if they chose not to stay in positions of responsibility. But if one thing is clear about the political system that the Constitution created, it is that it long failed to promote the stability of tenure that Federalists desired and anticipated. The

18. *Ibid.*, II, 283 n.1, 284, 288.
19. Benjamin Fletcher Wright, ed., *The Federalist* (Cambridge, Mass., 1961), 355–356.

evidence on this point is unambiguous. Well into the next century, the new system proved embarrassingly productive in its *recruitment* of aspirants to national office, but its record on *retention* was another matter entirely. The best that can be said for Congress is that its membership was marginally more stable than that of the state legislatures.[20] Throughout the entire first century of its history, members entered and left Congress with a frequency that stands in sharp contrast with modern standards. During this period, the median term of service in the House of Representatives fluctuated between two and four years, and the proportion of members who served more than four terms never exceeded 10 percent. From 1790 to 1870, the median age of departure from the House remained steadily fixed in the mid-forties. And although the reasons why men left the House are often hard to come by, death, old age, and electoral defeat clearly played far less of a role in attrition before the late nineteenth century than they do today.[21]

Some degree of mutability had, of course, been expected for the House of Representatives. Even so, it can hardly be argued that the framers had successfully compensated for the anticipated fluidity of that chamber by giving the Senate the stability inherent in a six-year term free from recall and the incentives to serve provided by its additional powers over foreign affairs and appointments. For had that truly been their expectation, the early history of the chamber that Antifederalists feared would be the real nursery of aristocracy would have been doubly disappointing. "Career data on the early Senate is a morass of resignations, short-term appointments, elective replacements, and more resignations," Douglas Price has observed. "There are *no* notable careers in terms of long service." Far from emerging as the

20. See L. Ray Gunn, "The New York State Legislature: A Developmental Perspective: 1777-1846," *Social Science History*, IV (1980), 276-282; and Ballard Campbell, *Representative Democracy: Public Policy and Midwestern Legislatures in the Late Nineteenth Century* (Cambridge, Mass., 1980), 31-32.

21. Allan G. Bogue *et al.*, "Members of the House of Representatives and the Processes of Modernization, 1789-1860," *Journal of American History*, LXIII (1976-1977), 291, 294-296. Other comparable findings are presented in the seminal essay of Nelson W. Polsby, "The Institutionalization of the House of Representatives," *American Political Science Review*, LXII (1968), 144-168; and in Morris P. Fiorina *et al.*, "Historical Change in House Turnover," in Norman J. Ornstein, ed., *Congress in Change: Evolution and Reform* (New York, 1975), 24-57. The impact of high rates of turnover on the conduct of congressional business is also emphasized in James Sterling Young, *The Washington Community, 1800-1828* (New York, 1966), chap. 5; and see Samuel Kernell, "Toward Understanding Nineteenth Century Congressional Careers: Ambition, Competition, and Rotation," *American Journal of Political Science*, XXI (1977), 669-693, which offers several hypotheses to explain why House careers became more attractive at the close of the nineteenth century.

great source of stability, prudence, and independence, "the Senate was an honorific nothing."[22] Moreover, there is some evidence to suggest that senators remained less independent of their legislative constituents than the framers had imagined they would be. State legislatures continued to issue instructions to the men they regarded as their elected representatives, and at least some senators felt bound either to honor those wishes or to treat instances of disagreement as an occasion, or even a pretext, for resigning.[23]

Perhaps because it is difficult to study the ambitions of men who are not ambitious, historians have generally ascribed little importance to this high rate of congressional turnover.[24] Within the scholarly literature, the principal problem has been to discover why Congress became more modern, or professional, toward the close of the last century rather than to understand why the boundaries between Congress and society remained so permeable so long. Yet this prior question is not without interest, and not merely because the realities of the early Republic did not conform to the expectations of 1787–1788. As Jack P. Greene has demonstrated, the tendency within the late colonial regime had been to produce higher levels of incumbency and cohesion within the provincial assemblies.[25] With the coming of Independence that tendency evidently was reversed, at both state and national levels of politics. Contemporaries sensed that an alteration in patterns of officeholding was taking place, and they struggled to explain its causes and correct its consequences. At first they interpreted the phenomenon of turnover as a reaction to the enormous burdens that public office now imposed.

22. Douglas Price, "Careers and Committees in the American Congress: The Problem of Structural Change," in William O. Aydelotte, ed., *The History of Parliamentary Behavior* (Princeton, N.J., 1977), 29–36 (quotation at 30).

23. The efforts of state legislatures to use instructions and other political devices to regulate senatorial behavior are discussed in Clement Eaton, "Southern Senators and the Right of Instruction, 1789–1860," *Journal of Southern History*, XVIII (1952), 303–319; William H. Riker, "The Senate and American Federalism," *Am. Pol. Sci. Rev.*, XLIX (1955), 452–469; and see Daniel P. Jordan, *Political Leadership in Jefferson's Virginia* (Charlottesville, Va., 1983), 186–190.

24. Thus an otherwise valuable recent survey of American legislative history devotes only a few rather tentative paragraphs to the general subject of recruitment and incumbency, but focuses instead on problems having to do with voting behavior. Joel H. Silbey, "'Delegates Fresh from the People': American Congressional and Legislative Behavior," *Journal of Interdisciplinary History*, XIII (1982–1983), 616–617. For a more sensitive consideration of the problem, see the comments in Young, *Washington Community*, 61.

25. Jack P. Greene, "Legislative Turnover in British America, 1696 to 1775: A Quantitative Analysis," *William and Mary Quarterly*, 3d Ser., XXXVIII (1981), 442–463. There was, of course, no counterpart to Congress during the colonial era.

Later, those who were most critical of the democratic excesses of the state constitutions began to conclude that the problem could be at least partly alleviated by departing from the sacred principle of annual elections.[26] But if by 1787 Federalists hoped that the prescriptive example of the new Constitution would promote stability at all levels of government, the evidence suggests their confidence was misplaced. For reasons that remain obscure, the Constitution failed to reverse the changes in behavior that the Revolution inaugurated. The turning point that made high rates of legislative incumbency so central a feature of modern American politics occurred only in the context of the much later developments associated with professionalization.

Irrelevant as these later developments may be to explaining why the framers at Philadelphia acted as they did, the disparity between the expectations of 1787–1788 and the behavior of candidates and incumbents nevertheless raises important questions about the making of the Constitution. For rather than continually confining our inquiries to the arguments that were bandied back and forth while the Constitution was being adopted, we should ask how well these original conceptions corresponded to the subsisting and persisting currents of American politics, to the world that contemporaries sought both to describe and to shape. What is at issue is whether the framers and ratifiers of 1787–1788 understood the range of ambitions that would actually carry men into office once the Constitution took effect, or whether their expectations reflected only the highly charged and distortive atmosphere within which they acted.

Is it possible to characterize the range of ambitions that carried men to Congress after the Constitution took effect? To explain why men entered and left Congress during the entire preprofessional period of its history obviously lies beyond the scope of this essay—and perhaps beyond the scope of even the most sustained inquiry. The relative obscurity of the large numbers of state-oriented politicians who circulated through Congress ironically compounds the difficulty of gathering all but the most rudimentary data about members.[27] It is not surprising that the few attempts at collective biography that have been made for the early national era tend to focus on ascertaining the social status and prior experience of officeholders, an em-

26. Thus in 1785, when he was already troubled by the shortcomings of state legislation, Madison could write (in his letter offering advice for a constitution in Kentucky) that while annual elections were still regarded as "indispensabl[e] . . . some of the ablest Statesmen and soundest Republicans in the U States are in favor of triennial" (to Caleb Wallace, Aug. 23, 1785, in Hutchinson *et al.*, eds., *Papers of Madison*, VIII, 354).

27. See the useful observations on the limits of collective biography in Lawrence Stone, "Prosopography," *Daedalus* (1971), 46–79, esp. 57–65.

phasis that betrays a tendency to measure the democratic character of our political system in terms of access to office.[28]

The key to understanding the sources of political ambition in the early period of national history lies, in any event, elsewhere. Ambition is, in some fundamental sense, an attitude, and the evidence that best testifies to its character and force includes articulate expressions of personal intention as well as the more obvious indexes of status. Moreover, such efforts as have been made to trace congressional career patterns have tended to indicate that the social background and experience of congressmen have changed little over time and that, indeed, the principal reason for the decline in turnover rests with the motives of the officeholders themselves, particularly with the willingness of incumbents to seek reelection.[29] The issue, in other words, is not so much who was elected to Congress, but, rather, why men wished to enter Congress in the first place and what considerations thereafter governed their decisions to retire or seek reelection. What makes the answer to this question so particularly elusive is that ambition is a subject upon which people are rarely candid with themselves, much less with friends or even spouses. The sorts of candid, self-conscious testaments historians would most like to consider, accordingly, do not come readily to hand.

The one group of congressmen whose ambitions can be described most easily are the ninety-odd members of the First Federal Congress of 1789–1790. Their experience in gaining and holding office marked the first test of the various predictions that had been vented while the Constitution was being adopted. The First Congress, of course, numbered fewer members than all but its immediate successor, and its ranks almost certainly included a higher proportion of prominent personalities than any later congress. To some extent, it is true, the likelihood that many of these first congressmen had taken major parts in both the Revolution and the debate over the Con-

28. For examples see Jordan, *Political Leadership in Jefferson's Virginia*, 34–84; Sidney H. Aronson, *Status and Kinship in the Higher Civil Service: Standards of Selection in the Administrations of John Adams, Thomas Jefferson, and Andrew Jackson* (Cambridge, Mass., 1964); Carl E. Prince, *The Federalists and the Origins of the U.S. Civil Service* (New York, 1977); Paul Goodman, "Social Status of Party Leadership: The House of Representatives, 1797–1804," *WMQ*, 3d Ser., XXV (1968), 465–474; and Richard D. Brown, "The Founding Fathers of 1776 and 1787: A Collective View," *WMQ*, 3d Ser., XXXIII (1976), 465–480. For the period when political behavior was becoming more modern, see David J. Rothman, *Politics and Power: The United States Senate, 1869–1901* (Cambridge, Mass., 1966).

29. Kernell, "Understanding Congressional Careers," *Am. Jour. Pol. Sci.*, XXI (1977), 690–692; and see Bogue *et al.*, "Members of the House," *JAH*, LXIII (1976–1977), 300–301, 281–292, on continuity in the basic social characteristics of congressmen.

stitution would suggest that their motives did not accurately represent the range of ambitions that came into play once the age of the founding patriarchs gave way to the era of mass political parties. Yet even during the Revolution, decisions about the depth of political involvement—as opposed to simple allegiance—often reflected personal concerns, and by the late 1780s, recovery from the turmoil and dislocation of the war was well enough advanced to enable potential candidates to weigh the benefits and costs of office quite carefully according to the dictates of individual interest and ambition. Finally, although one cannot fault the framers of the Constitution for failing to anticipate how "change of circumstances, time, and a fuller population of our country" would affect the character of representation, the "moderate period of time" separating the drafting of the Constitution from the first elections allows us to ask how well the arguments of 1787-1788 corresponded to certain aspects of what might be called, with all due respect to Sir Lewis Namier, the structure of American politics at the accession of George Washington.[30]

By any criterion, including those criteria that contemporaries would have applied, the victors in the first federal elections were a distinguished group. The roster of the First Congress included twenty members of the Federal Convention—among them Madison, Elbridge Gerry, Rufus King, Roger Sherman, William Samuel Johnson, Oliver Ellsworth, William Paterson, and Robert Morris—as well as a number of other men who had held prominent military or political positions during the war, such as Philip Schuyler, Elias Boudinot, Jeremiah Wadsworth, John Langdon, Richard Henry Lee, and Egbert Benson.[31] Prestige alone offers no proof of legislative talent, but most members of the First Congress shared another trait that would have enabled contemporaries to agree that they possessed what Madison had called for in *Federalist* No. 10: "the most attractive merit, and the most diffusive and established characters."[32] For in the milieu of the late 1780s, a

30. Both quotations are from *Federalist* No. 55, in which Madison discusses the size of the House of Representatives (Wright, ed., *The Federalist*, 377).

31. Egbert Benson's role in the New York assembly illustrates particularly well how the Revolutionary constitutions had affected the character of legislative politics. See Edward Countryman, "Some Problems of Power in New York, 1777-1782," in Ronald P. Hoffman and Peter J. Albert, eds., *Sovereign States in an Age of Uncertainty* (Charlottesville, Va., 1981), 157-184.

32. Exactly what Madison meant by "diffusive" is not clear, but I would follow Garry Wills, who suggests that it "must mean 'general' or 'widespread,'" in the sense of possessing a "reputation [that] is not only established but reaches out across larger stretches of the extended republic" (Garry Wills, *Explaining America: The Federalist* [New York, 1981], 232).

notable record of involvement in the Revolution was itself the first and perhaps even sufficient test of political merit. In this respect, it is striking that fully half of the members of the First Congress were politically active before Independence, with no fewer than a third entering politics during the final crisis of 1774–1776, and an additional quarter first holding office during the remaining years of the war. Only twenty members of the First Congress had launched their political careers since the treaty of peace—and twelve of these were aged twenty-eight years or less when the war ended.[33] Not all of these patriots had compiled distinguished *political* records: what helped to send men like Thomas Sumter of South Carolina and James Jackson of Georgia to Congress were the reputations they had earned in vicious combat in the South.[34] But, again, these were deeds that offered conclusive evidence of public-spiritedness. As one writer who promoted the (unsuccessful) candidacy of General John Sullivan observed, "No man can be more safely intrusted with the administration of a government than him who has risked his life to establish it."[35]

There is another sense in which authentically public-spirited motives can be readily imputed to those who sought election to the First Congress. Because the issue of amendments to the Constitution was widely expected to head the congressional agenda, the first federal elections were, in effect, an extension of the struggle over ratification.[36] A large proportion of congressional candidates—both Federal and Antifederal—stood for office in

33. In addition to an imposing list of biographies of the most prominent members, which will not be cited here, other biographical sources relied upon include Billy Bob Lightfoot, "The State Delegations in the Congress of the United States, 1789–1801" (Ph.D. diss., University of Texas, 1958); *Biographical Directory of the American Congress, 1774–1961* (Washington, D.C., 1971); *Dictionary of American Biography*; Clifford K. Shipton, *Sibley's Harvard Graduates: Biographical Sketches of Those Who Attended Harvard College*, Vols. XII–XVII (Boston, 1962–1975); James McLachlan, *Princetonians, 1748–1756: A Biographical Dictionary* (Princeton, N.J., 1976); Richard A. Harrison, *Princetonians, 1769–1775: A Biographical Dictionary* (Princeton, N.J., 1980); Walter B. Edgar *et al.*, eds. *Biographical Directory of the South Carolina House of Representatives*, Vol. III (Columbia, S.C., 1981); and Edward C. Papenfuse *et al.*, eds., *A Biographical Dictionary of the Maryland Legislature, 1635–1789*, 2 vols. (Baltimore, 1979–1985).

34. Anne King Gregorie, *Thomas Sumter* (Columbia, S.C., 1931); William Omer Foster, Sr., *James Jackson: Duelist and Militant Statesman, 1757-1806* (Athens, Ga., 1960).

35. *New Hampshire Spy*, June 6, 1789, in Merrill Jensen *et al.*, eds., *The Documentary History of the First Federal Elections, 1788–1790* (Madison, Wis., 1976–), I, 845.

36. Steven R. Boyd, *The Politics of Opposition: Antifederalists and the Acceptance of the Constitution* (Millwood, N.Y., 1979), 139–167.

part because either conscience or the urgings of friends persuaded them to view the election of a right-minded representative in terms of protecting or remedying the verdict of ratification. Ambition could still have played a part in their decisions, yet often it must have been subordinated to a sense of commitment generated by the intense politics of ratification. What brought the otherwise obscure Jonathan Grout of Massachusetts to Congress in 1789 was neither conspicuous experience nor ambition—he had served only two scattered terms in the General Court before his election to the state senate in 1787—but his record in Worcester as an Antifederalist. Grout enjoyed service in the House enough to seek reelection, but after his defeat in 1790, there is no record of his holding higher office again.[37] Aedanus Burke also gained election on the basis of his Antifederal credentials, but his interest in Congress waned once it completed drafting amendments to the Constitution; rather than seek a second term, he returned to South Carolina and his seat on the bench of the Court of Common Pleas and Sessions.[38]

Finally, if high social status and wealth were expected to be concomitant attributes of political distinction, the members of the First Federal Congress were eminently qualified. At least two of every five representatives and half of the first Senate can be said to have inherited high social status from their parents or earlier generations. Some, like Philip Schuyler or Richard Bland Lee, came from families whose right to leadership had long been assumed; others could readily convert conspicuous wealth into political influence, like Daniel Huger of South Carolina, whose inheritance included two plantations and 113 slaves. Such holdings could not be rivaled by Frederick A. Muhlenberg, the speaker of the first House, or his brother Peter, but their status was no less secure for being the eldest sons of their prominent clergyman father, which gave them enormous influence among the German community of Pennsylvania.[39] At the opposite end of the scale, only a handful of the ninety-odd members had risen from the lower ranks of white society, like Timothy Bloodworth of North Carolina, sometime wheelwright and cobbler, and Thomas Sumter, a common soldier during the Seven Years' War and a reputed fugitive from a debtors' prison, who had found prosperity through his marriage to a wealthy widow and prominence from his wartime record. The remaining members came from middling families of

---

37. Grout was so obscure—because lacking a Harvard education—that when Clifford Shipton found his name in a letter he wished to print, he could only place a question mark after it (Shipton, *Sibley's Harvard Graduates*, XIV, 544).

38. Edgar *et al.*, eds., *Biog. Dir. of S.C. House*, III, 105–107.

39. George A. Billias, *Elbridge Gerry: Founding Father and Republican Statesman* (New York, 1976); for Huger, see Edgar *et al.*, eds., *Biog. Dir. of S.C. House*, II, 340–341; and for the Muhlenbergs, *DAB*.

varying degrees of respectability. Many of them, of course, had acquired wealth and status in their own right, like Sumter and Thomas FitzSimons, the Philadelphia merchant-congressman who, hardly off the boat from Ireland, married the daughter of a prominent merchant and went into partnership with her brother in the same year.

All of these considerations of prior experience, principled engagement, and social status could be taken as evidence that, at the outset at least, the electoral system was working much as it had been hoped or expected to do. Indeed, they even seem to suggest that habits of deference were functioning reasonably well within the newly extended Republic. Yet if one looks at the first elections and their results from a slightly different perspective, other impressions come into view. Two sets of examples—one drawn from northern Federalists, the other from congressmen representing the southern periphery—illustrate the complex ways in which private circumstances and ambitions could fuse with prevalent notions of republican duty to make men eligible for national political office.

Historians generally agree that the two Federalist movements of the 1780s and 1790s were committed to the preservation or restoration of traditional principles of deference and that their leadership (at least in the northern states) tended to be drawn from an established elite whose superiority was endangered by the democratizing impulses the Revolution had released. Yet among the "dual Federalists" who sat in the First Congress,[40] it is striking to see how many fit the image of new men who had themselves struggled to gain—and not simply inherit—prestige and influence. Recognizing that their own rise to political power and higher social status had derived from participation in the Revolution, they were no less its products for resisting what they regarded as its excesses.

By way of example, consider the uncannily parallel paths that had led Oliver Ellsworth of Connecticut and William Paterson of New Jersey to the Senate in 1789. Both were born in 1745; both were graduates of the College of New Jersey; both served terms as state legal officers; both were delegates to the Federal Convention, where they collaborated on the making of the Great Compromise; and as the capstones of their political careers, both later accepted appointments to the Supreme Court, where they served together until Ellsworth's retirement in 1800. Both came from families with solidly middle-class credentials. Ellsworth's father was a respectable farmer, selectman, and militia captain who intended his second son for the ministry but saw him turn to law instead. Paterson emigrated with his family from Ireland in 1747; by 1750 his father was established in Princeton, where he

---

40. "Dual Federalists" here are those who supported both ratification of the Constitution and Hamiltonian policies.

prospered as a storekeeper and helped his eldest son take advantage of all the opportunities education could bestow.[41]

The promise of education was one thing, however; success was another matter again. When war broke out in 1775, both men were still struggling to make a respectable career at law. Ellsworth had earned all of three pounds sterling during his first three years of practice; the one promising step he had taken was to marry a Wolcott and move to Hartford, where he could profit from his in-laws' connections and status. Paterson, too, had remained a poor country lawyer. Rather than take his chances in Philadelphia or even one of the larger neighboring towns, he pursued a thankless practice in rural New Jersey; most of his work involved protecting his father's debt-troubled property.

Perhaps native ability would have brought eventual success to these two future justices had the Revolution not intervened in their lives. Certainly they did not support the Revolution because they foresaw how their careers could benefit from Independence: neither had shown any ardent interest in politics before 1775 (though Ellsworth did serve a term in the Connecticut assembly in 1773). With Paterson and Ellsworth, as with so many of their colleagues, the events of the mid-1770s can be said, not so much to have furthered ambitions previously thwarted, but rather to have created ambitions which had hardly existed. Yet while their commitment to the whig cause enabled them to acquire substantial political influence within their states, in many ways professional prominence remained their deeper object. Paterson held no office at the time of his election to the Senate; he was busy instead pursuing a hefty legal practice that had expanded enormously upon the basis of his record as wartime attorney general. For his part, Ellsworth accepted election grudgingly, informing Governor Samuel Huntington that he would have preferred to retain his seat on the Connecticut Superior Court. "Considering, however, that in the present scituation of our publick affairs, it may be a duty, for a time, to waive personal considerations, I have concluded, by the leave of Providence, to attend the Congress at its first, and perhaps two or three of its first, sessions."[42] Ellsworth went on to serve a full six-year term before replacing John Jay as chief justice; Paterson resigned even before the First Congress expired to accept election as governor of New Jersey.

Legislation and debate appealed little to Ellsworth and Paterson, but

41. Ronald John Lettieri, *Connecticut's Young Man of the Revolution: Oliver Ellsworth* (Hartford, Conn., 1978); John E. O'Connor, *William Paterson: Lawyer and Statesman, 1745–1806* (New Brunswick, N.J., 1979).

42. Ellsworth to Huntington, Dec. 29, 1788, in Jensen *et al.*, eds., *Documentary History of the First Federal Elections*, II, 30.

there were other attorneys who relished these activities to a degree that irked congressmen drawn from other occupations. Few, if any, members of the First Congress commanded greater respect in these areas than the two leading Federalist representatives from Massachusetts, Theodore Sedgwick and Fisher Ames. They, too, came from moderately respectable families that had struggled to maintain an estate and improve their social standing in the cramped and jealous world of a New England town. Having lost their fathers at an early age, both were forced to rely on a college education (Sedgwick at Yale, Ames at Harvard) and the diligent pursuit of legal studies to establish their own livelihoods. Like Paterson and Ellsworth, both had experienced the pangs of disappointment and idleness that were the dues of young attorneys, and like colleagues throughout America—including William Paterson—they knew the kind of resentment, not to say enmity, that their profession attracted. They naturally equated animosity against lawyers with aversion to the rule of law itself, and they viewed Shays's Rebellion of 1786 as proof of the need to restore a due sense of obedience to the restless citizenry of Massachusetts (a lost cause if ever there was one). Having relied upon their own talents and fortitude to make their way, with some success, in the world, they found it difficult to look sympathetically on the social jealousy and resentment of class that the Shaysite uprising embodied. For Sedgwick and Ames, as for so many other attorneys to come, election to Congress provided a welcome opportunity to escape the routine bickering of court appearances while continuing to practice the professional arts of draftsmanship and oratory. To his despondent and domestically overburdened wife— "a sufferer from chronic pregnancy and loneliness," his biographer has noted —Sedgwick wrote tender letters lamenting his confinement in Congress; but his correspondence with male friends reveals his pride in the legislative art.[43]

A final variation on this theme can be found in the careers of the three Philadelphia merchant-politicians who sat in the First Congress: Robert Morris in the Senate and George Clymer and Thomas FitzSimons in the House. Their camaraderie must have been instinctive, for there are striking similarities in their life histories. Clymer was orphaned when he was only a year old, Morris when he was sixteen; Morris and FitzSimons both immigrated to America in their teens; Clymer and FitzSimons both married

43. Richard E. Welch, Jr., *Theodore Sedgwick, Federalist: A Political Portrait* (Middletown, Conn., 1965), quotation at 66; Winfred E. A. Bernhard, *Fisher Ames: Federalist and Statesman, 1758–1808* (Chapel Hill, N.C., 1965). The Sedgwick Papers in the Massachusetts Historical Society contain a large number of revealing personal letters between Theodore and Pamela Sedgwick and are an excellent source for understanding the strain that politics placed on married life.

daughters of prominent Philadelphia merchants and used these connections to advance their own commercial activities. Since Clymer had been reared by a wealthy uncle and Morris had a family inheritance upon which to build, arguably only FitzSimons can be cast in the classic upwardly mobile mode; yet one suspects that each of these men looked back on his rise to economic prominence and social prestige with much the same sense of pride.

What of their attitude toward politics? Though all three are customarily lumped with the moderate whigs who favored reconciliation over independence, there was nothing equivocal about the support they gave the Revolution. Yet there is little evidence that they either sought political power or enjoyed political activity for its own sake, or in quite the way that one suspects the attorneys did. All three had represented Pennsylvania in the Federal Convention, but there they had been content to let James Wilson and Gouverneur Morris, their lawyer colleagues, do the talking. Their activities in Congress were largely an extension of their mercantile and financial concerns. Morris focused his attention on the task of bringing the national capital back to Philadelphia, and Clymer and especially FitzSimons were preoccupied with the framing of revenue measures. The subject of constitutional amendments, by contrast, left them cold. They knew they were in Congress to protect the interests of their city and their class, and when pending bills touched those concerns, they were quick to confer with their intimate constituents. No other congressmen acted on a more informed notion of what it meant to bring knowledge of local interests into the legislative arena.

These examples fall well short of explaining the social sources of the two Federalist movements,[44] nor do they complete a catalog of congressional ambitions circa 1789. Yet they help to suggest something of the *range* of considerations that actually came into play when specific individuals had to make choices about seeking and accepting office. All of these men were susceptible to the call of republican obligation; all subscribed to the central Federalist tenets. Yet their careers illuminate a set of motives more diverse— and in some ways more familiar—than the public language of 1788 would have recognized. Ellsworth and Paterson understood how useful politics had been to their careers at law, but in the care with which they weighed congressional service against professional pursuits, they illustrated how difficult it would be to maintain a stable corps of legislators even in the Senate. Ames and Sedgwick also understood the connection between law and politics; but finding the business of legislation attractive in its own right, they

44. The possibility that leading Federalists of the 1790s shared the conservatism of the self-made man, stereotypical as that image may be, is nevertheless worth pursuing.

came to prefer its demands to those of private practice. Their experience perhaps conforms most closely to the expectations of 1788. Morris, Fitz-Simons, and Clymer, on the other hand, never came to prefer the debating chamber to the countinghouse; but as they assiduously pursued the good of their constituents, they demonstrated just how readily congressmen would seek to direct the new federal system toward the promotion of particular interests.

When service in Congress interfered with the pursuit of private concerns, the Philadelphians—and others who lived reasonably close to the capital—could simply return home to adjust their affairs. At a critical point in the consideration of the assumption of state debts, Sedgwick complained that FitzSimons and Clymer had been called away to Philadelphia, while Jeremiah Wadsworth of Connecticut "has thought it more for his interests to speculate than to attend his duty in Congress, and is gone home."[45] Members coming from more distant states—especially those of the lower South—enjoyed no such advantage. For them, an important component of eligibility was often availability, which could be defined in various ways. Unmarried men, for example, could be said to be doubly available: it may not be a statistical quirk that at least twelve of the sixty-six men who sat in the first House fit that status. And there were other ways in which absence of domestic obligations enhanced eligibility.

A striking number of the early congressmen from the Carolinas and Georgia were men who apparently did not feel much at home in the states they represented. Senator Pierce Butler of South Carolina, for example, was the soldier son of an Irish baronet; after serving in Ireland and Canada, a posting to South Carolina made him aware of the colony's advantages, especially those to be garnered by marrying a Middleton whose own mother was a Bull. Butler assembled an enormous estate and fought actively in the bitter Carolina campaigns; but after his wife died in 1790, he was content to remain in Philadelphia even when he was out of Congress, returning home only to assure himself that his plantation affairs were going well.[46] His colleague Ralph Izard had been born at Goose Creek itself, but after receiving an English education and marrying Alice De Lancey (of New York) in 1771, he and his bride settled in London.[47] After Independence Izard remained in

45. Theodore Sedgwick to Pamela Sedgwick, Mar. 23, 1790, Sedgwick Papers, II, box 5, MHS.

46. Edgar *et al.*, eds., *Biog. Dir. of S.C. House*, III, 108–114.

47. After Congress moved to Philadelphia, Sedgwick had a memorable encounter with Alice Izard at an "assembly where I have seen all the Beauties and Belles of Philadelphia. Indeed they are not many. . . . At the assembly for the first time since I have been in town I saw Mrs Izard, I addressed her with all the politeness of which I

Europe, representing the United States as commissioner to Tuscany while leaving to others the management of the great estate he had inherited as the only surviving son of his wealthy planter father. Izard's son-in-law, William Loughton Smith, represented Charleston in the House in 1789; but though his roots in the state also ran deep, he had been sent to England for education in 1770, when he was twelve and newly orphaned, and remained abroad throughout the war. Among his four colleagues in the delegation, Thomas Tudor Tucker was Bermuda-born and British-educated, and Aedanus Burke was a lifelong bachelor whose lack of dependents spared him the familial concerns others felt.[48]

Congressmen from neighboring states could rarely match the wealth that the South Carolinians typically possessed, but they, too, showed something of the same mobility. Abraham Baldwin of Georgia was a transplanted Connecticut Yankee who (like Burke) never married but took a deep paternal interest in raising and supporting a flock of younger siblings and half-siblings—something that was easier to do from a seat in Congress than a residence in distant Georgia. Hugh Williamson, the Pennsylvania-born son of a Scots-Irish clothier, trained as a physician at Edinburgh and Utrecht and pursued interests in astronomy before settling in North Carolina in 1777, at age forty-one. From 1782 to 1785, and again from 1787 through 1789, he represented the state in the Continental Congress, eventually becoming one of a cohort of delegates to marry (at age fifty-three) a New York heiress. Supported by her wealth, he served two terms in the House and then remained in New York pursuing his scientific interests even after his wife and their two sons predeceased him. There he may often have encountered William Few, first senator from Georgia, who made New York his permanent residence after 1799.[49]

In certain ways, congressmen who did not feel too deeply attached to their constituencies could fit the original Madisonian ideal of representation better than those whose political loyalties never rose above their parochial roots. Yet to survey the diverse paths that brought the members of the First Congress to New York in 1789 is to realize how little relevance that ideal had to the actual recruitment and retention of national legislators. Even in 1789, when the existing political nation was still aroused over the character and fate of the Constitution and when the heady debates of the preceding

---

was master, but could scarcely procure in return an inclination of the head" (Sedgwick to Pamela Sedgwick, Feb. 10, 1791, Sedgwick Papers, II, box 5, MHS).

48. George C. Rogers, Jr., *Evolution of a Federalist: William Loughton Smith of Charleston (1758–1812)* (Columbia, S.C., 1962); Edgar *et al.*, eds., *Biog. Dir. of S.C. House*, III, 105–107.

49. *DAB*.

months still resounded clearly, it is clear that men sought national office for various reasons, public and private, patriotic and self-interested. It is easy enough to explain why men so long committed to public life as Madison and Roger Sherman wished to attend Congress in 1789, nor is it much more difficult to gauge the balance of public and private concerns that brought Baldwin, Williamson, and the Philadelphia merchants (all members of the Federal Convention) there as well. But it is no less revealing to examine the motives of Benjamin Contee of Maryland, who may have hoped a seat in Congress would help him stave off his Philadelphia creditor, or Thomas Scott of Pennsylvania, who balked at taking his seat until he was assured that his son would inherit his position as prothonotary of Washington County. Rather than seek reelection to the Second Congress, Scott sought to retain his clerkship of the county court, but after Governor Thomas Mifflin removed him from this position, he ran successfully for the Third Congress and then, apparently, refused to run again.[50]

In point of fact, of course, there was never a time when the political system operated solely as a filter of talent or when expedient calculations did not enter forthrightly into decisions to enter or leave Congress. Legislation was a tedious and often frustrating task that kept one away from family and business. Such appeal as it exerted in the early years of the new regime was probably felt most strongly either by those whose prior experience of the Revolution had already converted them to what John Jay called "the charms of liberty" or by those who (like Fisher Ames and William Branch Giles) were young enough to enter politics before finding themselves bound to another career.[51] The great majority of congressmen acted on different calculations. If they sought election out of some sense of engagement with public issues, their commitment was far from permanent. And if, on the other hand, they hoped a term or two in Congress might redound to their personal advantage, the rewards they hoped to garner were more likely to come in the form of an appointment to the bench or, better yet, a customs collectorship — positions that were more secure and less demanding. Whatever the framers of 1787 may have intended, they could not alter the underlying character of political activity by constitutional fiat. At the close of the Revolution, politics remained more of an avocation than a profession. Over

50. Levi Hollingsworth to Benjamin Contee, Philadelphia, May 28, June 1, 2, 8, 10, 23, 26, 30, 1789, Levi Hollingsworth letterbook, HSP; for Scott, see Jensen *et al.*, eds., *Documentary History of the First Federal Elections*, I, 426.

51. In this respect it may be significant that Virginia congressmen, who composed what was far and away the most stable delegation in the early House of Representatives, also tended to be among the youngest (as they had been in 1789). Jordan, *Political Leadership*, 197–200.

time, the emergence of the political party system provided a more reliable channel of recruitment than the powerful but erratic impulses of patriotism. But the persistence of high rates of turnover both in Congress and the state assemblies suggests that the dividends of legislative service were still found elsewhere, in a later appointment to a more comfortable sinecure. These were not quite the ambitions that the framers had hoped to evoke.

IV. MADISON'S SECOND THOUGHTS

On March 1, 1789, the day before he left Virginia to take his own seat in the First Federal Congress, James Madison stole a few moments to send Edmund Randolph a long-overdue letter. Three months earlier, Randolph had believed that Madison could gain election without returning to Virginia. At the time, Madison confessed, that advice had "coincided" with his own "inclination" and "judgment"; but the "pressing exhortations" that had led him back to Virginia, he now understood, had been justified, for otherwise he would never have been able "to repel the multiplied falsehoods which circulated" against his candidacy.[52] In the end, his victory over James Monroe came only after a campaign that had been as enterprising as it was difficult. Not only had the two candidates engaged in a series of debates, but Madison had been impelled to publish letters affirming his support for the adoption of amendments to the Constitution. For this indiscretion he was later criticized by Robert Morris, who scoffed that Madison "got frightened in Virginia and 'wrote a Book.'"[53] Madison did not regret the steps he had taken, but he surveyed the results of the first federal elections with his usual sobriety. "Whether I ought to be satisfied or displeased with my success, I shall hereafter be more able to judge," he informed Randolph. "My present anticipations are not flattering." Scanning the list of his colleagues in the House, he found only "a very scanty proportion who will share in the drudgery of business," and as he looked ahead to the tasks they would confront, he foresaw "contentions first between federal and antifederal parties, and then between Northern and Southern parties, which give additional disagreeableness to the prospect." On March 29, with Congress almost four weeks late to muster a quorum, Madison was still awaiting "experimental

52. Madison to Randolph, Mar. 1, 1789, and see Edward Carrington to Madison, Dec. 2, 1788, in Hutchinson *et al.*, eds., *Papers of Madison*, XI, 453, 378–379.

53. Morris to James Wilson, Aug. 23, 1789, Willing, Morris, and Swanwick Papers, Pennsylvania Historical and Museum Commission, Harrisburg; and see Morris to Richard Peters, Aug. 24, 1789, Richard Peters Papers, HSP.

instruction" as to the true "genius" of the government he had done so much to establish. "Were I to advance a conjecture," he wrote Jefferson, "it would be, that the predictions of an anti-democratic operation will be confronted with at least a sufficient number of the features which have marked the State Governments."[54]

These predictions and Madison's experience on the hustings obviously do not accord well with many of the ideas he had expressed only months earlier, while the Constitution was being adopted. They seem rather to contradict than confirm those aspects of his theory which held that the extended republic would be immune from "the vicious arts by which elections are too often carried" or that federal elections would yield an enlightened corps of legislators, or that factional divisions along sharply drawn ideological or sectional lines were not likely to appear. It would be easy enough to dismiss his doubts as momentary expressions of his cautious temperament or as an ironic footnote to the compelling arguments he had developed while the Constitution was being framed and adopted. Yet Madison, who could dissect contingencies and alternatives so rigorously, was a master of the allusive understatement; and precisely because he typically expressed himself with such care, his rare bursts of candor always deserve to be taken seriously.[55]

One would particularly like to know what Madison had in mind by intimating that the federal government might well bear "a sufficient number of the features which have marked the State Governments." Is it possible that he privately doubted whether members of the new Congress would serve longer than their counterparts in the state assemblies? He had in fact considered the problem, at least abstractly, in *Federalist* No. 62. There Madison had in part justified the existence of the Senate by complaining of "the mutability in the public councils arising from a rapid succession of new members," noting by way of evidence that "every new election in the States is found to change one half of the representatives." This in effect was an invocation of the same problem that had so preoccupied his thinking immediately before the Federal Convention: the "multiplicity" and "mutability" of legislation. A potential equation between state legislatures and the House of Representatives was implicit throughout this essay, especially when Madison contrasted the stability of a senate with the errors likely to be committed by "an assembly of men called for the most part from pursuits of a private

---

54. Madison to Randolph, Mar. 1, 1789; Madison to Jefferson, Mar. 29, 1789, in Hutchinson *et al.*, eds., *Papers of Madison*, XI, 453, XII, 38.

55. This remark applies as well to the weight to be given to Madison's early letters to Jefferson of Sept. 6, Oct. 24, 1787, in Hutchinson *et al.*, eds., *Papers of Madison*, X, 163–164, 206–219.

nature, continued in appointment for a short time, and led by no permanent motive to devote the intervals of public occupation to a study of the laws, the affairs, and the comprehensive interests of their country."[56]

It would, of course, push the argument too far to suggest that in 1789 Madison already foresaw that Congress would prove little more stable in its membership than the state assemblies. But there were at least three other respects in which he could already have plausibly sensed that Congress would be subject to pressures little different from those operating within the states.

There was, in the first place, the experience of the first federal elections themselves. Madison was neither surprised nor dismayed at the diversity of procedures the states had adopted to elect representatives. He had conceded their right to do so at the Federal Convention, and in October 1788, with the states beginning to frame election laws, he had recognized that some experimentation was useful.[57] Since the debates at the convention had addressed the apportionment of representation only *among* the states and not *within* them, some diversity was to be expected. Yet, pleased as he was that so few outright Antifederalists had been returned, Madison could not ignore the evidence that electoral procedures would remain highly susceptible to the manipulation of dominant political interests within the states. By allowing the state legislatures such broad authority over the election of federal congressmen, the Constitution guaranteed that elections would not operate solely—if at all—as impartial mechanisms for advancing the best men into office. For the procedures that the legislatures adopted for the first elections revealed not only the absence of a theoretical consensus as to just what it was that representatives were representing but also an immediate awareness of the calculated partisan uses to which this power could be put.

In Pennsylvania, for example, the assembly vote mandating a statewide election of representatives was the work of Federalists who, like Benjamin Rush, could confidently predict that this would enable them to "prevail by a majority of two to one." In Massachusetts, notwithstanding a clause in the electoral resolutions calling for a division of the state into eight districts containing "as nearly as may be" equal numbers of "polls," the actual apportionment favored the urban areas that could be expected to elect Federalists. The decision to divide South Carolina into electoral districts was taken to

56. Wright, ed., *The Federalist*, 410–411; cf. the discussion in *Federalist* No. 53, where Madison suggests that the problem with inexperienced legislators is the likelihood of their "fall[ing] into the snares that may be laid for them" by designing "members of long standing" (*ibid.*, 368).

57. Madison to Jefferson, Oct. 8, 1788, in Hutchinson *et al.*, eds., *Papers of Madison*, XI, 276.

prevent a presumed Antifederal majority in the backcountry from sweeping the delegation, and the Maryland plan of statewide voting for district nominees enabled Federalists to sweep the delegation just as effectively as their allies in Pennsylvania were able to do.[58] And in Virginia an Antifederal assembly drew an electoral map designed to discourage the election of Federalist congressmen: Madison was its foremost intended casualty. Since Madison was convinced that factious majorities would continue to be able to coalesce within states, he could well have realized that future elections would remain equally subject to political manipulation.[59]

A second respect in which congressmen would find themselves exposed to familiar but unseemly pressures also became immediately apparent as soon as the election results were announced. Within days of his election, Madison began receiving the first of a stream of requests for federal patronage. In this experience he was hardly alone. The Constitution may have delegated formal authority over appointments to the president and Senate, but masses of office seekers expected representatives to weigh in with a good word. Some of these requests came from military veterans and public officials who saw appointment to federal office as a handy means of restoring fortunes battered during the Revolution. A host of state officials who feared their positions would become redundant with the creation of federal customs and revenue service spoke in equally pressing terms. And then there were others, the vanguard of generations to come, who hoped a position in the public sector would make good the losses they had suffered in the marketplace. One of Pierce Butler's constituents put the point directly: "Having been formerly unsuccessful in Trade and having lately met with some unexpected losses and disappointments," wrote one Jonathan Mitchell, "I am induced to make application for some office under the Federal Government and I now earnestly solicit your kind and friendly aide and support in procuring any office you think me capable of filling with Justice to my Country." Christopher Leffingwell rang all the changes while asking William Samuel Johnson to help him secure federal reappointment as naval officer of Norwich, Connecticut: "having nine Children to support, having early in

---

58. Benjamin Rush to Jeremy Belknap, Oct. 7, 1788, in Jensen *et al.*, eds., *Documentary History of the First Federal Elections*, I, 302. Relevant materials for nine of the states are available in the two volumes of this work that have been published to date.

59. Nor is it difficult to surmise how Madison would have regarded the practices of malapportionment that prevailed before *Baker* v. *Carr*. In his 1785 letter discussing a constitution for Kentucky, he called for altering the number of representatives accorded legislative districts within a state to reflect changes in population (Madison to Caleb Wallace, Aug. 23, 1785, in Hutchinson *et al.*, eds., *Papers of Madison*, VIII, 353–354.)

the late Warr loaned the United States the greatest part of my Property, being now far advanced in Life, dependant on improvement of a little Land, a Paper Mill and a few Stocking Looms (all insufficient)," he pleaded for a post "that will give bread to a sober industrious deserving Family."[60]

Adventurous supplicants pursued their quarry in person, leaving their competitors who could not afford to do so all the more nervous. "Living so far from the capital gives a man a poor chance in any application," one of Philip Schuyler's Albany constituents lamented, "considering how many hunters there are under the very muzzle of Congress."[61] The metaphor might be muddled, but the thought was clear enough. A few applicants and congressmen found this entire process of solicitation distasteful and embarrassing, but what is more striking is the candor and directness with which such claims were pressed and treated. Congressmen were quick to grasp the importance of patronage to their constituents and to appreciate its potential political uses. As Carl Prince has demonstrated in his survey of Federalist appointments, political considerations were taken into account from a very early point.[62] At first, possession of an honorable Revolutionary record and support of the Constitution were the most important criteria for appointment, but the administration needed little time to establish further and more expedient calculations. Madison and his Republican allies may have resented but could not have been surprised by the partisan uses to which these appointments were later put.

The importance that election laws and patronage could play in public life was not something that had to be discovered in 1789. They had been part of the structure of American politics for a long time, and all the Constitution had done was to extend their scope and possibilities. But in the spring of 1789 Madison may have sensed that there was a third and arguably more critical area in which national affairs would be conducted along lines rather different from those he once hoped the Constitution would establish.

For in many ways the most innovative aspect of the legislative deliberations that began when Congress finally convened was their *publicity*, which seemed to leave representatives and even senators far more accountable to popular opinion and constituent influence than Federalists had ideally imagined would prove the case. Debates in the House were published almost immediately in the New York press and quickly circulated throughout the

60. Jonathan Mitchell to Pierce Butler, May 21, 1789, Pierce Butler Papers, HSP; Christopher Leffingwell to William Samuel Johnson, Norwich, Conn., May 21, 1789, William Samuel Johnson Papers, Connecticut Historical Society, Hartford.

61. John Fairlie to Philip Schuyler, Aug. 16, 1789, John and Philip Schuyler Papers, box 36, New York Public Library.

62. Prince, *Federalists and Origins of the U.S. Civil Service.*

rest of the country, and so were the texts of the bills that had been submitted to both houses. This practice elicited mixed reactions. On the one hand, as William Ellery informed one congressman, publication of debates left the people "more contented than they would otherwise have been," free from "the jealousies and suspicions" that would have arisen had Congress "shut themselves up and concealed their proceedings." Congressmen who feared that the public was impatient with the dilatory pace of business were sometimes less sanguine, however. Benjamin Goodhue of Massachusetts complained of the delay in business produced by "the needless and lengthy harangues" given by colleagues "who have been frequently actuated by the vain display of their Oritorical abilities." Representatives certainly were aware that the public was following their proceedings closely: Peter Silvester of New York, eager to be heard (or seen) to "say something clever in favor" of Madison's proposed amendments, asked a correspondent to "draw up some suitable speech for me, not to[o] long nor to[o] short."[63]

Only rarely, however, did anyone question the propriety of publishing House debates or the texts of pending bills. Curiously enough, it was left to the printer-journalist John Fenno to observe that there was "a gross absurdity in publishing Bills while on their passage thro' the Legislature; this has been done with respect to some which are now so altered, that they are quite a different affair."[64] But Fenno had missed the point. For bills were revised in response not only to the objections that congressmen would in any event have raised during the normal course of debate but also to those which they found themselves impelled to offer after constituents who had been reading their newspapers registered their own opinions. Representatives from New England knew quite well that their constituents wanted them to hold the line on congressional salaries and to reduce the proposed duty on molasses, just as Virginia congressmen soon found themselves under intense pressure to oppose the assumption of state debts. When the maverick Elbridge Gerry sided with southern representatives in seeking higher salaries, his friend James Sullivan took him to task for being so rash as to remark that "a representative ought to have more than a doorkeeper."[65]

63. William Ellery to Benjamin Huntington, July 21, 1789, Thomas C. Bright Autograph Collection, Jervis Public Library, Rome, N.Y.; Benjamin Goodhue to Cotton Tufts, July 20, 1789, Miscellaneous Mss., New-York Historical Society; Peter Silvester to [Peter van Schaack], [June 1789], Van Schaack Collection, Columbia University Library.

64. John Fenno to Joseph Ward, New York, June 6, 1789, Joseph Ward Papers, Chicago Historical Society.

65. James Sullivan to Elbridge Gerry, Boston, Aug. 18, 1789, Elbridge Gerry Papers, MHS.

Nor was receptivity to constituent opinion solely a function of extensive newspaper coverage of Congress. Members of both houses sent texts of pending bills off to their correspondents and solicited their comments and reactions. Thus Thomas FitzSimons dispatched a draft of the bill regulating the coasting trade to a committee of Philadelphia merchants, and William Maclay conveyed a copy of the judiciary bill to Tench Coxe, noting, "We wish to obtain assistance in our deliberations, on that subject, from all quarters."[66] Where the extant correspondence of men like Gerry, Goodhue, and George Thacher enables us to canvass the range of concerns about which they both sought and received advice, it is apparent that the entire congressional agenda was open for discussion. Some of these letters touch upon such general topics as the residual suspicions of Antifederalists and the lingering anxieties of Federalists, but many more are concerned with highly specific points of legislation: the proposed duties on salt and other commodities, congressional salaries, the location of ports of entry and federal courts, and other seemingly mundane details. Next to the volume of correspondence on these matters, little attention seems to have been paid to the once anxiously discussed issue of constitutional amendments.

By the standards either of the Continental Congress or the state legislatures (whose own debates were themselves only beginning to be published), the members of the First Federal Congress appear to have been remarkably sensitive to popular opinion. More to the point, they apparently took this sense of accountability as a matter of course. Madison's notion of representation had indeed presupposed that members would bring an informed understanding of their constituents' interests and circumstances into Congress. He had been careful in *The Federalist* to show that congressmen would have strong incentives to act as their constituents would wish. Yet, when he originally blocked out his ideas on representation in 1787, or when he wrote the corresponding essays for *The Federalist* early in 1788, he had not imagined that the interplay between congressional debate and opinion out-of-doors would be so effective or continual.

Could this have been what Madison foresaw when he hinted that the new regime might not reveal the "anti-democratic operation" that its opponents had feared and he had himself at least partly desired? If so, one has to ask what might have led Madison to recognize that certain structural features of American politics lay beyond merely constitutional repair. One answer at least may be suggested, and it involves considering what impact the very

66. FitzSimons to Samuel Meredith, Aug. 24, 1789, Drew Collection, HSP; Maclay to Coxe, June 16, 1789, Tench Coxe Papers, incoming correspondence, box 43, HSP.

process of ratifying and implementing the Constitution had on the understanding of what national politics would actually entail.

When the Federalists of 1787–1788 found themselves "using the most popular and democratic rhetoric available to explain and justify their aristocratic system," Gordon Wood has argued, they did so because "they were public officials and social leaders fully immersed in the currents of American politics—a politics that would no longer permit the members of an elite to talk only to each other." Only by carrying to their logical conclusion such notions as popular sovereignty and the representative character of all branches of government could the Federalists secure ratification of the Constitution. But in "attempting to confront and retard the thrust of the Revolution with the rhetoric of the Revolution," Wood concludes, the Federalists wound up legitimating the very democratic doctrines they hoped in part to check. The American science of politics that had crystallized with the adoption of the Constitution was thus at once innovative and "impoverished," advancing the bold ideas of "democratic radicalism" while denying "the real social antagonisms of American politics."[67]

This argument, which is concerned with the intellectual legacy of the struggle for the Constitution, can be carried one step further. For the *political* lessons to be drawn from the campaign for ratification and the first federal elections were in their own way no less important than its *intellectual* consequences. Conceived though the Constitution may have been to check populist excesses, its ratification came to depend on a form of popular politics that marked almost a quantum leap beyond what had proved practical theretofore. The year and a half that separated the adjournment of the Federal Convention from the assembling of the First Congress had provided a remarkable education in the possibility of conducting politics on a scale that would have seemed inconceivable as late as 1786, when the Continental Congress was still hoping, in vain, that even one of the amendments it had proposed to the Articles of Confederation would be adopted by the states. The events of 1787–1788 had demonstrated, as nothing else had since 1776, that there was such a thing as national politics: that is, that national issues could provide the basis for mobilizing large numbers of people both within their parochial communities and in coalitions that stretched across state and even regional lines. More than that, the ratification campaign had evoked innovative forms of political action and expression, all designed to shape popular opinion on a mass scale, to affect the elections of delegates to the ratifying conventions, and then to influence their votes when assembled. The lessons of that remarkable episode in constitutional politics would be

---

67. Wood, *Creation of the American Republic*, 562–563, and chap. 15.

recalled when organized political conflict took a new course in the mid-1790s; but to the perceptive, they could have been apparent in 1789. The idea that the deliberations of Congress could be safely insulated from interests and pressures arising within the states and individual constituencies was one of the casualties of the adoption of the Constitution.

☆ ☆ ☆ ☆ ☆

The Persistence
of Antifederalism
after 1789

RICHARD E. ELLIS

I

The Antifederalists, like most of history's losers, have not been treated very kindly. Until fairly recently, the tendency has been either to ignore them or simply to dismiss them as "men of little faith," who have only a peripheral place in the American political or constitutional tradition.[1] In the past two decades, however, a growing number of professional scholars have taken a fresh look at the Antifederalist opposition to the Constitution; they have concluded that they were an articulate and formidable group who not only offered a searching, intelligent, and coherent criticism of the proposed new government but also spoke the views of a substantial portion of the population, perhaps even a majority of Americans.[2] It still remains unclear, however, what happened to the Antifederalists and their opposition to the Con-

---

1. Edmund S. Morgan, *The Birth of the Republic, 1763–89* (Chicago, 1956), 131; Cecelia M. Kenyon, "Men of Little Faith: The Anti-Federalists on the Nature of Representative Government," *William and Mary Quarterly*, XII (1955), 3–43; Benjamin Fletcher Wright, *Consensus and Continuity, 1776–1787* (Boston, 1958); Stanley M. Elkins and Eric McKitrick, "The Founding Fathers: Young Men of the Revolution," *Political Science Quarterly*, LXXVI (1961), 181–216.

2. Michael Lienesch, "In Defense of the Anti-federalists," *History of Political Thought*, IV (Spring 1983), 65–87; Jennifer Nedelsky, "Continuing Democratic Politics: Anti-Federalists, Federalists, and the Constitution," *Harvard Law Review*, XCVI (1982), 340–360; John P. Kaminski, "Antifederalism and the Perils of Homogenized History: A Review Essay," *Rhode Island History*, XLII (Feb. 1983), 30–37; Herbert J. Storing, ed., *The Complete Anti-Federalist*, 7 vols. (Chicago, 1981); Jackson Turner Main, *The Antifederalists: Critics of the Constitution, 1781–1787* (Chapel Hill, N.C., 1961); Robert Allen Rutland, *The Ordeal of the Constitution: The Antifederalists and the Ratification Struggle of 1787–1788* (Norman, Okla., 1966).

stitution after the new government went into effect. For at this point the Antifederalists have generally been abandoned by scholars. Most students of the 1790s tend to deny that there is any connection between the struggle over the adoption of the United States Constitution and the party battles that followed, or they argue that the Antifederalists generally accepted the Constitution as a fait accompli and abandoned the struggle.[3] Sometimes the struggle over the ratification of the Constitution is traced through Congress's adoption of the Bill of Rights, but this is viewed exclusively as an aftermath of the ratification struggle, and not as a harbinger. A few historians have begun to examine the first congressional elections and have found some indication that Antifederalism persisted, and others have suggested that the political alignments that existed on the state level during the 1780s continued into the early 1790s. But the significance of these findings has not been fully explored, and they have not had much impact.[4]

This is unfortunate. For while it is understandable now, nearly two hundred years later, that the United States Constitution should inspire awe and even reverence, and it is comforting to some to believe that it has always

3. See, in particular, Lance Banning, "Republican Ideology and the Triumph of the Constitution, 1789-1793," *WMQ*, 3d Ser., XXXI (1974), 167-188; and *The Jeffersonian Persuasion: Evolution of a Party Ideology* (Ithaca, N.Y., 1978). Most treatments of the 1790s generally ignore the question of what happened to the Antifederalists after the adoption of the United States Constitution. Joseph Charles, *The Origins of the American Party System: Three Essays* (New York, 1961); Noble E. Cunningham, Jr., *The Jeffersonian Republicans: The Formation of Party Organization, 1789-1801* (Chapel Hill, N.C., 1957); Richard Buel, Jr., *Securing the American Revolution: Ideology in American Politics, 1789-1815* (Ithaca, N.Y., 1972); Rudolph M. Bell, *Party and Faction in American Politics: The House of Representatives, 1789-1801* (Westport, Conn., 1973); Mary P. Ryan, "Party Formation in the United States Congress, 1789 to 1796: A Quantitative Analysis," *WMQ*, 3d Ser., XXVIII (1971), 523-542; Paul Goodman, *The Democratic-Republicans of Massachusetts: Politics in a Young Republic* (Cambridge, Mass., 1964); Carl E. Prince, *New Jersey's Jeffersonian Republicans: The Genesis of an Early Party Machine, 1789-1817* (Chapel Hill, N.C., 1967); William Nisbet Chambers, *Political Parties in a New Nation: The American Experience, 1776-1809* (New York, 1963).

4. Steven R. Boyd, *The Politics of Opposition: Antifederalists and the Acceptance of the Constitution* (Millwood, N.Y., 1979); Merrill Jensen *et al.*, eds., *The Documentary History of the First Federal Elections, 1788-1790* (Madison, Wis., 1976-); John Zvesper, *Political Philosophy and Rhetoric: A Study of the Origins of American Party Politics* (Cambridge, 1977), esp. 88-93; Joyce Appleby, *Capitalism and a New Social Order: The Republican Vision of the 1790s* (New York, 1984); Norman K. Risjord, *Chesapeake Politics, 1781-1800* (New York, 1978); Jerome J. Nadelhaft, *The Disorders of War: The Revolution in South Carolina* (Orono, Me., 1981); Alfred F. Young, *The Democratic Republicans of New York: The Origins, 1763-1797* (Chapel Hill, N.C., 1967).

inspired awe and reverence, it is undeniable that the Constitution was not very popular when it was first adopted. Moreover, the opposition to the kind of central government created by the Constitution and the desire to alter its structure fundamentally were an integral and dynamic part of American political culture well into the nineteenth century.

II

To understand why the Antifederalists remained an influential (if not quite dominant) force in American politics in the years after 1788, one must examine the amendments they proposed to the United States Constitution at the various ratifying conventions (Massachusetts, South Carolina, New Hampshire, Maryland, Virginia, New York, and North Carolina) and compare them with the Bill of Rights, for there were important differences. The amendments proposed by the states fall into two categories. The first limited the authority of the central government over individuals in a number of key areas by providing protection for freedom of religion, freedom of the press, and the rights to assemble, petition, and bear arms. Prohibitions were demanded against the quartering of troops and unreasonable search for and seizure of evidence. Still others guaranteed due process in criminal trials by demanding grand jury indictments, speedy public trials, the assistance of counsel, the right of a jury trial, and protection from excessive bail and fines and cruel and unusual punishments.

The amendments of the second group were both substantive and structural. They expressed Antifederalist concern about the centralizing tendencies inherent in the new government, the federal government's control of the purse and the sword, the various limitations placed upon the power of the states, the way the president was elected, the long terms of United States senators, the authority of the federal judiciary, and the ratio of representation in the House of Representatives. Among other things they provided limitations upon the federal government's power to levy taxes, restricted the jurisdiction of the federal courts, and stipulated that the militia remain under the control of the states. Every state convention that submitted amendments also included one, often at the top of its list, stipulating that all those powers not "expressly" delegated to the federal government be retained by the states.[5]

5. The proposed amendments may be found in Jonathan Elliot, ed., *The Debates in the Several State Conventions on the Adoption of the Federal Constitution* . . . (Philadelphia, 1836), II, 177, 550–553, III, 657–661, IV, 243–247. U.S. Department of State, *Documentary History of the Constitution of the United States, 1786–1870* (Wash-

The First Congress took up the matter of amendments to the Constitution in September 1789. Although the supporters of the new government had pledged themselves to do this and President George Washington even alluded to it in his inaugural address, many Federalists were extremely apprehensive of what the results might be. They feared, in particular, that the adoption of amendments might destroy what had been accomplished at Philadelphia. Some even suggested that the question of amendments be permanently tabled. But James Madison, who was more responsible than any other individual for the final form the Constitution had taken, insisted that the issue of amendments be directly faced. In pursuing this course, Madison was motivated by a mixture of reasons. His honor was at stake, since he had personally guaranteed the Virginia ratifying convention that he would support the move to amend the Constitution. He also recognized that failure to amend the Constitution would fuel the movement for a second constitutional convention, which was in many ways a more dangerous alternative. Finally, in 1789, Madison could have few illusions about the extent of Antifederalist strength, especially in Virginia, where Patrick Henry had blocked his election to the United States Senate. In addition, Madison had won his seat in the House of Representatives only after a close contest with James Monroe, who had opposed the adoption of the Constitution.[6]

To deal with the dilemma of how to go along with amendments to the Constitution without fundamentally altering either the power or structure of the newly created central government, Madison arranged to be appointed head of the committee considering the recommendations of the state ratifying conventions. Carefully culling the various proposals, Congress under Madison's leadership submitted twelve amendments to the states for approval. Of these, ten were eventually adopted. Of the two rejected amendments, one increased the number of representatives, and the other prevented members of Congress from benefiting from increases in compensation. Of the ten amendments that make up the Bill of Rights, the first nine protected the rights of individuals. Only the tenth dealt with the problem of distributing power between the states and the federal government, and the way it was written did not satisfy many Antifederalists. The Tenth Amendment stipulates, "The powers not delegated to the United States by the Constitution,

---

ington, D.C., 1894–1905), II, 139–142, 190–192. There is an incomplete but convenient list of the proposed amendments in Edward Dumbauld, *The Bill of Rights and What It Means Today* (Norman, Okla., 1957), 173–205.

6. For Virginia policies following the adoption of the United States Constitution, see Richard R. Beeman, *The Old Dominion and the New Nation, 1788–1801* (Lexington, Ky., 1972). This is one of the few attempts to look at the persistence of Antifederalist thought after 1788. It has not received the attention it deserves.

nor prohibited by it to the States, are reserved to the States respectively, or to the people." Taking their cue from the second article of the Articles of Confederation, the Antifederalists tried to alter it to read, "The powers not *expressly* delegated to the United States by the Constitution . . . are reserved to the states . . . ," but they were unsuccessful.[7]

Richard Henry Lee described the amendments finally proposed by Congress as "mutilated and enfeebled," and William Grayson judged them to be "good for nothing."[8] In other words, the Bill of Rights, as finally adopted, did not lay to rest the concerns of many Antifederalists about the kind of central government created by the United States Constitution. As a result, the question of how power was to be distributed between the state and federal governments was to remain the central constitutional and political issue in American history until the Civil War.

Careful analysis of the fight over ratification indicates that, once local and special considerations are taken into account, the main division was between the cosmopolitan and commercial-minded Americans who favored adoption and the provincial rural types who were either outside or on the periphery of the market economy that opposed the new government. The opponents of the Constitution were strongest in those areas farthest away from urban areas and navigable waterways, areas to be found in northern New England, western Massachusetts, central and western Pennsylvania, backcountry South Carolina and Georgia, New York, Virginia, and North Carolina.[9]

The social, economic, and geographical conditions that undergirded Antifederalism and made its localist appeal so attractive to so many people did not suddenly change after 1789, but continued to exist well into the nineteenth century. In many ways Antifederalism was much more than simple opposition to the United States Constitution or a demand for amendments. It was a way of viewing the world. It was the political and constitutional expression of tradition-oriented people who distrusted change and who de-

7. On the drafting of the Bill of Rights, see Bernard Schwartz, *The Great Rights of Mankind: A History of the American Bill of Rights* (New York, 1977); and Robert Allen Rutland, *The Birth of the Bill of Rights, 1776–1791* (Chapel Hill, N.C., 1955); Dumbauld, *The Bill of Rights*, 206–222. Almost nothing has been done on the ratification procedure followed in the different states.

8. Richard Henry Lee to [Francis Lightfoot Lee], Sept. 13, 1789, in James Curtis Ballagh, ed., *The Letters of Richard Henry Lee* (New York, 1911–1914), II, 500; William Grayson to Patrick Henry, Sept. 29, 1789, in William Wirt Henry, ed., *Patrick Henry: Life, Correspondence, and Speeches* (New York, 1891), III, 406.

9. Main, conclusion to *Antifederalists*, 249–281; and *Political Parties before the Constitution* (Chapel Hill, N.C., 1973). See also Orin Grant Libby, *The Geographical Distribution of the Vote of the Thirteen States on the Federal Constitution, 1787–8* (Madison, Wis., 1894).

sired to live in a society and under a government that was as simple and immediately under their control as was possible. It was a world view that was also in many ways decidedly anticommercial and precapitalist.[10]

III

The struggle over the adoption of the United States Constitution did not so much create divisions as reflect them, and this caused problems for Jefferson and Madison, who had their own vision for the economic development of the United States and who became unhappy over many of the domestic programs and the foreign policies that were adopted by Alexander Hamilton and the Federalists in the early 1790s. For their opposition to the government did not include a desire to alter the Constitution fundamentally. It is for this reason that their criticism of Federalist policies took the form of a demand for a strict, or a literal, interpretation of the powers granted by the Constitution, and not for clarifying amendments.

Throughout the early 1790s Jefferson's and, especially, Madison's opposition to Federalist policies tended to be cautious and measured. Although they sometimes recognized the Antifederalists as useful allies, they also tended to dissociate themselves carefully from many of their forms of opposition. For example, Madison was critical of Hamilton's proposal to fund the domestic portion of the national debt at face value with back interest. But instead of adopting the Antifederalist position, which would have repudiated that portion of the debt which provided enormous profits for speculators and would have reduced the amount of taxes to be levied, Madison instead *ineffectively* and confusedly proposed that the federal government discriminate between original holders and speculators. Madison wanted to pay the speculators the highest market value at the time of their purchase and to give the balance to the original holder. This proposal would not have reduced either the total amount of the national debt or the amount of taxes needed to pay it off.[11]

Slowly and haltingly, the Republican party was formed between 1792 and 1796. The consolidating tendencies evinced by the passage of the Judiciary Act of 1789, the assumption of the state debts, the creation of the national bank, and the levying of internal taxes bore out to many the fears expressed by the Antifederalists during the ratification struggle, and most

10. Richard E. Ellis, *The Jeffersonian Crisis: Courts and Politics in the Young Republic* (New York, 1971), 250–284.

11. E. James Ferguson, *The Power of the Purse: A History of American Public Finance* (Chapel Hill, N.C., 1961), 297–342.

Antifederalists became Republicans. But the Republican party was made up not only of Antifederalists but also of people who had supported the adoption of the Constitution. It was not so much an absorption or even an amalgamation of the two groups, but an uneasy alliance. The differences between them were real enough in 1792, when George Clinton decided to oppose John Adams for the vice-presidency. Jefferson and Madison were, at best, lukewarm to this development, because they viewed the governor of New York as the Antifederalist candidate.[12]

Tension between the two groups also emerged during the struggle over the Jay Treaty. Madison, who started out as a vigorous opponent of its adoption, became increasingly hesitant and eventually withdrew from the fight at a key point, as extremist elements on the Republican side, both on the state level and in Congress, turned the battle into a struggle over the Constitution itself. The Virginia legislature proposed a series of amendments that would have required the approval of both houses of Congress (not just the Senate) for a treaty to go into effect, limited the term of senators to three years, removed the power to try impeachments from the Senate, and prohibited federal judges from holding any other office at the same time. Although these proposals were not formally endorsed by the legislature of any other state, they did gain the approval of a number of prominent Antifederalists, including Samuel Adams, then governor of Massachusetts. Within the House of Representatives there were various proposals which, had they been adopted, would have seriously weakened the power of the president.[13]

Despite the tensions that existed between the two wings of the party, the coalition in opposition to the policies of the Washington administration made sense. Disunited, each group would remain an ineffective minority. In particular, for the Antifederalists, an alliance with former supporters of the adoption of the Constitution would mean help from leaders who had the experience and the connections to launch a national campaign. This is something at which the Antifederalists, who tended to be ideologues lacking in

12. Thomas Jefferson to James Madison, June 10, 1792, in William T. Hutchinson *et al.*, eds., *The Papers of James Madison* (Chicago, Charlottesville, 1962–), XIV, 316.

13. Stephen G. Kurtz, *The Presidency of John Adams: The Collapse of Federalism, 1795–1800* (Philadelphia, 1957), 21–23, 35–36, 40–45, 48–50, 64–65; Bell, *Party and Faction in American Politics*, 54–56; Thomas J. Farnham, "The Virginia Amendments of 1795: An Episode in the Opposition to Jay's Treaty," *Virginia Magazine of History and Biography*, LXXV (1967), 75–88; "To the Legislature of Massachusetts, January 19, 1796," in Harry Alonzo Cushing, ed., *The Writings of Samuel Adams* (New York, 1904–1908) IV, 386–393.

organizational skills and particularist in outlook, were not very adept, as the struggle over the adoption of the United States Constitution had revealed.

Equally important, it allowed the opponents of the Constitution to shed the name "Antifederalist," which they themselves had not chosen. It had been successfully foisted on them by the supporters of ratification in the 1787–1788 struggle, who preempted the term "Federalist" for themselves, even though, in many ways, it more accurately described their opponents. That the term "Antifederalist" stayed with the opponents of the Constitution through the early 1790s and generally down to this day is part of the penalty for losing perhaps the most crucial political battle in American history. Therefore, when the Antifederalists, with only a few key exceptions moved into the Republican party, they eagerly embraced the opportunity to be known as Republicans.[14]

The coalition of the two most important groups opposed to the policies of John Adams's administration in the latter part of the 1790s proved to be a formidable development that culminated not simply in the defeat of the Federalists but in their permanent vanquishment. The high point of Republican opposition came in 1798–1799 with the adoption of the Kentucky and Virginia resolutions (drafted by Jefferson and Madison, respectively), with their emphasis upon fear of the central government's power and upon the rights of the states.

These resolutions not only denounced the Alien and Sedition Acts as unconstitutional but also contained an elaborate theory of the Union. The federal government, they argued, was one of limited and specifically delegated powers and a product of the compact made between the different states in 1787–1788. The Kentucky and Virginia resolutions also took issue with the Federalist claim that the United States Supreme Court was the exclusive and final arbiter of constitutional questions. The Court, it was asserted, was a creature of the Constitution, and to give it the power of judicial review would be to make, as Jefferson argued in the Kentucky Resolutions, "its discretion, and not the Constitution, the measure of its powers." According to the Kentucky and Virginia resolutions, should the federal government assume a power not granted to it, each state as a party to the compact had the right to declare the law unconstitutional; and since Congress exceeded its constitutional powers when it adopted the Alien and Sedition Acts, the state of Kentucky declared these to be "not law" and "altogether void and of no force."[15]

---

14. Those exceptions were Patrick Henry, Luther Martin, and Samuel Chase, whose conversions to the Federalist party have never been adequately explained, but who appear to have been motivated by personal and idiosyncratic reasons.

15. Adrienne Koch and Harry Ammon, "The Virginia and Kentucky Resolutions:

In actuality, at least where Jefferson and Madison were concerned, the rhetoric of the Kentucky and Virginia resolutions was a good deal more extreme than their reality. They were never meant to be a prescription for action. Even though both states declared the Alien and Sedition Acts to be unconstitutional, no official attempt was actually made to prevent the enforcement of the laws by federal officials within the boundaries of Kentucky and Virginia. The resolutions were issued for political effect to rally the Republican opposition, to reaffirm the Revolutionary tradition whereby the defense of personal and civil liberty was joined to states' rights, and to offer a theory of the origins and nature of the national government that undercut the constitutional basis for the Federalist program of centralization. In this sense the resolutions were an enormous success, as they played an important role in helping Jefferson obtain the presidency in 1800.

But other Republicans wanted more than simply a victory for Jefferson in 1800. John Randolph, an influential Virginia congressman, expressed the feelings of this group when he observed, "In this quarter we think that the great work is only begun: and that without *substantial reform*, we shall have little reason to congratulate ourselves on the mere change of *men*." These Republicans wanted substantive changes in the Constitution and a definite weakening of the principles of nationalism that had been unleashed by the achievement of 1787–1788. In particular, they wanted to reduce the power of the president and the federal judiciary, make the latter more amenable to popular control, and more precisely define and restrict the prerogatives of the central government.[16] In later years these demands became known as the Spirit, or Principles, of 1798, and for many Jeffersonians, especially those who became known as Old Republicans, the base from which they were to measure the apostasy, as they viewed it, of the leaders of the Republican party after 1801.

As president, Jefferson refused to launch an attack on the Constitution. He removed some Federalists from office and repealed the Judiciary Act of 1801, but did not ask for amendments to weaken the power of the federal government. Instead, he established the precedent that, when the out party comes to power in the United States, it changes the personnel and the policies of the government, but not the government itself. Disappointed but undaunted, the Old Republicans, led by John Randolph, who from 1801 to 1805 was the Spirit of 1798 incarnate, proceeded to attack the federal judi-

---

An Episode in Jefferson's and Madison's Defense of Civil Liberties," *WMQ*, 3d Ser., V (1948), 145–176.

16. John Randolph to Joseph H. Nicholson, July 26, 1801, Nicholson Papers; William Branch Giles to Thomas Jefferson, June 1, 1801, Jefferson Papers, both at Library of Congress, Washington, D.C.; *Examiner* (Richmond), Oct. 20, 1801.

ciary by broadly defining the impeachment process and thereby raising constitutional questions about the nature of judicial independence. But this, too, was thwarted in the impeachment trial of Samuel Chase when Jefferson made no attempt to impose party regularity and allowed enough Republican senators to vote not guilty and put an end to the attack on the federal judiciary. If anything, Jefferson, as president, expanded the powers of the national government, through the purchase of Louisiana, the building of a national road, and the adoption and enforcement of his controversial embargo policy.[17]

When Jefferson stepped down from the presidency in 1808, a vigorous, if uncoordinated and unsuccessful, attempt was made to prevent Madison, who clearly was the leader of the pro-Constitution wing of the Republican party, from succeeding him. George Clinton and James Monroe, both of whom opposed the adoption of the Constitution in 1787–1788, were his chief rivals, but the congressional caucus, which had the final say, stuck by Madison.[18] During his first term in office Madison revealed his constitutional nationalism in a number of important ways. When the governor of the state of Pennsylvania, with the approval of the legislature, moved to prevent the enforcement of the Supreme Court's decision in *United States* v. *Peters*, Madison threatened to use force and compelled the state to back down. In fact, the militia officer who, under the authority of the state, had led the resistance to the federal marshal in charge of enforcing the high court's decree was arrested, tried, and convicted.[19] Although he was eventually pardoned by the president, for humanitarian reasons, this pardon did not come until the principle of federal supremacy had been established. Madison also, over the objections of many Republicans, even Jefferson's, appointed Joseph Story, who turned out to be an even more extreme nationalist than John Marshall, to the United States Supreme Court.[20] Madison also endorsed the move to recharter the first Bank of the United States.

17. Ellis, *The Jeffersonian Crisis*, 19–107; Richard Hofstadter, *The Idea of a Party System: The Rise of Legitimate Opposition in the United States, 1780–1840* (Berkeley, Calif., 1969), 122–169. On Jefferson's attitude toward the Constitution and the related problem of the economic development of the United States, see also Richard E. Ellis, "The Political Economy of Thomas Jefferson," in Lally Weymouth, ed., *Thomas Jefferson: The Man, His World, His Influence* (London, 1973), 81–95.

18. Harry Ammon, "James Monroe and the Election of 1808 in Virginia," *WMQ*, 3d Ser., XX (1963), 33–56.

19. Kenneth W. Treacy, "The Olmstead Case, 1778–1809," *Western Political Quarterly*, X (1957), 675–691; William O. Douglas, "Interposition and the *Peters* Case, 1787–1809," *Stanford Law Review*, IX (1956–1957), 3–12; Sanford W. Higginbotham, *The Keystone in the Democratic Arch: Pennsylvania Politics, 1800–1816* (Harrisburg, Pa., 1952), 177–204.

20. Morgan D. Dowd, "Justice Story and the Politics of Appointment," *American*

Despite the ability of nationalist-oriented Republicans to preserve the integrity of the Constitution and increase the power of the federal government, their need to stay in power, their constant fear of a Federalist revival, and their desire to avoid, if at all possible, an open division in the party required that some recognition be given to those Republicans whose roots lay in Antifederalism. Consequently, the person selected to be vice-president came from that wing of the party. Aaron Burr, the unsuccessful Republican vice-presidential candidate in 1796 and the vice-president from 1801 to 1805, had been very circumspect during the struggle over the adoption of the Constitution in New York, but he was viewed by many as basically opposing its adoption and was initially proposed for the post by Melancton Smith, a prominent Antifederalist. George Clinton, vice-president from 1805 to 1812, was, of course, a vigorous and open opponent of the Constitution in 1787–1788. And Elbridge Gerry, vice-president from 1813 until his death in 1814, although a member of the Philadelphia Convention in 1787, had refused to endorse the new government. Neither Burr nor Gerry had much impact on Republican policy, but Clinton definitely made his presence felt when, as presiding officer, following a tie vote in the United States Senate, he killed, for constitutional reasons, the bill to recharter the first Bank of the United States.

Beginning in 1811, a major political revolution, one that has barely been touched on by historians of the period, began to take place in the Republican party.[21] After several years of drifting on foreign policy issues, which were further complicated by various personal and policy differences among the more nationalist Republicans, Madison decided to take control of matters by going to war with Great Britain in 1812. Before doing so, however, he had to make his peace with the old Antifederalist wing of the party. He did this by reconciling with James Monroe and making him secretary of state and his heir apparent. Madison also developed good relations with Governor Daniel Tompkins of New York, known as "the farmer's boy," who had inherited George Clinton's political supporters, and gained the support of Governor Simon Snyder of Pennsylvania, the political leader of the small farmers from the more economically backward areas of the state. He also obtained the backing of Spencer Roane, the politically influential judge of the Virginia Court of Appeals who had had close political and personal ties to Patrick Henry (Roane married Henry's daughter) and who had actively opposed the adoption of the Constitution by the Old Dominion.

Journal of Legal History, IX (1965), 265–285; R. Kent Newmyer, *Supreme Court Justice Joseph Story: Statesman of the Old Republic* (Chapel Hill, N.C., 1985), 70–71.

21. Although the events leading to the War of 1812 have been closely examined, almost no work has been done on the effect of the coming of the war on the Republican party.

The country was swept by a spirit of nationalism following the end of the War of 1812, but there was more opposition to the expansion of the federal government's power than is generally recognized. To be sure, the second Bank of the United States was chartered, but the vote was a close one (eighty to seventy-one in the House and twenty-two to twelve in the Senate). Most of those who voted against the bank were Old Republican types, and the measure passed only when it received the support of a number of states' rights Republicans who abandoned their constitutional scruples and voted in favor of the bank because they believed it was the only way to achieve economic stability following the chaos of the war years and the proliferation of state banks since 1811. The nationalists, or New Republicans (as they were beginning to be called), were much less successful in establishing a federal program of internal improvements. The bonus bill vote was eighty-six to eighty-four in the House and twenty to fifteen in the Senate; and Madison, who supported the measure on policy grounds, vetoed it because he believed it unconstitutional. In his veto message he specifically rejected the "necessary and proper" clause, the federal government's "power to regulate commerce among the several states," and its obligation "to provide for the common defense and general welfare" as justification for such a program.

Why did Madison do this? There is no question but that he was motivated by a genuine belief in a truly federal system of government in which there was "a definite partition of powers between the General and State Governments" and was fearful "that no adequate landmarks would be left by the constructive extension of the powers of Congress as proposed in the bill" should the extreme nationalist arguments of John C. Calhoun and Henry Clay, who were the bill's chief supporters, be followed.[22]

He also was aware, however, that there was considerable opposition to the measure from Old Republicans and other advocates of states' rights, a group whose support had been crucial for the recent war effort. In addition, it is clear that by 1817 there existed considerable popular discontent with the nationalist direction in which Congress was taking the country. A number of states moved to try to tax the second Bank of the United States out of existence. But the opposition to congressional policies found an even more effective way to express itself. In 1816, the Fourteenth Congress voted to increase the salaries of its members, and there was an enormous reaction in the fall elections. Incumbents ran into so much hostility at home that most members of Congress decided not to run for reelection or were defeated if they did run. Two-thirds of the members of the House of Representatives were replaced in what is probably the largest single turnover in American

22. "Veto Message," Mar. 3, 1817, in Gaillard Hunt, ed., *The Writings of James Madison* (New York, 1900–1910), VIII, 386–388.

history.[23] What makes this development significant is that the right of congressmen to increase their own salaries had been prohibited in one of the amendments that had actually been submitted to the states by Congress as part of the Bill of Rights, but that amendment had not been ratified. It is yet further indication that the issues and the resentments that had been raised in the fight over the adoption of the Constitution continued to smolder and even explode well into the nineteenth century. The huge turnover that took place in the congressional election of 1816 put a halt to any further nationalist legislation. What few internal improvement bills did squeak through as a consequence of logrolling activities were generally vetoed by James Monroe, who had succeeded Madison in 1817. John Quincy Adams, who urged Congress not "to be Palsied by will of its Constituents," was the first president to support the view that Congress had the authority to create a federal program of internal improvements, but by the time he entered the White House in 1825, the Jacksonian revolution had already begun, and relatively few measures were adopted.

IV

The 1820s saw a major revival of democratic, agrarian, and states' rights thought. Much of it was directed against the postwar nationalist decisions of the Supreme Court, particularly *Martin* v. *Hunter's Lessee* (1816), *McCulloch* v. *Maryland* (1819), *Cohens* v. *Virginia* (1821), and *Osborn* v. *Bank of the United States* (1824). Several of the Supreme Court's decisions, *New Jersey* v. *Wilson* (1812), *Green* v. *Biddle* (1823), and *Worcester* v. *Georgia* (1832), proved unenforceable and were successfully resisted or ignored by the states. These decisions also brought forth a series of unsuccessful but widely supported demands that amendments to the Constitution be adopted to limit the powers of the federal judiciary and to make sure the states, rather than the Supreme Court, were the final arbiter in disputes between the states and the federal government. Another proposal authorized the United States Senate to act as a final court of appeals to determine disputes between the states and the nation. There also were attempts in Congress to

23. George Dangerfield, *The Awakening of American Nationalism, 1815–1828* (New York, 1965), 16; Henry Adams, *History of the United States of America during the Administrations of Thomas Jefferson and James Madison, 1801–1816* (New York, 1891–1896), IX, 119–122, 134–138, 144–146; George T. Blakey, "Rendezvous with Republicanism: John Pope vs. Henry Clay in 1816," *Indiana Magazine of History*, LXII (1966), 233–250. See also Gerald Gunther, ed., *John Marshall's Defense of McCulloch v. Maryland* (Stanford, Calif., 1969).

increase the size of the Supreme Court, to require more than a bare majority decision by the Court to invalidate a state law, and to repeal Section 25 of the Judiciary Act of 1789, which allowed the Supreme Court to hear appeals of state court decisions involving the Constitution, laws of Congress, or treaties of the United States. Also at this time, especially after the election of 1824 — when Andrew Jackson received a plurality of the popular and electoral vote, but was denied the presidency by the House of Representatives, which selected John Quincy Adams instead — various amendments were proposed stipulating that the president and vice-president be directly elected.[24]

On the state level, where events were fueled by the Panic of 1819, the first truly national depression, the 1820s saw a revival of those struggles that had convulsed the country in the 1780s. Several states, in clear violation of Article I, Section 10, of the Constitution, passed debtor legislation that interfered with the obligation of contracts through stay and replevin laws and legal tender acts. Further, a number of state-owned loan offices were created which, in effect, issued paper money.[25] Also, at this time there was a growth of demands to make state governments more immediately and directly responsible to the will of the people. The changes desired included an increase in the number of elective officers, an expansion of the suffrage, a more proportionate form of representation, and ways of making judges more responsive to popular sentiment.[26]

This movement culminated in Andrew Jackson's election to the White House in 1828. Because the campaign was a particularly scurrilous and bitter one and much of it centered on Jackson's controversial personality, it has, in recent years, been argued that personalities rather than issues were the key ingredients in the election of 1828 and that Jackson's victory is to be explained mainly through his personal magnetism and his party's superior organization. Although there is some truth in this viewpoint, it ignores the fact that constitutional-ideological considerations played a real and impor-

24. Charles Warren, "Legislative and Judicial Attacks on the Supreme Court of the United States—A History of the Twenty-Fifth Section of the Judiciary Act," *American Law Review*, XLVII (Jan.-Feb. 1913), 1-34, 161-189; and Warren, *The Supreme Court in United States History* (Boston, 1922), I, 474-564, 633-687; Charles Grove Haines, *The Role of the Supreme Court in American Government and Politics, 1789-1835* (Berkeley, Calif., 1944), 427-537; Paul W. Gates, "Tenants of the Log Cabin," *Mississippi Valley Historical Review*, XLIX (1962), 3-31.

25. Frederick Jackson Turner, *Rise of the New West, 1819-1829* (New York, 1906); Murray N. Rothbard, *The Panic of 1819: Reactions and Policies* (New York, 1962).

26. Merrill D. Peterson, ed., *Democracy, Liberty, and Property: The State Constitutional Conventions of the 1820's* (Indianapolis, Ind., 1966); Fletcher M. Green, *Constitutional Development in the South Atlantic States, 1776-1860: A Study in the Evolution of Democracy* (Chapel Hill, N.C., 1930).

tant part in the election of 1828. For John Quincy Adams, Jackson's opponent, had guided his whole administration and run for reelection on what
was a platform of the American System, a loose interpretation of the Constitution and the need for a strong and active national government. Adams's
constitutional views were a major issue in the election of 1828, and opposition to them explains much of the support that Jackson received. Francis P.
Blair, a product of the relief struggle of Kentucky who was soon to become
editor of the *Washington Globe* (the semiofficial Jackson administration newspaper), broke his alliance with Henry Clay in 1827 to support Jackson,
justifying his disaffection thus: "I never deserted your banner until the question on which you and I so frequently differed in private discussion—(State
rights, the Bank, the power of the Judiciary, etc.)—became the criterions to
distinguish the parties, and had actually renewed, in their practical effects,
the great divisions which marked the era of 1798." [27]

Jackson had served in Congress in 1798 as a Republican, though he
had not been very active. As president, however, he stressed the need to
return to plain republican principles, and he often evoked the Spirit of '98.
Throughout his first administration he urged that the Constitution be
amended to eliminate the role of the House of Representatives in presidential elections, limit the tenure of president and vice-president to a single
term of four or six years, and provide self-government for the District
of Columbia; and there are indications that, if Congress had supported
these proposals, Jackson's closest advisers had other, much more substantial
changes in mind. But these proposals were never endorsed by Congress,
which was at odds with Jackson throughout most of his presidency. [28] Consequently, Jackson was forced to enunciate his views of the Constitution
through his various annual addresses, veto messages, proclamations, and
nonresponses to Supreme Court decisions. In these various ways Jackson
made clear his opposition to a federal program of internal improvements on

27. Francis P. Blair to Henry Clay, Oct. 3, 1827, in James F. Hopkins *et al.*, eds.,
The Papers of Henry Clay (Lexington, Ky., 1959–), VI, 1106–1107. See also Hugh
L. White to Andrew Jackson, Apr. 20, 1831, in John Spencer Bassett, ed., *Correspondence of Andrew Jackson* (Washington, D.C., 1926–1935), IV, 267. For a useful
account of what groups supported Jackson in 1828 and why, see Richard B. Latner,
The Presidency of Andrew Jackson: White House Politics, 1829–1837 (Athens, Ga.,
1979), 7–30. Also valuable is John William Ward, *Andrew Jackson: Symbol for an Age*
(New York, 1955), which stresses Andrew Jackson's agrarian appeal in the election
of 1828.

28. James D. Richardson, ed., *A Compilation of the Messages and Papers of the Presi-
dents, 1789–1897* (Washington, D.C., 1896–1899), II, 448, 518–519, 557, 605.
See also Amos Kendall to Francis Preston Blair, Jan. 9, 1829, Blair-Lee Papers,
Princeton University Library, Princeton, N.J.

both constitutional and policy grounds, stressing that it would be both safer and more efficient to let the states build roads and canals wherever necessary. He vetoed the bill to recharter the second Bank of the United States because it impinged upon the rights of the states. In addition to declaring the bank unconstitutional, Jackson took direct issue with the nationalist claim that the Supreme Court was the final arbiter of constitutional questions. He also sided with the states in their claim that they had jurisdiction over Indian tribes living within their boundaries, despite federal treaties that stipulated otherwise. And he appointed justices to the Supreme Court who were unsympathetic to the broad construction and nationalist tendencies of the Marshall court. Jackson, who was a product of the South and North Carolina backcountry areas where Antifederalism had been strong in 1787–1788, failed to make substantive changes in the Constitution itself, but he effectively dismantled the American System and was the most important and vehement proponent of states' rights to occupy the White House up to that time.[29]

Jackson also advocated the principle of rotation of office. This had been an important concept in the years immediately following Independence, finding expression in both the Pennsylvania Constitution of 1776 and Article V of the Articles of Confederation, which stipulated that no one could be a delegate to the Continental Congress "for more than three years in any term of six years." Failure to include the principle in the United States Constitution had been a source of considerable concern to Antifederalists in 1787–1788,[30] and Jackson's espousal of it in regard to presidential appointments was considered by many of his opponents tantamount to a direct assault on the Constitution.

But what of Jackson's attack on the doctrine of nullification? Was not this an attack upon states' rights? The answer is no.[31] Historians have tended to misconceive the nullification crisis by viewing it as a rehearsal for the coming of the secession crisis of 1860–1861. In so doing they have viewed the constitutional issues involved solely in terms of the nationalist–states' rights dichotomy of the famous Webster-Hayne debate. But Jackson had a different

29. This and following paragraphs based on Richard E. Ellis, *The Union at Risk: Jacksonian Democracy, States' Rights, and the Nullification Crisis* (New York, 1987).

30. Gordon S. Wood, *The Creation of the American Republic, 1776–1787* (Chapel Hill, N.C., 1969), 87, 140–141, 521–522.

31. Ellis, *The Union at Risk.* See also Merrill D. Peterson, *The Jefferson Image in the American Mind* (New York, 1960), 36–66; Charles Sellers, ed., *Andrew Jackson, Nullification, and the State-Rights Tradition* (Chicago, 1963); Andrew C. McLaughlin, "Social Compact and Constitutional Construction," *American Historical Review*, V (1899–1900), 467–490; Arthur M. Schlesinger, Jr., *The Age of Jackson* (Boston, 1945), 510–518.

view of the constitutional issues involved, and he was a far more important protagonist in the crisis than the senator from Massachusetts. Jackson viewed the nullification crisis as a contest between *different* versions of the states' rights doctrine, one version traditional, constitutional, and democratic and the other illegitimate, contrived, and subversive.

Throughout his first administration, in his annual addresses and in his private correspondence, Jackson articulated the difference between the two kinds of states' rights. The traditional kind of states' rights, which Jackson espoused, stressed the need to decentralize power in order to protect the rights of the people and the importance of majority rule. John C. Calhoun and his supporters in South Carolina, on the other hand, promulgated their doctrine as a way of protecting the rights of a minority.

The significance of this difference can be clearly seen when one compares the position of Jackson and the traditional proponents of states' rights with that of Calhoun and the nullifiers on the question of who should amend the Constitution and when. The former group believed that, if a power or act of the central government was believed to be unconstitutional or dangerous, they would have to take upon themselves the responsibility of obtaining an amendment to the Constitution. Since this required the approval of two-thirds of both houses of Congress and three-quarters of the states, it was a very difficult kind of majority to obtain, and they never were really success-ful in this endeavor. The nullifiers, on the other hand, argued that, once a single state nullified a federal law (that had been passed by both houses of Congress and signed by the president), its proponents would have to assume for themselves the responsibility of obtaining the requisite constitutional majority needed to alter the Constitution, thus shifting, in a decisive way, the burden of obtaining the amendment.

Jackson was also hostile to Calhoun's version of the states' rights doctrine because he believed it threatened the existence of the Union. The right of a state to secede from the Union had not traditionally been a part of the concept of states' rights. For example, the Articles of Confederation in 1777 bound the individual states together in "perpetual Union," and rather than destroy the Union that had been created by independence from Great Britain, many Antifederalists had reluctantly gone along with the ratification of the Constitution. Jackson's commitment to the rights of the states in no way precluded a belief that the Union was perpetual or that within its properly limited sphere of power the federal government was sovereign. Jackson completely rejected the nullifiers' claim that secession was a legal right which could be peacefully exercised, insisting instead that it was only a natural or revolutionary right that had to be fought for and that could be suppressed.

The two versions of states' rights also had different social, economic, and geographical roots. Jackson's appeal was mainly to small farmers and others who favored a weak, inactive, and frugal government that would leave them alone and not engage in grandiose social and economic programs that would cost a great deal of money. Recognizing that some kind of authority was necessary, they believed power should be placed in the hands of local officials who could be closely watched. Deeply suspicious of a strong, active, and distant central government, the beliefs and feelings of these people were summed up in such aphorisms as "That government is best, which governs least" and "The world is too much governed." From this, of course, it followed naturally that on the question of how to distribute power between the states and the federal government, they wanted most of the power to be placed in the hands of the states.

The nullifiers, on the other hand, got their chief support from planters who had a strong commercial outlook. Their involvement in the market economy had made them sensitive to the benefits of governmental activism. Consequently, starting in the 1830s, they used the concept of states' rights not simply as a way of denying the authority of the federal government, but as a way of getting the federal government to protect and even endorse the institution of slavery, particularly on the question of its expansion into the territories and on matters involving comity. In the years leading up to the Civil War, the nullifiers and their proslavery allies used the doctrine of states' rights and state sovereignty in such a way as to try to expand the power of the federal government so that it could more effectively protect the peculiar institution; and this, in turn, laid the groundwork for the charge that the South was an aggressive slavocracy, an argument that was to play an extremely important role in galvanizing antisouthern feeling in the North during the 1850s.[32]

Two other presidents shared Jackson's view of the world. The first was Martin Van Buren, whose administration was overwhelmed by the Panic of 1837 and the prolonged depression that followed, but who was a vigorous proponent of the traditional form of states' rights. His father had been an Antifederalist; he himself was a product of the economically backward and politically isolated areas north of New York City and east of the Hudson River (Columbia County); and his closest political allies came from what is known as Northern New York and the Adirondack region, rural areas that did not benefit from the economic growth and prosperity created by the Erie Canal. Van Buren entered politics during the 1790s by becoming a Democratic-Republican. He later claimed, "The old anti-federalists . . . constituted more than three-fourths of that party." In 1828 he threw his support behind Andrew Jackson for the presidency because he recognized that his political creed came from the "old republican the anti-federal and demo-

---

32. I have elaborated and documented this argument in *The Union at Risk*.

cratic parties." On the state level Van Buren and his friends tended to be openly suspicious of those engaged in the unbridled pursuit of wealth, and they opposed the creation of too many banks, the building of questionable feeder canals, and deficit spending by the state. It was this group that enacted the famous New York Safety-Fund law of 1829, which limited the number of banks and subjected them to legislative control. On the national level Van Buren was a strong proponent of states' rights, opposed to a federally sponsored program of internal improvements, and an important ally of the Old Republicans. The powerful Virginia–New York alliance that played such a dominant role in the politics of the early Republic had its roots in the strong Antifederalist tradition that existed in both these states.[33]

James K. Polk was the other president. He was an unusually effective and successful chief executive, who is best known for his aggressive expansionism. But he also was an old-fashioned, doctrinaire Democrat. He prevented the creation of a third Bank of the United States, reinstated the independent treasury system, and circumscribed even further the federal government's spending on internal improvement projects and appropriations for harbor and river improvements. Polk's perception of the world and his constitutional-ideological views can be traced back to the provincial and economically backward areas of rural North Carolina (Mecklenburg County) and East Tennessee where he grew up and which had a strong Antifederalist tradition.[34]

Polk died shortly after leaving office and never got around to writing his memoirs or putting his beliefs in historical perspective, but Van Buren lived a long time after he left the presidency in 1841. He spent a fair amount of his time writing. His *Autobiography* is a well-known and frequently cited source. In addition he wrote a more systematic work (published posthumously in 1867), *Inquiry into the Origin and Course of Political Parties in the United States*. The book has many faults. It is a partisan work, and it avoids discussing the differences that existed within the Republican party and criticizing anyone who was part of the Jeffersonian tradition. Despite these omissions, it is an important work, because it is a major attempt by a major political figure to trace the political development of the nation from the founding of the Republic through Jackson's administration.

33. John C. Fitzpatrick, ed., *The Autobiography of Martin Van Buren*, Vol. II of *Annual Report of the American Historical Association for the Year 1918* (Washington, D.C., 1930), 432, 695. See also Donald B. Cole, *Martin Van Buren and the American Political System* (Princeton, N.J., 1984), esp. 9–31; and John Niven, *Martin Van Buren: The Romantic Age of American Politics* (New York, 1983), esp. 21.

34. Charles Grier Sellers, Jr., *James K. Polk: Jacksonian, 1795–1843* (Princeton, N.J., 1957), esp. chap. 1; and *James K. Polk: Continentalist, 1843–1846* (Princeton, N.J., 1966).

In the book Van Buren stresses, not the organizational links between the different parties, but the principles, issues, and the similar ideological sources of the different struggles. It is also a very cautious book. For, while Van Buren talks about the Antifederalists in fairly generous terms, he also makes it clear that he believes they had made a mistake in opposing the adoption of the Constitution, since almost everyone at the time agreed that the central government created by the Articles of Confederation was inadequate to meet the needs of the country and since the Antifederalists had no alternative plan to meet the crisis that was developing in the 1780s. And the book is certainly not an attack on the Constitution itself. But then, it could hardly have been otherwise, since it was written on the eve of the Civil War, when the Constitution and the Union had become increasingly intertwined in many peoples' minds and both were facing their severest test. Van Buren, like most traditional states' rights advocates, endorsed Abraham Lincoln's decision to use force to preserve the Union.

Nonetheless, despite the guarded approach of the book, it is clear from its structure and from its argument that Van Buren believes the struggle over the adoption of the Constitution was the central event in the founding of the young Republic and that the issues there raised affected political alignments and policy decisions for years to come. As Van Buren observes:

> The political feelings which lay nearest to the hearts of the great body of the people . . . were those of veneration and affection for their local governments as safeguards of their liberties and adequate to most of their wants; endeared to them as their refuge from the persecutions of arbitrary powers and hallowed by the perils and triumphs of the Revolution. Allied to these feelings, and nearly co-extensive with in point of duration, was a distrust . . . on the part of the masses, of what they called an overshadowing general government.[35]

Van Buren was right. Because the Antifederalists chose to align themselves against some of the nation's most important and revered figures— George Washington, Alexander Hamilton, James Madison, Benjamin Franklin, John Jay, and John Marshall—it does not follow that they are not an important part of the American political tradition or that their ideas are irrelevant to our history after the adoption of the Constitution. In many ways the Antifederalists were truer to the spirit of 1776 than their Federalist opponents, and the fear of centralized governmental authority remains a central and effective theme of popular political thought even to this day.

35. Martin Van Buren, *Inquiry into the Origin and Course of Political Parties in the United States* (New York, 1867), 35–57, 62–63, 174–178, 190, 195–201, 235, 240, 261, 270–272, 299, 331, 379–380.

☆ ☆ ☆ ☆ ☆
Religious Dimensions of the Early American State

STEPHEN BOTEIN

When the "surprise issue" of the 1984 presidential election first attracted notice on front pages and covers of American periodicals, most professional historians were caught as unprepared as most political pundits.[1] Although the constitutional relationship of "church and state" promised to enliven late twentieth-century public debate, this was a historical subject that in its very wording seemed quaintly antiquarian. It did not even figure in the list of "Thirteen Enduring Constitutional Issues" drawn up by the organizers of Project '87 on behalf of the American Historical Association and the American Political Science Association to provide an agenda for celebrating the bicentennial of the Philadelphia Convention.[2]

With all due respect for the usual noteworthy exceptions, it was striking how little of substance had been written over the previous two decades on the place of religion in early American constitutional law.[3] Gordon S. Wood's massive *Creation of the American Republic*, which had already achieved the status of a classic since its appearance in 1969, passed quite lightly over the question in a couple of paragraphs. That was consistent with the politely indifferent reception of Mark DeWolfe Howe's last book, *The Garden and the Wilderness*, published four years previously. Proffering some friendly

The research for this essay was completed during the term of a National Endowment for the Humanities Fellowship at the American Antiquarian Society.

1. See, for example, "God and Politics," in *Newsweek*, Sept. 17, 1984, 24–35.

2. See various early numbers of *This Constitution: A Bicentennial Chronicle*, beginning in Winter 1983.

3. Of the works cited below, particular mention should be made of those by McLoughlin (n. 13) and Cord (n. 16).

advice, Howe had called on his liberal contemporaries to avoid "superficial and purposive interpretations of the past." Most readers apparently chose to ignore that challenge. Or, if Howe was right to emphasize the evangelical contribution to disestablishment in the post-Revolutionary period, perhaps they concluded that it would be prudent to do without history altogether.[4]

Such a pattern of deliberate neglect may have reflected a sense of relief in certain quarters that at long last the church-state issue seemed on the way to satisfactory resolution. Milton R. Konvitz, one of the leading civil libertarians of the day, was understandably pleased that the *Everson* decision of 1947, after a period of some hesitation by the Supreme Court, was resulting in a kind of mop-up of undesirable practices at the state level — school prayers included. With the religious clauses of the First Amendment "incorporated" into the Fourteenth, whether by dubious reasoning or not, the Court appeared to be leading the American public toward rigorous separation of church and state. The less said about history, the better. John F. Kennedy's election in 1960 was another favorable sign, not simply because of what it might show about the decline of religious prejudice in America but because of the obvious appeal to commentators like Konvitz of Kennedy's formula for dealing with such prejudice — which was to insist that his religious beliefs were purely private.[5] The weaknesses of that formula became painfully evident in 1984.

Meanwhile, a new approach emerged to the study of religion in American public life. This was presented most influentially by Robert N. Bellah, in a provocative article of 1967 that identified an American "civil religion." The founding fathers, according to Bellah, gave the country a God on the side of "order, law, and right," who was "actively interested and involved in history, with a special concern for America." As Bellah acknowledged, this was an interpretation of American religious and political culture that went back at least as far as Tocqueville; in the 1970s, it would draw strength from a growing literature about the religious components of American Revolutionary thought. By defining civil religion in extrainstitutional terms, as "a collection of beliefs, symbols, and rituals with respect to sacred things," Bellah invited scholars to focus on a religious dimension of the American political tradition to be found not in constitutional law, nor usually for that matter in law of any kind, but (for example) in the psychometaphoric

4. Gordon S. Wood, *The Creation of the American Republic, 1776–1787* (Chapel Hill, N.C., 1969), 427–428; Mark DeWolfe Howe, *The Garden and the Wilderness: Religion and Government in American Constitutional History* (Chicago, 1965), 4, and chap. 2 generally.

5. Milton R. Konvitz, *Expanding Liberties: Freedom's Gains in Postwar America* (New York, 1966), chap. 1.

content of presidential inaugural addresses. The founding fathers were quick to develop such metaphor, which was later revived and intensified under Lincoln.[6]

There can be no doubt that the concept of civil religion has contributed valuably to historical understanding of the broader cultural context surrounding political institutions in the new American republic. For students of early American constitutionalism, however, the very breadth of Bellah's interpretive strategy has obscured as well as enlightened. It has obscured, first, a subtle but significant change in modes of religious reference at the federal level of government during and after the second quarter of the nineteenth century. Therefore, too, it has obscured the historical reasons for what continues in our own time to be the awkwardly illogical relationship of such religious reference to written fundamental law. If one rather old-fashioned premise of what follows is that constitutional language must be assigned special weight in any analysis of political culture, another is that the "original intent" underlying such language is likely to become inaccessible to subsequent generations confronting markedly different circumstances. Recognition of the historical realities may be the beginning of present-day political wisdom.

The most important reality of American constitutional history has surely been the document framed in Philadelphia in 1787. Whatever else may be said about American political culture in that period, it cannot be denied that the Constitution was a perfectly secular text—if, by that term, nothing more or less is signified than the absence of manifest religious content.[7] That is, the Constitution contained no reference to God and none to religion except in the prohibition of a religious test for federal office in Article VI. Furthermore, whatever may or may not have been intended between the lines, the text of the First Amendment merely added two more prohibitions in confirmation of the new government's secularity. One historian has observed wryly that the closest thing to a religious reference in the United States Constitution was the formal dating of the document by the Christian

6. Robert N. Bellah, "Civil Religion in America," in Bellah, *Beyond Belief: Essays on Religion in a Post-Traditional World* (New York, 1970), 175 (this essay originally appeared in *Daedalus* [Winter 1967]). On Revolutionary thought, see, for example, Nathan O. Hatch, *The Sacred Cause of Liberty: Republican Thought and the Millennium in Revolutionary New England* (New Haven, Conn., 1977). On presidential religion, see Dwight G. Anderson, *Abraham Lincoln: The Quest for Immortality* (New York, 1982), chap. 3.

7. In other words, "secular" is used here for literary convenience, without any implication of programmatic hostility to or rejection of religion.

calendar—a procedure that escaped the vigilant attention even of James Madison.[8]

As of 1787, within the whole of Western political culture, the secularity of the United States Constitution might have seemed starkly anomalous. Religious establishment was the rule on the continent of Europe, and in the former mother country. There, in January 1787, at a great meeting of the deputies of three dissenting denominations, it was decided to petition Parliament for repeal of the Test and Corporation acts, which technically excluded all non-Anglicans from public office. By 1790, this campaign had failed miserably. According to the younger Pitt, speaking on behalf of triumphant hard-line Anglicans, the American constitution resembled England's "neither in church nor state." In defense of the Test and Corporation acts, Lord North insisted that religious establishment was "necessary to the happiness of the people and the safety of the constitution."[9] Similar reasoning informed policy toward what remained of Britain's North American empire. In 1791, Parliament proceeded to pass an act providing a constitutional framework of government for Canada's upper and lower provinces. The thirty-sixth section of this act set aside one-seventh of the land grants in the territories involved for the support of "a Protestant clergy," which by law then could have meant only Anglicans. Although this measure caused dissension and sometimes violent turmoil in Canada, it survived through the middle of the nineteenth century.[10]

Furthermore, within the new American republic itself, the constitutions of the separate states were anything but secular. One incident at the Constitutional Convention of 1787 indicates the strength of establishmentarian religion at the state level. In early September, a peripatetic German Jewish merchant named Jonas Phillips, then located in Philadelphia, wrote to the president and members of the convention to complain of a requirement in the otherwise fairly liberal Pennsylvania constitution that every public officeholder acknowledge the divine inspiration of the New Testament. Without that provision, wrote Phillips, "the Israeletes will think them self happy to live under a goverment where all Relegious societys are on an Eaquel footing— I solecet this favour for my self my Childreen and posterity and for the benefit of all the Isrealetes through the 13 united States of america."[11] From

8. E. R. Norman, *The Conscience of the State in North America* (London, 1968), 46.

9. T. C. Hansard, *The Parliamentary History of England* . . . , XXXVIII (London, 1816), 413, 17; and see, generally, Anthony Lincoln, *Some Political and Social Ideas of English Dissent, 1763-1800* (Cambridge, 1938).

10. Norman, *Conscience of the State*, 48-74.

11. Max Farrand, ed., *The Records of the Federal Convention of 1787* (New Haven, Conn., 1911), III, 78-79.

the convention came no useful response to this plea, although a few years later the specific Christian content of Pennsylvania's religious test was eliminated. None of the delegates at Philadelphia, not even Madison, seems to have given serious thought to the possibility of using national constitutional law to prohibit official religiosity at the state level.[12]

Indeed, such intervention would have been politically unthinkable, in view of the commitment to religion already written into the early constitutional record of the states. Despite the lamentable tendency of most constitutional historians to downgrade or ignore the importance of that record, it is readily available; its religious provisions need only brief summary here.[13] Except for Rhode Island, which had gone its own way from the time of Roger Williams, the New England states maintained or, at any rate, permitted multidenominational religious assessment systems. In some other states, such systems were proposed or even authorized constitutionally, if never in fact implemented. From the evidence of state constitutional law, it could be concluded (1) that there was a near consensus in America for toleration of all religions, and against assistance to religious organizations if such assistance discriminated against any Protestants; (2) that opinion was divided on the question of nondiscriminatory assistance, with opposition coming from both latitudinarian and evangelical sources; and (3) that preponderant opinion, also coming from diverse sources, favored some provisions of written fundamental law that acknowledged public office and government generally to be under or of God.

It would be an error to disregard this last category of constitutional provisions on the grounds that they seldom involved tangible costs or benefits. Fundamental attitudes toward civil authority were at stake. Most states required officeholders to profess some kind of religious faith, ranging from Delaware's elaborate trinitarian statement to Massachusetts's oath of belief in "the Christian religion." And it was the norm for state constitutions to make preambulary references to God. South Carolina's constitution included the unusual flourish of declaring "the Christian Protestant Religion" to be "the established religion of this State." No one has ever been sure what that meant. Such provisions often went unenforced or were in their nature un-

---

12. Madison did toy with the idea later. See Irving Brant, "Madison: On the Separation of Church and State," *William and Mary Quarterly*, 3d Ser., VIII (1951), 19.

13. Any state constitutional provision may be easily enough located in Francis N. Thorpe, comp., *The Federal and State Constitutions . . .* , 7 vols. (Washington, D.C., 1909). Material in this paragraph and the next is drawn from William G. McLoughlin, "The Role of Religion in the Revolution: Liberty of Conscience and Cultural Cohesion in the New Nation," in Stephen G. Kurtz and James H. Hutson, eds., *Essays on the American Revolution* (Chapel Hill, N.C., 1973), 211–228.

enforceable, but they affirmed in constitutional terms the official religious dimension of state government. At the state level, then, constitutional law expressed the broader political culture, which included such other formal features as blasphemy prosecutions, Sabbatarian rules, official thanksgiving and fast days, and a large miscellany of localistic informal practices that gave religion a recognizable public role. These practices were so much a part of the fabric of American social life as to be above (or beneath) controversy. One good example, which could not have escaped the attention of some delegates to the Constitutional Convention, was the old Philadelphia custom—observed in the name of guaranteeing freedom of worship—of putting chains across the street at service time to prevent coaches or carts from disturbing a congregation.[14]

Appearances to the contrary, it can be argued that for all its textual secularity the United States Constitution was not really inconsistent with this culture. Certainly it was not the product of an irreligious cabal. Although the outlook of most delegates was in tune with the rationalistic and empirical spirit of the British Enlightenment, Edmund Randolph was the only overt deist present; old Benjamin Franklin made a rather embarrassing display of piety. Madison, whose personal background combined Chesapeake-style Anglicanism with the dissenting tradition at the College of New Jersey, was idiosyncratic in the severity of his separationist logic, to the point where few of his countrymen could always understand him, much less follow his lead.[15] (Jefferson, for one, had needed careful instruction from Madison before he was able to appreciate why the cause of separation was not advanced, but damaged, by excluding ministers from a state legislature, as provided by a number of state constitutions.) But even Madison was capable of allowing some very limited public role for religion, and, anyway, the text of the United States Constitution was by no means owing only to the opinions of the man who is honored as its "father."[16] There is no evidence whatsoever that its framers left God out with the intention of boldly repudiating the conventional political assumptions of their era. To the extent that they may be said to have had a common purpose in writing so secular a document,

14. Charlotte Erickson, *Invisible Immigrants: The Adaptation of English and Scottish Immigrants in Nineteenth-Century America* (Coral Gables, Fla., 1972), 268.

15. Henry F. May, *The Enlightenment in America* (New York, 1976), 96–97, 371; Farrand, ed., *Records*, I, 450–452; William Lee Miller, *The First Liberty: Religion and the American Republic* (New York, 1986), 87–96.

16. Thomas E. Buckley, *Church and State in Revolutionary Virginia, 1775–1787* (Charlottesville, Va., 1977), 70; Robert L. Cord, *Separation of Church and State: Historical Fact and Current Fiction* (New York, 1982), 20–36.

presumably it was to forestall criticism from sectarians fearful of oppression by a national religious establishment.

In fact, the church-state issue was not especially conspicuous in the debates over ratification of the Constitution. Some Antifederalists pressed demands for express guarantees of religious liberty, which Madison among others thought quite unnecessary because of both the reserved powers clause and the extraordinary diversity of sects in America.[17] There were also sporadic attacks on the religious test prohibition. The vote in the convention for Article VI had not been unanimous, with North Carolina opposing and Connecticut and Maryland dividing. Evidently, however, the objection from Connecticut was that the prohibition seemed superfluous, since no one could foresee the possibility of a test ever being imposed. On the other hand, Maryland's Luther Martin reported back to his state legislature with heavy sarcasm that a few members of the convention were "*so unfashionable*" as to think it "*at least decent* to hold out some distinction between the professors of Christianity and downright infidelity or paganism." In the North Carolina ratifying convention, concern was expressed that in time deists, Jews, pagans, Mahometans, even the pope himself might hold federal office.[18] From New England also came scattered grumbling on another count, about the "sinful omission" in the preamble of "not looking to God for direction." One critic of the Constitution devised a new introductory paragraph that began as follows: "We the people of the United States, in a firm belief of the being and perfections of the one living and true God, the creator and supreme Governor of the world, in his universal providence and the authority of his laws..."[19]

But these were unsystematic minority criticisms that never amounted to much. In view of the pattern of religious reference pervading the state constitutions, it is most curious, not that the United States Constitution was faulted for its secularity, but that so few people appear to have cared. The problem, in other words, is to explain the prevailing indifference to the secularity of what was framed in Philadelphia. Negative historical propositions are notoriously hazardous, but it is reasonable to speculate that more was involved than sectarian fear of religious tyranny. In the late 1780s, only the most pessimistic of Antifederalists understood the new federal government

17. Jackson Turner Main, *The Antifederalists: Critics of the Constitution, 1781-1788* (Chapel Hill, N.C., 1961), 159, 230, 260.

18. Farrand, ed., *Records*, II, 468; III, 227; Louise Irby Trenholme, *The Ratification of the Federal Constitution in North Carolina* (New York, 1932), 178-180.

19. Edward Frank Humphrey, *Nationalism and Religion in America, 1774-1789* (Boston, 1924), 462-463.

to be a true nation-state, on the European model, for which some traditional religious identity might have been desirable. It was, instead, a government designed for certain general purposes. It did not police or educate; it did not embody the immediate will of the people. Compared with the governments of the several states, conceivably it was too distant from the citizenry and too restricted in the scope of its responsibility to require an official religious dimension. By the very nature of its limitations, it did not have to be directly associated with "sacred things." It was not so much that church and state had to be separated at the federal level, then, as that there was no federal state to be kept separate.

The point is, of course, unprovable. Such thinking cannot be documented, perhaps because such ideas were too elemental either to have been proposed or to have been disputed at the time. They do help to account for what happened, however, not only at the Philadelphia Convention and in the ratification debates but also afterward. Hence, arguably, the willingness of Congress to allocate federal funds for religious purposes in the Northwest and Southwest territories, where there were no reserved powers. Madison might be appalled, but, after all, he was as likely to be offended by official religion at the state as at the federal level. When, as president in 1811, he vetoed a bill to incorporate a church in the District of Columbia, where also there were no reserved powers, he revealed again that his assumptions about official religion in America were sui generis.[20]

This is not to underestimate the religious dimension of early American public life, as manifested in discourse by leaders holding high federal office. However tepidly or insincerely, as Garry Wills would have us know, George Washington produced or signed his name to presidential rhetoric that from the beginning laid out the vocabulary of civil religion.[21] America was a land and a people and a "nation" (depending on what was meant by that last term) overseen by Providence. But nothing in the Constitution or in any credible early interpretation of that document indicated that God could or should be directly implicated in the official apparatus of the newly established government. The public religiosity of the United States continued to consist primarily of verbal exhortation, as it had under the Continental Congress.[22] Two features of the new government struck some contemporaries as anomalous because they appeared to partake of official religion:

20. McLoughlin, "Role of Religion," in Kurtz and Hutson, eds., *Essays*, 211; Brant, "Madison," *WMQ*, 3d Ser., VIII (1951), 18.

21. Garry Wills, *Cincinnatus: George Washington and the Enlightenment* (Garden City, N.Y., 1984), 23–25.

22. Humphrey, *Nationalism and Religion*, chap. 14.

congressional chaplains and presidential thanksgiving proclamations. In each case, there was less to the problem than met the eye.

It seems clear that the chaplains were not understood by most people to be ministering to the government at all. Instead, they were supplying personal pastoral assistance to individuals—for instance, as one of their defenders would later explain, by visiting the bedside of a sick or dying member of Congress "who may have arrived . . . a stranger from some remote part of the country."[23] For the makeshift boardinghouse community that was Washington after the turn of the century, this was spiritual aid not so greatly dissimilar to that provided by military chaplains, whose role was relatively uncontroversial. During the 1790s, when the federal government was still lodged in Philadelphia, two local clergymen served almost continuously as congressional chaplains: the Presbyterian Ashbel Green (for the House of Representatives) and William White (for the Senate), the latter becoming Episcopal bishop of Pennsylvania within the decade. Both stayed inconspicuous, alternating at morning prayer services for the benefit of about one-third of the membership of Congress, at other times scurrying about to retail minor morsels of gossip. As president, Washington treated them much as he might have treated clergymen in the vicinity of Mount Vernon, summoning them to dinner once a month while Congress was in session. Usually, on such occasions, the president remembered not to ask the preliminary blessing himself.[24]

Before the turn of the century, there were four presidential proclamations for days of thanksgiving—a usage (along with proclamations for days of humiliation) that Madison himself would adopt as president, though only with the deepest misgivings. All four were rich in religious sentiment and imagery. (Ashbel Green reportedly wrote Adams's second proclamation, giving it a decidedly "evangelical character." As if to settle the issue of sincerity for all future historians, Green subsequently remarked that "the sanction given it by the President made it virtually his own act.")[25] Following a formula that originated with the Continental Congress, the operative language of these proclamations merely "recommended" observances. Except for Washington's first, none began with the standard "whereas" introducing a paragraph of legal authorization. Even within the federal government itself, the proclamations had no official force whatsoever. And with good reason. As one member of the House of Representatives put it in 1789: "If a

23. Lorenzo D. Johnson, *Chaplains of the General Government* . . . (New York, 1856), 24.

24. Joseph H. Jones, *The Life of Ashbel Green, V.D.M.* (New York, 1849), chap. 15.

25. H.S.J. Sickel, *Thanksgiving: Its Source, Philosophy, and History* . . . (Philadelphia, 1940), 153–159; Jones, *Ashbel Green*, 270–271.

day of thanksgiving must take place, let it be done by the authorization of the several States." Jefferson, partly for partisan political purposes, rejected the practice entirely, saying that the "enjoining" of such exercises was "an act of discipline." [26] But it had never really been anything like that.

Two sermons preached by chaplains Green and White in 1795, upon the day recommended by Washington's second thanksgiving proclamation, show how thoroughly unofficial such occasions were at the federal level of government. Both men preached simply as the regular ministers of and in their Philadelphia churches. Green emphasized that the thanksgiving proclamation left everyone "to his own inclination"; it was not a command, but a "signal to a *willing people*," as he put it. White, for his part, said that he was preaching "within his privileges as a citizen." Washington himself was in attendance. White called attention to the president as a frequenter of Christ Church during the occasions of "his temporary residence in this city, within the twenty years last past," but the sermon made no specific reference to the federal government—although its topic was "the Reciprocal Influence of Civil Policy and Religious Duty." In fact, it was to the states that White looked for support of religion. Just the previous year, in a private letter, he had praised highly the multidenominational assessment systems of New England.[27]

As of 1800, then, Hamilton's observation in *Federalist* No. 69 could be said to have been borne out. The king of England was "the supreme head and Governor of the national church," according to Hamilton, whereas the American president had "no particle of spiritual jurisdiction." [28]

Ever so gradually, however, this situation began to change, as formalistic religious expectations came to focus on the federal government. One reason for the failure of most historians to appreciate this development is that it occurred while there was a superficial trend toward secularity in constitutional law at the state level. The latter trend was by no means uniform, nor did it testify to any general decline in American piety. Rather, it was the outcome of miscellaneous practical accommodations among competing sects.

Although Connecticut disestablished in 1818 and Massachusetts in 1833, New Hampshire's constitution retained Article VI, authorizing general religious assessments, through and beyond the Civil War. Almost every state constitution preserved some form of preambulary reference to God, and a

26. W. DeLoss Love, Jr., *The Fast and Thanksgiving Days of New England* (Boston, 1895), 404; Cord, *Separation*, 40.

27. Ashbel Green, *A Sermon . . .* (Philadelphia, 1795), 18; William White, *A Sermon . . .* (Philadelphia, 1795), 5; Bird Wilson, *Memoir of the Life of the Right Reverend William White. . .* (Philadelphia, 1839), 165.

28. Jacob E. Cooke, ed., *The Federalist* (Middletown, Conn., 1961), 470.

total of eight appear to have held on to vague religious tests throughout the nineteenth century. (Tennessee and Mississippi did so despite inclusion of seemingly contrary provisions that prohibited religious tests.)[29] Massachusetts, in 1821, voted to abolish its religious test by a very narrow margin. The preceding December, in the state's constitutional convention, no less a political luminary than Daniel Webster had addressed the issue. Typically cautious, he said he was willing to retain the test, having heard of "no practical evil resulting," yet he did not consider it "essential" because—as he explained, referring to the controversial Article III, which provided for a general religious assessment—"there is another part of the constitution which recognizes in the fullest manner the benefits which civil society derives from those Christian institutions which cherish piety, morality and religion." Webster then went on to articulate what was obviously still a widely held opinion. "I am conscious," he said, "that we should not strike out of the constitution all recognition of the Christian religion. I am desirous, in so solemn a transaction as the establishment of a constitution, that we should keep in it an expression of our respect and attachment to christianity."[30] Strong sentiment persisted that state government should have a religious dimension.

By the 1830s, for many people, the federal government was itself apparently beginning to reveal enough attributes of a true state to warrant some semblance of the official religious identity Webster had wanted to retain in Massachusetts. No longer was the nation's capital along the Potomac just a muddy little village where, in the words of one newspaper editor, an ineffectual chief executive sat "like a pelican in the wilderness." The operations of the federal government were expanding and were being covered more intensively by newspapers that reached greater numbers of readers throughout the country. Having mastered new techniques of communication, politicians in Washington learned how to mobilize followers on a national scale.[31] Though still far from powerful, the odd political entity designed half a century before in Philadelphia seemed noticeably less remote from the citizenry of the United States.

29. Humphrey, *Nationalism and Religion*, 499–501; for a systematic update through and beyond the middle of the twentieth century, see Chester James Antieau *et al.*, *Religion under the State Constitutions* (Brooklyn, N.Y., 1965).

30. *Journal of Debates and Proceedings in the Convention of Delegates, Chosen to Revise the Constitution of Massachusetts* . . . (Boston, 1853), 163.

31. James Sterling Young, *The Washington Community, 1800–1828* (New York, 1966), 41, 252–254; Michael Schudson, *Discovering the News: A Social History of American Newspapers* (New York, 1978), chap. 1; Richard P. McCormick, *The Presidential Game: The Origins of American Presidential Politics* (New York, 1982), chap. 6.

An early manifestation of new attitudes had come in the unsuccessful Sabbatarian movement of the late 1820s, which pitted evangelical clergymen and some others against a congressional regulation of 1810 ordering postmasters to conduct business on Sunday if necessary.[32] Quixotic as this crusade may have been, it did appropriately and perhaps shrewdly spotlight the one major territorial function of the federal government—which was delivery of the mail. Earnest Sabbatarians stressed that theirs was the cause of "eight thousand postmasters," a veritable army of federal officials. Sensing the more participatory mood of national politics, they also made a special point of insisting that their elected representatives in Washington ("whom we have clothed with power by our suffrage") should "not stop their ears against the supplication, nor disappoint the hopes, of millions." Sunday mail delivery, according to one outraged pamphleteer, was "a disgrace to the nation, and an insult to the Supreme Lawgiver."[33]

That was none other than Lewis Tappan speaking. Within a few years, as he launched a successful business career that demonstrated a national vision of resources and markets,[34] Tappan would pour his energies into another movement, which criticized the United States Constitution precisely on the grounds that it had established a state that should be but was not accountable to God. To an abolitionist like William Lloyd Garrison, the Constitution was a "national compact" in which each individual participated, by virtue of his oath to support it. That oath bound individuals, in Garrison's view, "to have no other God before them than a CONSTITUTIONAL GOD." If the God of the Constitution was in fact not God but Satan, as evidenced by constitutional recognition of slavery, then personal consent to the federal government would have to be suspended, until such time as the government could make a valid claim to divine right.[35] To be sure, the abolitionists began as a fringe movement, and Garrison was regarded by many people as something of a lunatic even on that fringe. But Judge William Jay, a former leader of the Sabbatarian cause, was definitely not. Jay was a "True Christian Patriot," in the phrase of one eulogist. He was an evangelical Episcopalian who believed that a "just and Christian government" could not be permitted to

32. See Bertram Wyatt-Brown, "Prelude to Abolitionism: Sabbatarian Politics and the Rise of the Second Party System," *Journal of American History*, LVIII (1971–1972), 316–341.

33. Lewis Tappan, *Letter to Eleazer Lord . . .* (New York, 1831), 9, 7, 15.

34. See Leonard L. Richards, *"Gentlemen of Property and Standing": Anti-Abolition Mobs in Jacksonian America* (New York, 1970), 166–170.

35. *Selections from the Writings and Speeches of William Lloyd Garrison* (Boston, 1852), 302–315; and see, generally, Lewis Perry, *Radical Abolitionism: Anarchy and the Government of God in Antislavery Thought* (Ithaca, N.Y., 1973), 33–34, 44–46, 189.

maintain an unholy alliance with slavery. "Our Fathers in forming the Federal Constitution," lamented Jay, "entered into a guilty compromise . . . , and heavily is their sin now visited upon their children."[36]

Judge Jay is of particular interest here because his critics accused him of repudiating the practical constitutional wisdom of his father. William Jay vehemently denied the charge, citing John Jay's record in 1785 as president of the first antislavery society to be formed in the state of New York. As president of that society, according to the son, John Jay drafted a petition to the legislature of the state requesting legal relief for those held in slavery "though FREE BY THE LAWS OF GOD." John Jay had indeed wanted government to be under or of God, but the relevant government for the father ("never out of my mind nor heart") was that of New York. There, as governor (for which office he had abandoned the chief justiceship of the United States), he pressed for statutes to prevent profanation of the Sabbath, and—rather provocatively, given the political climate—hinted that he might like authority to "*require and enjoin*" observance of a public day of thanksgiving. By the evidence of *Federalist* No. 3, on the other hand, John Jay had seen the federal government principally as an instrument of diplomacy.[37]

In 1848, preaching at the funeral of John Quincy Adams, one conservative New England clergyman exclaimed: "Are Church and State, in our country, right, each in itself, and both in their reciprocal relations? Are we becoming the true theocracy, the end of promise?"[38] Adams might have stirred uncomfortably at that, but there could be no question that his nationalistic vision had somehow stimulated new religious hopes for the federal government, to be exploited by both old-style theocrats and fervently patriotic evangelicals. One significant expression of a new outlook was the well-established custom by mid-century that the congressional chaplains would preside regularly at Sunday services in the Capitol, for the general public as well as members of Congress. Not surprisingly, old Bishop White had taken a dim view of this practice when it first came to his notice, in 1830, long after he had left the chaplaincy.[39] But his understanding of his former office

36. George B. Cheever, *The True Christian Patriot . . .* (Boston, 1860), 12; William Jay, *A View of the Action of the Federal Government, in Behalf of Slavery* (New York, 1839), 2.

37. William Jay, *Reply to Remarks of Rev. Moses Stuart . . .* (New York, 1850), 10; Henry P. Johnston, ed., *The Correspondence and Public Papers of John Jay . . .* , I (New York, 1890), 407; William Jay, *The Life of John Jay . . .* (New York, 1833), I, 401, 385–386; Cooke, ed., *Federalist*, 13–18.

38. John R. Bodo, *The Protestant Clergy and Public Issues, 1812–1848* (Princeton, N.J., 1954), 60.

39. Johnson, *Chaplains*, 24; Wilson, *Memoir*, 312–322. It should be noted that preaching in the Capitol in the 1850s differed from the makeshift arrangements for

was going out of fashion by then. A guide to Washington churches published in 1857 duly listed "Services every Sabbath morning in the Capitol, conducted alternately by each of the chaplains." According to one memoir of the decade, "great audiences" attended. At about the same time, after impassioned debate, the House of Representatives overwhelmingly voted down a proposal to abolish the chaplaincies and proclaimed "the belief of our people in the pure doctrines and divine truths of the Gospel of Jesus Christ" to be "the great vital and conservative element in our system."[40]

In the 1850s, the religious identity of the federal government loomed large in public discourse because of controversy over the Fugitive Slave Act, which William Jay for one thought was "unexampled in the legislation of any Christian country." He said it amounted to a "mass of iniquity," to which the only suitable response was civil disobedience. The Fugitive Slave Act allowed abolitionists like Jay to reach out to a larger antislavery audience. Simultaneously, if Arthur Bestor's exposition of southern constitutional theory is to be credited, the act committed proslavery political leaders to an agenda of consolidation, even to expansion of the federal government as a nation-state exercising territorial police powers—this despite traditional southern rhetoric taking a contrary line.[41] The logic of nationalism, carrying with it implications for the religious identity of American government, seems with the advantage of hindsight to have been inexorable. As it turned out, the Constitution of the Confederate States of America consolidated a central government in at least one important respect. Though loosely imitative of what had been framed in Philadelphia in 1787, it allowed none of its supposedly sovereign units any local control over the institution of slavery. In its preamble, this constitution referred to the people of the Confederacy as "invoking the favor and guidance of Almighty God."[42]

On the other side, President Lincoln renewed the practice of proclaiming

---

religious services there in the very early years, as described by Young in *Washington Community*, 72. Young's account is only a partial representation of the rather confused and unreliable memories recorded in Margaret Bayard Smith, *The First Forty Years of Washington Society*, ed. Gaillard Hunt (New York, 1906), 13–17.

40. Lorenzo D. Johnson, *The Churches and Pastors of Washington, D.C.* . . . (New York, 1857), 127; Byron Sunderland, "Washington as I First Knew It, 1852–1855," *Records of the Columbia Historical Society*, V (1902), 208; De Alva Stanwood Alexander, *History and Procedure of the House of Representatives* (Boston, 1916), 98–99.

41. William Jay, *Miscellaneous Writings on Slavery* (Cleveland, Ohio, 1853), 622, 630; Arthur Bestor, "State Sovereignty and Slavery: A Reinterpretation of Proslavery Constitutional Doctrine, 1846–1860," *Journal of the Illinois State Historical Society*, LIV (1961), 117–180.

42. *Journal of the Congress of the Confederate States of America, 1861–1865*, I (Washington, D.C., 1904), 909.

days of national thanksgiving or humiliation. It must be left to the professors of literature, or religion, to expound on themes of guilt and retribution in Lincoln's proclamations. Here, what deserves consideration is a small change registered in his formal phraseology. Not altogether consistently, he began to do more than "recommend" observances. He "appointed" or "designated" or "set apart" particular days; he "invited" or "requested" or "desired" people to pray; and, on one occasion, in a proclamation of 1864, he specified that the "heads of the Executive Departments of this Government," along with other public officials, were to participate in his call for a day of worship.[43]

No dramatic transformation of political theory was achieved, but the difference was revealing—and symptomatic. By the Civil War, it can be said that religious reference in America had been redefined at the federal level, to the point where it was sometimes at a minimum quasi-official. In this context, it is unsurprising that agitation for an amendment to correct the mistake made at the Philadelphia Convention and put God into the Constitution of the United States reached a climax in 1863–1864. The new preamble would be unequivocal: "Recognizing Almighty God as the source of all authority and power in civil government, and acknowledging the Lord Jesus Christ as the Governor among nations, His revealed will as the supreme law of the land, in order to constitute a Christian government..."[44] Nothing definitive came of this effort, for lack of solid support in Washington, but the vitality of the campaign was one more sign that Americans were reconceiving the nature of their federal government.

One unavoidable result of redefining the religious dimension of public life at the federal level of government was a certain tension with the original secular language of the Constitution. That tension remains to this day. Normally it has made no great difference in judicial decision making, beyond once in a while prompting the kind of vaporous statement contributed by Mr. Justice Douglas to the *Zorach* case ("We are a religious people whose institutions presuppose a Supreme Being").[45] What must be recognized, however, is the irony of asking a people that *are* religious—unusually so, by the standards of the modern Western world—to swear by a written constitution that is strictly secular, for reasons peculiar to the era and circumstances of its adoption. This is one consequence of the relative infrequency, unforeseen by the founding fathers, with which the American people have

43. Sickel, *Thanksgiving*, 148–149, 162–166.

44. Morton Borden, *Jews, Turks, and Infidels* (Chapel Hill, N.C., 1984), 58–74 (quotation on 63).

45. See Howe, *Garden*, 13; Konvitz, *Expanding Liberties*, 20–25.

managed to amend the work of the Philadelphia Convention. Perhaps, there-fore, written constitutional law has come to be perceived by many Americans as unexpressive of fundamental principles in their political culture. For better or worse, this is a situation that encourages loyalty to a shadowy *un*written constitution, which, confusingly, is a habit of thought that runs against the American grain.

In 1953, Senator Ralph Flanders of Vermont, proceeding in footsteps that stretched back into the eighteenth century, introduced the following joint resolution to amend the Constitution: "This Nation devoutly recog-nizes the authority and law of Jesus Christ, Saviour and Ruler of Nations through whom are bestowed the blessings of Almighty God."[46] No doubt that was mischievous. But there is something to be gained from knowledge of the long history behind this proposal, however little Senator Flanders himself may have been aware of it. It is worth recalling, too, what happened in 1980 when word spread that John Anderson had long before sponsored another Christian amendment, one of many proposed in the early 1960s.[47] The outcry of incredulity from Anderson's admirers in response to that revelation suggests why it is useful to inquire into the religious context of early American constitutional law.

For those who demand straightforward lessons from the study of history, there is little comfort to be taken from the story of official religiosity in post-Revolutionary America. Although the original secularity of the United States Constitution did not reflect general secular intent in the political cul-ture of the time, it is still the only constitution we have—and there are some good reasons for wanting to keep it secular. But that is subject matter for another essay. What may be said here, by way of conclusion, is that anyone wishing to insulate religion from government and government from religion would be well advised to maintain a constant watch for those unwritten fundamentals embedded in the political culture of the nation. Despite *Everson* and Milton R. Konvitz, they are still out there, not about to go away. If liberals expect their own principles to prevail, they must be prepared not only for courtroom battles but for strenuous political engagement in the heartland.

46. Konvitz, *Expanding Liberties*, 34.
47. Mark Bisnow, *Diary of a Dark Horse: The 1980 Anderson Presidential Cam-paign* (Carbondale, Ill., 1983), 222, 251.

Epilogue

☆ ☆ ☆ ☆ ☆

A Roof
without Walls
The Dilemma of American
National Identity

JOHN M. MURRIN

The United States Constitution, as we have come to realize, provided an innovative answer to the legal problem of sovereignty within a federal system. This difficulty had destroyed the British Empire by 1776, and by 1787 it seemed likely to reduce the Congress of the United States to impotence. The Federalists solved this dilemma by applying on a continental scale the new principles of revolutionary constitutionalism that the states had explored and developed between 1776 and 1780, the year in which the Massachusetts Constitution completed the model. To be fully legitimate, a constitution had to be drafted by a special convention and ratified by the people. By so institutionalizing the premise that the people alone are sovereign, and not government at any level, Americans made it possible for a sovereign citizenry to delegate some powers to the states, others to the central government. We still live happily, more or less, with the benefits of this discovery.[1]

But the Constitution was also a more tentative answer to a broader cultural problem. It established what Francis Hopkinson called a "new roof" over an American union of extremely diverse states. Opponents of the Constitution often warned that "the several parts of the roof were so framed as to mutually strengthen and support each other," he contemptuously declared, "and therefore, there was great reason to fear that the whole might stand independent of the walls." With heavy logic, he refuted this possibility.[2]

1. Gordon S. Wood, *The Creation of the American Republic, 1776–1787* (Chapel Hill, N.C., 1969).
2. In Paul M. Zall, ed., *Comical Spirit of Seventy-Six: The Humor of Francis Hopkinson* (San Marino, Calif., 1976), 186–194, esp. 190.

Hopkinson had the right image but the wrong alignment. The Federalists, not their opponents, were building a roof without walls.

I

The American Revolution was not the logical culmination of a broadening and deepening sense of separate national identity emerging among the settlers of North America. The sprawling American continents had taken a remarkably homogeneous people, the Indians, and divided them into hundreds of distinct societies over thousands of years. America was quite capable of doing the same to Europeans. The seventeenth century created, within English America alone, not one new civilization on this side of the Atlantic, but many distinct colonies that differed as dramatically from one another as any of them from England. Even the Revolution would establish, not one new nation, but two distinct polities: the United States and Canada. A century later the Civil War nearly added a third. The Latin America wars for independence produced twenty-two nations from a few vice-royalties.

For the English, the Atlantic functioned much as a prism in the seventeenth century, separating the stream of immigrants into a broad spectrum of settlements from the Caribbean to New England. Most colonies shared many important traits with immediate neighbors (Massachusetts with Connecticut, Maryland with Virginia, St. Kitts with Barbados), but differences became cumulative as one advanced farther along the spectrum. At the extremes — Barbados and Massachusetts, for instance — the colonies had almost nothing in common.

Historical demography suggests the larger pattern. For complex reasons that included climate and settler motivation, the farther north one went, the greater that life expectancy generally became, the higher the percentage of women in the colony, and the sooner population growth by natural increase set in. The extent of population mixture also followed the spectrum. New Englanders really were English. The Middle Atlantic colonies threw together most of the peoples of northwestern Europe. The Chesapeake added a significant African population, which would expand dramatically from the 1690s on. Africans eventually outnumbered Europeans by two to one in South Carolina and by much greater ratios in the islands. Climate and demography also affected local economies. Apart from the fur trade, few settlers north of Maryland engaged in economic activities strange to Europeans. As rapidly as possible, they even converted to European crops (without abandoning maize), grown mostly through family labor. But the staple colonies specialized in the growth and export through unfree labor of non-

European crops, especially tobacco and sugar. The West Indies did not even try to raise enough food to feed the settlers and their servants and slaves.[3]

Government and religion also followed the spectrum. At the province level, New England gloried in its corporate autonomy, which Rhode Island and Connecticut would retain until the Revolution. Royal government, by contrast, really defined itself in the Caribbean during the Restoration era. On the mainland south of New England, most settlers lived under proprietary governments that eventually became royal, but Virginia had been royal since 1624, and Maryland and Pennsylvania regained their proprietary forms after losing them for a time following the Glorious Revolution. In local government, the New England town—a variation of the traditional English village—spread no farther south than East Jersey. English counties, not villages, became the dominant form of local organization from West Jersey through North Carolina, and parishes prevailed in South Carolina and the islands. In general, the farther north one traveled, the higher became the percentage of local resources that settlers were willing to spend on religion. Formally, the Old World established church, the Church of England, became the New World establishment everywhere from Maryland south by 1710. In the Middle Atlantic region, dissent and establishment fought to a standstill, with toleration the big winner. In New England except for Rhode Island, Old World dissent became New World establishment.[4]

Some uniformities different from England's did emerge to bridge these cultural chasms. Except in the smaller sugar islands, all of the colonies enjoyed a more widespread distribution and ownership of land. No colony successfully reproduced a hereditary aristocracy. Indeed, younger sons enjoyed liberties in North America hard to match in any European society. Similarly, England's complex legal system was everywhere simplified and

3. For strong examples of this extensive demographic literature, see the essays in Stanley N. Katz and John M. Murrin, eds., *Colonial America: Essays in Politics and Social Development*, 3d ed. (New York, 1983), 122–162, 177–203, 290–313; and in Thad W. Tate and David L. Ammerman, eds. *The Chesapeake in the Seventeenth Century: Essays on Anglo-American Society* (Chapel Hill, N.C., 1979), 96–182. See also Richard S. Dunn, *Sugar and Slaves: The Rise of the Planter Class in the English West Indies, 1624–1713* (Chapel Hill, N.C., 1972), esp. 300–334.

4. John M. Murrin, "Political Development," in Jack P. Greene and J. R. Pole, eds., *Colonial British America: Essays in the New History of the Early Modern Era* (Baltimore, 1984), 408–456. John M. Murrin, Mary R. Murrin, and Gregory E. Dowd are engaged in a study, still in progress, that will enumerate colonial clergymen, colony by colony and year by year. The data show that the ratio of clergy to people generally rose from south to north, which also provides a rough index of each society's financial support for organized religion.

streamlined. And except in Quaker communities, the settlers also adopted a ferocious style of waging war. For Europe's more limited struggles among trained armies, they substituted people's wars of total subjection and even annihilation. Their methods were deliberately terroristic. They, not the Indians, began the systematic slaughter of women and children, often as targets of choice. Finally, the English language became more uniform in America than in England simply because no colony was able to replicate the mother country's rich variety of local dialects.[5]

Nevertheless, the overall differences stand out more starkly than the similarities. The spectrum of seventeenth-century settlement produced, not one, but many Americas, and the passage of time threatened to drive them farther apart, not closer together. Most of what they retained in common—language, Protestantism, acquisitiveness, basic political institutions—derived from their shared English heritage, however institutionally skewed, and not from their novel encounters with the continent of North America.

II

Between the Glorious Revolution of 1688–1689 and the Peace of Paris of 1763, the colonies grew more alike in several respects. As newer generations adjusted to climate, life expectancy improved south of Pennsylvania, population became self-sustaining, and family patterns grew more conventional. Warfare retained its original brutality in conflicts with Indians, but it too Europeanized as the primary enemy became the settlers and soldiers of other European empires. The widespread imposition of royal government through the 1720s gave public life structural similarities it had lacked in the seventeenth century.

As these examples suggest, British North America in fundamental ways became more European, more English, in the eighteenth century. The growth of cities, the spread of printing and newspapers, the rise of the professions, and the emulation of British political culture all encouraged

5. Daniel J. Boorstin provides a good starting point on language in *The Americans: The Colonial Experience* (New York, 1958), chaps. 41–43. For an excellent introduction to early legal history, see David H. Flaherty, ed., *Essays in the History of Early American Law* (Chapel Hill, N.C., 1969). On war, see John Shy, *A People Numerous and Armed: Reflections on the Military Struggle for American Independence* (New York, 1976), 225–254; Edmund S. Morgan, *American Slavery, American Freedom: The Ordeal of Colonial Virginia* (New York, 1975), 73–74; Francis Jennings, *The Invasion of America: Indians, Colonialism, and the Cant of Conquest* (Chapel Hill, N.C., 1975), esp. chaps. 9, 13; and Allen W. Trelease, *Indian Affairs in Colonial New York: The Seventeenth Century* (Ithaca, N.Y., 1960), 60–85.

this trend. But the colonies did not all change in the same way. New England anglicized at the core. On the fringes of the social order, it retained much of its original uniqueness, such as the Puritan Sabbath and annual election sermons. The southern colonies anglicized on the fringes while remaining unique at the core, which now more than ever was characterized by plantations and slave labor. A planter's economic base had no English counterpart, but his daily behavior closely imitated gentry standards. In the Middle Atlantic region, where emulation of England always had ethnic and class overtones, the pattern was less clear.[6]

A few examples will have to suffice in illustrating this process. New England increasingly replicated basic European institutions. Southern provinces, by contrast, imported much of what they needed and did not acquire the same capacity to produce their own. Thus, for instance, every college but one was north of Maryland in 1775. New England trained virtually all of its own clergy, lawyers, and physicians. By contrast, no native-born South Carolinian (and only a few dozen Virginians out of the several hundred men who took parishes in the colony) became Anglican clergymen. All of South Carolina's bar and much of Virginia's was trained in England. Similarly, New Englanders wrote their own poetry, much of it bad, while Maryland imported poets, a few of them quite good (such as Richard Lewis).[7]

Perhaps the change was most conspicuous in public life. In the seven-

6. The process of anglicization in the Middle Colonies is too complex to pursue here, but an adequate account would have to examine and compare the different ways that particular ethnic groups were assimilated into the larger culture. For example, see Randall H. Balmer, "Dutch Religion in an English World: Political Upheaval and Ethnic Conflict in the Middle Colonies" (Ph.D. diss., Princeton University, 1985). Balmer argues that New York City Dutch settlers cultivated close ties with the classis of Amsterdam and retained a rather sentimental attachment for the Dutch language while intermarrying with Anglicans and assimilating to upper-class English standards. The Jersey Dutch rejected both the authority of Amsterdam and elite English norms. They adjusted to an English world by going evangelical and aligning with the Presbyterians. Ned C. Landsman's Scots who settled in central New Jersey were commercially active and largely succeeded in capturing and defining the Presbyterian church. In the process they forged a new Scottish-American identity, which, like that of the Jersey Dutch, was linked to revivalism. But Ulster Scots who settled in Pennsylvania's Susquehanna Valley were less commercial and were antirevival. See Landsman, *Scotland and Its First American Colony, 1683-1765* (Princeton, N.J., 1985); and Elizabeth I. Nybakken, "New Light on the Old Side: Irish Influences on Colonial Presbyterianism," *Journal of American History*, LXVIII (1981-1982), 813-832.

7. John M. Murrin, "The Legal Transformation: The Bench and Bar of Eighteenth Century Massachusetts," in Katz and Murrin, eds., *Colonial America*, 540-572, illustrates this process.

teenth century many colony founders had tried quite consciously to depart from and improve upon English norms. They attempted to build a city upon a hill in Puritan Massachusetts, a viable autocracy in ducal New York, a holy experiment of brotherly love in Quaker Pennsylvania, a rejuvenated feudal order in Maryland, and an aristocratic utopia in Carolina. But from about the second quarter of the eighteenth century, colonial spokesmen expressed ever-increasing admiration for the existing British constitution as the human wonder of the age. Improvement upon it seemed scarcely imaginable. North American settlers read British political writers, absorbed their view of the world, and tried to shape their provincial governments into smaller but convincing replicas of the metropolitan example.[8]

One conspicuous consequence was imperial patriotism. The generation in power from 1739 to 1763 fought two global wars and helped to win the greatest overseas victories that Britain had ever seized. Despite frequent disputes in many colonies, royal government achieved greater practical success in America than at any other time in its history to 1776. Colonial expressions of loyalty to Britain became far more frequent, emotional, intense, and eloquent than in earlier years. To the extent that the settlers were self-conscious nationalists, they saw themselves as part of an expanding *British* nation and empire. Loyalty to colony meant loyalty to Britain. The two were expected to reinforce one another.[9]

Occasionally a new vision of a glorious future for the American continent would appear in this rhetoric, but almost without exception these writers confined their exuberance to an Anglo-American context. North America would thrive *with* Britain, Nathaniel Ames's almanacs excitedly told New Englanders. Because population grew faster in America than in Europe, mused Benjamin Franklin, the colonies would one day surpass the mother country, and perhaps crown and Parliament would cross the ocean to these shores.[10]

8. For a survey, see Murrin, "Political Development," in Greene and Pole, eds., *Colonial British America*, 408–456.

9. Max Savelle, "Nationalism and Other Loyalties in the American Revolution," *American Historical Review*, LXVII (1961–1962), 901–923; Paul A. Varg, "The Advent of Nationalism, 1758–1776," *American Quarterly*, XVI (1964), 169–181; Judith A. Wilson, "My Country Is My Colony: A Study in Anglo-American Patriotism, 1739–1760," *Historian*, XXX (1967–1968), 333–349; Nathan O. Hatch, "The Origins of Civil Millennialism in America: New England Clergymen, War with France, and the Revolution," *William and Mary Quarterly*, 3d Ser., XXXI (1974), 407–430.

10. Sam Briggs, ed., *The Essays, Humor, and Poems of Nathaniel Ames, Father and Son* . . . (Cleveland, Ohio, 1891), esp. 284–286, 308–311, 313, 324–325; Benjamin Franklin, *Observations concerning the Increase of Mankind* (1755), in Leonard W.

In other words, political loyalties to an entity called America scarcely yet existed and could not match the intensity with which settlers revered either their smaller provinces or the larger empire. Despite the frequent worries voiced in the British press or expressed by British placemen in America, native-born North Americans showed no interest in political union, much less independence. Every colony involved rejected the Albany Plan of Union of 1754 regardless of the manifest military peril from New France.

This reality was far from obvious to the British. They, not the settlers, imagined the possibility of an independent America. Imposing new patterns of uniformity on colonies that they had to govern routinely, few London officials grasped the extent or significance of local differences three thousand miles away. The British worried about the whole because they did not understand the parts, and they reified their concerns into a totality they called America. Debate over the Canada cession focused these anxieties more sharply than ever before and also revealed that British writers almost took it for granted that one day the American colonies would demand and get their independence. Wise policy required that Britain avert this result for as long as possible.

In a word, America was Britain's idea. Maybe it was even Britain's dream, but if so, it soon became her nightmare. Every countermeasure taken to avert the horror seemed only to bring it closer. Nothing is more ironic in the entire span of early American history than the way in which Britain finally persuaded her North American settlers to embrace a national destiny that virtually none of them desired before the crisis of 1764–1776.[11]

There was, in short, nothing inevitable about the creation and triumph of the United States. Rather, the American nation was a by-product that at first nobody wanted. The British believed that they were doing everything they could to avoid such a thing. The settlers until almost the last moment denied that they had anything of the kind in mind. Only British oppression, they insisted, could drive them from the empire.[12]

Labaree *et al.*, eds., *The Papers of Benjamin Franklin* (New Haven, Conn., 1959–), IV, 227–234.

11. See J. M. Bumsted, "'Things in the Womb of Time': Ideas of American Independence, 1633 to 1763," *WMQ*, 3d Ser., XXXI (1974), 533–564. Close examination of Bumsted's sources will show that this was a debate among Europeans, including British placemen and travelers in America. Only an occasional native-born colonist participated, often with some bewilderment about why this dialogue was taking place at all.

12. For a classic statement, see Benjamin Franklin, *The Interest of Great Britain Considered, with Regard to Her Colonies, and the Acquisition of Canada and Guadaloupe* (1760), in Labaree *et al.*, eds., *The Papers of Benjamin Franklin*, IX, esp. 90–91. For a shrewd analysis of the role that Independence did play for a major patriot in his

At one level the Revolution was thus the culminating moment in the process of anglicization. The colonists resisted British policy, they explained with increasing irritation and anger, because London would not let them live *as Englishmen*. They demanded only the common rights of Englishmen, such as no taxation without representation and trial by jury, and not unique privileges for Americans. (At the same time, they did believe that the availability of land in North America gave them unique benefits unavailable to fellow subjects at home.) Britain demanded that North Americans assume their fair share of common imperial obligations and embarked on a reform program after 1763 that was designed to centralize and rationalize the empire. Beginning with the Stamp Act crisis of 1764–1766, London thus polarized the needs of the whole and the rights of the parts. She was never able to put them together again.

Precisely because public life in America was so thoroughly British, the colonists resisted Britain with all the available weapons of eighteenth-century politics—ideology, law, petitions, assembly resolves, grassroots political organizations, disciplined crowd violence. Until 1774, when the Continental Congress finally provided an American institutional focus for general resistance, patriot leaders looked to the radical opposition movement in London as the logical center of their own. Not surprisingly, until the Congress met, more of its members had visited London than Philadelphia. The Revolution, in short, was a crisis of political *integration* and centralization that Britain could not master. Britain could not control politically the forces that were drawing the parts of the empire closer together. That failure left patriots on this side of the ocean alone with America. They had shown that they would fight and even confederate to protect the rights of the parts. They had yet to discover whether they could create enough sense of common identity to provide for the needs of the whole. The challenge was exhilarating—and terrifying.[13]

III

Perhaps we can now appreciate the dilemma of American national identity. To the extent that North Americans were more alike by 1760 than they had

strategy of resistance, see Pauline Maier, "Coming to Terms with Samuel Adams," *AHR*, LXXXI (1976), 12–37.

13. See, generally, Pauline Maier, *From Resistance to Revolution: Colonial Radicals and the Development of American Opposition to Britain, 1765–1776* (New York, 1972); David Ammerman, *In the Common Cause: American Response to the Coercive Acts of 1774* (Charlottesville, Va., 1974); H. James Henderson, *Party Politics in the Continental Congress* (New York, 1974).

been in 1690 or 1660, Britain had been the major focus of unity and the engine of change. To repudiate Britain meant jeopardizing what the settlers had in common while stressing what made them different from one another. Older patriots quickly sensed the danger. If goaded into the attempt, the colonies would indeed be able to win their independence, John Dickinson assured William Pitt in 1765. "But what, sir, must be the Consequences of that Success? A Multitude of Commonwealths, Crimes, and Calamities, of mutual Jealousies, Hatreds, Wars and Devastations; till at last the exhausted Provinces shall sink into Slavery under the yoke of some fortunate Conqueror."[14] Younger patriots were more confident about America. They welcomed the chance to become fabled heroes in their ironic quest to prove that the British had been right about America all along and that their own doubts and hesitations were unworthy of their lofty cause. At his Yale commencement of 1770, John Trumbull predicted the eventual supremacy of America in the arts and sciences, called the colonies a nation, and exulted in the deluge of blood that would accompany this transition to greatness.

> See where her Heroes mark their glorious way,
> Arm'd for the fight and blazing on the day
> Blood stains their steps; and o'er the conquering plain,
> 'Mid fighting thousands and 'mid thousands slain,
> Their eager swords promiscuous carnage blend,
> And ghastly deaths their raging course attend.
> Her mighty pow'r the subject world shall see;
> For laurel'd Conquest waits her high decree.

The colonists would inherit from Britain, not just their own continent, but the world. America's fleets would "Bid ev'ry realm, that hears the trump of fame, / Quake at the distant terror of her name." Trumbull hardly needed to announce the moral, but he did anyway. Although the process would take some centuries to complete, America's triumphs would hide "in brightness of superior day / The fainting gleam of Britain's setting ray."[15]

This bloodcurdling rhetoric probably concealed real anxieties. Any task that sanguinary—that worthy of heroes—was quite daunting. Not only would an American national identity have to be forged in a brutal war with the world's mightiest maritime power, but the settlers would have to do so without the usual requisites of nationhood. Sir Lewis Namier has contrasted

14. Dickinson to Pitt, Dec. 21, 1765, in Edmund S. Morgan, ed., *Prologue to Revolution: Sources and Documents on the Stamp Act Crisis, 1764–1766* (Chapel Hill, N.C., 1959), 119.

15. John Trumbull, *An Essay on the Use and Advantages of the Fine Arts* . . . (New Haven, Conn., 1770), 3–6, 11–12, 14.

two basic types of European nationalism from the eighteenth century to the present. Both reduce to a question of human loyalties. To what social collectivity do people choose or wish to be loyal? One pattern was traditional and, at root, institutional. England was a nation because it possessed reasonably well defined boundaries and a continuity of monarchical rule for about nine hundred years. The crown had created Parliament, which became both a reinforcing and a competing focus for loyalties as the two, together with their public, defined England's distinct political culture in the seventeenth century. Switzerland provided Namier with another example. This mountainous republic forged a common institutional identity among its several cantons despite their division into three languages and two major religions.

The other model, just beginning to find important spokesmen in late-eighteenth-century Germany, was linguistic nationalism. Among a people who shared no common institutional links, language seemed an obvious focus for loyalty. Even though the boundaries between competing languages were by no means clear-cut, this type of nationalism would come to dominate Central and Eastern Europe in the nineteenth and twentieth centuries. Whereas institutional nationalism had the potential to absorb waves of reform without internal upheaval, linguistic nationalism recognized no obvious geographical boundaries and had to replace existing political institutions with new ones to achieve full expression. Although it began with warm sentiments of benign humanitarianism, it was far more likely to become militaristic and destructive, and by the twentieth century it could be deflected into overt racism whenever it seemed necessary to distinguish true Germans, for example, from outsiders who had merely mastered the language over several generations.[16]

The most fascinating and troubling feature about the American case is that neither model could work here. The American continent could boast no common historic institutions other than crown and Parliament. It had acquired no shared history outside its British context. Likewise, the American settlers possessed only one language in common: English. In both cases, the logic of national identity pointed back to Britain, to counterrevolution, to a repudiation of the bizarre events of 1776. From this perspective, the loyalists were the true nationalists. Many older patriots implicitly agreed, at least to the extent that they too equated nationhood with the institutionalization of centralized power. To them centralization meant a severe challenge to liberty, a threat to the Revolution itself. Yet all patriots understood that, unless they could unite and fight together effectively, they would lose the war. Their early answer to this dilemma was virtue. Americans had

16. Sir Lewis Namier, "Nationality and Liberty," in Namier, *Vanished Supremacies: Essays on European History, 1812-1918* (New York, 1963), 31-53.

it; the British had lost it. Virtue, or patriotism, would inspire the settlers to sacrifice their private interests, even their lives, for the general welfare.[17]

As the struggle progressed into a seemingly endless war and the North Americans (often for the first time) came into intimate contact with each other, this conviction wore thin. The shock of recognition was uncomfortable and disturbing, for it was just as likely to expose differences as similarities. It revealed, in effect, the underlying spectrum of settlement. Too often the Americans discovered that they really did not like each other very much, but that they needed common trust to survive. Mutual suspicion and fascination jostled for preeminence in the hearts of patriots. The language of virtue may have intensified the sense of hostility, for it became all too easy to explain any annoying cultural differences as someone else's lack of virtue and commitment. The terms of opprobrium that Americans hurled at each other may even have contained more venom than did the anti-British polemics of the period, many of which reflected the anguish of an ancient and real affection now inexplicably betrayed.

The most conspicuous fault line divided New Englanders from everyone else, although other antagonisms surfaced as well. Yankees could not conceal their sense of moral superiority, which often seemed rankly hypocritical to observers from other regions. "We Pennsylvanians act as if we believe that God made of one blood all families of the earth," complained William Maclay; "but the Eastern people seem to think that he made none but New England folks."[18] One New York merchant, Gerard G. Beekman, thought that nearly everyone in Connecticut "has proved to be d—d ungreatfull cheating fellows." Thirteen years later he was still denouncing "the best of them out of that damd Cuntry" for defaulting on their debts.[19] Lewis Morris, Jr., could not even keep a similar sense of disgust out of his last will and testament in 1762. He ordered that his son Gouverneur Morris (the later patriot) receive

the best Education that is to be had in Europe or America but my Express Will and Directions are that he be never sent for that purpose to the Colony of Connecticut least he should imbibe in his youth that

17. For recent efforts to understand the patriots in generational terms, see Pauline Maier, *The Old Revolutionaries: Political Lives in the Age of Samuel Adams* (New York, 1980), esp. chap. 6; and Peter C. Hoffer, *Revolution and Regeneration: Life Cycle and the Historical Vision of the Generation of 1776* (Athens, Ga., 1983), which studies younger revolutionaries.

18. Edgar S. Maclay, ed., *Journal of William Maclay, United States Senator from Pennsylvania, 1789–1791* (New York, 1890), 210.

19. Quoted in Philip L. White, *The Beekmans of New York in Politics and Commerce, 1647–1877* (New York, 1956), 223–224.

low Craft and cunning so Incident to the People of that Country, which is so interwoven in their constitutions that all their art cannot disguise it from the World tho' many of them under the sanctified Garb of Religion have Endeavored to Impose themselves on the World for honest Men.[20]

When John Adams passed through New York City in 1774, he heard Yankees castigated as "Goths and Vandalls," infamous for their "Levelling Spirit." He retaliated in the privacy of his diary by speculating on the shocking lack of gentility and good breeding among the New York elite. To Abigail Adams, Virginia riflemen seemed every bit as loathsome and barbaric as British propaganda claimed.[21]

Sometimes regional hatreds became severe enough to reduce the northern department of the Continental army to near impotence. Yankees showed such complete distrust of New York's General Philip Schuyler that he virtually lost the ability to command. Soldiers from other parts of America, reported Captain Alexander Graydon of Pennsylvania, retaliated in kind. They regarded the eastern men as "contemptible in the extreme," in part because their officers were too egalitarian. In 1776 a court-martial acquitted a Maryland officer accused of showing disrespect to a New England general. "In so contemptible a light were the New England men regarded," explained Graydon, who sat on the court, "that it was scarcely held possible to conceive a case, which could be construed into a reprehensible disrespect of them."[22]

IV

American national identity was, in short, an unexpected, impromptu, artificial, and therefore extremely fragile creation of the Revolution. Its social

20. Quoted in Max M. Mintz, *Gouverneur Morris and the American Revolution* (Norman, Okla., 1970), 15.

21. L. H. Butterfield *et al.*, eds., *Diary and Autobiography of John Adams* (Cambridge, Mass., 1961), II, 107, 109; Abigail to John Adams, Mar. 31, 1776, in L. H. Butterfield *et al.*, eds., *Adams Family Correspondence* (Cambridge, Mass., 1963–), I, 369. Abigail asked whether the common people of Virginia were "not like the uncivilized Natives Brittain represents us to be?" The rest of the letter shows that she believed they were.

22. See, generally, Don R. Gerlach, *Philip Schuyler and the American Revolution in New York, 1733–1777* (Lincoln, Nebr., 1964). For the quotations, see Alexander Graydon, *Memoirs of His Own Time, with Reminiscences of the Men and Events of the Revolution*, ed. John Stockton Littell (Philadelphia, 1846), 158, 179; see also 147–149.

roots were much weaker than those that brought forth the Confederate States of America in 1861, and yet the Confederacy was successfully crushed by military force.[23]

At first Congress tried to govern through consensus and unanimity. That effort always created strain, and it finally broke down in 1777–1778. Thereafter no one could be certain whether the American union could long outlast the war. In June 1783 a mutiny in the Pennsylvania line drove Congress from Philadelphia. The angry delegates gathered in the small crossroads village of Princeton, New Jersey, where they spent an anxious four months in uncomfortable surroundings. They found that they had to contemplate the fate of the Union. Could the United States survive with Congress on the move and its executive departments somewhere else? Charles Thomson, secretary to Congress since 1774, doubted that the Union could endure without British military pressure to hold the several parts together. This worry obsessed him for months.[24] By 1786 New England delegates were talking openly of disunion and partial confederacies, and this idea finally appeared in the newspapers in early 1787.[25]

Instead, a convention of distinguished delegates met in Philadelphia that summer. It drafted a Constitution radically different from the Articles of Confederation. By mid-1788 enough states ratified the plan to launch the new government in April 1789. This victory followed a titanic struggle in which the Constitution had almost been defeated by popularly chosen conventions in nearly every large state. Among the small states, New Hampshire and Rhode Island also seemed generally hostile.

Ratification marked a victory for American nationalism, as folklore has always told us, but it also perpetuated political conflict, which continued without pause into the new era. Most patriots equated union with harmony and were quite upset by the turmoil of the 1790s. The only union they could

23. For a fuller discussion, see John M. Murrin, "War, Revolution, and Nation-Making: The American Revolution versus the Civil War," in Murrin, ed., *Violence and Voluntarism: War and Society in America from the Aztecs to the Civil War* (forthcoming, Philadelphia, 1987).

24. Eugene R. Sheridan and John M. Murrin, eds., *Congress at Princeton, Being the Letters of Charles Thomson to Hannah Thomson, June to October 1783* (Princeton, N.J., 1985), 19, 29–30, 66–67, 73, 83, 86, 91–92.

25. Edmund C. Burnett, ed., *Letters of Members of the Continental Congress* (Washington, D.C., 1921–1936), VIII, 247–248, 282, 415–416, 533, for some of the major correspondence on this subject. The first public call for separate confederacies appeared in Boston's *Independent Chronicle*, Feb. 15, 1787. Cf. William Winslow Crosskey and William Jeffrey, Jr., *Politics and the Constitution in the History of the United States*, Vol. III, *The Political Background of the Federal Convention* (Chicago, 1980), 395.

maintain was accompanied by intense political strife, a pattern of contention that did, however, observe certain boundaries. It had limits.[26]

The actions of the Washington administration in its first few years seemed to vindicate the gloomiest predictions of the Antifederalists, but these proud patriots did not respond by denouncing the Constitution. Instead, they began the process of deifying it. They converted it into an absolute standard and denounced their opponents for every deviation from its sublime mandates. In effect they returned to their anchorage in British political culture to find a harbor in which their ship might float. They converted the Constitution into a modern and revolutionary counterpart for Britain's ancient constitution. To keep the central government going at all, they embraced the venerable antagonism between court and country, corruption and virtue, ministerial ambition and legislative integrity. The Federalists claimed only to be implementing the government created by the Constitution. Their Jeffersonian opponents insisted that they, in turn, were merely calling the government to proper constitutional account. But they both accepted the Constitution as their standard, a process that kept the system going and converted its architects into something like popular demigods within a generation.[27]

The lesson taught by the first American party system was curious in the extreme. Americans would accept a central government only if it seldom acted like one. The British Empire had crumbled while trying to subordinate the rights of the parts to the needs of the whole. The Continental Congress had brought American union to the edge of disintegration by protecting the rights of the parts at the expense of common needs. The Constitution seemed to provide an exit from this dilemma, a way of instilling energy in government while showing genuine respect for revolutionary principles. But it did not work quite that way. Vigorous policies by the central government always threatened to expose the underlying differences that could still tear America apart. The spectrum of settlement had been muted, warped, and overlaid with new hues, but it was still there. Thus, although everyone soon agreed that the new government was a structural improvement on the Articles, it exercised very few substantive powers in practice that people had not been happy to allocate to the old Congress. In a word, the Constitution became a substitute for any deeper kind of national identity. American nationalism is distinct because, for nearly its first century, it was narrowly

26. See, generally, Richard Hofstadter, *The Idea of a Party System: The Rise of Legitimate Opposition in the United States, 1780–1840* (Berkeley, Calif., 1969).

27. Lance Banning, "Republican Ideology and the Triumph of the Constitution, 1789 to 1793," *WMQ*, 3d Ser., XXXI (1974), 167–188.

and peculiarly constitutional. People knew that without the Constitution there would be no America.[28]

In the architecture of nationhood, the United States had achieved something quite remarkable. Francis Hopkinson to the contrary, Americans had erected their constitutional roof before they put up the national walls. Hovering there over a divided people, it aroused wonder and awe, even ecstasy. Early historians rewrote the past to make the Constitution the culminating event of their story.[29] Some of the Republic's most brilliant legal minds wrote interminable multivolume commentaries on its manifold virtues and unmatched wisdom. Orators plundered the language in search of fitting praise. Someone may even have put the document to music.[30] This spirit of amazement, this frenzy of self-congratulation, owed its intensity to the terrible fear that the roof could come crashing down at almost any time. Indeed, the national walls have taken much longer to build.

The very different Americas of the seventeenth century had survived into the nineteenth after repudiating the Britain from whom they had acquired their most conspicuous common features in the eighteenth. While the Republic's self-announced progenitors, New England and Virginia, fought out their differences into the Civil War, the middle states quietly eloped with the nation, giving her their most distinctive features: acceptance of pluralism, frank pursuit of self-interest, and legitimation of competing factions.

The Constitution alone could not do the job, but the job could not be done at all without it. The Constitution was to the nation a more successful version of what the Halfway Covenant had once been to the Puritans, a way of buying time. Under the shade of this lofty frame of government, the shared sacrifices of the Revolutionary war could become interstate and intergenerational memories that bound people together in new ways.[31] Ordi-

28. For fuller discussions, see John M. Murrin, "The Great Inversion, or Court versus Country: A Comparison of the Revolution Settlements in England (1688–1721) and America (1776–1816)," in J.G.A. Pocock, ed., *Three British Revolutions: 1641, 1688, 1776* (Princeton, N.J., 1980), 368–453; and Lance Banning, *The Jeffersonian Persuasion: Evolution of a Party Ideology* (Ithaca, N.Y., 1978).

29. Peter C. Hoffer, "The Constitutional Crisis and the Rise of a Nationalistic View of History in America, 1786–1788," *New York History*, LII (1971), 305–323.

30. See Edward S. Corwin, *Court over Constitution: A Study of Judicial Review as an Instrument of Popular Government* (Princeton, N.J., 1938), 229–230 n. This incident was probably an example of Confederate humor, not a real event.

31. Charles Royster, "Founding a Nation in Blood: Military Conflict and American Nationality," in Ronald Hoffman and Peter J. Albert, eds., *Arms and Independence: The Military Character of the American Revolution* (Charlottesville, Va., 1984), 25–49.

nary citizens could create interregional economic links that simply were not there as late as 1790, until a national economy could finally supplant the old imperial one. Like the Halfway Covenant, the Constitution was an ingenious contrivance that enabled a precarious experiment to continue for another generation or two with the hope that the salvation unobtainable in the present might bless the land in better times.[32]

32. Kenneth M. Stampp, *The Imperiled Union: Essays on the Background of the Civil War* (New York, 1980), 3–36, shows how tentative the idea of a perpetual union really was.

Index

☆ ☆ ☆

Notes on Contributors

LANCE BANNING is Professor of History at the University of Kentucky and the author of *The Jeffersonian Persuasion: Evolution of a Party Ideology* as well as numerous articles on James Madison and on the Constitutional Convention.

RICHARD BEEMAN is Professor of History at the University of Pennsylvania and the former Director of the Philadelphia Center for Early American Studies; he is the author of *The Old Dominion and the New Nation, 1788-1801.*

STEPHEN BOTEIN was Professor of History at Michigan State University and the author of *Early American Law and Society* and of articles on colonial printers and booksellers. In 1985-1986 he was Visiting Editor of Publications at the Institute of Early American History and Culture.

RICHARD D. BROWN is Professor of History at the University of Connecticut and the author of *Revolutionary Politics in Massachusetts: The Boston Committee of Correspondence and the Towns, 1772-1774*, of *Modernization: The Transformation of American Life, 1600-1865*, and of a forthcoming study of the diffusion of information in early America.

EDWARD C. CARTER II is Librarian of the American Philosophical Society, Editor in Chief of *The Papers of Benjamin Henry Latrobe*, and Adjunct Professor of History, and of the History and Sociology of Science at the University of Pennsylvania.

RICHARD E. ELLIS is Professor of History at the State University of New York, Buffalo, and the author of *The Union at Risk: Jacksonian Democracy, States' Rights, and the Nullification Crisis* and *The Jeffersonian Crisis: Courts and Politics in the Young Republic* (National Historical Society First Book Award).

PAUL FINKELMAN is Assistant Professor of History at the State University of New York, Binghamton, and the author of *An Imperfect Union: Slavery, Federalism, and Comity* and *Slavery in the Courtroom* (Joseph T. Andrews Award from American Association of Law Libraries).

STANLEY N. KATZ is President of the American Council of Learned Societies, President of the Organization of American Historians (1987-1988), Senior Fellow, Woodrow Wilson School of International Affairs, Princeton University, and author of *Newcastle's New York: Anglo-American Politics, 1732-1753.*

RALPH LERNER is Professor, Committee on Social Thought, and the College, the University of Chicago, and the coeditor (with Philip B. Kurland) of *The Founders' Constitution.*

DREW R. McCOY is Associate Professor of History at Harvard University and the author of *The Elusive Republic: Political Economy in Jeffersonian America.*

JOHN M. MURRIN is Professor of History at Princeton University and is coeditor and coauthor of *Saints and Revolutionaries: Essays in Early American History.*

JACK N. RAKOVE is Associate Professor of History at Stanford University and the author of *The Beginnings of National Politics: An Interpretive History of the Continental Congress.*

JANET A. RIESMAN is Assistant Professor of History at the State University of New York, Stony Brook, and at work on a study of the commercial revolution in America, 1690-1830.

GORDON S. WOOD is Professor of History at Brown University and the author of *The Creation of the American Republic, 1776-1787* (Bancroft Prize, John H. Dunning Prize).